MAKING THE CHINESE MEXICAN

# Making the Chinese Mexican

GLOBAL MIGRATION, LOCALISM,
AND EXCLUSION IN THE
U.S.-MEXICO BORDERLANDS

*Grace Peña Delgado*

STANFORD UNIVERSITY PRESS

STANFORD, CALIFORNIA

Stanford University Press
Stanford, California

This book has been published with the assistance of The Pennsylvania State
University.

Printed in the United States of America on acid-free, archival-quality paper

Library of Congress Cataloging-in-Publication Data
Delgado, Grace, author.
  Making the Chinese Mexican : global migration, localism, and exclusion in
the U.S.-Mexico borderlands / Grace Peña Delgado.
      pages cm
  Includes bibliographical references and index.
  ISBN 978-0-8047-7814-5 (cloth : alk. paper)
  1. Chinese--Mexican-American Border Region--Ethnic identity--History--20th
century. 2. Immigrants--Cultural assimilation--Mexican-American Border
Region--History--20th century. 3. Mexican-American Border Region--Race
relations--Political aspects--History--20th century. 4. Mexico--Emigration and
immigration--Government policy--History--20th century. 5. United States--Em-
igration and immigration--Government policy--History--20th century. I. Title.
  F1392.C45D45 2012
  305.800972'1--dc23                                              2011040196

Typeset by Bruce Lundquist in 10.5/12 Sabon

*For my mother,*
*Sandy Delgado*

# Contents

# List of Illustrations

# Acknowledgments

This book was made possible by the generosity and kindness of others. My first thanks go to friends and family members who sustained me through various phases of writing, researching, and rewriting. I cannot begin to express the critical role they played through this book's rather long gestation period. I am deeply grateful for the loving-kindness of Mary McClanahan, Troy Johnson, the late Xiaolan Bao, Julie Rivera, Lauren Walton, Tom Magnetti, Sharon Corl, Peter Marshall, Lisa Kilpatrick and Keith Burch, Donnan Stoicovy, Ron Zimmerman, and Ron Mize. Each in his or her own way encouraged my scholarship with the perfect antidote to the tedium of writing and research. Special gratitude goes to the members of my family, who were patient and caring throughout: Mom, Sylvia, Alyssia, Rose, Scott, Kyle, Aaron, Carol, Jeff, and my twin brother, David. I have finally finished "that paper."

In 2006 I threw caution to the wind and moved from southern California to central Pennsylvania to join the History Department at the Pennsylvania State University. I was hopeful that there a community of lively scholars, institutional resources, and some time away from teaching would help catapult my book to completion. And they did! What was most gratifying—and completely unanticipated—was the manner in which my ideas grew, deepened, and in the end, came together. Matthew Restall read multiple drafts of the introduction and provided perceptive comment and encouragement—and at a critical moment, opened doors for me at Stanford University Press when I was overwhelmed with tenure pressures. I am incredibly fortunate to have Matthew as my colleague. Philip Baldi, Cary Fraser, A. Gregg Roeber, Sally McMurry, Nan Woodruff, Tobias Brinkmann, Mrinalini Sinha, and Lori Ginzburg read parts of the manuscript at various stages of its development. I am thankful for their comments and their insights. With their usual enthusiasm, Amy Greenberg and Ronnie Po-chia Hsia read the entire manuscript. For their generous expenditure of time and their keen observations I am deeply grateful. Hongyan Chiang and Xinmin Lin checked and rechecked my Chinese translations and helped me navigate the murky waters of the Qing Dynasty and Republican-era calendars. Colleagues at other institutions have been equally gracious. Evelyn Hu-Dehart, Samuel Truett, K. Scott Wong, Erika Lee, Alexandra Minna Stern, and Alexis McCrossen read early parts of the manuscript and pushed me, however kindly, to clarify and develop my ideas. I am especially indebted to Katherine Benton-Cohen for her expeditious and painstaking (literally line-by-line) critique of the manuscript. Thank you, Katie, for a yeowoman's work.

Equally critical in the shaping of this book were the contributions of several archivists in Mexico City, Tucson, Berkeley, Hermosillo, and Laguna Niguel. A few stand out as being especially dogged and wonderfully helpful. Paul Wormser, director of archives at the National Archives and Records Administration's Pacific Region, took particular interest in the project in its early stages. He led me to unculled documents on Chinese immigration and border crossing. Equally helpful was Rose Byrne, who at the time was an archivist at the Arizona Historical Society (AHS). To my great delight, she found source material on borderlands Chinese in unexpected places. Her tenacity as a researcher has enriched this book. Benjamín Alonso Rascón at the Archivo General del Estado de Sonora shared his deep knowledge of Sonoran history and the archive's key archival holdings. In Mexico City, Jaime Vélez Storey guided me through the maze of rich archival material at the Archivo General de México. Toward the end of the project, Jill McCleary, a librarian at AHS; Scott Cossel, from Library Technologies at the University of Arizona; and Chrystal Carpenter, an archivist at the University of Arizona Libraries, employed superhuman-like powers to secure permissions and images. Cartographer extraordinaire Erin Greb drew all the maps quickly and beautifully. I am so fortunate to have Erin's creative and artistic contribution to the book. Generous subvention monies provided by the Pennsylvania State University's College of Liberal Arts, headed by Dean Susan Welch, made all the maps and images possible.

Late in the process I had the pleasure of meeting two energetic members of the Tucson Chinese Cultural Center (TCCC): Robin Blackwood, chair of the History Program; and Patsy Lee, president of the Tucson Chinese Association. Both Robin and Patsy embraced me and the book project with immediate enthusiasm and warmth. I was honored to be among a small group of academics and community scholars whom Robin and Patsy invited to speak at the TCCC's First Annual Chinese American Immigrant History Program in September 2010. My experience at the TCCC reminded me that writing history must never be a project of mere intellectual curiosity or indulgence. Wherever possible, social histories must be shared with communities of origin and, if plausible, coproduced in a meaningful and exacting manner. Along these same lines I want to acknowledge the generosity of Esther Don Tang. Known throughout Tucson for her long-standing record of social activism and intrepid spirit, Esther graciously allowed the use of a family photograph in this book. The stories about Esther and the Don Wah family are among several personal accounts that grant us a better understanding of how southern Arizona Chinese indelibly shaped the history of the U.S.-Mexico borderlands.

As this book neared its final stages, it benefited especially from the help of two friends, Barry Kernfeld and Mary McClanahan. Barry's talent as an editor and as a widely read scholar in many fields helped me clarify arguments and pay close attention to word choice. I always looked forward to receiving his penciled edits on paper recycled from his many books on jazz. I also treasure the friendship and editorial prowess of Mary McClanahan. During the dog days of completing this book, her wit and warmth inspired me to continue writing even when it meant returning to my office on cold winter nights. She kept me company, kept me fed, kept me laughing, and encouraged my sports-watching habit. With Mary I knew it was all possible.

As I hope I have made clear, I have been immensely blessed throughout this process. I must reserve my deepest gratitude, however, to Norris Pope, director of scholarly publishing at Stanford University Press. Norris understood the urgency of getting this book to press and extended both the graciousness and expertise to advocate on its behalf. He brought all of his resources and energy to bear on bringing this book to completion. There simply are no words that can adequately convey my appreciation. In addition, Sarah Crane Newman and Alice Rowan skillfully commanded the editorial process, gently drawing my attention to the smallest detail, and Mariana Raykov adroitly shepherded this book to publication.

This book is dedicated to my mom, Sandy Delgado. I can only aspire to achieve her strength and wisdom.

# A Note on Language Use

This book was written from sources in English, Spanish, and Chinese. Drawing on three languages brought to bear a myriad of decisions that warrant explanation. In keeping with scholarly convention, all Romanized and Cantonese Chinese names were converted to pinyin, the official spelling system adopted by the People's Republic of China in 1958. One exception to this was Zhou Ren (Chapter 5). I used his name in Cantonese, Zhenran, to offset other similar-sounding names and for easier readability. When Chinese names appeared in British, Spanish, U.S., and Mexican legal documents, I retained the original spelling and name order used in these official records. For the most part, Mexican Chinese wrote in Spanish, although on occasion they wrote in Chinese and in pidgin Spanish-Chinese. In the former case, I translated the Chinese to Spanish and then into English, and in the latter case, I translated the pidgin into Spanish and then into English-Spanish-Chinese pidgin (Chapter 4).

# MAKING THE CHINESE MEXICAN

# Introduction

By 1993, Cheng Chui Ping could claim she helped hundreds of Chinese immigrants achieve the American Dream. Cheng, most commonly known as "Sister Ping," proved to be a reliable conduit to jobs and housing in New York City, Los Angeles, and San Francisco for would-be immigrants. Sister Ping's generosity was without comparison and her resourcefulness was unsurpassed. When destitute immigrants were unable to afford the transportation cost from China to the United States, Ping financed the journey and arranged work for those who could not immediately repay the loan. For her deeds, the Fujianese native earned a reputation as a modern-day Robin Hood and was once described as "a living Buddha."[1] Ping's benevolence seemed befitting of one called "Sister." She promised hope and prosperity to those who believed that hard work and dependability would secure jobs and relieve debts.

Ping, though, was not a "sister" of goodwill. Rather, she was a kingpin, often dubbed the "Mother of All Snakeheads," who organized and financed the most notorious human-smuggling network in the history of the United States. Her scheme, which included packing hundreds of Chinese into the sweltering holds of cargo ships, netted millions of dollars for the immigrant financier and members of the Fuk Ching, a New York City–based gang with whom Ping worked closely for more than fifteen years.[2] "Customers" paid as much as $40,000 for a circuitous, often treacherous trip from Hong Kong through Thailand and across the Pacific Ocean to Guatemala and Belize. From Central America, immigrants either continued by sea to the port of New York City or trekked overland and across the Mexican border to the United States. Once they landed in the United States, they were either harbored or housed, depending on the travel debt owed to Sister Ping. After years of immigrant smuggling, Ping's enterprise finally met its end when the off-loading of would-be border crossers went awry a mile from the Mexican coast and fourteen immigrants drowned trying to swim ashore.[3]

When one thinks of the history of unauthorized immigration through the U.S.-Mexico borderlands, the story of Sister Ping is hardly the first to come to mind.[4] Instead, our common image of border crossers is of weary Mexicans who slog through blistering deserts and scale walls partitioning one nation from another. A mental picture emerges of migrants so desperate to reach the United States that they enlist the services of "coyotes," that is, human smugglers of varying scruples who promise safe passage— but for a steep price.

Despite the familiarity of these images, our common views of immigration through the U.S.-Mexico borderlands are curious mostly for what they reveal about the writing and silencing of history. That we summon pictures of stark national division and treacherous border crossings when we think of immigrants originating from Mexico indicates that history has effaced many stories from the record. This book seeks to tell these stories. Until 1924, when the National Origins Act placed stringent new restrictions and means of exclusion on would-be immigrants, Mexicans were subject to some scrutiny from American immigration officials but, for the most part, entered the United States almost unfettered. Chinese border crossers, however, faced a different reality. After the passage in 1882 of the Chinese Exclusion Act, which barred Chinese laborers from entering the United States, virtually all Chinese were subject to intense inspection and surveillance by an immigration bureaucracy designed to exclude and deport. But immigration officials at the Mexico border discovered early on that exclusion laws were often too general for effective enforcement at the southern U.S. boundary. U.S. lawmakers had not anticipated the manner in which the myriad legal and social complexities presented by Chinese immigrants continuously prompted the reconfiguration of enforcement strategies at the Mexico border. Networks of migration comprising Chinese family and business relationships that reached deeply into the trans-Pacific world mutated in constant adaptation to immigration restrictions, serving to offer ever-changing means of undocumented entry into the United States. These means of migration persist to the present day.

Sister Ping's story, an example of the illegal immigration that occurs at the southern U.S. boundary, reminds us that the images that constitute the common borderlands narrative rarely if ever capture the entire history of any given group. Over the last thirty years, scholars have worked attentively to retrieve the histories of native peoples, women, and working-class *fronterizos* (borderlanders) from the oblivion of official narratives. We now take as a given the larger webs of race, gender, class, and nation that have ultimately defined who becomes American and Mexican and who does not.[5] But as much as this body of scholarship has helped us better understand the intricacies of border life and the discreet adjustments made by *fronterizos* in times of momentous social change, the history of Chinese borderlanders has yet to be adequately told.

There were noteworthy entries in the early scholarship of Chinese in Mexico.[6] Evelyn Hu-Dehart's pioneering research, for example, invited scholars to look through a revisionist lens focused on Chinese living in Mexico's northern states. Advancing the work of Leo Michel Jacques Dambourges and Charles Cumberland, Hu-Dehart made visible the rhetoric of Sinophobia (the unfounded fear and intense dislike of Chinese persons) and economic competition as justifications for the official expulsion of Sonoran Chinese in 1931.[7] At the same time, Hu-DeHart posited that Mexico's revolutionary period was a crucial historiographical watershed, a time of national and racial consolidation that worked alongside anti-Chinese crusades. Since then, new studies about Chinese Mexicans have emerged, generating rich social and cultural histories.[8] But as Chinese borderlanders became more visible in scholarly literature, they did so almost exclusively within the context of nation-centered histories, Asian American studies, and Latin American studies. Their full significance for U.S.-Mexico borderlands history is still inadequately understood.[9]

I initiated writing this book because the omission of Chinese *fronterizos* from borderlands history did not square with my knowledge of the region, which resided in the everyday, in anecdotes, and in places where individuals and communities created identity. For a time, I relied on my own neighborhood experiences, the transmission of family stories, and the pursuit of hunches, which proved to be as effective in reconstructing this story as did a small collection of historians' essays. A patchwork of memories distilled from my childhood through my early adulthood guided my initial investigation. Growing up in southern California some two hundred miles from the U.S.-Mexico divide I experienced the border initially through a series of short visits from my grandmother, a native of Magdalena, Sonora, Mexico, a border town just south of Nogales, Arizona. I was perplexed that each visit culminated in a formal meal of Chinese food and not my favorite rice and beans. The meal, shared only among the adults, who would dress up for the occasion, seemed to transport my grandmother to places in her past as only a particular cuisine and ambience could. When rice and beans gave way to Chinese food, I invariably turned to a more reliable source to satisfy my palate—the corner grocery store. Here a family of Chinese, all of whom spoke Spanish, supplied me with far too many sodas and candies. While I dedicated myself to getting my fill of junk food, they proved equally dedicated to pestering me to improve my awkward Spanish. The irony was not lost on me.

Years later, as a college freshman, I ran into this story again. On a whim, I ventured into Mexicali, Baja California, Mexico, expecting to find a smaller and calmer version of Tijuana, but instead I chanced upon three square blocks of Chinese-owned restaurants, groceries, *carnicerías* (meat markets), and dry-goods stores. The dusty red facades of *la chinesca* (the Chinese neighborhood) lingered in my memory. Some years after that, teaching sixth, seventh, and eighth-grade immigrant students from Mexico, Vietnam, Laos, and Cambodia taught me that no matter how much emphasis was placed on the distinct histories, cultures, and languages of Southeast Asia and China, some Mexican students still believed that all Asians were Chinese, and that all Chinese deserved ridicule and humiliation.

When I stopped teaching middle school, I began to search for this story as a graduate student and then as an American historian, but I encountered nothing more than fragments lodged between Mexican and U.S. national histories. As I mined archives on both sides of the border, a deeper, interlocking, and fascinating history appeared, one that seemed to account for some of my earlier experiences and observations. Telling this story has raised new questions, and to answer them has required looking beyond and between the Mexican and U.S. national narratives that had obscured it.

What follows is a history of Chinese *fronterizos* that offers a way to understand how the current images of the border came to be, and why our constructs of the U.S.-Mexico border do not include the Chinese. The answer is both complicated and simple. Clearly one can point to the enforcement of the Chinese Exclusion Act, or one may conclude that the violence of the Mexican Revolution (1910–1917) permanently drove out the Chinese. Restrictionist laws and civil war, however, were social realities that occurred almost everywhere Chinese settled; they alone cannot adequately explain the absence of Chinese from our border imagery. Some scholars have diminished the presence of Chinese *fronterizos* in their histories because of the modest size of the Chinese communities along the U.S.-Mexico border. When compared to the larger populations in San Francisco, Cuba, and Peru, the Chinese story of transborder communities seems like a marginal tale and one that historians can justify as numerically inconsequential.

I propose instead a more complicated explanation, one that has to do with writing history and recalling the past, which Michel-Rolph Trouillot and Prasenjit Duara suggest is mutually constitutive. In *Silencing the Past*, Trouillot argues that the production of historical knowledge involves power and that this power often determines what history includes and what history neglects. The basis of underrepresented, unconventional, or unpopular stories, contends Trouillot, is a lack of equal access to history telling, from the assembling and retrieval of facts to the selection of certain themes over others.[10] Trouillot's insights about the "silences and mentions" of the Haitian Revolution can be similarly observed about the Chinese in the U.S.-Mexico borderlands: Mexican and American histories of westward expansion (imperialism), nationalism, and immigration have all but neglected Chinese *fronterizos* and say little about how these border-landers openly challenged laws and practices that cast them as foreign and dangerous.

The silencing of people of Chinese descent is especially apparent in the prevailing historiography on race in Mexico, which for the most part has upheld the view that national identities were forged from the racial mix-ture of European *criollos* (creoles) and indigenous peoples. The discourse of *mestizaje* (racial mixture) by José Vasconcelos, its most eloquent pro-genitor, offered postrevolutionary Mexican elites a foundation for national unity and race homogeneity based on the triumph of the Europeanized *mestizo*.[11] By overcoming African, Asian, and Indian cultures to favor the Europeanized *mestizo*, the discourse of Vasconcelos placed a special emphasis on *mestizaje* as the ideal synthesis of racial diversity on which Mexico's national identity hinged. *Mestizaje* guided the efforts of post-revolutionary architects to assimilate native populations into mainstream Mexican society, to exclude blacks from the national image, and to expel most Chinese from the country. But as Ben Vinson II shows, scholars in postrevolutionary Mexico—notably Alfonso Toro, Germán LaTorre, and Gonzalo Aguirre Beltrán—celebrated blacks as colonial missionaries, early abolitionists, and rightful citizens of Mexico. These accounts, Vinson contends, were partially successful in restoring Afro-Mexicans into the national-racial imaginary.[12] Scholars, however, rarely extolled the contri-butions of Chinese Mexicans, instead casting them mostly as either inter-lopers or tragic victims of virulent xenophobia (the unfounded fear and intense dislike of persons perceived to be foreign or alien).[13] Chinese Mexi-cans are nearly absent from the Mexican national narrative.

Omissions of history, however, are only one part of the equation. The predilection for nation-centered history is the other. Prasenjit Duara makes this point explicit in his critique of the writing of history as a project of modernity. "Linear history," contends Duara, "allows the nation-state to see itself as a unique form of community which finds its place in the oppositions between tradition and modernity, hierarchy and equality, and empire and nation."[14] In challenging the constructs of history, Duara urges scholars to "rescue history from the nation" by reevaluating how pre-national identities shaped national ones. "Nationalism is rarely the nation-alism of *the nation* [his italics]," argues Duara, "but rather marks the site where different representations of the nation contest and negotiate with each other."[15] The concept of nationalism as a modern form of conscious-ness gained wide currency in the work of Karl Deutsch, Ernest Gellner, and

Benedict Anderson, but Duara is quick to challenge perspectives that privilege the nation as a cohesive, collective subject.[16] Duara's rethinking of the past reminds us to account for the contingent nature of national identity and the fluid communities that emerge in the process of nation-building.

This book builds on Duara's insights. It shows not only how the strategies, adjustments, and practices of Chinese *fronterizos* reveal nationalism at work along the U.S.-Mexico borderlands, but also how Chinese, British, and Spanish imperial influences, regionalism, and localism mediated the nation-making process and shaped Chinese Mexican identities. Significantly, the late nineteenth-century borderlands world in which the Chinese settled was crafted in the *absence* of exclusionary nationalisms. After 1854, when the Arizona Territory was cleaved from northern Sonora, many features of late Spanish colonial society and early Mexican national society persisted. Without the ideological stronghold of American or Mexican nationalism in place, relationships based on kinship lines and friendship ties organized social and cultural interaction among borderlanders. Over time, Chinese *fronterizos* came to rely on relationships with Mexicans that not only counteracted the misgivings that had often accompanied their arrival in greater Mexico and the United States, but also transfigured a system of mutual trust that underscored the ways in which they responded to the challenges of living in the Arizona-Sonora borderlands.

What continued steadily into the early twentieth century at the Arizona-Sonora borderlands was a reliance on relationships that derived from Chinese, British, and Spanish imperial societies and were malleable and durable in national landscapes. Some of these relationships originated on the other side of the world. Western imperialism in South China bore the unmistakable imprint of the colonizers' power, as Qing officials and Chinese emigrants knew all too well. Britain and later the United States left their mark by embedding structures of migration in South China that linked Chinese to various colonies and nations in the Americas and the U.S.-Mexico borderlands. The world of Chinese *fronterizos* was shaped by the convergence of trans-Pacific networks and local borderlands arrangements, showing that, in often indirect ways, a wide range of collective practices deepened cultural interactions among *fronterizos*, solidified networks of regional and hemispheric migration for border crossers, and preserved a sense of social fluidity in the region.

The configuration of relationships had profound consequences for Chinese on both sides of the border. In the absence of American citizenship by naturalization for Chinese migrants, networks—and the types of relationships they fostered—gave value to a type of civic participation that had less to do with voting and holding elected office than with creating neighborhood bonds. On the other hand, Mexican citizenship among Sonoran

Chinese helped to fend off anti-Sinitic (that is, anti-Chinese) attacks. These relationships worked for the Chinese until the mid-1920s, but thereafter, ties among *fronterizos* began to erode and were replaced by exclusionary nationalisms that resulted in a hardening of racial identities and in a more clearly defined border. On the U.S. side, adjustments to nation-building projects brought a measure of social mobility to southern Arizona Chinese, but on the Sonora side, the Chinese became perpetual foreigners. *Making the Chinese Mexican* reveals these processes by telling stories of the exceptional, the obscure, and the in-between, as well as the mundane, the predictable, and the unfortunate. These stories reveal that our common contemporary image of the U.S.-Mexico borderlands represents not what actually was but what nation-centered histories have made it.

*Making the Chinese Mexican* argues for a rigorous rethinking of the history of U.S. and Mexican borderlands traditions by broadening the temporal and spatial boundaries of the region. In moving this story into several social and cultural worlds, the concept of *borderlands* is expanded chronologically and geographically so that the continuous life of Chinese *fronterizos* through imperial and national states in the U.S.-Mexico borderlands is captured. In this book, *borderlands* designates a physical place between the shared national boundary of the United States and Mexico, a place that was also influenced by pressures originating from European empires and the Qing Dynasty. By using this term in this manner, I illustrate that Old World patterns from Britain, Spain, and dynastic China were not easily toppled by new political and cultural configurations in the U.S.-Mexico borderlands.[17] Within these cultural landscapes, *fronterizos*, sometimes separately and sometimes together, mediated centralized authority to hold on to their place in the borderlands or to move freely within them. Importantly, these activities, at some distance from colonial and national metropoles, occurred where power wielded by the British, Qing, and Spanish, and later the Mexican and American central states, were often relational, exercised from numerous sites and subject to local permutations and arrangements. Thus, whereas the periodization of this work—the 1870s to the mid-1930s—corresponds with the rise of nationalism in Mexico and the United States, interaction among *fronterizos* shows that the origins of the modern border were wrought from the overlapping worlds of empires and alternative visions of national belonging.

Approaches and arguments in this book shift the intellectual underpinnings of U.S.-Mexico borderlands history from nation-centered narratives to transnational and global history. Viewed broadly, Chinese transnational communities reveal much about borderlands, and they magnify the cultural and political ambiguities of burgeoning nation-states. Putting forth this perspective is crucial. To move away from nation-centered narratives requires nothing short of writing Mexican and U.S. history from the perspective of multilayered empire-state and nation-state processes.[18] Calls to internationalize American and Mexican history have long been in play, and although many studies have adopted transnational approaches, few have pushed the boundaries of the nation into other realms. Thomas Bender's *A Nation Among Nations*, an influential rewriting and reimagining of the American past, stands as a substantial revision of U.S. history. Bender's work reinterprets national processes as transnational ones.[19] The "default narrative" that Bender and countless other historians wish to unseat and replace with a more cosmopolitan, less "exceptionalist" view of American history is but a partial solution to writing beyond nation-centered history. Instead transnationalism must also acknowledge and explore its imperial origins by recognizing globalization as a determining influence both spatially and temporally, and as a consistent subject of history.

One consequence of bridging empires and nations may be that the American West and the Mexican North become less hermetic fields. The exploration of connections to imperial Spain and Britain and dynastic China links colonial worlds to national ones at the U.S.-Mexico borderlands. Within such a frame, Asian American history and Latina/o history unite discrete areas of study and explore an array of previously unknown relationships among various peoples in the Americas.[20] This perspective may help explain how relationships among indigenous people, blacks, South Asians, Caribbean creoles, and Latin Americans have co-created discourses to counter racism and immigration hierarchies, thus revealing a more thorough telling of people's lives within global and local landscapes. Such an approach not only opens up nation-centered history to divergent cultural bonds, ties to a homeland, and temporal and spatial realms, but also captures the complexities of everyday tensions, revealing nations as historically constructed and variously contested entities.

## Movements and Migrations

Several overlapping processes converge in this book to tell a new story about the U.S.-Mexico borderlands, not least of all how webs of support created everyday meaning for Chinese borderlanders and how that meaning was part of a deep multilayering of local and global systems of migration. Thus, global, local, and transborder movements of people tie together this study. They bridge disparate epochs and geographies, and they reveal distinctions between imperial and national projects.[21] Chapter One traces the reliance on diasporic networks and local structures that linked Chinese migrants from imperial worlds to national worlds. Existing networks tied Chinese migrants to each other through kinship, friendship, and membership in social or lineage associations. Once in place, these networks reproduced or were transformed in order to facilitate channels of interconnectivity so that people, commodities, and ideas circulated almost seamlessly and continuously from homeland to adopted country.[22]

The movements of migrants organize this book in an additional manner. They help us to understand how local relationships and transnational arrangements profoundly influenced the reception and treatment of Chinese migrants in the Arizona-Sonora borderlands. Chapter Two examines personal and economic ties between Chinese and Mexican *fronterizos* that afforded Chinese newcomers a home abroad. Everyday bonds among *fronterizos* and the relationships those bonds engendered deepened, changed, and gave new meaning to community and family life. In the midst of the enforcement of Chinese exclusion laws and the monitoring of southern Arizona Chinese communities by immigration officials, kith and kinship networks reinforced claims of social belonging and highlighted personal and practical relationships between people of Chinese and Mexican origin en route to becoming ethnic Americans.[23]

Relationships also served to keep the border open. For Sonoran Chinese, claims of Mexican citizenship prompted border officials to extend, rather than deny, the right of entry into the United States and reentry into Mexico, whereas southern Arizona Chinese caught at the border relied on Mexican and Chinese kith and kin for support. By the turn of the twentieth century, however, the fluidity and flexibility of the region began to give way, albeit unevenly, to a growing regime of immigration restrictionism. Chapter Three discusses myriad inconsistencies of border enforcement at the southern U.S. border and the manner in which Chinese smugglers blazed illegal pathways across the Arizona and California lines. The backdoor route was so successful that it spurred American politicians to seek a diplomatic solution to end illegal entry of Chinese at the country's northern and southern borders, although Canada was more inclined than Mexico to accommodate American requests. By the turn of the twentieth century, enforcing Chinese exclusion laws remapped the U.S.-Mexico borderlands on the basis of a new sense of territoriality.

After 1917, local and regional attachments began to give way to restrictionist immigration policies in Mexico as well, as cross-border movements provoked political persecution and dislocation more than social freedom and autonomy. The new Mexican nationalism cast Chinese as both race contaminators and stalwarts of Porfirian liberalism (which dominated a period between 1876 and 1911 characterized by liberal immigration laws, foreign investment, and capitalist economic development). State-makers sought to remedy Chinese influence by ousting the Chinese from Mexico in general and from Sonora in particular. Chapter Four explores the rise of José María Arana's anti-Chinese movement and the dynamics it created between Mexican women, Chinese men, and revolutionary state-makers. In reinforcing women's primary role in the revolutionary project, state-makers simultaneously cast women at two extremes of the moral-political tandem: as traitors of the Mexican state by way of marriage to Chinese men, and as gatekeepers of the revolutionary state by way of marriage to Mexican men. To choose one over the other circumscribed women's relationship to Mexico's revolution. The ability of women to retain Mexican citizenship was dependent on *mestizo* marriages, whereas those who married outside the socially ascribed racial structure (in this case the Chinese) suffered the loss of citizenship. Revolutionary fervor also constrained the lives of Sonoran Chinese men, many of whom began to flee Mexico as victims of Sinophobic violence. The influx of Sonoran Chinese into the United States induced heightened policing of the Arizona border, and by 1917, excluding Chinese from U.S. shores as well as imposing new measures for legal entry on Mexicans placed greater emphasis on immigration officials as America's gatekeepers.

Chinese in southern Arizona dealt with the reinscription of nativism similarly, but from a different position. Chapter Five examines these distinctions. Whereas *mestizaje* and Sinophobia shaped the Mexican nationalist imagery in opposition to Sonoran Chinese, numerical immigration quotas, specifically the National Origins Act of 1924, created and privileged "whiteness" as a race category and as a criterion for legal entry into the United States. With the near exclusion of all Asians from U.S. shores and the virtual closure of the U.S. southern border to unrestricted crossing, relations between Chinese and Mexican *fronterizos* grew strained. Differences in legal status, political power, and resources began to distinguish Chinese from Mexicans even as each group had become, in the words of historian Mae Ngai, "impossible subjects," a people whose presence in the United States was a political reality and economic necessity but whose legal membership in the nation was unattainable.[24] In the absence of citizenship through naturalization and in the face of harsher immigration laws, southern Arizona Chinese recast the boundaries of community and family life toward Chinese-based social networks.

If American immigration law widened the divide between Mexicans and Chinese in southern Arizona, Sonorans effectively purged themselves of the so-called "yellow peril" by attacking what had made the Chinese Mexican: citizenship by naturalization, the formation of nuclear families, and business ownership. Chapter Six examines the dimensions of postrevolutionary Mexican nationalism and the expulsion of Sonora Chinese. In legal and extralegal maneuverings at the local and federal levels, anti-Chinese agitators successfully endeavored to counter most claims of social and political belonging. State-makers and policymakers utilized a brand of nationalism that constructed and drew on highly racialized and gendered identities. Beset by the enforcement of Chinese-Mexican marriage annulments, severe labor laws, and barrioization (the forced relocation of Sonoran Chinese to designated sections of the state), the Chinese fled Sonora under a state order of expulsion in 1931, with many taking flight into southern Arizona. Objections to the expulsion decree prompted a flurry of correspondence between Chinese ministers and Mexican and American officials, but in the end the only concession granted to Sonoran Chinese was temporary admission to the United States.[25] By August and September of 1931, the peak months of expulsion activity, a steady stream of Sonoran Chinese were temporarily housed in southern Arizona jails, in Nogales, Naco, Bisbee, Tucson, and Douglas (see Figure I.1).[26]

For Mexican women married to Chinese men, the prospect of leaving the western border region of Mexico for China seemed less terrifying than remaining in Sonora. Although legally able to stay in their native land, the vast majority of Mexican women departed for China with their husbands and children.[27] Once in China, however, many Mexican women and their children found themselves stateless, unprotected by Chinese or Mexican law; others returned to their homeland with the help of Mexican consuls during the presidency of Lázaro Cárdenas (1934–1940).[28] By 1943, only 155 Chinese remained in Sonora, once a dynamic borderlands community, whereas on the other side, southern Arizona Chinese become ethnic Amer-

FIGURE I.1  Chinese Fleeing Sonora, Circa 1931. Courtesy of the Arizona Historical Society/Tucson. Photo no. 42945, Fallis Photograph Collection, PC 042, folder 7, box 1. http://www.arizonahistoricalsociety.org

icans.[29] As southern Arizona Chinese differentiated themselves from Mexicans and as Sonoran Chinese steadied themselves from the 1931 expulsion decree, the modern conceptualization of the border began to crystallize. Nation-centered policies—and histories—were on the ascent.

The idea that some people belong to nations more easily than others is powerful, yet it is subject to the political construction and cultural imaginings of the nation-state. National borders arbitrate state control as much as they mediate identities. This book's Epilogue ponders the use of state power in the U.S.-Mexico borderlands after 1931, and the manner in and degree to which cross-border interaction persisted even as the American state limited immigration and Mexican officials sought to contain emigration. The expulsion of approximately 3,500 Sonoran Chinese to China and the repatriation of approximately 500,000 Mexicans and Mexican Americans to Mexico marked the beginning of a regime of border control predicated on territorial sovereignty during the early years of the Great Depression. Despite some semblance of bilateralism, evidenced in the pan-Americanism of the Good Neighbor Policy (1933) and the Bracero Program (a series of initiatives between 1942 and 1964 to facilitate the importation of Mexican workers to the United States for agricultural labor), Mexico and the United States emerged as sole arbiters of the composition, communication, and enforcement of their shared border. The Epilogue meditates on the tension between late twentieth- and early twenty-first-century globalization forces by placing this present-day configuration in the *longue durée* of U.S.-Mexico borderlands history.

In the late nineteenth and early twentieth centuries, the U.S.-Mexico borderlands was a world of overlapping cultures and epochs of Chinese, native peoples, and Mexicans who saw one another pragmatically: at various times as neighbors, as rivals, and as outsiders, but most often as intensely "in between." Chinese *fronterizos* reconciled the turbulence of a changing trans-Pacific-borderlands landscape while creating lives that corresponded at once with disparate spaces and times. Between transimperial and transnational movements, Chinese *fronterizos* countered exploitation and race hatred in multiple and contingent ways. Many adjusted on their own terms, coexisted, and built new communities that integrated all that was around them. What follows is a history that draws attention to movements, relationships, and tensions. In doing so, it places the U.S.-Mexico borderlands and Chinese *fronterizos* at the crossroads of imperial and national worlds.

# 1 From Global to Local

There was nothing in the lofty diplomatic career of Matías Romero to suggest that he would become a tireless advocate of Chinese immigration to Mexico (see Figure 1.1). Romero, a lawyer by training, joined the Liberal Party of Benito Juárez during the War of the Reform (1857–1861), when the influence of military leaders and the power of the Roman Catholic Church were replaced with a constitution-based civil society. In this period, Romero quickly climbed Mexico's diplomatic ranks.[1] At twenty-five years of age, the Oaxaca native had already served as Mexico's *chargé d'affaires* and minister to the United States, where he tenaciously lobbied the Lincoln administration to arbitrate the French Intervention, in which France had invaded Mexico in 1862 under the leadership of Napoleon III. A dauntless proponent of liberalism, Romero facilitated U.S. investment in Mexico, earned the respect of Lincoln's secretary of state, William H. Seward, and engendered a close friendship with General Ulysses S. Grant. Romero proved equally effective as secretary of the treasury, offering, among many suggestions, that the United States assist Mexico in settling its debts with Britain, France, and Spain.[2]

Neither Romero's extensive diplomatic résumé nor his trust in free-market solutions inspired the young attaché to turn to Chinese labor. In fact, Romero's plan transpired from his own frustration with growing coffee in Soconusco, Chiapas, which he pursued after poor health steered him temporarily away from politics in 1872. In his estimation, the *tierra caliente*, Mexico's tropical hotlands abutting Guatemala and Belize, held immense potential, but the region lacked a steady workforce to make coffee profitable. After all, Romero's ambition was not to provide Mexicans with the rich, aromatic drink, but to supply Americans with high-quality coffee beans, produced from the drudgery of Chinese laborers.

When Romero returned to politics as senator of Chiapas in 1875, he conveyed his plans in two essays that were circulated in Mexico City-based

FIGURE 1.1   Portrait of Matías Romero, 1863. Image presented to the U.S. Government in 1863/Civil War Series. http://www.civil-war.net/cw_images/files/images/184.jpg

newspapers: *Revista Universal* and *El Correo del Comercio*. Romero's writings were consistently optimistic, appealing to the popular belief that where Chinese toiled in cane and cotton fields and filled mining and railroad camps, progress occurred. The former coffee grower stirred optimism that development was possible even in the most remote, most arid parts of the world. "It seems to me," he surmised, "that the only colonists who could establish themselves or work on our coasts are Asians, primarily from climates similar to ours, primarily China. . . . This is not an idle dream. Chinese immigration has been going on for years, and wherever it has occurred prudently, the results have been favorable."[3] Enamored with China, Romero also added Japan to the mix of countries from which Mexico stood to benefit as a source for immigrant laborers.[4]

If Romero's vision represented one possible pathway to modernity, it did so within a global context, one rich in international migration amid competing imperial and national worlds. Within this uncertain landscape, Romero pursued his conviction that the solution to Mexico's labor shortage lay across the Pacific Ocean. In 1882, an appointment as Mexico's minister plenipotentiary under the presidency of Porfirio Díaz finally afforded the physically fragile but politically stalwart public servant the influence to promote Chinese immigration.

Vigorous discussion ensued between Romero and a range of Qing Dynasty officials. Diplomats traded gifts: chocolate, rope from the fibers of the henequen plant, and Veracruz coffee beans in exchange for porcelain vases, tea, and cloth made from hemp.[5] Eventually, Chinese laborers arrived in Mexico under official treaty protection, but not until 1899, twenty-four years after Romero first advocated for such immigration, and one year after the intrepid politician succumbed to an appendicitis attack.[6] The delay in China-Mexico diplomacy was in no way due to a lack of effort or forethought on the part of Romero, who had distinguished himself as an astute observer of the mid-nineteenth-century world. The tireless immigration advocate could never, however, have anticipated the dynamic of overlapping empire-states and nation-states that would both produce and delay the very scope and manner of the arrival of Chinese into Mexico and its borderlands with the United States.

## Opium Networks and Imperial Unrest

The complexities bearing on Romero's pursuit of opening up Mexico to Chinese immigration were a reaction to and emblematic of sweeping transformations occurring at the global, national, and local levels in the Pacific world at that time. Within South China and on its adjacent seas, the trading of British commodities and Spanish silver for South Asian opium established durable systems of illegal drug trafficking in the early nineteenth century. Decades later, these systems would evolve into trans-Pacific migration networks to facilitate the labor needs of transitioning imperial and national economies. After the 1820s, as Chinese, British, and American smugglers solidified mutually trusting relationships, the opium trade developed into a tightly organized cartel, the strength of which lay in the structure of its business alliances. To move the drug efficiently and into local and international markets, small, independent opium syndicates formed strong connections with experienced ship captains, who in turn hired large crews of men to help transship opium. The highly organized network also relied on the latest innovations in maritime communication and shipping technology, which made the smuggling of opium from India to South China and into Western markets remarkably efficient. Schooners arrived from Bengal at Kumsing Moon off the coast of Macao in May or June to transfer chests

of "black-earth," "white-skin," and "red-skin" opium to Chinese interme-
diaries.[7] Opium merchants then made their way into South China's inner
harbors by collaborating with local sailors, who transported opium to their
customers through the meandrous and narrow Canton Delta region using
agile sampan ships. By late October, the selling and distribution of opium
was complete. Schooners anchored at the harbor of Lintin, an island just
north of Hong Kong, until late spring of the following year, when merchants
and smugglers followed the same seasonal routine to acquire and sell opium.

Heu Kew, a subcensor in the Qing Military Department, described in
frustration the scheming of opium cartels, which he was powerless to break:
"The traitorous natives who sell the opium cannot altogether carry on the
traffic with the foreign ships in their own persons. To purchase wholesale,
there are brokers. To arrange the transactions, there are the Hong merchants.
To take money and give orders to be carried to the receiving ships, that from
them the drug may be obtained, there are resident barbarians. . . . And to ply
to and fro for its conveyance, there are boats called 'fast-crabs.'"[8] Within the
taut, highly efficient organization of the trade, annual importations in opium
rose gradually from two thousand chests in 1800, five thousand in 1820,
and sixteen thousand in 1830, to twenty thousand chests in 1838.[9]

The robust trading networks impressed many, especially those who
were profiting from the cartel, but the durability and forcefulness came
at a high cost. The strength of the opium networks sowed deep enmity
between Chinese natives and British interlopers. Choo Tsun, a member of
the council of the Board of Rites, expressed a common viewpoint: "The
natives of this place were at first . . . active. . . . But the people called
Hung-maou [red-haired], came thither and . . . in introducing opium into
this country, their purpose has been to weaken and enfeeble the Central
Empire."[10] Repeated bans, the burning of pyres of opium, and harsh penalties for merchants, smugglers, and users failed to end the trade. Whereas
the interests of opium smugglers demanded bonds of common trust, the
Qing and British officials harbored deep misgivings for one another. For
lack of a diplomatic tradition on which to draw and for want of a middle
ground on which to meet, the far-reaching evils of opium led to war, and
the status quo in China gave way to British imperialism.

The spoils of the First Opium War, as codified in the Treaty of Nanking
(1842), bestowed British control over the ports of Canton (Guangzhou),
Amoy (Xiamen), Fuzhou (Foochow), Ningbo, and Shanghai, and later
eleven others, including Shantou (Swatow) and Qiongshan.[11] The dealings
of the British Empire with the Qing Dynasty proceeded from the conviction that the so-called treaty ports were, and should remain, bastions of
unencumbered global exchange in order to benefit the Crown directly and
the United States, Portugal, the Netherlands, Russia, France, and China
obliquely (see Map 1.1). After the First Opium War in 1842, the emer-

MAP 1.1 China Treaty Ports and South China. Drawn by Erin Greb.

gence of Hong Kong and Canton as British-controlled treaty ports shifted commerce firmly into South China. Markets gradually reoriented southward from Shanghai, Hangzhou, and Wenzhou, while contraband trade in opium continued unabated.[12]

Aside from a small number of merchants who applied their management skills from the opium trade to emigration brokering, few Chinese benefited from the new economic configuration. Dislocation and poverty caused by continuous war and village strife constrained the lives of most Chinese. Hong Kong, which was ceded to the British Crown in 1842, quickly acquired a reputation for unfettered commerce and as a hub for opium trafficking.[13] The colony's 21,514 inhabitants—mostly native Chinese and British merchants and their families—seemed well equipped to handle the turbulence of legal and illegal market exchange, until British and Qing authorities called Hong Kong's status as a duty-free zone into question. With piracy going nearly unchecked in and around the colony, legal trade languished while illicit exchange in opium flourished.

In nearby Canton, the opposite blueprint emerged. Merchants from around the globe descended on the Guangdong capital city to trade and receive goods, paying duties on both imported and exported items. *Hongs*—Chinese franchised merchants licensed by the Qing emperor to trade with Westerners—mixed and competed with the thirteen European and American commercial houses on China Street. As foreigners and *hongs* prospered, Chinese boat merchants suffered the inequities of the new trade regime, and some fell into medicating themselves with "poisonous liquors" in the hovels of adjacent Hog Lane.[14]

The terms of trade positioned the British Empire quite favorably in South China. British envoys worked alongside Qing customs officials to collect duties on imports and exports and to tender fines on wayward merchants. But as relations among Qing and British imperial authorities edged tentatively toward conciliation, efforts at accommodating post-war labor demands brought to bear old tensions from within and introduced fresh problems from without. Overpopulation, the shift to commercial agriculture, and export manufacturing displaced subsistence farmers from traditional landholdings. Cheaper British textiles drove Chinese clothmakers out of business, while many porters and warehouse employees lost their jobs when new treaty ports opened to export exchange.[15]

Ethnic violence and civil war exacerbated the changing economic regime in South China. Commencing in 1851, the Taiping Rebellion claimed more than twenty million lives by 1864, when Qing forces quashed the advocates of the "Heavenly Kingdom of Great Peace."[16] During the same period, the so-called Red Turban Rebellion divided loyalties between the Qing and anti-dynastic Triad organizations in the Canton region.[17] More than one million Chinese lost their lives in battle, while the Qing army executed an additional seventy thousand Red Turban sympathizers. To make matters worse, ethnic tensions between the Hakka minority and the Punti majority plagued the Guangdong districts of Xinhui, Taishan, Kaiping, and Enping, known collectively as *Siyi* or the Four Districts. In 1855, Hakka claims to scarce arable lands set off a twelve-year clan war with *Siyi* residents, and thousands more Chinese died.[18] British imperial control, ethnic violence, and the durability of the opium trade combined to create a national landscape in which migration became an ever-greater probability. Hundreds of thousands of Chinese would take up this path, voluntarily or not.

### Between Slavery and Freedom:
### Migration Networks and Coolieism

The collision of the British Empire and the Qing Dynasty yielded to new arrangements of power that remade South China into a locus of transoceanic migration. The forces of rapidly shifting empire-states and nation-states and their transitioning economies configured transoceanic networks that were initially created from the early to mid-nineteenth century opium trade. In a little less than a decade, opium transportation networks matured to accommodate both the imperial appetite for semi-free labor and the demand for wage labor on the part of nation-states. After the British ended the African slave trade in 1807 and abolished the use of slavery in its colonies in 1833, plantation owners turned to Chinese and South Asian contract laborers.[19] The switch to Chinese laborers supported the abolitionist claims of British authorities, and this strategy seemed to appease antislavery advocates. But the British commitment to rid its colonies of any form of slavery yielded to pressure from the Caribbean planter classes—mostly owners of large sugarcane plantations—to retain additional labor that was both cheap and tractable. Planters' profits fell precipitously after the so-called free-trade movement (1846–1849) equalized duties on foreign and colonial sugar. To restore the profitability of Caribbean sugar, British authorities turned to so-called coolie labor. The term *coolie* derived from the Urdu word *qulī*, meaning "day laborer." By the eighteenth century, the term came to be synonymous with cheap South Asian and Chinese labor, whether imported or hired locally. However, by the mid- to late nineteenth century, *coolie* came to be understood as an indentured laborer, especially one who worked on a plantation.[20] Coolie labor squared the needs of planters for tractable, low-cost labor with the conflicting demands of the British public for the complete abolition of slavery. The Spanish branch of this planter class, compelled less by humanitarian dictates than by a desire for profits in sugar, cotton, and guano (fertilizer made from bird droppings), exploited the British coolie network by adding Chinese to their existing force of African slaves.[21]

Both the British system and the Spanish system worked in tandem with private individuals who held no national or imperial allegiances. The recruitment and transportation of coolies and the selling of contracts were in the hands of entrepreneurs or private firms operating within the logic of slave societies as French, American, Portuguese, Cuban, Peruvian, and British ship owners organized the coolie trade from both treaty and non-treaty ports.[22] At Macao, Amoy, Swatow, Canton, and Hong Kong, migrant firms sold coolie contracts to Cuban and Peruvian planters at a far lower price than the cost of African slaves.[23]

From the beginning of the coolie trade, Chinese migrants were left virtually unprotected. The Crown's first secretary of state for the Colonies, Lord Edward Stanley, sought to guard against possible abuses. He believed that "the apprehensions [of the coolie trade] may be removed by increased vigilance and new precautions."[24] These precautions included Qing regulation of emigration, but this was not a realistic possibility given the centuries-long ban on emigration from China. Qing authorities, and the Ming before them, steadfastly maintained the *hai jin*, a prohibition on overseas travel.[25] The Manchus, after their conquest of China in 1644, continued to guard against outside influences first by banning foreign trade, and later, by reinforcing their prohibition on emigration. Dynastic authorities perceived Chinese abroad as traitors (*hanjian*), deserters, rebels, and conspirators who had rejected their filial duties. When, after 1847, several thousand Chinese began departing for the Americas under dubious circumstances, the *hai jin* continued to be enforced, leaving émigrés vulnerable to abuse at points of procurement and transit and while under contract abroad.

Despite Lord Stanley's optimism, authorities paid no real attention to labor conditions or to the techniques of labor procurement.[26] At the same time, Qing officials refused to regulate emigration, because doing so would sanction it as permissible. When Lord Stanley authorized the coolie trade, the Qing approach to emigration did not figure into the new British scheme. This union of well-meaning but misplaced intentions and regulatory incompetence on the part of the British had disastrous results: the emergence of unfettered and privatized migration networks.

With neither the Qing nor the British as regulators of emigration, Chinese immigrants suffered from the whims and needs of empire-states accustomed to slavery. Immigrant brokers, unscrupulous imperial consuls, and Chinese migrant *hongs* emerged as a motley crew of emigration overseers. Planters, labor contractors, and recruiters composed the main links, creating new sorts of bonds. Within South China, private shipping firms from the United

States and Europe, along with Chinese migrant *hongs*, organized the recruitment and transportation of Chinese laborers, whether free wage workers or indentured servants. Operations stretched across the Pacific Ocean and were enmeshed with the enterprises of Spanish and British planters and American railroad and mining companies, or linked to the designs of smugglers' rings and kinship associations throughout the Americas (see Map 1.2).

When in need of laborers, British and Spanish planters, for example, drew on contractors who had the sea-faring experiences and financial wherewithal to transport thousands of Chinese migrants across the Pacific Ocean. Still, they needed help. On the ground in South China, labor contractors obtained the services of recruiters or coolie brokers, "men of the lowest possible character . . . to supply the wants of the merchants."[27] These brokers resorted to coercion, fraud, and trickery. When traffic was slow, coolie brokers often paid unemployed Chinese to deceive neighbors and acquaintances into the indenture.

Such deceptive practices also characterized the procurement of ostensibly free labor under the credit-ticket system, sometimes referred to as the bargain-ticket system. In this manner of labor procurement, emigrants who could not afford passage borrowed transportation expenses from sponsoring agents. Circulars portended in image and in scrawled Chinese the wealth to be had overseas, including opportunities in the United States and Mexico. "Laborers are wanted in the land of California," announced collie broker Ah Lung. "Great works to be done there, good houses, plenty of food." Just as labor recruiters promoted California in 1868, so they boosted Mexico as early as 1870. Coolie broker Clang Wo wrote, "China colony for Mexico. All get rich there, have land. Make first year $400; next year $1,000. Have quick more money than mandarins. Plenty good rice and vegetables cheap. Nice ship, no sickness, plenty of room."[28] Once landed, emigrants repaid auxiliary overseers the cost of passage from wages earned, at least in theory. Villages in China also sponsored the emigration of their members. Under this system, a designated kinsman traveled with the emigrants and bore responsibility for collecting payments and interest for transportation expenses. By the 1870s, approximately 49,277 Chinese were listed as California residents. Ostensibly all were free wage laborers, and a few thousand more found their way to Idaho, Oregon, Utah, and Nevada.[29]

Yet not all was as it appeared. In describing the procurement of laborers for California under the bargain-ticket system, W. Caine, the British lieutenant governor at Hong Kong, detailed similar features of the contract labor system. "A passage-broker (not unfrequently [sic] a man of straw who is not to be found a few hours after the vessel leaves) sends out his crimps to the mainland, and these on the payment of about five dollars as bargain money. [He] gives to each candidate for shipment a bargain-ticket,

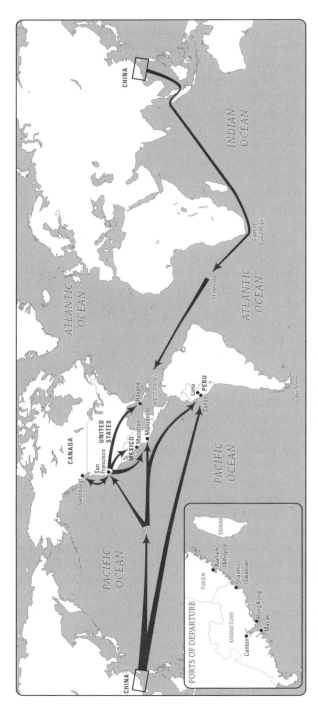

MAP 1.2 Chinese Migration into the Americas, the Mid-Nineteenth and Early-Twentieth Centuries. Drawn by Erin Greb.

sealed with the seal of the broker."[30] The expectation of quick wealth on the part of Chinese gold rush miners and railroad workers met the reality of hardship, exploitation, and increasing debt obligation, especially among those unable to repay transportation costs to migrant agents. In theory, coolies, who operated under the contract labor system, stood in contrast to wage laborers, who operated under the credit-ticket system. In practice, these distinctions were blurred.

The passage of both free and contract laborers into the Americas was organized by a system of networks employing coercive tactics at the level of acquiring workers. The networks, although seemingly structured for diametrically different types of labor—one operating under the calculus of free labor in nation-states and the other under the logic of slavery in colonies of empire-states—became conflated with one another, with the subsequent crucial consequence that the perception of Chinese labor in Mexico and the United States eventually became that of coolies, not free laborers. Regardless of the actual or intended status of any given group of Chinese workers in any given locale, unscrupulous actions served to tilt the balance and to shift public perceptions toward the notion that all such workers were coolies.

Under pressure from both Caribbean planters and American capitalists (and later, Mexican state-makers), the dualism of free and unfree was undermined in several early instances of deceptive and coercive labor procurement. The *Robert Bowne* incident constituted the first significant example. On March 21, 1852, the *Robert Bowne* left Amoy in South China, ostensibly bound for San Francisco. As it turned out, the four hundred Chinese migrants on board were not destined for San Francisco, nor had they been obtained for the purposes of wage work; rather, they were meant to toil as coolies in Peru's infamous guano islands. Outrage took hold after the news broke of the coolies' actual fate and after the ship's captain, Lesley Bryson, supposedly as a matter of public hygiene, "cut off the tails of a very large number of Chinese" and scrubbed down his human cargo with "hard brooms."[31] After nine days of cruelty, the coolies rose up against their captors and killed Bryson, two officers, and four crew members. Similar accounts of deception and mutiny on the British vessels *Lady Montague*, *Victory*, and *Susannah* were registered.[32]

Extreme abuses at the point of procurement served further to fix attention on Chinese workers as coolies rather than as free laborers. John Bowing, British consul and diplomat in China (1850–1857), reporting from Amoy, witnessed hundreds of coolies corralled in barracks, or barracoons, "stripped naked, and stamped or painted with the letter C (California), P (Peru), or S (Sandwich Islands) on their breasts, according to the destination for which they were intended."[33] The abduction of Chinese men and boys was rampant practice throughout South China port cities, and the barracoons—operated by British, Spanish, Portuguese, and American coolie traders—were filled with the victims of kidnapping schemes.

Tseen-a-koon, a vegetable farmer, was among those tricked into the trade by coolie brokers working for an American shipping company. Assured by an acquaintance that a job was to be had in Canton, Tseen-a-koon embarked on a passage boat and then a sampan to Honam Island, a gateway to Canton. Instead of landing in Canton as promised, the sampan continued to the deep-sea anchorage at Whampoa, where Tseen-a-koon was forced aboard a coolie broker's boat. Threatened with murder if he did not consent to the contract, the vegetable farmer remained confined on the ship for nearly a month with 250 other coolies until Chinese officials uncovered the ploy.[34]

Most who were coerced into the barracoons for transportation to the Americas were less fortunate than Tseen-a-koon. Once abroad, Chinese laborers under the contract system were at the mercy of their plantation overseers or beholden to migrant agents, and a variety of strategies of labor control took hold. Typically, contracts ran eight years and pay remained atrociously low—approximately four pesos a month in the Spanish indenture and two dollars a month in the British indenture.[35] In a push for profits in British Guiana, planters retained control over indentures by attaching criminal sanctions to work discipline and by instituting a pass law system—a means of social control that originated in South Africa in the eighteenth century—marking South Asian coolies (of which there were 429,623) and Chinese coolies (of which there were 10,022) as veritable chattel. The labor conditions were equally treacherous in Peru, especially after the abolition of slavery in 1854. The newly installed Peruvian regime greatly benefited from the new nation's diverse agricultural economy, especially on its coastal isles, where Chinese painstakingly scraped dried guano from rocky surfaces of the Chinchas, Ballestas, and Guañape islands.[36]

Just as in Peru, Chinese labor in Cuba was reduced to slavelike conditions. In Cuba, approximately 142,000 Chinese worked the sugar cane plantations to supplement an increasingly contraband trade in African slaves, although the manumission of slaves in Cuba did not occur until 1886.[37] When compared with the costs of African slaves, Chinese coolies were cheaper.[38] As they worked alongside African slaves, Chinese coolies rarely received adequate food, recourse for mistreatment, or pay. Owners usually afforded the Chinese a three-day respite during the Chinese New Year, but Sunday rest was rare. After 1860, a royal Spanish decree reinforced the servile status of coolies by further limiting the options of the Chinese to leave the island after meeting the terms of their contracts. Because previous ordinances guaranteeing Chinese a free passage to South China were eliminated by this decree, few actually had the resources to return home.[39] In the absence of official state supervision, and through overwork and the forced renewal of contracts, Chinese and African slaves made Cuba the world's foremost producer of sugar by the mid-nineteenth century, far outdistancing competition in Puerto Rico, Jamaica, and Brazil.[40]

In free labor markets, controversies swirled over the use of coolie labor and its abuses. With rumors running rampant about the severity of the Spanish indenture system, British authorities prompted an imperial mission to investigate instances of abuse, murder, and suicide among Cuba's Chinese. The *Cuba Commission Report*, an 1871 testimony, detailed the viciousness of worker brutality in the sugar cane plantations in the Spanish colony. Knowing about these abuses, the British government attempted to rein in renegade coolie ships by passing the Merchant Shipping Act of 1872. The act forbade emigrant passenger ships from proceeding to sea until cleared and certified by surveyors of the British Board of Trade.[41] The United States also guarded against the Chinese indenture. By outlawing coolies, American politicians took steps to protect the working classes from the Chinese indenture, and as historian Moon-Ho Jung argues, to extirpate slavery from the American South.[42] A Republican-dominated Congress, acting at the behest of the Lincoln administration's report on the Chinese indenture that confirmed the perniciousness of the trade and the failure of government regulation, proposed legislation to end U.S. involvement in the trade.[43] In outlining the terms of the Anti-Coolie Act of 1862, Congress prohibited Americans and foreigners residing in the United States from engaging in the importation of "subjects of China, known as 'coolies.'"[44] On the other hand, immigration of Chinese wage laborers was consistent with American notions of universal inclusion and free labor ideology. To extend these ideals into the Pacific world, the United States signed the Burlingame Treaty with Qing dynasty officials in 1868, further emphasizing the requisite that all Chinese heading toward and entering into the United States were free and voluntary immigrants. Immunities, exemptions, and privileges "enjoyed by subjects of the most favored nation" were also extended to the Chinese living in the United States.[45]

Yet protection ostensibly provided in the Burlingame Treaty was more rhetoric than reality. Throughout the United States, Chinese laborers confronted exploitation and racially motivated violence with few safeguards in place. In the United States, the Chinese could expect no official defense as politicians and the working classes joined to cast them as coolies.[46] At the same time, Qing government officials continued to regard Chinese abroad as traitors to the dynasty and therefore did not protect them. As international condemnation gathered strength, the coolie trade—despite all the profit it garnered for planters and capitalists—grew increasingly untenable. British and American officials identified Macao, a Portuguese-controlled port city, as the largest supplier of coolie labor to the Americas and lobbied for its closure. In countering the criticism, the Portuguese charged that Chinese coolies embarking from Macao were no different from those laborers boarding American and British ships from Hong Kong and Canton: all were workers under the contract system, some involuntarily so. In 1874, due mostly to pressure exerted by British and American diplomats, Macao was closed and, later, Amoy, effectively ending the trade in unfree laborers into Latin America and the Caribbean.[47] Migration of Chinese into the Americas continued, and by 1877 new diplomatic conventions between China and Spain abolished contract labor in Cuba and declared free the emigration of Chinese to any Spanish colony, even as such labor was shadowed by the stigma of coolieism.[48]

### Contrasts and Commonalities: Chinese Immigration into the United States and Mexico

Even as the coolie trade was abolished in Latin America and the Caribbean, the United States and Mexico struggled to reconcile the need for Chinese immigrant labor with working-class hostilities in the former and racial anxieties in the latter. As would be the case in many other facets of their immigration policies, the two nations shared perspectives on Chinese immigration even as they diverged greatly in certain practices. Both were poised for considerable development, the pace of which depended in part on the labor available to them. Both were also explicit regarding the preferred racial makeup of their growing populations, with Mexico preferring European descent but begrudgingly allowing for Middle Eastern and Chinese immigrants, and the United States enforcing its Chinese exclusion laws. One critical difference, however, was the presence of a post-emancipation American working class that was active and vocal in protecting its livelihood from the threat of Chinese labor, and from politicians who, by virtue of the 1882 Chinese Exclusion Act and its subsequent 1892 expansion, were inclined to accommodate that demand. By contrast, Mexico's need for a cheap, tractable labor force ultimately clashed with the racial ideals of the Porfirian intelligentsia. The resolution of that clash—a liberal immigration policy that tacitly held to the expectation that Chinese would provide labor to but not intermarry with Mexicans—proved infeasible. A primary factor in Mexico's inability to attract immigrants was the intended destination of those immigrants. Mexican officials hoped that Chinese would settle and work in the most remote regions of the country—its coasts and jungles. But there were virtually no transportation systems by which to convey workers and products, and would-be immigrants balked at settling in the most inhospitable regions of Mexico. One plan after another failed to lure Chinese immigrants in sufficient numbers to provide the desired labor, a failure that left the country outside the orbit of trans-Pacific migration networks and ultimately delayed widespread immigration from China until the mid-1890s. Mexico's development would suffer for the delay. By the mid-1880s, no more than one thousand Chinese had found their way into Mexico. Conversely, trans-Pacific migration networks reached well into the United States, especially the Pacific states, where most Chinese settled. By the late 1880s, more than 105,000 Chinese had arrived in the United States, 75,132 in California alone.[49]

The differing approaches to immigration in the United States and Mexico unfolded in an era ostensibly dedicated to using free labor, a commitment that would have profound consequences for Chinese immigration into the two nations. Although African slavery had been abolished in the United States in 1863 and in Mexico in 1829, considerable fear remained among American and Mexican officials and the U.S. working class with regard to Chinese labor.[50] In the United States, far more than in Mexico at that time, Chinese immigrants posed considerable competition for menial jobs as a highly exploitable, if not semi-free, labor force that employers tended to prefer to their own citizens. Yet employers escaped public criticism for their decisions, and the stigma of coolieism followed Chinese laborers wherever they arrived. In 1869, approximately 400 Chinese coolies from South China and 145 Chinese indentures from Cuba arrived in New Orleans.[51] The infamy of coolieism surrounded their presence. Even in St. Louis, Missouri, arguments to exclude Chinese from U.S. shores were based on the assumption that "not one . . . came in an 'entirely voluntary' manner and in every respect [was] the Cooly [sic] type."[52] Just before the completion of the transcontinental railroad in 1869 at Promontory Point in Utah, many Chinese remained in the United States, settling in the Pacific Coast and Rocky Mountain regions of the country. In California they constituted one-twelfth of the state's population and one-fifth of the workforce, whereas in other areas of the American Southwest and in the Pacific mountain states far fewer had arrived. The cant of coolieism was most vociferous in San Francisco, where the Chinese population increased from 2,719 in 1860 to 12,022 in 1870.[53] Benjamin E. Lloyd was just one of many observers to comment on the city's reliance on coolie labor. Writing in the mid-1870s, he observed, "The slavery that exists—its propagators being in San Francisco—is the system of 'contract labor' practiced by both Americans and Chinese. It may be liberty to the Chinaman . . . but it is slavery when construed in the spirit of justice."[54] Lloyd's comments were no doubt influenced by a massive influx of Chinese workers who had landed in California to labor on the transcontinental railroad for the Central Pacific Railroad Company in the previous decade, and by contin-

ued suspicions that newly arriving Chinese were also coolies. Reports that
Chinese women were slaves were also pervasive. According to this commentary—much of it true—Chinese emigrant agents, conspiring with prostitution rings, received reimbursement for travel from the owners of the
prostitutes—either wealthy individuals or members of a Chinese guild.[55]

As small groups of Chinese came to reside in the Arizona Territory during the 1860s and early 1870s, stories comparable to those of other cities,
that they were akin to slaves, also followed. Local residents viewed the
Chinese with skepticism, but also layered their anti-Chinese rhetoric with
criticism of mining owners. When, in the late 1870s, a crew of one hundred Chinese laborers arrived in the adjacent mining towns of Clifton and
Morenci, Henry Lesinsky, the mining proprietor, was condemned by locals
for his decision to use Chinese labor: "That shows the true character of the
man, putting Chinese against American labor. Let it be remembered as a
matter of Arizona history that one Mr. Lesinsky made the first importation
of Chinese cheap slave labor into Arizona."[56] To most white residents in
early territorial Arizona, Chinese were coolies who accepted "slave wages."
They were not coworkers, small-shop owners, and potential settlers.

Despite these distinctions, by the end of the 1870s the Chinese had
become objects of suspicion and racially charged commentary. Their growing population in the Arizona Territory, often as unskilled workers and
modestly capitalized merchants and farmers, generated controversy over
immigration and colonization projects and policies. Territorial boosters,
keen for European-origin immigrants and white Americans, painted the
barren landscape of Arizona as a modern-day oasis and extolled the qualities of pastoral and mineral resources and the open-air comforts of rural
living.[57] To encourage white immigration even more aggressively, Arizona
legislators created the office of commissioner of immigration in 1885.
Among carrying out other responsibilities, the commissioner provided
maps of stage routes and "emigrant roads" to direct immigrants from eastern states and Canada into the Territory, and pamphlets and circulars to
advertise mining, farming, and agricultural projects.[58]

For a decade, the immigrant population met the hopes and expectations
of territorial boosters to attract European and white Americans. Alongside
a large percentage of settlers originating primarily from New York, Ohio,
and Texas, the foreign-born population of the Arizona Territory comprised a growing number of Europeans amid a majority of Mexicans from
Sonora; in 1870, of the 5,809 persons listed as foreign-born white, 4,368
were born in Mexico and the second largest white foreign-born population (686 people) originated from Great Britain and Ireland.[59] In ten years
the Territory's population increased dramatically, from 9,658 in 1870 to
40,440 in 1880. The most dramatic increase in population during this time
occurred among the Chinese—from 20 in 1870 to 1,630 in 1880.[60] Migra-

tion from China was virtually unimpeded in the Arizona Territory, despite the stigma of coolieism that adjoined Chinese laborers.

To be sure, opposition against the Chinese influx took hold. In the estimation of James Chester Worthington, a resident of Tucson, Arizona, the Chinese figured dubiously among those who stood to benefit from the celebrated vision of the Arizona Territory. While corresponding with his brother Dan in 1880, Worthington addressed possible solutions to the Chinese arrival at a time when, in his estimation, "the Anti-Chinese feeling is much stronger here [than in San Francisco]." Yet he considered, among many possibilities, as a response to the recent influx of Chinese that they be enfranchised, asserting:

I have come to believe in restricting immigration from China, or obliging the Chinese to become citizens . . . and then making them stay and keep there [sic] money they earn in the country as all other foreign emigrants. I believe that the Chinese are better for servants and laborers than natural Americans, or even any Europeans and they would not make very bad citizens—[they] would always vote with their employers as they ought to do and against Dennis [sic] Kearny [sic] and his ilk—and so counteract the "sand lot man" influence. . . . I can't see any other remedy than to enfranchise the Chinese. . . .[61]

Worthington's remarks about Denis Kearney, leader of the Workingman's Party of California, reflected a persistent tension between workers and capitalists that underscored anti-Chinese campaigns throughout the United States, including the Arizona Territory. During "sand lot" rallies, Kearney's fiery speeches and evocation of the Party's slogan, "The Chinese Must Go!" roused thousands of followers to demonize Chinese laborers, despite his own ambivalence toward the working class.[62] Kearney, in keeping with his groundless reputation as the "workingman's friend," cried out for the expulsion of monopolists, industrialists, and Chinese alike, but never explicitly advocated a laborers' platform for the party.[63] Despite Kearney's faults and Worthington's considerable dislike for the Irish-born party leader, the Tucson resident eventually retreated from earlier consideration to enfranchise the Chinese. Worthington grew more skeptical about the benefits of Chinese naturalization, instead adopting a common view that the Chinese were, at best, competitive with white labor and, at worst, "slaves, sent over on speculation by contracts made between their masters and the 6 Cos."[64] By "6 Cos" Worthington meant the Chinese Consolidated Benevolent Association, commonly known as the Six Companies, a San Francisco-based political organization formed by wealthy merchants from the Ning Yuen, Hop Wo, Kong Chow, Yeung Wo, Sam Yup, and Yan Wo *huigan* or district associations. The Six Companies assisted the Chinese community by arbitrating disputes among individuals and by representing the community's interests to both the U.S. and Chinese governments.

Worthington's approach was less rancorous than that of ardent exclusionists. Despite his views that the Chinese made for better servants than "natural" Americans or Europeans, Worthington initially preferred to grant them citizenship, whereas others advocated for a complete restrictionist platform. Regardless of one's place on the spectrum—to make Chinese U.S. citizens or exclude them altogether—Worthington's rhetoric of coolieism was a sign of the times in the United States. Such discourse underscored a virulent anti-Chinese perspective that culminated in the passage in 1882 of the Chinese Exclusion Act, which barred laborers from entering the United States for ten years.[65] For the first time, certain classes and races of immigrants were excluded by federal legislation. Although Chinese merchants, diplomats, teachers, travelers, and students were permitted entry, they would face considerably greater difficulty ten years later when the exclusion law was amended to add further restrictions. After the passage of the Geary Act in 1892, even those Chinese who held exemption status had to provide documentation from the Chinese government to certify that they were not laborers.

Yet as the United States enacted legislation to restrict the entry of Chinese, the need for tractable labor south of the U.S. border encouraged liberal immigration laws, although the international controversy over indentured servitude and free labor seemed not to instruct Mexican views on Chinese immigration directly. In objecting to Mexican officials'—mainly Romero's—original plan to attract Chinese into the country, nary a word was mentioned by the Mexico City press or by the general public about the cries of coolieism emanating from San Francisco and Louisiana, or about the brutal treatment of contract laborers in Peru or Cuba. Mexicans instead derived their objections to Chinese immigration from indirect experience with coolieism and couched these objections mostly in terms of miscegenation, the genetic mixing of races.[66] "[The Chinese] have perverse tendencies," warned the editors of the *Gaceta Internacional*, a Mexico City newspaper. "Any race mixture like those in Cuba and Peru will produce a generation [in Mexico] whose quality we will have to leave to the judgment of ethnographers."[67] Similar characterizations of the Chinese were to be found in *La Libertad* and *El Monitor Republicano*, also Mexico City newspapers. The latter newspaper claimed that because Chinese would come to Mexico as single men, miscegenation—and by extension, race contamination—would inevitably ensue. The editors of *La Libertad* extolled the unspoiled beauty of the Mexican Indian that stood to be blemished by degenerate Chinese.[68] Alberto Mertes, writing for *El Monitor Republicano*, was brutal. He cast the Chinese as "indolent, cruel, and arrogant" while asserting that Mexico did not stand to benefit from these "usurious immigrants."[69]

The Mexican government was particularly interested in luring European immigrants from abroad, because the *científicos*, Porfirio Díaz's brain trust, believed that the Chinese were racially unfit for intermarriage and that the Mexican peasant was inherently incapable of building and participating in a modern, industrial society. The *científicos* saw European immigrants, especially those who practiced Roman Catholicism, as ideal.[70] Indigenous peoples, already identified as the bane of Mexico, could hardly be entrusted with such lofty aspirations. "For only European blood can keep the level of civilization . . . from sinking," exhorted Social Darwinist and leading *científico* Justo Sierra.[71] In the view of the Mexican intelligentsia, nothing short of an influx of European immigrants could jump-start Mexico's stalled journey toward industrial development. While the *científicos* gushed over the preeminence of the European immigrant, Vicente Riva Palacio, Mexico's minister of development, kept prospects realistic, reminding Porfirian intellectuals that whereas most Mexicans remained unaccustomed to the lifestyles of people in advanced countries, Europeans knew well the living standards of most Mexicans—they were *peones* (landless ranch hands), laborers, and farmers. In Palacio's estimation, Europeans would inevitably reject the lifestyle of the Mexican, wanting instead to settle in urban areas amid transportation networks and cultural centers.[72]

Racial anxieties, however, were not the sole factor holding Chinese immigration in check. Accompanying Mexico's fears about miscegenation were its failed colonization and immigration schemes of the mid-nineteenth century, which left the country outside trans-Pacific migration networks. The project of Jacob P. Leese of the San Francisco-based Lower California Company (LCC), for example, failed due to a lack of interested colonists. Baja California's vast potential in commercial fishing, mining, and agriculture seemed to offer an ideal opportunity for would-be colonists. In 1863, the Mexican government granted Leese more than 45,000 square miles of land on the peninsula, including the coastline, for $100,000 in gold bullion and the promise that Leese would populate Baja California with colonists. Of particular value in Mexico's charter with Leese were the generous terms guaranteeing to the company's colonists, regardless of race, the same civil and political rights as those enjoyed by Mexicans. Leese and his colonists were granted autonomy from the Mexican government as the LCC was permitted "quasi-government powers" to establish and govern municipalities and to raise taxes.[73] Chinese settlers were at the center of Leese's scheme, but because the San Francisco-based businessman could not raise enough funds to charter steamers from China to Mexico, no Chinese arrived in Baja California under the LCC, and those few immigrants who did undertake the voyage had abandoned the operation by 1871. Over the next few years, only a few hundred Chinese immigrants trickled into

Mexico, certainly not enough to meet labor demands for agricultural and industrial projects. Other efforts to attract colonists to Mexico met with longstanding failure, and with the exception of colonies of Russians and European Jews in Baja California, greater opportunities pulled immigrants of European descent into the United States, even though Mexican immigration laws and colonization projects were much more generous than those of its northern neighbor.[74] More broadly speaking, refusal by most Arabs, Egyptians, African Americans, former confederate soldiers, Chinese, and Europeans to colonize Mexico's far-flung regions dampened even the most enthusiastic proponents of the Mexican liberal cause.[75]

That few immigrants of the Porfirian ideal actually settled in Mexico sharply modified the nation's stance on immigration. In tacit recognition of Mexico's difficulty in attracting newcomers to its shores, some *científicos* became, out of necessity, less selective when it came to accepting menial laborers. By the late 1870s, according to historian Moisés González Navarro, "the positivists [*científicos*] had no preference when it came to peones. They were interested not in the origin but in the efficacy of the labor. . . . [They] omitted all racial and aesthetic considerations, and noted only economic criteria."[76] Taking advantage of the changing political winds among the Porfirian intelligentsia, Romero persuaded a reluctant Mexican Congress to accept Chinese immigration, but as would often be the case, these projects had few tangible results.

Without well-established migration networks that had otherwise channeled thousands of Chinese laborers into the Pacific Americas, Mexico's colonization and immigration projects stood to fail. But in 1874, Mexican officials took steps to place their country within the orbit of trans-Pacific migration networks even as they held deep apprehension about Chinese laborers. Under contract with the Mexican government, the New York-based Pacific Mail Steamship Company (PMSC) established northward passage routes from Panama to San Francisco via Acapulco, and southward travel from San Francisco to Panama via Cabo San Lucas, Salina Cruz, Mazatlán, and Acapulco.[77] Despite these routes and Mexico's agreement with the PMSC, the pursuit of Chinese immigration did not begin in earnest until a decade later, in 1884, when PMSC steamers began making regular trips from Acapulco to Hong Kong via Honolulu and Yokohama, Japan. For each voyage, the PMSC received $17,000 from the Mexican government (approximately $62,900 in 2012 terms) to transport up to one thousand Chinese laborers into Mexico and to trade coffee, sugar, and tobacco for silks and tea. Potentially, the most lucrative aspect of the PMSC was procuring Chinese labor. After the PMSC received its official subsidy, the shipping company would collect additional compensation of thirty-five pesos per Chinese worker. At the same time, and under the same contract,

Mexico offered PMSC sixty-five pesos per European worker.[78] Although the contract did not specify where the new arrivals would toil, their most likely duty would have been to work on the Tehuantepec railroad line.

But this scheme for Chinese immigration never got off the ground. (The European scheme also failed.) In fact, the PMSC lost money. When *Mount Lebanon*, a PMSC-owned steamer tried to set off for Acapulco from Hong Kong with six hundred Chinese laborers on board, British officials did not permit the steamer to leave the harbor, in the belief that once the Chinese landed in Mexico, they would have no legal recourse in the slave-like conditions that awaited them. Ignacio Mariscal, who at the time was in London negotiating the resumption of diplomatic relations with Great Britain, reminded British officials that slavery had long been abolished in Mexico and, because of this, there would be no reason to prohibit the emigration of Chinese to Mexico. The British nonetheless refused the diplomat's appeal. Moreover, according to PMSC attorney Theodore Schneider, British government officials would continue to prohibit Chinese emigration until they were satisfied that Chinese migrants were protected from abuse.[79] At first Schneider thought that the order to block the landing of the *Mount Lebanon* was a simple mistake. When this proved not to be the case, it became clear to Schneider that British officials were unwilling to risk putting the welfare of Chinese laborers into the hands of a nation that did not enjoy diplomatic relations with Great Britain or China. Moreover, without an official treaty between China and Mexico, the British objected to Chinese emigration and would not support emigration to Mexico until such a treaty was accorded.[80]

The British put forward a possible solution to the impasse. Spenser St. John, the British representative to Mexico, proposed to José Fernández of the Ministry of Foreign Relations (SRE) that the protection of Chinese laborers in Mexico should fall to the British. In making his recommendation, St. John avoided any direct reference to labor conditions that the Chinese could encounter in Mexico, and instead extolled the necessity of Chinese labor for Mexican development.[81] St. John contended: "I cannot but think that it is of the very highest importance to the prosperity of the Mexican State . . . that Chinese immigrants should be encouraged to settle there, and that the acceptance of this . . . proposal made on behalf of China, will enable the Mexican Company to procure an excellent class of labourers. . . . No people can give a better revenue to a government than the Chinamen."[82] But with equal significance, St. John also pointed to the necessity of having in place some diplomatic recourse for Chinese workers and the Qing government if abuses were to occur.[83]

Mexican officials offered a counterproposal that China appoint representatives to oversee its subjects in Mexico rather than allow the British to represent them, an option that would not compromise Mexico's future dip-

lomatic relationship with Great Britain.[84] China turned down this proposi-
tion and insisted that the British stand as official overseers of Chinese in
Mexico. The stalemate produced frustration among Mexican, Qing, and
British diplomats. A compromise was finally reached when Schneider threatened to abandon his agreement with Mexico for lack of international cooperation. Mexico responded to the PMSC agent's latest gambit by accepting
the "good offices of England," and rejected the absolute British protection of
Chinese in Mexico.[85] After it was finally agreed that the British government
would serve as the unofficial advocate of Chinese in Mexico, treaty talks
began in earnest in July 1885. From the beginning, negotiations languished
in miscommunication, misunderstanding, and frustration. Díaz accommodated China's request to negotiate a treaty through their only North American legation, which was located in Washington, DC, because appointing one
for Mexico stood to delay the process further. But as it turned out, the negotiations would encounter seemingly innumerable obstacles anyway.

When Romero's diplomatic counterpart, Chinese Minister Cheng Tsao
Ju, fell ill, he was replaced by Chang Yen Hoon, who was apparently not
prepared to broker a treaty with Mexico. The sudden turnabout caught
Romero off guard. Until a commission was convened to aid in the process,
Chang contended that he could do very little to instigate negotiations.[86]
Chinese and Mexican diplomats stalled talks for another year, only to be
stymied yet again when talks resumed. Chang raised apprehensions that
Romero believed had been resolved in reaching good-office protection for
Chinese workers two years prior. Romero dealt steadily and patiently with
each concern raised by Chang, reiterating that Chinese workers would
receive protection against possible abuse and that the location of treaty
talks in Washington, DC, favored no country over the other. Chang, after
receiving Romero's correspondence in December 1887, was replaced by
Tsui Kwo Yin, and for five more years the stalemate continued.[87]

Some progress was made after China recommenced communication with Mexico in 1893, but it would take an additional six years for
the two countries to come to an official agreement. Chinese migration,
however, was not completely thwarted by the lack of an official treaty
between Mexico and the Qing government or by the enforcement of U. S.
exclusion laws beginning in 1882. Generous opportunities to naturalize as Mexican citizens and to own land fostered a small but continuous
stream of migrants from China, despite the lack of official protection.
In the three years leading up to official Mexico-Qing diplomacy, more
than 4,100 Chinese arrived in Mexico, lured mostly by the Colonization
Law of 1883 and the Law of Alienage and Naturalization (*Ley de extran-
jería y naturalización*) of 1886.[88] The new immigration laws structured
the duties of the newly created Ministry of Development (*Ministerio de*

*Fomento*), in which Mexican officials supervised immigration and over-saw all modernization and development projects throughout the nation. Generous incentives were granted to immigrants seeking to colonize Mexico, and there were no limits on the location of settlements or the number of immigrants who could enter the country. The only restriction that the Colonization Law of 1883 made was for Mexico's island territories. There, settlers could not exceed 50 percent of the islands' population.[89] Foreigners residing in Mexico for more than six months became immigrants, and immigrants were eligible for naturalization if they remained for an additional two years.[90]

These efforts worked well, and the Porfirian regime considered Chinese immigration a success. To foster progress, Díaz lured foreign investors with promises of profits, and immigrants with favorable circumstances of opportunity. The Mexican approach ran counter to the immigration policies of the United States, which had barred the entry of Chinese laborers. Furthermore, China, until 1893, continued to enforce the *hai jin*, even though many thousands had returned home from abroad, and in so doing risked their lives. Repatriation occurred only when imperial authorities realized the value to their nearly bankrupt regime of remittances from overseas Chinese.[91] Mexico's open immigration policies were in direct contrast to those adopted in both China and the United States, a divergence that would yield considerable results for the Chinese in Mexico. There, civil law granted them Mexican citizenship, with rights equal to those of Mexicans.

In 1899, one year after the death of Romero, China and Mexico formalized relations with the signing of the Treaty of Friendship, Commerce, and Navigation (*Tratado de Amistad, Comercio, y Navegación*) in Washington, DC, where the only Chinese legation in North America was instituted.[92] The most vivid outcome of this diplomacy was its support for Chinese immigration to Mexico. Treaty provisions stipulated free and voluntary movement between nations, and assigned civil rights and privileges to émigrés.[93] China and Mexico also enjoyed most-favored-nation status and were accorded "perpetual, firm, and sincere friendship . . . between their respective citizens and subjects."[94] The treaty seemed agreeable enough, but Mexico tipped the political scales in its favor by negotiating protection for Mexican nationals charged with crimes in China. Mexicans in China suspected of criminal activity were to be held at the Mexican Consulate in Beijing, whereas justice for Chinese in Mexico was to be vetted in Mexican courts and among Mexican government officials.[95] But if the aim of the treaty, which China and Mexico took more than twenty-five years to ratify, was to equalize relations and secure equal political rights for Mexican and Chinese subjects, the actual outcome would later have dubious results.

The treaty immediately paid off in terms of Mexico's immigration goals, but the agreement proved to be a rather flimsy safeguard against exploitation. Chinese in Tampico and Veracruz, try as they might to escape the trappings of coolieism, endured slavelike conditions, poor pay, and a lack of food while building railroads and harvesting henequen. Some Chinese laborers left the port of Hong Kong believing they would land in Victoria, British Columbia, to work in canneries or fisheries but instead found themselves working for the *Ferrocarril Nacional de Tehuantepec* (National Railroad of Tehuantepec) at the San Luis Potosí–Tampico line. Construction of the railroad, which would run from the Atlantic Ocean at Coatzacoalcos, Veracruz, to the Pacific coast at Salina Cruz, Oaxaca, was completed in 1907 at the expense of the Chinese. An official petition to Mexican government officials from 480 Chinese in Tampico revealed a conspiracy to kidnap laborers through deception, fraud, and physical coercion. Workers claimed that the On Wo Company was principally to blame for their condition by deducting twenty pesos from their monthly earnings of twenty-six pesos for food and clothing and exposing them to the quick whip of overseer Ma Chok. "We endured all types of hardship," a laborer revealed, "without raising our eyes."[96] Mexican officials responded that fines would be levied against the railroad company but if workers wanted further justice, they would have to adjudicate their cases in the Mexican court system. During the same period, the Chinese withstood harsh working conditions in the henequen fields of the Yucatán, spurring outrage from Chinese officials but almost no protective action from the Mexican government.

Despite numerous other complaints directed against planters and recruiters, and the cavalier responses of the Díaz regime, Chinese immigration into Mexico was deemed to be a plausible immigrant project. Chinese laborers, after all, conformed to Porfirian development goals of linking people to markets and once-distant places with the backing of foreign capital. If the Díaz regime measured success as Chinese laborers building railroads or harvesting crops and then departing for home, then what transpired in the U.S.-Mexico borderlands at the turn of the twentieth century would place the dictator's liberal immigration policies in doubt.

## Destabilized Nations and the
## Chinese Diaspora at the Border

By the time China and Mexico formalized relations in 1899, Chinese migrants had already arrived in Mexico, mostly in the northern states. By 1900, Sonora was home to the largest Chinese population in Mexico, with more than 850 settlers. Contrary to what Mexican officials had anticipated and desired, many Chinese came not to labor but to set up shop, cross into the United States, or both. In theory, the U.S. southern boundary may have been closed to Chinese immigration, but in actuality, the Chinese, occupying a range of positions between Mexican citizen, national, sojourner, and merchant-laborer, were uniquely poised to cross into the United States almost unfettered. The various statuses amassed by Chinese border crossers, however, were not the most significant outcomes of their experience, although the myriad of options helped them mediate immigration bureaucracies and combat the notion that they were coolies. Of greater impact was the trans-Pacific Chinese migration networks that converged with an existing borderlands society long defined as a place of fluid movement and political autonomy. Persistent movements of indigenous peoples in Sonora, in conjunction with the border crossings of Chinese migrants beginning in the late nineteenth century, destabilized national projects at the U.S.-Mexico borderlands (see Map 1.3).

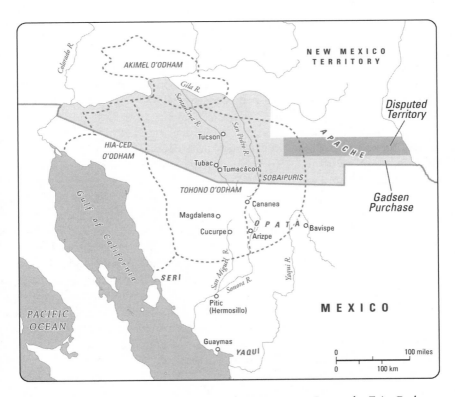

MAP 1.3 Arizona and Sonora Borderlands, Circa 1854. Drawn by Erin Greb.

The state-building projects of the Spanish Crown and, later, of the United States and Mexico, were not clear-cut undertakings in the sense that boundaries were drawn, sovereignty was recognized, and subjects were held in allegiance. From the earliest days of colonial intrusion to the last decades of the nineteenth century, the tempo of resistant adaptation—defined by physical mobility and the reconstitution of indigenous communities—allowed native peoples to preserve a strong sense of ethnic space even as confrontations with other frontier peoples over land, water, and labor continually challenged their survival. Physical mobility reworked customary patterns of territory and language, while bonds of marriage, lineage, and kinship unified native communities among the Eudeve, Opata, Tohono O'odham, Seris, Sobapuri, and Yaqui, the most common wandering peoples (*naciones errantes*) of the borderlands landscape.[97] Thus, when Spanish explorers initially confronted native peoples in the early 1600s, they witnessed a complicated cultural terrain of shifting ethnic and territorial boundaries that withstood some of the more exigent demands of colonialism. Under Spanish rule, the *naciones errantes* maintained access to communal plots by brokering compromises over labor availability and the use of land that sustained the needs of the Crown for surplus production. Simultaneously, these arrangements preserved native peoples' time-honored seasonal migrations to *aldeas* (compact semi-sedentary villages) or *rancherías* (scattered shifting settlements) in the Sonoran piedmont. By returning to geographies of origin, native peoples continued centuries-long customs while buffering mission settlements from Indian incursions. Such practices—a dual process that historian Cynthia Radding calls "fragmentation and nucleation"—sustained the birth and rebirth of indigenous cultures amid colossal restructurings of government bureaucracies and provincial and state boundaries.[98]

The fluid movements of indigenous peoples persisted well into the mid-nineteenth century. Because of this, when Mexican and American state-builders sought to transform the Arizona and Sonora landscapes into national borderlands, they initially wielded faint power to do so. Indigenous peoples steadily undermined the nation-making project on both sides of the border, a trend that was also intensified by shifting political currents from without. Yaqui and Mayo collaboration with Sonoran centralist Manuel María Gándara in the 1830s and 1840s, and Opata and Yaqui cooperation with French magistrates in the 1850s and 1860s, made clear a deep enmity toward the liberalizing schemes of Sonoran federalists. Other efforts impeded state-building enterprises as well. The geographic dislocation and near bankruptcy caused by the Mexican American War (1846–1848) and by Apache raiding had further destabilized the state. A brief interlude of solidity and calm, achieved only because of Mexico's postwar financial crisis, carved out Sonora's present-day boundaries with Arizona as south of the Gila and Mesilla Rivers.[99]

After the Gadsden Purchase, if one discerned a sense of nationhood at the Arizona-Sonora borderlands, it was indeed an unstable fiction. Mexican and American efforts to reappropriate land and remake indigenous peoples into exemplars of the new social order produced dubious results, due in large part to the persistence of kinship networks held together by *indios* (indigenous peoples) and *mestizos*.[100] For indigenous peoples, kinship lines, whether matrilineal, patrilineal, or bilateral, structured familial relations and spiritual practices on both sides of the border. Mexican kinship networks served a similar purpose as native systems, with the exception that the basis of familial and community arrangements in Mexico was almost always patriarchal. Kinship networks elaborated cultural and economic exchange and were not severely weakened by market forces in the late nineteenth century.[101] Among indigenous peoples and Mexican *fronterizos*, kinship ties and the identities they engendered blurred a sense of national belonging even as European Americans came to reside in the region in greater numbers at the turn of the twentieth century. Society was constructed not from totalizing ethnic identities, but rather from interchangeable political, cultural, and kinship communities that had distinguished these borderlands from greater Mexico and the United States, as a more racially diverse, more politically fluid, and proportionately less settled region.

Within those cultures, Mexican and indigenous peoples had already rejected rigid and bounded concepts of nationhood. It would come as no surprise, then, that the existing fluidity of the borderlands, when combined with trans-Pacific migration networks, likewise sustained cross-national movements through Arizona and Sonora. The concept of the Chinese diaspora—already intricate by virtue of its multiple political and physical geographies—was rendered all the more complex by the myriad factors shaping its structure and development at the borderlands. Chinese diasporic communities, whether in Mexico or in the United States, embodied the experiences of individuals and families who left their homelands to settle in new regions where identities were both reaffirmed and remade. Just as they brought their culture with them, the Chinese were equally transformed in turn by the culture they encountered in the borderlands. In the process, they became *fronterizos*—Chinese Mexicans.

The interlacing movements and linkages that kept borders porous and identities fluid would also serve to complicate Matías Romero's vision for Chinese immigration into Mexico. The diplomat's foray into coffee farming in Chiapas, no less ambitious for its ultimate impossibility, offers some insight into Mexico's development aspirations and the limitations that global realities imposed. No doubt Romero distinguished himself as a discerning observer of his country and his times, but he could not have foreseen that the arrival of Chinese into the Americas would bear so heavily in Mexico. Although silhouetted by its colonial past, the political machinery and orientation of the Mexican nation changed markedly after 1854. Throughout a forty-year period that witnessed social upheaval and ongoing movements from within and outside of Mexico, the need for Chinese labor was a constant one. Entrepreneurs, labor recruiters, corporations, and state-builders on both sides of the border and in China attempted to entice Chinese migrants into Mexico's most remote regions. Whereas Romero and his cohorts anticipated a Chinese labor force that would toil under the harshest conditions and for meager wages, far removed from the more urbane Mexican citizenry, the eventual reality would prove to be quite different: the persistence of vibrant Chinese *fronterizo* communities. For the Chinese, theirs was a world shaped by the quality and content of social relationships among neighbors, friends, and kin, revealing the U.S.-Mexico borderlands as a historically constructed and contested crossroads of immigration, settlement, and fluidity.

# 2 Of Kith and Kin

CHINESE AND MEXICAN RELATIONSHIPS
IN EVERYDAY MEANING

Don San Wo was well connected up and down southern Arizona. He had some firm attachments in Tucson, including friendship ties to Don Chun Wo,[1] who was considered the unofficial mayor of Tucson's Chinese community.[2] Connections aside, Don San Wo was in good spirits over what the near future held: the soon-to-be merchant was on the cusp of acquiring a new grocery store for himself and a new home for his family in Tucson. Before actually entering into a lease in mid-spring of 1902 with Dolores Serón, a Mexican resident of the Old Pueblo (another name for Tucson), Wo was careful to sketch out several provisos. The terms of the agreement would yield a store and a home for him, a four-hundred-dollar advance for Serón, and new neighbors for the residents of downtown Tucson. And the stakes were high. For all to go well, Serón had to deliver, in a little over a month, a newly constructed, adobe-style building suitable for selling groceries and housing Wo's family. Wo's demands of Serón did not stop there. Before Wo took possession of the Sixth Avenue property and assumed responsibility for the lease, Serón was to make sure the storefront had two glass doors through which customers could come and go, and that each room in the attached house had a window. The payoff for Serón was long-term. After the ten-year lease expired, the downtown building would be Serón's, to let again or to occupy as a resident. For Wo the payoff was both short-term and long-term. For three years he would not pay rent, in exchange for having advanced $400 to Serón for the construction of the dwelling and for building materials. The arrangement at once secured for Wo and his family a place among neighbors and a modest standing as a grocery-store-owning family in a predominately Mexican *barrio*.[3]

At the turn of the twentieth century, the relationship between Don San Wo and Dolores Serón was an ordinary one. When Wo assumed the lease and moved into the new adobe dwelling in downtown Tucson, relation-

ships between Chinese and Mexican neighbors were already twenty years
in the making.[4] In the late 1870s and early 1880s, as Chinese workers
wrapped up their obligations to the Southern Pacific Railroad Company
outside Tucson, they began the work of cultivating kith ties, or bonds of
friendship, with Mexicans and some European Americans. At times, relations among neighbors were burdened with some apprehension because
of Chinese exclusion laws, but discreet arrangements and daily interactions among *fronterizos* created everyday meaning and helped to mili-
tate against virulent Sinophobia.[5] This was no minor issue. The passage of
the Chinese Exclusion Act prohibited skilled and unskilled workers from
entry, even as 39,579 Chinese rushed to enter the United States before
the 1882 law went into effect. To strengthen the original exclusion law,
Congress passed an amendment in 1884 that sought to protect the West
Coast states, particularly California, from "surreptitious arrivals" while
shipmasters whose vessels originated from the English treaty ports of Singapore and Hong Kong risked imprisonment and fines if they landed or
intended to land Chinese at American port cities. Furthermore, in 1888 an
additional amendment barred any returning Chinese laborer from entry
unless he was lawfully married, had a child or parent in the United States,
or was owed debts valuing more than $1,000. When in 1892 the original
act came up for renewal, Congress extended exclusion another ten years.
Immigration from American insular possessions, Hawaii, and later the
Philippines was also barred. By 1904, just two years after Don San Wo
and Dolores Serón agreed to a ten-year business arrangement in downtown Tucson, Chinese exclusion laws were made permanent, until their
repeal in 1943.[6]

In this period of far-reaching immigration restriction in which the
Bureau of Immigration assumed extraordinary legal power to enforce the
Chinese exclusion laws, relationships between Chinese and Mexican borderlanders such as Wo and Serón developed in response to transnational
forces and local arrangements. From the outside, trans-Pacific migration
networks, which channeled Chinese laborers into the western United
States, the Caribbean, South America, and greater Mexico, converged with
kith and kin networks—connections born of blood, friendship, and business contacts—in the U.S.-Mexico borderlands. In southern Arizona, kith
networks between Chinese and Mexicans, and the relationships they fostered, gave value to a type of social belonging that had less to do with formal political mechanisms than with leasing land, peddling vegetables, and
cultivating personal bonds with neighbors and friends. By making everyday connections out of arrangements that were fundamentally economic
but profoundly social, Chinese in Tucson first imagined and then made the
southern Arizona borderlands into a place of permanence.

Relationship dynamics between Chinese and Mexicans were decidedly different just across the border in Sonora. Whereas Chinese in Tucson created close bonds with their Mexican neighbors, Sonoran Chinese drew on more formal relationships with Mexicans to facilitate their movement both within and outside of Mexico. In Sonora, kith relations with Mexicans rarely engendered bonds of kinship as did they across the border because the lives of Sonoran Chinese were not proscribed by immigration restriction laws and confined to limited national geographies (see Map 2.1). The conventions prevailing on interactions between Chinese and Mexicans in Sonora were based primarily in diplomatic relations and in a concern for political rights rather than in everyday interactions among friends and neighbors. Those who could not prove Mexican citizenship or merchant status drew on institutionally arranged relationships with U.S. consuls and Mexican officials. These relationships sustained legal cross-border movements and prevented deportation to China. Yet even though the dimensions of border life in northern Sonora were neither materially equivalent to nor culturally synonymous with those in southern Arizona, the most human of all inclinations—to make, maintain, and draw on relationships—organized borderlands communities as fluid and transnational in a time of harsh American exclusion laws.

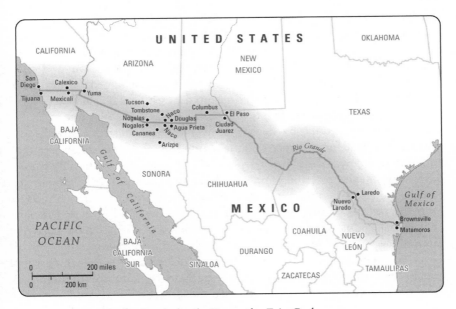

MAP 2.1  U.S.-Mexico Borderlands. Drawn by Erin Greb.

*Kith Relations and* Guanxi

Tucson was a critical place for Chinese newcomers. In the context of the American Southwest during the 1880s, the Old Pueblo was a large town with neither the trappings of big cities like San Francisco or Los Angeles nor the drawbacks of mining camps like Bisbee or Tombstone. Tucson's population comprised an admixture of ethnic groups that "could not be well gotten together anywhere else—Jews, Swedes, Irish, English, Germans, Chinese, French, Yankes [sic], Spaniards, [and] Indians. . . ."[7] Among the 7,007 residents, Mexicans were the majority population, making up 64 percent of all Tucsonans, while Chinese residents numbered just over 180.[8] For Chinese immigrants, establishing a sense of social belonging and residential permanency was initially tethered mostly to relationships with Mexicans and, after 1900, with Chinese kin in general. In the absence of generational ties on which to draw, Chinese immigrants were then compelled to create alternative mechanisms to establish connections with their new home and neighbors. Truck farming and small-scale commerce structured relations among Chinese and Mexican neighbors and fostered *guanxi* relations (關係, pronounced *kuan hsi*) among Chinese in particular. Bonds of kinship through *guanxi* inextricably linked Chinese to one another through the expectation of *bao* (reciprocity) and *ganqing* (affection).[9] Yet in the initial years of settlement there were moments in the making of friendships when Chinese felt bonds with their Mexican neighbors more deeply than they felt them with their kin. These kith relations would be made and remade in no small part against the imposition of exclusion laws that assigned great importance to the mundane routines of Chinese truck farmers, grocers, and merchants. Visibility, everyday interaction, and reliance on neighbors for fresh produce and dry goods sustained and brought *tucsonenses* (Mexican residents of Tucson) and Chinese denizens together through friendship and familial ties.

A transitioning, cross-border economy—one moving from subsistence to market dependence—structured the manner in which Tucsonans related with Chinese newcomers. Before the mid-1880s, the international border posed few hurdles to selling and obtaining goods in Sonora, Chihuahua, and the American Southwest. Intimate familiarity with the regional geography as well as family-based commercial networks in northern Mexico kept transnational trade in the hands of the *hispano* merchant class in Tucson. By controlling the freighting of goods in the region, and with a knack for avoiding payment of duties to Mexican and American custom houses, many Tucson-based Mexican merchants came to operate some of the most lucrative businesses and to own the largest tracts of land. Estevan Ochoa, in his partnership with Mississippi-born trader Pinckney Randolph

Tully, for example, amassed a significant fortune supplying Army posts, mining camps, and isolated townspeople with *mezcal*, cigarettes, nails, and lumber, and the well-to-do with fine linens, silverware, and cheeses.[10] By the early 1880s, Tully, Ochoa, and Company had accumulated more than $100,000 in machinery and employed many local residents as teamsters and wheelwrights.[11]

Against the backdrop of this transnational economy linking Tucson to Mexico City in the south and to San Francisco in the north, ordinary Mexican, European, and Chinese households maintained subsistence farming and a traditional way of life in the Old Pueblo. A visitor to 1880s Tucson might ride his horse past the adjoining Santa Cruz River households of Telles, León, Davis, Cerilio, Wing, and Fish and witness farmers maintaining economies of exchange based largely in harvesting crops for family consumption. Some, including the Chinese, cultivated crops for their own eating, as well as vegetables to truck to town, by leasing land from their neighbors. Farming was the keystone of kith and kin bonds. In the 1880s, leasing land from Mexicans helped to reestablish community and familial life in the Old Pueblo. In several cases, the web of kith relations between Mexicans and Chinese extended through generations, with women as the principal agents. In 1881, Gertrudes Pacheco and Wing Mow Yun chartered the earliest recorded lease between Chinese and Mexicans in Tucson.[12] Gertrudes, the fifty-five-year-old wife of Ramón Pacheco, leased approximately eleven acres to Wing in El Barrio for six years at $150 a year. Although the agreement listed no other tenants, Wing almost certainly cultivated the plot with other Chinese, who would have helped him with the steady daily routines of plowing fields and laying smooth furrows by hand.[13] Four years later, Mateo Pacheco, the twenty-two-year-old great grandson of Gertrudes and Ramón, leased ten acres of land to Lee Ding for five years. The agreement included provisions for building a two-horse stable as well as a one-room house sufficient to shelter four Chinese men. Under the oddly configured terms of the lease, Ding would pay Mateo Pacheco $50 upon signing the agreement in March, followed by $62.50 on the first day of June and October. Thereafter, Pacheco fixed Ding's rent at $58.33 each March, June, and October.[14] As kith ties with Chinese persisted in the Pacheco family, Ding's five-year commitment to farm Pacheco land suggested that he followed the practice of *guanxi* and eventually hired other Chinese men to help grow and harvest crops. More to the point, Lee Ding's lease contained explicit stipulations for housing additional Chinese farmers. Together, Ding and Wing established the bases of mutual interest, shared benefit, and affection—the cornerstones of Chinese society in Tucson—by leasing land from their Mexican neighbors.

Economic arrangements, however, did not portend romantic relationships between Mexican women and Chinese men. Anti-miscegenation laws prohibited marriage between Chinese and Mexicans, whom territorial law and regional custom recognized as racially white. In 1865, Arizonans passed an anti-miscegenation bill that voided all marriages between whites and blacks, Hindus, mulattos, Indians, and Chinese.[15] Designing Arizona's laws to mirror those of the American South and Midwest, officials privileged marriage as a social and economic unit by attaching conjugality to respectability, legitimacy for children, and financial benefit. Few romantic relationships between Mexican women and Chinese men ever blossomed, but those that did challenged Arizona's marriage laws after the turn of the twentieth century.[16]

To guard against miscegenation, leases drawn up between Mexican women and Chinese men in Tucson always noted the marital and racial status of both parties. Close living arrangements underscored the personal-legal descriptions of the female Mexican landlord and the male Chinese tenant; in other leases, these distinctions were not made. The Pacheco-Wing lease, like a subsequent 1887 agreement between Angela de López and Yuen Lee, left little room for ambiguity: Doña Pacheco was recorded as the wife of Don Ramón, whereas the 1887 lease between Angela de López and Yuen Lee described Doña Angela as "*casada* [married] and of age" and Lee as a "(Chinaman) single and of age."[17] For ten dollars a month, Yuen Lee rented a room in the southwest section of López's house at North Meyer and Telles Streets. The two parties agreed that Lee would have access to the back house, where he was allowed to draw water for his personal hygiene and where he could wash and iron his clothes. López further stipulated that Lee should "not have washing and ironing going on in his room." Before Lee agreed to these terms, he requested that López repair the front door of the back house. Such stipulations against romantic involvement were understood to apply to relations between Chinese and Mexican men. Nearby on Meyer Street, the incentive to live together was as practical for Jesús Munguía and Tim Chong as it was for López and Lee, although the arrangement did not suggest anything beyond two men sharing a living space. Tim Chong's three upstairs rooms in Munguía's home reflected what was probably an affable relationship between the two men. Their housing arrangement implied that living together would be sensible, but no less friendly for its practicality.[18]

Besides renting rooms and land from *tucsonenses*, Chinese migrants settled in El Barrio (which means "the neighborhood"), a racially mixed but predominately Mexican area that encompassed South Meyer, Main, Pennington, Pearl, Congress, and Alameda Streets.[19] Considered Tucson's first area of Chinese residential concentration, the neighborhood was also home to many Mexicans. By 1883, Tucson Chinese were most heavily concentrated in this district west and south of the presidio gate known as either the Walled City or the Plaza de las Armas. Chinese railroad workers occupied the original buildings of the neighborhood, which were constructed of wood and adobe. Mexican tenants inhabited stone dwellings next to the homes of the Chinese railroad workers. The Mexican-Chinese portion of the neighborhood comprised four large buildings, two washhouses, three stores, two opium dens, and a block-long adobe structure that "lost all its Spanish-American attributes, and [became] wholly oriental."[20] Residents in this area also included young male Chinese migrants who sought refuge alongside poor Mexican families in rundown buildings.[21]

## Farming the Land

After 1883, with the completion of the railway from Guaymas, Sonora, to Nogales, Arizona, the southern Arizona region was transformed from a local economy to one with access to more lucrative markets on the West and East Coasts. Speculators from eastern cities, "kid-gloved men . . . full of the idea of plundering Arizona, and going back to enjoy the results" and "stock-men from California, inquiring quietly for large land grants," found their way into Tucson and put residents on notice that local agriculture would soon go national. In 1885, the water rights case of Leopoldo Carrillo and traditional farmers would come to represent how the new economic order drove a wedge between Mexicans and Chinese.[22] In *W. A. Dalton et al. v. Leopoldo Carrillo et al.*, traditional Mexican irrigation methods employed to harvest chili peppers, garbanzo beans, and watermelons for local consumption came into conflict with the water demands of commercial farming. While some Chinese practiced traditional farming alongside their Mexican neighbors, others, including those who worked for Carrillo, farmed for the market. The man at the center of the dispute, Leopoldo Carrillo, was a self-described merchant, farmer, and real estate developer who had earned a reputation as a "hard man with a dollar."[23] Proclaimed an "urban entrepreneur," Carrillo owned more than $75,000 in assets that included an ice cream parlor, a bowling alley, and one hundred houses and parcels of farmland along the Santa Cruz River. Carrillo's fondness for horticulture and the profit he had amassed from prior dealings combined in a rare display of philanthropy for Tucsonans to enjoy. His gesture came in the form of a public garden resort that transformed eight acres of desert scrub into an oasis of man-made lakes and green areas fed from local water sources (see Figure 2.1).

FIGURE 2.1  Carrillo's Gardens. Courtesy of the Arizona Historical Society/Tucson. Photo no. 17795. http://www.arizonahistorical society.org

By the mid-1880s, the general public was crowding into Carrillo's gardens to enjoy music and dancing. Spring-fed ponds and a desert esplanade landscaped with grapevines and peach, quince, and pomegranate trees drew praise from even the most cosmopolitan residents. Despite his philanthropy, Carrillo's penchant for turning a quick profit often brought him into conflict with his neighbors, who wished to retain a semblance of traditional agricultural practices and access to water from *acequias de communes* (community irrigation ditches). In the instance that led to the water-rights court case, Carrillo took advantage of the region's growing demand for fresh vegetables by renting 150 acres of land south of Sisters Lane on the west bank of the Santa Cruz River to Chinese farmers, who both trucked vegetables to El Barrio and sold to regional markets. The substantial water demands of market-based agriculture placed Carrillo and his tenants at odds with other farmers, including many Chinese who had leased land from Mexicans and employed traditional irrigation methods to raise subsistence crops.[24]

W. A. Dalton, a former *zanjero* (water overseer), and several communal landowners sued Carrillo over the disproportionate amount of water consumed by the so-called Chinese gardens on land principally owned by Carrillo. Dalton charged that at Carrillo's directive the newly appointed *zanjero*, Lorenzo Rentaría, had granted priority water rights to Chinese farmers working for Carrillo, despite the past practice of equal and adequate water distribution for subsistence farmers. At the time, water laws in the Arizona Territory were based on the law of prior appropriation, which held that water was *publici juris*, or a matter of public right. The concept of prior appropriation held that any individual who owned the land adjacent to or containing a water source had the right of first use, with the proviso that the water be applied toward some beneficial purpose, such as agriculture or mining. A landowner who had access to an irrigation source could not simply bar others from using it if he were not putting it toward some tangible purpose himself.[25] Carrillo argued that, as the owner of the lands at the source of the Santa Cruz River, which unlike most rivers flowed south to north, he was under no obligation to share the water equally with his neighbors north of Sisters Lane.

Dalton countered that whereas Carrillo may have had right of first use, the merchant's disproportionate consumption of water left the farmers north of Sisters Lane with an inadequate supply with which to cultivate subsistence gardens. Traditional farmers also contended that the irrigation techniques of Carrillo's tenants, the Chinese commercial farmers, were wasteful, consuming up to three times the amount of water used to irrigate traditional plots. To make matters worse, if the amount of water was insufficient, Chinese farmers working for Carrillo were apt to steal from the common irrigation ditch to water their seedbeds. "They are wanting [water] every day and continuously," charged Dalton. "Besides what is allowed to them they steal; I am suffering from that."[26] The former *zanjero* explained that the Chinese filled five-gallon containers to keep their seedbeds well-irrigated while subsistence plots often went without water.

These practices seemed reasonable to Carrillo. After all, the Chinese gardens raised everything from garlic to artichokes and the region's largest cabbages, making their plots into a viable business. The much smaller *huertas* (gardens), on the other hand, produced little more than garlic and onions for family consumption.[27] Despite testimony from Eusebio Telles, Francisco Munguía, Miguel Ortíz, Feliciano Romero, Leonardo Romero, Dolores Gallardo, and Mateo Pacheco, the court ruled that traditional farmers had not established a legal record of equitable water distribution. It upheld the interests of Carrillo and his Chinese farmers, who raised produce for commercial markets.

To many Tucsonans, *Dalton v. Carrillo* ushered in a new way of life, while demonstrating once again Carrillo's penchant for amassing wealth by shutting out the poor. The court's decision solidified a long-standing relationship between Chinese commercial farmers and the Carrillo family. A few years later, in 1892, Quong Sang's five-year lease of fifteen acres from Joaquin Carrillo, the grandson of Leopoldo Carrillo, indicated that the Chinese gardens persisted adjacent to Sisters Lane.[28] Sang's lease, although it explicitly outlined terms of payment, was silent on irrigation practices. An 1893 agreement between Alejandro Molina and Wing Wo Yuen, on the other hand, specifically addressed water rights. Yuen's seventeen acres would receive water once a week during a twenty-four-hour period commencing every Sunday at 6:00 AM; if Yuen's gardens required more water, he would have to pay seven cents an hour to irrigate.[29]

The interactions that mattered most between Mexicans and Chinese were those that were fixed in place by everyday engagement. When Gertrudis and Jesús Montejo Sr. leased plots in Fort Lowell to Lee Gin Kuan's Wing Fat Company in 1898, the Chinese had already established a foothold in farming throughout Tucson (see Figure 2.2). Farmers harvesting crops along the Santa Cruz River often went into partnership with kin members to extend the efficiency and longevity of their businesses and to develop bonds of reciprocity and trust. Truck farming filled out most seasons with heavy work, but during the summer the routines were especially arduous. Kuan's neighbors—Chinese laborers of the Sun Sing Company to the south and those of the Wah Hop Company to the north—had mastered the arduous routine of truck farming and spent long hours cultivating surplus crops for market. Truck farming filled out most seasons with heavy work, but during the summer the routines were especially taxing. To avoid the sun's withering power, the produce needed to be transported early and sold door-to-door.

Beginning at dawn, farmhands pushed steadily behind the plow, sometimes stopping to smooth over the furrows by hand. There was no time for slacking. Farmhands loaded "strong but shabby wagons" with fresh vegetables, kept cool on ice for the trip to town.[30] María Uriquides, whose father rented to Chinese gardeners in Tucson during the late nineteenth century, recalled that as a little girl she witnessed how "they'd clean the carrots and onions and the *calabitas* [little squashes] and they'd arrange them on their wagons, cover them with gunny sacks, and wet them."[31] Selling house-to-house required at least two men, one who had some knowledge of both Spanish and English to do the peddling, the other to reshuffle the produce into freed-up cart space. Special customers—usually those who paid on time—had first pick of the tomatoes, watermelons, and artichokes in the summer, and of the carrots, turnips, cabbage, and lettuce during the winter.[32] At day's end, truck farmers tallied their bills and recorded the day's proceeds on the wagon's casement. As an adolescent growing up in El Barrio, Clera Ferrin Bloom observed the painstaking routine of Chinese truck farming in the Santa Cruz River region. The reward for a hard day's work, she observed, was time to spend having breakfast with "one of their city 'cousins' in a

FIGURE 2.2  Chinese Vegetable Vendor on Meyer Street, 1904. Courtesy of the Arizona Historical Society/Tucson. Photo no. 25734. http://www.arizonahistorical society.org

grocery store."³³ A few Chinese farmers sold their produce to Chinese grocers, and later became grocers themselves. Wing Wo Yuen, who had leased land from Alejandro Molina, was one such farmer-turned-grocer.³⁴

For Tucson Chinese, truck farming proved to be a stabilizing business. Although the Carrillo water rights case reinforced the new economic order in Tucson, the ability of the Chinese to continue farming at Sisters Lane had far greater implications for border society at the turn of the century.³⁵ After the legal case, those who farmed on a large scale—that is, for commercial sale and profit—enjoyed an ongoing advantage over those who cultivated the land primarily for family consumption. In keeping with these prevailing market forces, Chinese commercial farmers intensified production in their gardens to meet regional demand for produce. Chinese traditional farmers also began to grow their fruits and vegetables for the market, although to a far lesser extent than did commercial farmers. Despite the dramatic changes in the economic environment, truck farming was not only a stable business, it was also the keystone of kin and kith relations. As Tucsonans gradually left their subsistence farms for more urbanized areas, they relied increasingly on Chinese commercial and traditional farmers to provide much-needed produce. Through the everyday routines of their work, Chinese farmers forged economic, residential, and social ties with *tucsonenses*, which proved to be especially significant in the last decades of the nineteenth century by providing an occupational "safety net" for them in times of anti-Chinese pressures.

The acts of leasing land and growing produce for both local and regional consumption contributed to a diverse labor market where the Chinese worked in various types of settings. Of the 211 Chinese residents in Tucson in 1890, thirty-one were listed as laundry men, thirty-four as cooks, thirty-six as farmers, and forty as merchants.³⁶ Such occupational diversity provided Tucson Chinese with a viable alternative to the laundry business, which had become an increasingly volatile place of employment in port cities such as San Francisco, Los Angeles, and Galveston, and in southern Arizona mining towns. Chinese in Bisbee, for example, competed for laundry work with the widows of copper miners. Shortly after the founding of Bisbee in 1877, several hard rock workers lost their lives on the job. Left without any other means of support, their widows took up work as washerwomen. A few years later, when they began settling in Bisbee, the Chinese set up laundry businesses, and because of their "natural ability to do work cheaply and efficiently," they out-competed the washerwomen and forced the widows out of work.³⁷ For a while, some patrons remained steadfast about keeping the women employed and independent from public aid, so they continued to frequent their laundries, although the washerwomen charged more for services than did the Chinese. Though the threat to white labor was not direct, miners protested against Chinese launderers "because they would deprive these women of a means of supporting their families." The miners wanted some reassurance that if they were suddenly killed in a mining accident, their wives would be able to support themselves in their husbands' absence. In response to the miners' concerns and protests, Bisbee's newly appointed Justice of the Peace passed an ordinance prohibiting the Chinese from staying overnight in the town. The law effectively barred any Chinese-owned businesses from operating in the city and prevented the Chinese from continuing to reside in Bisbee.[38]

In other areas of the United States there were similar objections to Chinese laundries. In Galveston, Texas, for example, black women rallied against the Chinese, who they said "had no business coming here taking our work from us."[39] The washerwomen spelled out their threats about what they would do if the Chinese did not leave the laundries to black female labor. One woman warned, "Mr. Slam Sling Chinamen you better sling your shirt short cause we mean what we say. . . . We are coming with our jockets fasten tite and our shoes fasten tite cause we mene what we say cause we expect to sail through bloody seas and we will die for our company."[40]

In the nearby mining town of Tombstone, locals fought the same battle. Alarmed by a "Chinese invasion" the likes of which San Francisco had witnessed, the residents of Tombstone loathed Chinese workers as adjunct labor to the mining boom, especially in the service of laundering clothes. John Clum, former Apache agent, future Tombstone mayor, and then-editor of the *Tombstone Epitaph*, conceived of a strategy to oust the despised Chinese: "There are but three ways of getting rid of John: First, by modification or repeal of the [Burlingame] treaty; second by violence; and third, by denying them employment and patronage."[41] Rejecting the first two options, property owners and workers united in their preference for peaceful efforts to rid the town of the perceived evil. Any violent protests or threats made against the Chinese were openly and directly discouraged by most citizens of Tombstone. Even Clum, though contending that the "Chinese must go," adamantly opposed acts of bloodshed and murder. Good citizens, the former Apache agent asserted, must take a positive stand against such heinousness. Clum believed in the promises made by Chinese launderers to leave Tombstone once they were ready or "when the washing gave out."[42]

In Tombstone, the tenor of anti-Chinese agitation was much more subdued than in Galveston and Bisbee, but in all cases the outcomes were the same. Those in southern Arizona returned to truck farming when laundering clothes had become a politically defended domain of non-Chinese "women's work." Curiously, the same law that banned the overnight stay of Chinese also allowed them to sell fresh vegetables in the mining camp during the day. To avoid violating the law in Bisbee, Chinese launderers-turned-truck farmers settled in neighboring Fairbank and cultivated vegetables to sell in the mining town. During the early morning hours, gardeners drove to the top of the divide and waited at that location until sunrise before entering the town. Farmers sold carrots, turnips, cabbage, and lettuce during the winter, and tomatoes and artichokes in the summer.[43] Chinese truck farmers made their efforts profitable. For example, Hop Sing, a gardener from south of Tucson, reported a profit of $1,000 from selling his goods in Bisbee a few years after the turn of the century.[44] Mou Op came to be known throughout Tucson for his extraordinary ability to grow the tastiest strawberries in the southern region of Arizona. The local press reported on Op's gardening skills and on his rise to affluence. According to the *Arizona Daily Star*, Op's strawberries garnered such a high price that Op, if he wanted, could travel back to China "on a special steamer and be a wealthy member of the emperor's court for the rest of his days."[45]

Apprehensions toward Chinese in Tucson tended to play out in different ways than they did in southern Arizona mining towns and in other places in the South. Because the Old Pueblo was not a mining town, the anti-Chinese sentiment of Mexicans there gained few adherents and, except in the slightest ways, was not as pervasive as it was in places where Mexicans and the white working classes fought for jobs and equality. This is not to say that such sentiment did not exist. The editors of *El Fronterizo*, a Tucson-based circular aimed at Mexicans with middle-class sensibilities, accused the Chinese of being racially unfit for marriage, characterizing them as "a fungus that lives in isolation, sucking the sap of the other plants."[46] Although *El Fronterizo* enjoyed a considerable audience, anti-Chinese views were not the elements that most defined Mexicans' attitudes toward their Chinese neighbors. The interactions that mattered most between Mexicans and Chinese in Tucson were those fixed in place by the mundane and the everyday.

While launderers moved into the ranks of cooks and engine cleaners, truck farming remained remarkably constant over the next few years. Even though farmers who toiled on plots near Silver Lake lost their fields to promoters of irrigation schemes, this loss represented an exception to a typically profitable rule.[47] Merchants did not fare nearly as well. More than half of the forty Chinese merchants in Tucson in the 1890s left the Old Pueblo by 1900. The twenty-one who headed out may have been drawn elsewhere—for example, across the border to Sonora, where conditions were more favorable for business investment; or to China, where families reunited. For those who stayed, a different set of challenges marked their experience in Tucson.

## Merchants and the Ties That Bind

The formalities of kinship through *guanxi* relations made living in Tucson among Chinese residents a bond all its own. Visibility, everyday interaction, and reliance on Chinese neighbors for fresh produce and dry goods sustained Tucsonans and brought them together. Solidifying friendships and family ties and maintaining businesses proved to be an easier task for truck farmers, who enjoyed the freedom to traverse the town at large, than for merchants. After the passage of the Geary Act in 1892, Chinese merchants with few or no *guanxi* relations on which to rely had to consider their choices carefully because drawing on relatives from great distances was a colossal risk. The Geary Act required all Chinese laborers currently living in the United States to register within one year with the federal collector of internal revenue and obtain a certificate of residence.[48] Each certificate contained a photograph of its holder and recorded that person's name, age, address, occupation, and residential and work histories. The certificate also documented any distinguishing physical characteristics (such as "mole on right ear") that would set laborers apart from one another. If a laborer did not obtain a certificate of residence, he risked immediate arrest and a deportation hearing with a U.S. judge or, in the case of Arizona before statehood, a district commissioner. Although merchants were exempt from registering with the federal government, they were frequently mistaken to be laborers without certificates, especially when they were away from home or working in their stores.[49] Considering the potential consequences of detainment, relations with neighbors proved crucial in the Geary Act era. Establishing residency and long-standing social ties meant the difference between remaining in the United States or receiving an order of deportation. The passage of the Geary Act reinforced the importance of establishing residential histories and relations with neighbors in Tucson.

Chin Tin Wo enjoyed considerable success selling dry goods in the Old Pueblo (see Figure 2.3). However, when the former railroad cook-turned-prominent-merchant, who had no sons or Chinese neighbors on whom to rely, decided to return to Hong Kong in 1895, he faced the challenge of finding a suitable heir to take over and maintain his Tucson businesses. Safeguarding and adding to his reputation and substantial ventures, which included holdings from fishing and mining industries, was no small order.[50] For years he had managed without kin, drawing on relationships with Mexican and Jewish suppliers to stock his store, and he accumulated most of his wealth by striking deals with middlemen suppliers such as Julius Goldbaum, an immigrant who made sure that plenty of whiskey, cigars, and vinegar lined the shelves of his grocery store.[51] He also drew on Mexican neighbors, especially when jealousies arose between rival Chinese

FIGURE 2.3   Chin Tin Wo. Courtesy of the Arizona Historical Society/Tucson, Buehman Collection B8379. http://www.arizonahistoricalsociety.org

businessmen. Manuel Vasavelbaso, a friend of Chin Tin Wo and a business school teacher, foiled Chan Beet's plot to burn down Chin Tin Wo's store. Seeking revenge for a past dispute, Chan interrupted Vasavelbaso at his home in Tucson while the teacher was instructing his Chinese pupil, Charley Long, in English lessons. Chan, who had known Vasavelbaso from previous business dealings, requested a private conversation with the teacher. Once out of Long's earshot, Chan disclosed his plot to burn down Chin Tin Wo's store. "He put his hand in his pocketbook and showed me some gold and greenbacks," recounted Vasavelbaso. "He [Chan] told me this money is to pay the men to set fire to Chin Tin Wo's store, and if it is not innuf [sic], I [Chan] will get some more from my friends."[52] By notifying local law enforcement of Chan's scheme, Vasavelbaso saved his friend's store from fire. Given the stakes, it was clear that Chin Tin Wo's heir would need to be equally astute not only at developing *guanxi* relations, but also at cultivating those kith connections that had saved his uncle's store.

In his need to pass along his store and secure an overseer for his other holdings, Chin Tin Wo requested that his brother, Don Doan Yook, a goldsmith and jeweler, and his son relocate from San Francisco to Tucson to take up the task.[53] This reunion transformed the two brothers, long separated by hundreds of miles, into kin linked by *guanxi* relations. The risks of reconnecting California-area and Tucson-based kin in the Geary Act era were great, but the reward of firming up *guanxi* relations was worth the peril. The two San Francisco residents arrived in Tucson by rail in early 1895. Over the next seven months, Chin Tin Wo familiarized his brother and his twenty-two-year-old nephew with the grocery store that was soon to be theirs. Chin Tin Wo granted partial ownership to his brother, but the responsibility for daily operations fell into the hands of his nephew. Perhaps because of his U.S. citizenship, his fluency in English, and his education in the United States, Don Doan Yook's American-born son was more likely to excel at managing the day-to-day operations of the grocery store.[54] Bonds of kinship were forged when Chin Tin Wo's nephew and heir changed his name to Don Chun Wo.[55]

Like many Tucson Chinese, Don Chun Wo had numerous significant connections in China, not the least of whom was his uncle, Chin Tin Wo. Sustaining such connections necessitated frequent trips abroad. International travel in the Geary Act era was perilous, however, and had potentially dire consequences. Without proper documentation proving his merchant status, Don Chun Wo faced the possibility of being denied reentry into the United States. His first trip abroad involved taking his young family of five to China in 1904. With his wife, Leung Duan Goat, whom he married in Tucson in 1896, and his three sons—Jack Sam, Jack Fong, and Jack Han—the family visited China several more times for lengthy stays, and Don Chun Wo made additional trips from Tucson by himself during that time.[56] Don Chun Wo's travel began with seeking and acquiring permission from a local customs inspector, who at the time doubled as an immigration inspector. In Tucson, gaining this permission was crucial, especially if one continuously traveled, had a business, and expected that one's family members would gain unquestioned reentry into the United States after long stretches of time in China. At the time of Don Chun Wo's travel, 177 Chinese residents put down roots in Tucson. The vast majority (155) were adult males, seven were adult females, and fifteen were children.[57] The married couples among them collectively raised nine sons and three daughters as well as cared for a pair of grandparents and one adopted son. When Don Chun Wo courted his new bride in China after the death of his first wife, successful travel abroad from the United States was a constitutive bond of the Chinese community in Tucson.

Transnational comings and goings were critical dimensions of the community. At the turn of the twentieth century, Chinese began to pool their resources to finance businesses. Most of these were groceries, but some laundries still thrived.[59] Few businesses had the fortunate beginnings of Don Chun Wo's enterprise, but some could and did draw from San Francisco and China-based sources to stock canned goods, some staple items, and silks. Other business owners relied on securing a lease for a newly built grocery store like Don San Wo did in the center of El Barrio from Dolores Serón. Charley Lee's storefronts advertised *mantequilla de tempe*, *fruta*, *huevos frescas*, *pasteles*, *pan*, and *quequis* (room-temperature butter, fruit, fresh eggs, pies, bread, and cake). In 1893, two new joss houses and more Chinese gardens prompted some locals to call for the establishment of a Chinatown to keep those "wily Mongolians . . . in as small an area as possible." But the tending to business, as well as the affable relationships between most Tucsonans and their Chinese neighbors, also made it easy to anticipate that the locals' petition would be categorically rejected by the Tucson City Council as unconstitutional.[59] There was never a legally mandated Chinatown in Tucson.

Even as Tucson Chinese enjoyed a less hostile environment than that faced by Chinese elsewhere in the United States, the restrictions of the Geary Act nonetheless tightened around them. Urged not to comply with the Geary Act, they resisted. A well-organized national boycott was spearheaded by the Chinese Six Companies, prompting a majority of Chinese laborers to refuse to register with the federal government during the time allotted. According to historian Lucy Salyer, out of an estimated 85,000 Chinese laborers in the United States, only 13,242 initially complied with the Geary Act.[60] Nationally, the noncompliance boycott was a remarkable success, and Tucson was no exception. The Chinese Six Companies' campaign for noncompliance garnered considerable support, and Arizona and New Mexico issued only 429 certificates to the 1,610 Chinese residents in these territories.[61] Despite the boycott's effectiveness, some consequences were brought to bear on merchants, who when traveling were subject to blackmail, harassment, and detainment. In a time of immigration exclusion, proof of residency in the form of official documentation became the primary basis for determining a person's legal status, as mandated by the new law.

Efforts to get the Chinese to comply with the Geary Act failed miserably, although one Tucson resident became a visible exception to the political activity of the Six Companies. Long Kee, described as a "fat, good-natured looking chap" who owned a grocery store off Simpson and Convent Streets in Tucson, was the first individual in the Arizona and New Mexico territories to register for a certificate of residence. Although lauded by the local press for his willingness to register under the terms of the Geary Act, Kee ardently "refused to agree with any denunciation of [the Six Companies'] methods."[62] The merchant's immediate enrollment indicated that a particular set of circumstances was at play. Kee registered to avoid the consequences of being mistaken as an unregistered laborer and therefore subject to immediate deportation. Kee also obtained a certificate of residence to ensure his unobstructed reentry into the United States should he visit China in the future. Other Chinese laborers in Tucson wondered how and when immigration sweeps would take place and when the process of deportation would begin. Judge W. Wetford of San Francisco was puzzled as to why most Chinese refused to register, and he believed that the mandates placed on them were justified:

There is no reason why the Chinese could not have registered as required by the Geary Act. . . . American citizens are compelled to register in order to vote. Every ten years a census taker comes around [and] asks personal questions that people have to answer or pay a penalty for refusal. The Mongolians could easily have obeyed the law.[63]

In *Fong Yue Ting v. the United States* (1893), a Supreme Court case that upheld the Geary Act, Congress affirmed the right to deport Chinese laborers who did not possess a certificate of residence. More important, the act created the impression that all persons of Chinese ancestry who lived in the United States did so illegally, and were thereby compelled to document lawful residency. When coupled with earlier court decisions, which had yoked immigration and entry of aliens to Congress's undisputed authority over matters of national self-defense, the repercussions of *Fong Yue Ting* were clear: Chinese citizens and noncitizens alike were at risk for immediate deportation. Chinese laborers had a six-month extension from the passage of the amendment in 1894 to obtain a certificate.[64] Without it, arrest was imminent and deportation was probable. In southern Arizona, as elsewhere, Chinese residents had to meet the burden of proof of residency or needed to summon two white witnesses to confirm legal residency.[65]

Frequent immigration sweeps in southern Arizona apprehended several Chinese in Nogales, Yuma, Marana, Douglas, and Tucson.[66] No accurate figure exists for the total number of Chinese who made their way into the United States during this time, but the vast majority of criminal cases brought before the territorial courts of Nogales, Yuma, and Tucson were suits filed against Chinese for violating the exclusion laws.[67] Lee King was one of several Chinese arrested in Tucson for violating the Geary Act. His neighbors, Lee Foo and Lee Tan, posted the required $500 bond to free their friend from jail while he awaited trial. In court, fellow Tucsonans Kim Lee and Leo King, acting through interpreter Don Chun Wo, who had long enjoyed the esteem of Old Pueblo Chinese, managed to convince territorial commissioner W. H. Culver that their friend was a legal resident, even though at the time of his arrest Lee King possessed no certificate of residence.[68] Their success was extraordinary. The territorial courts of Nogales and Tucson often deported or harassed Chinese on the basis of scant evidence from "dutiful citizens" or the Chinese inspector, an immigration agent assigned to patrol U.S. borders for Chinese crossers and to investigate potential violations of the exclusion acts. From 1894 to 1903, the Tucson territorial court ordered the deportation of more than one hundred Chinese who had recently crossed the Mexican border.[69] Several Chinese who claimed to possess certificates of residence but were unable to produce them were also unable to find two white witnesses or to provide the necessary documentation in the period mandated by the court. In 1904 alone the Chinese Division at the Arizona border reported arresting 123 Chinese who had originated from the interior of Sonora. Of these individuals, 84 faced deportation, 23 awaited judgments, and the remaining 16 were discharged.[70] Almost inevitably the vast majority of Chinese arrested in Nogales, Yuma, and Tucson on the suspicion of illegal entry into the United States faced deportation.[71]

The battlefront of the Geary Act all but guaranteed that Chinese such as Joe Con would clash with the territorial courts over citizen and alien status. In 1902, Joe Con visited Nogales, Sonora, without a certificate of residence. Upon his return but before his arrest, he was asked for a certificate, which he did not possess. He affirmed, nonetheless, the right to reenter the United States because of his American citizenship. After spending more than three weeks in jail awaiting trial, Con's case was finally adjudicated by the territorial court in Nogales. Louis Levin and W. R. Mannsfield, two white witnesses on behalf of the Nogales court, testified to Con's presence in Mexico. Levin claimed that he saw Con at a "wedding on the Mexican side of Nogales," while Mannsfield, a cattle inspector, said he noticed Con approaching him from the Mexican side of the border.[72] Mannsfield and James Shaw, the owner of the cattle, spoke to Con as he passed through the cow field to Nogales, Arizona. "We spoke to him and recognized him as Joe Con. We rode to the monument to take observation and found out that he was inside of Mexico about 1,000 feet."[73] Con's fortune turned after Mannsfield's testimony. His attorney pointed out to the court that the conversation between Con, Mannsfield, and Shaw was in English. Con's fluent English held sway in light of the charges against him, and the territorial court found in favor of Con's claims.[74]

When the Geary Act was enforced and Chinese laborers were compelled to obtain certificates of residence, Tucson Chinese found that *guanxi* relations and connections to established borderlands residents became even more crucial. Business, kith, and family relations, the strongest ties binding together Tucson Chinese, encouraged more immigrants to settle in El Barrio, even though it would be four decades before the Chinese community numbered more than three hundred residents (see Table 2.1). Lim Bow's 1902 lease with Jesús Montejo Jr., the son of Gertrudis and Jesús Montejo, Sr., suggests one reason that Tucson's Chinese population remained stable. The agreement made clear that the seven Chinese men employed by Bow's Sun Sing Company "were all residents of Pima County."[75] Leases between whites and Mexicans did not distinguish place of residence; it was assumed that Mexicans were local and legal inhabitants. Chinese, however, were almost always considered itinerant denizens, and such specification about residency was thus deemed necessary to avoid deportation. Leases provided essential proof of local belonging.

Under growing pressure to enforce Chinese exclusion laws, residential and work histories proved critical for those who were suspected of illegal residency in the United States. Tucson's new Chinese inspector, Charles Connell, came to symbolize the U.S. immigration regime's aggressive and uncompromising approach to apprehending and deporting Chinese at the border. Appointed to the post in late 1903—the same year in which the

TABLE 2.1
*Chinese Occupations in Tucson, 1900*

| Occupation | Number | Occupation | Number |
|---|---|---|---|
| Truck farmers | 35 | Houseworkers | 2 |
| Cooks | 26 | Druggists | 2 |
| Launderers | 19 | Drugstore keepers | 1 |
| Merchants | 19 | Clerks | 1 |
| Grocers | 13 | Variety store keepers | 1 |
| Waiters | 12 | Water tank tenders | 1 |
| Engine and depot wipers | 12 | Dishwashers | 1 |
| (Day) laborers | 7 | Pastry cooks | 1 |
| General store keepers | 6 | Carvers | 1 |
| Restaurant keepers | 4 | Restaurant workers | 1 |
| Physicians | 3 | Capitalists | 1 |
| Servants | 3 | No employment listed | 5 |
| | | | Total: 177 |

Source: U.S. Census Bureau, *Twelfth Census of the United States*, 1900.

Bureau of Immigration was placed under the authority of the Department of Commerce and Labor in order to tighten the grip of the exclusion laws at the U.S. southern border—Connell was no stranger to the various ethnic communities in southern Arizona. Born in Mount Vernon, Iowa, and educated on the East Coast, Connell arrived in Arizona during its pioneering days. At the age of twenty-one, he administered the first census of the Apache Indians at the San Carlos Reservation in 1880. Considered a foremost authority on the tribe, Connell served as a "diplomatic agent" to the Apache on behalf of the federal government. Only a few years later, when the Spanish-American War broke out, Connell continued his government duties as a secret service agent along the U.S.-Mexico border. From this experience, Connell reportedly carried a mental map of the entire Mexican border between El Paso and San Diego and "knew every trail, road, pass, canyon, mountain and water hole." His experience as an Apache agent and wartime officer proved quite useful in his future duties for the federal government, especially in his role as Chinese inspector.[76]

While on surveillance duty in Tucson, Connell apprehended Ng Jan and Chan Cheong and charged them with violating the Geary Act because neither of them had a certificate of residence. The two laborers were visiting Tucson at the financial expense of Chun Kee, a San Francisco merchant who employed them. Kee, whose store dealt in Chinese and Japanese goods, testified at their hearing that he had purchased the train tickets for Jan and Cheong. Despite the testimony of Kee, William Watson, Teamster Chun Jay, and San Francisco merchants Ng' Sin Fa and Chan Yang Yick, Cheong and Jan were deported because they possessed no certificates and failed to prove their legal residency in the United States.[77]

Chinese migrants were often deported solely on the basis of the eyewitness testimony of one or two individuals. Wong Poy, arrested in Tombstone in February 1907, experienced such a fate. While visiting Cananea, Sonora, in January, Connell saw Poy. Concurring with Connell's testimony, Cananea resident and barber Frank Malone stated that he noticed Poy "in December and January at a wedding . . . and saw him [in Cananea] on several occasions."[78] A laborer who possessed a certificate of residence, Poy challenged the claims of Malone and Connell that he had visited Cananea. Although the witnesses for Poy convincingly traced his residential history back sixteen years to Los Angeles and to his recent associations with truck farmers in Fairbank, Arizona, they were unable to overturn the claims of Malone and Connell. Without an extensive residential history in southern Arizona and ties to long-standing Chinese in Tucson, Chinese such as Poy were especially vulnerable to politically expedient deportation hearings.

Travel from places other than Tucson or southern Arizona proved risky for Chinese. In the next few decades, when the Bureau of Immigration enforced the political border between Arizona and Sonora, those Chinese who were more established in Tucson were often shielded from the harsh reality of exclusion laws. As the machinery of the U.S. immigration regime grew in manpower and became more efficient at stopping Chinese from entering the United States at the southern border, bonds of neighborhood and kinship that connected Chinese to other *fronterizos* shielded them from being summarily deported. Their most enduring accomplishment was the kith bonds created between them and their Mexican neighbors in Tucson. For Tucson Chinese, kith bonds were based in the everyday relations of farming, commerce, and companionship. They cultivated ties with Mexicans, formed families, and socialized. Kith bonds meant that *guanxi* relations could, and did, secure bonds among the Chinese themselves and, by extension, the essential foundation of settlement was laid. The cultivation of kith and kin relations occurred in the midst of struggle with harsh immigration laws and the efforts of Tucson Chinese to fend off the enforcement of exclusion. These were largely unintended consequences of the enforcement of Chinese exclusion laws at the U.S.-Mexico border.

Some seventy miles south of Tucson, in Mexico, different types of relationships between Chinese residents and Mexicans would have implications for Sonoran Chinese similar to the implications they had for Tucson Chinese. Patterns of transnational travel, social ties, and economic activity were not so easily broken. Although at the beginning of the twentieth century crossing into the United States from Mexico assumed greater complexity, Chinese merchants and Mexican and American officials acted in tandem to maintain cross-border travel even as the path to open borders was fraught with uncertainty and confusion. Another factor was at work as well. Washington, DC, policymakers, although fully aware of Chinese communities in northern Mexico and the U.S. Southwest, had yet to rework exclusion laws to make them suitable for the borderlands context. Whereas immigration officials throughout the United States might use minor discretion in interpreting some aspects of the exclusion laws, customs collectors in southern Arizona went much further, deviating greatly from conventional understandings of the law. Instead of summarily practicing apprehension and exclusion—which was the approach taken by San Francisco and Los Angeles immigration inspectors—customs collectors at Tucson, Nogales, and Yuma often made decisions in favor of admission. With virtually no guidelines to direct decision making and no virulent anti-Chinese sentiment to sway their judgment, cross-border movement often prevailed. Mexican consular officials and U.S. customs authorities worked in partnership to maintain open borders for Chinese merchants in Mexico. Until the turn of the twentieth century, fluid and open borders trumped Chinese exclusion laws.

*Keeping Borders Open*

Lee Sing was among the first Chinese to settle in Tucson after initially arriving in Sonora. In 1879, Sing, an ambitious young merchant, established a dry-goods business with his brother in the Old Pueblo. The small store, stocked with items such as beef jerky, beans, and whisky, was quite enterprising in the context of the burgeoning Tucson economy. Financial connections with prominent Jewish businessmen made Sing's business prospects bright.[79] Sing's success inspired him to expand into the production and sale of shoes in Nogales, Arizona. Over the next few years, Sing's second business enterprise flourished along with the economy of this booming border town, but by 1889 the operation of his businesses took a back seat to his personal priorities. After some years of engagement to a Mexican woman, Sing decided to liquidate his assets and properties in Nogales and Tucson in order to relocate to Sonora, marry, and become a Mexican citizen.

After his wedding in Mexico, Sing established stores in the Sonoran towns of Ímuris, La Cienaga, and Santa Ana. Like many Chinese proprietors in northern Mexico, Sing lived in a transnational world. He established financial and familial ties in both the United States and Mexico, holding investments with his brother in Tucson while creating a home and family in Sonora. Yet his growing wealth and economic status did not necessarily guarantee trouble-free entry into the United States. During a routine trip north in 1893, Sing was detained by Arizona border inspectors and his status as a merchant was questioned. The thirty-two-year-old businessman was fortunate; he was able to call on Mexican and American officials for assistance. D. A. Moreno, president of the border city of Santa Ana, verified Sing's *ciudadanía* (citizenship), his eleven years of residency in Mexico, his marriage to a Mexican woman (and the fact that he was father to three Mexican children), his annual income of eight to ten thousand pesos, and his ownership of a local general store. Also persuasive were the confirmation of the merchant's real estate holdings by the prefect of Magdalena, Ignacio Bonilla, and Sing's affidavit to the American consul at Nogales, Sonora, Josiah E. Stone.[80]

Sing's overwhelming record of settlement held sway and officials permitted Sing to pass freely across the border over the next four years. No single aspect—merchant status, Mexican citizenship, or familial roots in Sonora—determined his entry. All were important and all would have an impact on local enforcement of Chinese exclusion laws. It is useful to compare Sing's situation to that of most Mexicans, who were relatively free to cross the border during the 1890s; they were stopped at the border only when customs officials suspected them of evading paying appropriate tariffs, or of smuggling contraband whiskey, cigars, and opium. Unlike for the Chinese, proof of citizenship or nationality was not required for Mexicans to pass into the United States. A Mexican national simply declared his name to U.S. customs officials and paid whatever duty or fine was due.[81] Chinese residents of Mexico, by contrast, were always stopped at the border, under the assumption that they were "aliens" in the region.[82]

Claims of Mexican citizenship and nationality yielded positive results when immigration officials stopped and detained Chinese border crossers. In fact, most Chinese merchants who asserted such privileges benefited from the rights bestowed on Mexicans at the southern U.S. border: they gained legal entry north. Moreover, conscious assertions of *mexicanidad* (Mexican-ness) on the part of Chinese border crossers indicated that membership in the Mexican polity had not yet assumed the narrow and ethnically confining requisites associated with the postrevolutionary identity of *mestizaje*. Although Mexican nationality, and its subsequent power at the southern U.S. border, continued to perplex immigration and customs officials attempting to make sense out of rather inept exclusion laws, Chinese merchants continued to cross, although their movements were not always effortless.

The 1897 murder of Lee Sing's brother in Tucson threw the orderly world of the shoe merchant into confusion. Sing began the difficult task of taking care of his brother's affairs, including selling his dry-goods store to a local Chinese merchant for three thousand dollars. Somewhere in this process Sing began to feel sentimental about his earlier life in the Arizona Territory and contemplated relocating his wife and their three young children to Tucson.[83] He returned to Ímuris and persuaded his wife of the virtues of Tucson, including the quality of its schools. Sing then left for Tucson to arrange for the move, leaving with his wife the money and documents related to the sale of his brother's property.

Sing passed without incident across the international border, but trouble began almost immediately upon his arrival in Tucson. After an eight-year absence, no one recognized Sing. He took up short-term residency at the Star Laundry, a downtown shop in the Old Pueblo owned by an elderly friend of Sing, Sam Lee. It was here that a local passerby, who had witnessed Sing ironing what were later determined to be his own clothes, mistook the merchant for a laborer. Not surprisingly, this type of manual activity threw Sing's status as merchant into question. In a matter of a day, Tucson immigration officials arrested Sing, believing he was a laborer illegally in the United States. As his lengthy testimony revealed, the exchange of money in the form of a wage never occurred between Sam Lee and Lee Sing. The proprietor of the laundry washed his guest's clothes free of charge, and if any ironing was to be done, Sing would have to do it himself.

Sing's experience was a common one among Chinese merchants in the United States. They were often stopped arbitrarily, and scrutiny of their status often ensued. A similar predicament held true for Mexican merchants Ah Suey, Hi Chung, Wong Nam, Wong Fong, and Mary Fong of southern Arizona.[84] All gained admission to the United States, albeit after a period of detention, questioning, and litigation. Declarations of citizenship and merchant status aided their disputes. The territorial court even recognized the dual residencies of merchants Mary and Wong Fong to be Tombstone, Arizona, and San Pedro, Sonora, Mexico. The couple operated stores on both sides of the border while maintaining their home in Tombstone.[85] Likewise, legal maneuverings and the assertion of Mexican citizenship eventually freed Sing from the grip of the territorial courts.[86]

After Sing's case, things seemed to get easier for Sonoran Chinese merchants traveling to the United States. By then, significant numbers of Chinese had begun arriving in Sonora with the intention of settling and establishing businesses, supported in large part by the Chinese Six Companies in San Francisco. The shoe and manufacturing firm of Tung, Chung, Lung, for example, had set up shop in 1873, and by the late nineteenth century they held extensive wealth and political clout.[87] These factors would come to matter significantly. In 1898, merchants Lau Chi, Lau Chan, and Chin Chan Jin, members of the prominent Sonoran firm of Juan Lung Tain and Company, obtained travel visas from J. F. Darnell, the American consul in Nogales, to enter the United States. To facilitate a trouble-free admission, Darnell requested that Chi, Chan, and Jin "establish the testimony of two credible witnesses other than Chinese." Each merchant possessed certificates from Mexican authorities as well as testimonies verifying their good character and the nature of their business. Once these evidentiary guidelines were settled, Darnell completed the petition for travel and the three businessmen were issued visas. Chan and Jin traveled to San Francisco to purchase goods for their firm. Chi traveled to China for the same purpose.[88] Citizenship, family, and merchant status would remain the cornerstones of Mexico's Chinese business community over the next five decades, even in the face of burgeoning anti-Chinese sentiment in Sonora.

In 1890, there were 229 Chinese in Sonora, working mostly in hotels as cooks, launderers, and gardeners.[89] The small community nonetheless caused Ramón Corral, the state's governor, a great deal of apprehension. In fact, the Chinese presence alarmed Corral so much he worried that immigration from China would eventually land millions in Mexico. What Corral feared never transpired, although his paranoia did motivate him to recommend a quota limiting the landing of Chinese in Mexico.[90] The number of Chinese migrants that Corral deemed to be the maximum acceptable limit was ten per year. But just as he was advocating a restrictionist stance, in 1895, a change took place at both the national and international levels that would prevent the governor's vision from taking hold. Porfirio Díaz's successful consolidation of power at both the federal and local levels meant that immigration from China would begin in earnest. Then, in 1899, official diplomacy and Mexico-to-China transoceanic lines made migration easier. Increased migration from China also meant that existing merchant activity in Sonora began to expand and Chinese-owned firms grew more influential and wealthier. The Siu Fo Chon Company, Fon Qui, and Tung, Chung, Lung for a time employed most Chinese migrants who came to work in Sonora. They also found themselves hiring workers who had previously tried their hand at mining but had abandoned that industry for more stable work in shoe and clothing manufacturing.[91]

Chinese merchants wielded considerable influence in Sonora, but it was most clearly evident in their relationships with Mexican officials. Enlisting the aid of Mexican and U.S. officials, merchants petitioned for entry north as Mexican citizens. This strategy suggests that the pliability of Mexican citizenship and nationality, at least for two decades, trumped the narrow confines of Chinese exclusion laws. Laborers, on the other hand, faced greater legal barriers to crossing the border, yet they also exercised more than nominal control over their deportation hearings. If they demonstrated Mexican citizenship or residency, they were deported to Mexico, not China. For both Chinese merchants and laborers, inclusion in the Mexican national community provided a means to contest exclusion laws and state-sponsored campaigns against them. As more Chinese from Sonora and Baja California insisted on traveling to the United States, customs officials stopped and detained Chinese merchants with growing frequency.[92] U.S. customs officials wrestled with this social reality, as well as with the ambiguities of enforcing exclusion laws. Some consular officials began to feel that temporary Chinese travel into the United States should be allowed within the framework of exclusion laws. Within this ambiguous and negotiable intersection between formal law and social reality, requests by Chinese to enter the United States were, more often than not, resolved in their favor (see Figure 2.4).

The inconsistencies in enforcing Chinese exclusion weighed heavily on customs collectors throughout the United States, but especially on those in San Francisco, from whom other collectors sought advice. "Commissioners along the southern border," charged San Francisco collector T. J. Phelps, "have all construed the law differently, and perhaps only one of them has made up anything like a proper judgment."[93] Improper judgments were made among Arizona's territorial commissioners, who did not automatically deport Chinese from Mexico to China. Territorial commissioners recognized the value of community life among Chinese in Mexico and made decisions to sustain it rather than find pat solutions to exclude in otherwise nebulous exclusion laws. With virtually no legal precedents to guide decision making and no political pressure to sway their judgment,

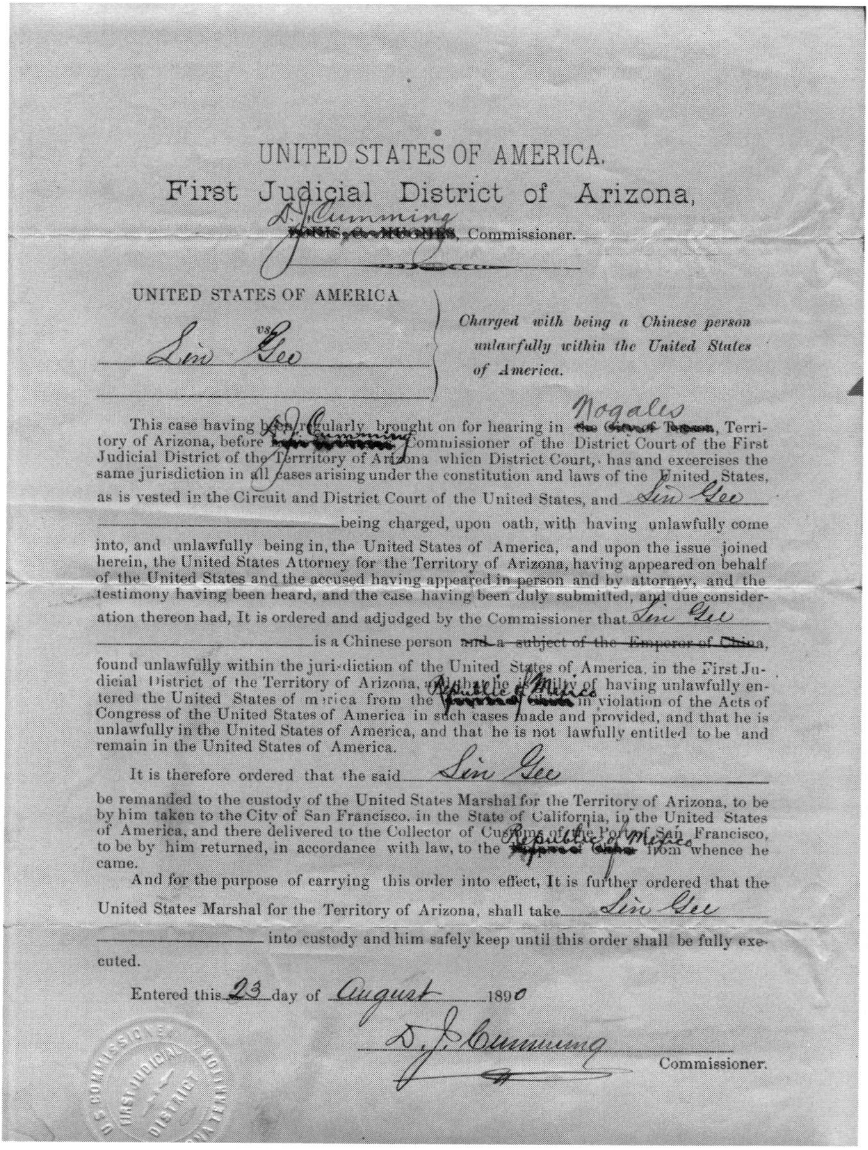

UNITED STATES OF AMERICA.

First Judicial District of Arizona,

*D. J. Cumming*

~~HON. C. NICHOLS,~~ Commissioner.

UNITED STATES OF AMERICA

vs

*Sin Gee*

> Charged with being a Chinese person
> unlawfully within the United States
> of America.

This case having been regularly brought on for hearing in ~~the Circuit Room~~ *Nogales*, Territory of Arizona, before ~~Hon. C. Nichols,~~ Commissioner of the District Court of the First Judicial District of the Territory of Arizona which District Court, has and excercises the same jurisdiction in all cases arising under the constitution and laws of the United States, as is vested in the Circuit and District Court of the United States, and *Sin Gee* _____being charged, upon oath, with having unlawfully come into, and unlawfully being in, the United States of America, and upon the issue joined herein, the United States Attorney for the Territory of Arizona, having appeared on behalf of the United States and the accused having appeared in person and by attorney, and the testimony having been heard, and the case having been duly submitted, and due consideration thereon had, It is ordered and adjudged by the Commissioner that *Sin Gee* _____is a Chinese person ~~and a subject of the Emperor of China~~, found unlawfully within the jurisdiction of the United States of America, in the First Judicial District of the Territory of Arizona, ~~and that he is guilty of~~ having unlawfully entered the United States of America from the ~~Empire of China~~ in violation of the Acts of Congress of the United States of America in such cases made and provided, and that he is unlawfully in the United States of America, and that he is not lawfully entitled to be and remain in the United States of America.

It is therefore ordered that the said *Sin Gee* _____ be remanded to the custody of the United States Marshal for the Territory of Arizona, to be by him taken to the City of San Francisco, in the State of California, in the United States of America, and there delivered to the Collector of Customs at the Port of San Francisco, to be by him returned, in accordance with law, to the ~~Empire of China~~ from whence he came.

And for the purpose of carrying this order into effect, It is further ordered that the United States Marshal for the Territory of Arizona, shall take *Sin Gee* _____into custody and him safely keep until this order shall be fully executed.

Entered this **23** day of *August* 189**0**

*D. J. Cumming*

Commissioner.

FIGURE 2.4 Sin Gee. This is one of several hundred certificates documenting the court proceedings of Chinese exclusion cases in the Arizona Territory. Note the many modifications, especially what previously read "and a subject of the Empire of China." Records of the District Court of the United States for the Territory of Arizona, First Judicial District, Criminal Case Files, 1882–1912, RG 21, case no. 410. Courtesy of the National Archives and Records Administration, Pacific Region, Laguna Niguel.

Arizona territorial customs officials found themselves in the position to interpret exclusion laws on the basis of their own understanding of Chinese life at the border.

Chinese laborers who were stopped at the Arizona-Sonora border were not always subject to the same exclusionary practices as those entering elsewhere. Territorial commissioners Louis C. Hughes, Allen R. English, and D. J. Cumming made distinctions between border crossers and border residents—those Chinese laborers who were sojourning *through* Mexico and those who were *from* Mexico. Until roughly 1900, Chinese laborers of Mexican citizenship or nationality who were crossing the border were simply deported to Mexico, the most favorable outcome possible for Chinese laborers at the time, and one that was consistent with San Francisco collector Phelps's judgment of exclusion laws.[94] "I don't think there is any doubt . . . of the law," Phelps asserted. "The law refers to all Chinamen, whether they come from China or whether they are citizens of Cuba [or] Spain. . . . If they had acquired citizenship in Mexico undoubtedly they would be entitled to be sent back to Mexico."[95] Chinese with no claims to Mexican residency or citizenship continued to risk crossing into the United States from Mexico, even if it meant deportation to China. The reason was fairly simple: although deportation was a certainty if they were caught, border crossers were more likely than not to evade detection.

In the hot summer months of 1890, twenty-two Chinese, including Ning Ah Goon, Ta Ho, Ah Cheong, Hom Jung, Gwan Gong, and Ning Saung Hoe, were captured and imprisoned in Nogales and Tucson. They were not residents of Mexico and had no other intention than to cross into the United States. Without any legal representation, each of the laborers signed an affidavit, translated into Chinese by San Francisco-based interpreter Carleton Rickards, about the nature of the circuitous journeys that landed them in Arizona. The testimony of Ning Ah Goon was typical: "My name is Ning Ah Goon. I am 42 years old, was born in China. I am a laborer. I arrived in San Francisco from China Jan. 20 to Feb. 17–1890 on S. S. City of Peking. I then went to Guaymas [sic] Mexico where I arrived Feb 27–1890, I do not know from which vessel."[96] By the time these laborers completed their declarations there was no longer any question as to their status—they were Chinese laborers and nationals illegally in the United States and had to be returned to China. A month after their arrest they were officially deported.

The fact that many Chinese laborers crossed the border with no claims to Mexican residence or citizenship did not deter territorial commissioners Hughes, English, and Cumming from seeking to verify Mexican citizenship and residency when possible. That same summer they held thirteen Mexican-based Chinese laborers for illegal entry into Arizona. Without the assistance of attorneys, Sam Hing, Chu Yun, Charley Quong, and Charley Ah Fong, asked to be deported to Mexico rather than to China.[97] Each defendant self-identified as a laborer and declared nationality or citizenship in Mexico. Support for Sam Hing was especially evident, because for years he owned and operated the Bird Cage Restaurant next to the famous Bird Cage Theater (see Figure 2.5). Tombstone residents Wong Lung and

FIGURE 2.5 Sam Hing at Fly's Gallery in Tombstone, Arizona. This photograph was part of the evidence submitted on behalf of Hing. Records of the District Court of the United States for the Territory of Arizona, First Judicial District, Criminal Case Files, 1882–1912, RG 21, case no. 413. Courtesy of the National Archives and Records Administration, Pacific Region, Laguna Niguel

James Reese posted a hundred-dollar bond on his behalf. They also testified to Hing's activities in Tombstone, and provided important documentation that Hing had resided in Mexico, hoping that their friend would escape deportation to China. After the proceedings were completed, territorial marshal R. H. Paul escorted Hing, Yun, Quong, and Fong to the border town of Nogales, Sonora.

The language of the territorial court suggested that deportation of laborers to Mexico was deemed to be not as punitive as the deportation of laborers to China. Hughes, English, and Cumming viewed sending laborers to Mexico as a mere discharge. The order of deportation by Commissioner English underscored this point: "I certify the order on the 26th day of June, AD 1890, by carrying the defendant, Chin Yan, to Nogales, State of Sonora, Republic of Mexico, and there discharging him."[98] That *deportation* meant returning to China and *discharge* meant a short escort to the border town of Nogales further undermined the intent of the law to prohibit entry. In effect, Chinese attempting to enter the United States at its southern border prompted territorial commissioners to weigh the significance of Mexican citizenship or nationality against exclusion laws that targeted Chinese originating from China. The largely informal category of discharge emerged from the need to know what to do with Chinese residents and citizens of Mexico who fell outside the official purview of exclusion laws.

Not everyone was satisfied with the practices of the Arizona territorial commissioners. Customs officials in San Diego were impatient with the Arizona practice of discharging Chinese, which they felt made a mockery of their exclusion efforts. "To take them to the line and turn them loose below it, does no good whatsoever, as they simply take the first opportunity to cross again," remarked San Diego customs collector John R. Berry. "The farce enacted [occurs] when officials' backs are turned [and] the opportunity is created for their returning again."[99] At the same time, Mexican immigration restriction narrowed opportunities for Chinese, although not on the same scale as in the United States. For some time, Chinese were accorded rights equal to those of Mexicans. The civil privileges enjoyed by Chinese merchants and laborers in Mexico, however, gradually began to erode after 1900. Over time, American immigration officials were less inclined to allow Mexican Chinese to cross legally, nor were they as easily disposed to discharge deportees to Mexico.

Ties among *fronterizos* on both sides of the border had a variety of unintended consequences for Chinese, both as border crossers and as settlers. Bonds afforded newcomers companionship, marriage, and cohabitation among friends and neighbors. They also reinforced mutual trust and reciprocity among kin members whose residential histories may have been suspect or less established. Among all kinds of ties in Tucson, the mundane and everyday endeavors of operating stores or laundering clothes, more than any other ties, tempered anti-Chinese sentiment, provided paths around the enforcement of harsh exclusion laws, and mitigated against the virulent Sinophobia of American urban settings, especially San Francisco. In Sonora, the lives of Chinese were also not always sharply constrained by social class, nationality, or race. Family ties, the search for work, and the maintenance of transnational economic exchange between Chinese merchants in northern Mexico and those in the United States softened exclusionists' calls for the closure of the American southern border. Merchant *fronterizos* continued to travel to Chinatowns in San Francisco, Tucson, San Diego, Los Angeles, and El Paso to supply their stores and cultivate economic and social relationships. In a similar fashion, the power of exclusion did not completely overtake Chinese laborers as they engaged in extraordinary measures to avoid deportation to China when caught at the border.

Chinese *fronterizos* made kith and kinship relationships succeed in myriad ways, all of which amounted to important successes, whether practical or personal. Relationships may have been overwrought by the pressure of exclusion laws and, at times, strained by breaches of confidence. But regardless of the ruptures that did occur, relationships structured on both sides of the border sustained fluid and transnational communities among Mexican borderlands populations. That Chinese *fronterizos* cultivated relations with neighbors and friends, considering the weight that bore down on them, was a feat not easily achieved. Chinese insulated their communities from exclusion politics that jeopardized personal moorings by making everyday bonds from intensely social arrangements. Out of this complex social landscape grew interethnic communities, even as attendant apprehensions weighed heavily on Chinese borderlanders. Although proponents of immigration restrictionism would have neither anticipated nor desired them, kith, kin, business, and diplomatic bonds were the most significant outcomes of Chinese exclusion laws at the Arizona-Sonora borderlands. For Chinese border crossers traversing into the United States illegally through California, other types of dynamics were at play to facilitate their passage north.

# 3 Traversing the Line

In 1890, Anthony Godbe had little idea that his days as American vice consul would be spent tracking the activities of Chinese smuggling rings operating at the Mexico-California line. The illegal entry of Chinese migrants baffled the seasoned government official, who by virtue of his consular duties in Baja California, Mexico, operated within a politically complicated landscape. Godbe spared no pride confessing his ignorance of the trafficking scheme. In a missive to John C. Fisher, the collector of customs at San Diego, Godbe expressed his bewilderment at the efficiency of the smuggling cartels: "It is evident the Chinamen were apprised of the fact that officers were on the lookout for them and therefore returned to Ensenada. But how?"[1] Fisher's response evinced no clues about the origins or day-to-day operations of the smuggling activity, but he did assure Godbe that a congressional subcommittee would soon launch an investigation into the illegal crossings of Chinese migrants through the Canadian and Mexican frontiers. There is no telling if the customs collector allayed any of Godbe's concerns. But when Fisher asked Godbe about the nature of Chinese mining activity in Alamos and Real de Castillo, small towns just outside the port city of Ensenada, Fisher mentioned that the colonization projects of the On Yick Company were legitimate ones, even as he hinted that they could also stand as fronts of illegal activity.[2]

If Fisher's hunches were correct, the ruse was ingenious. The 116–square mile mining concession, acquired by Yee Chong Long and financed by several wealthy Chinese associates, required large pools of manpower. Without constant replenishment of foreign labor, colonization projects stood to, and did, fail. Such ventures were risky business in Mexico, especially in the arid and mountainous desert terrain of Baja California, where time and time again colonization efforts collapsed because of the scarcity of labor and lackluster investment. The several dozen Chinese landing in Ensenada were in perfect keeping with the express intention to make colonization projects work, but what soon became evident to Godbe and Fisher was that the laborers, once acclimated to the routine of work, were promptly escorted over the Mexico border by smugglers employed by the On Yick Company.[3]

If these suspicions illustrate the ways in which American officials responded to the Chinese in Baja California, the reactions of American officials in Mexico revealed an even more complex set of circumstances in the Pacific borderlands states. American officials' first reaction to Chinese in Mexico was not suspicion but rather a tacit acknowledgment that the Chinese were a stock presence south of the border. In the early 1890s, Delos H. Smith, the American consul at Nogales, Sonora, was not alarmed by the Chinese in the state, nor did he proceed as if they posed an imminent threat to enforcing Chinese exclusion laws. Rather, Smith's preoccupation focused on taxing goods and settling disputes over stolen livestock and contraband *mezcal*. He was less urgent about conveying the presence of a large group of Chinese men at Altar, Sonora, near the U.S. border, to immigration officials. He remarked, "I hardly [knew] whether or not I was right in reporting this matter," but he later came to realize that the "Exclusion Acts seems to justify reporting the information."[4]

Smith's disinclination to immediately notify American immigration authorities about the northward movement of border crossers combined with his curious advocacy for Chinese in Sonora. The laws permitted Chinese merchants, who were among the so-called exempted classes, legal entry once a certificate verifying their status was issued by immigration authorities. Just as consular agent Josiah Stone would do a few years later, Smith petitioned U.S. government officials on behalf of Chinese merchants in Sonora who had requested permission to enter the United States by obtaining an exemption to the "Section Six" clause of the 1882 Chinese Exclusion Act.[5] Smith wrote, "It occasionally happens that Chinamen come to the consulate here for permission to visit the United States on business or pleasure and I desire to know if under the Treaties and Laws now in force, a Consul can issue such permit? I find no forms here, or in the Regulations for such permit, and enclose one for the consideration of the Department."[6] Smith was confident that his idea of an entry permit would quickly supply what was simply needed. Chinese merchants who wished to travel into the United States would only have to submit a photograph, testimony of "reliable and trusty" character, and Smith's entry permit.[7] Smith saw no contradiction between his actions and upholding the Chinese exclusion laws.

Both Fisher and Smith learned a good deal about the Chinese in Mexico, the former from the vantage of Baja California as a customs collector and the latter from Sonora as an American consular official. Telltale signs abounded that Fisher and Smith's approaches gained traction even as they seemed to be in conflict. As a trickle of Chinese border crossers turned into a constant stream of aliens smuggled illicitly into the United States by internationally organized rings, Fisher saw an increased need for more immigration agents to patrol the southern line whereas Smith sought greater clarification of exclusion laws for Mexican Chinese. The growing presence of Chinese in Mexico's port cities—principally Ensenada, Baja California, and Guaymas, Sonora—indicated that many were crossing illegally through one of the last frontiers of the United States. Patrolling the line for aliens coming up from Baja California and Sonora remained a fixture in the daily routine of immigration inspectors, just as finding a means to facilitate legal entry preoccupied American consular officials. Fisher's attention to so-called contraband Chinese focused on surveillance and apprehension because illegal crossings from Mexico embodied the danger that smuggling cartels would take firm hold in the region. Control over Chinese foot traffic sustained immigrant inspectors' sense of mastery over the borderlands even as many Chinese from Mexico were perfectly admissible into the United States. The tensions between exclusion and admission may have been embodied in Fisher and Smith, but their origins were grounded in the terms of early Chinese settlement and the successes and failures of Mexican colonization and immigration projects in Baja California and Sonora. Until 1910, many Chinese settlers lived alongside border crossers in Sonora, while in Baja California few settled and most were smuggled. Given these sets of circumstances and the proximity to several hundred miles of coastline and unguarded borderline, it was no small wonder that Baja California and Sonora would become ground zero in the American controversy over Chinese immigration into Mexico and border crossing into the United States.

## The Chinese Invasion from Mexico

By 1890, a brilliant scheme was in the works to evade Chinese exclusion laws at the southern U.S. border. Aided by ties to trans-Pacific migration networks, smugglers blazed illegal pathways through the unguarded coastline and boundary line at Baja California and Sonora.[8] While fears of a Chinese invasion loomed large throughout the United States, events on the ground seemed to confirm suspicions that the southern U.S. border was a veritable gateway for the illegal entry of Chinese. When, for example, eighty Cantonese travelers transferred from the *City of Peking* to the *New Bernal* at the port of San Francisco, en route to Mexico, it signaled the onset of a systematic movement of Chinese migrants traveling overland through Baja California and Sonora with the intent to cross the international line.[9] Smuggling continued almost unabated through the 1890s, with customs officials undermanned and overwhelmed with the task of enforcing the line.[10] The advantage held by smuggling rings was that they

were entrenched along the western coastal region of the United States and
Mexico long before American politicians and immigration inspectors had
caught up with their schemes.

Illegal trafficking had other practical advantages for Chinese border
crossers. By traversing the U.S.-Mexico border by way of Baja California
and Sonora, Chinese could avoid prolonged detentions at the barracks in the
port of San Francisco. These backdoor routes into the United States troubled American politicians so much that in May 1890, Congress called for
an immediate diplomatic solution to stop the illegal entry of Chinese at both
the southern and northern U.S. borders. Armed with nothing more than an
unfounded fear that the *City of Peking–New Bernal* scheme was emblematic of widespread smuggling, Republican senator William W. Morrow
from California exhorted President Benjamin Harrison to secure treaties
with the country's southern and northern neighbors. Morrow underscored
the urgency of diplomacy, insisting that Chinese exclusion laws had been
"vigorously enforced" from within, but stood tenuously relative to outside
forces. "To police these frontiers," Morrow argued, "will require a much
greater force than has been provided for."[11] And the force needed here was
to be diplomatic, not martial.

If Morrow had had his way, there would have been no confirmatory
investigation. Instead, diplomacy would have been the initial and only
course of action, assuming that both Mexico and Canada would be agreeable partners. But rumors of a Chinese invasion called for an official Senate investigation before diplomatic channels could be considered. Herman
Lehlbach, a Republican congressman from New Jersey, chaired the Select
Committee on Immigration and Naturalization, which was charged with
investigating the immigration of Chinese from Mexico and Canada. This
committee would recommend, if necessary, a course of action to curb the
entry of Chinese across the northern border from Canada and across the
southern border from Mexico.[12]

Lehlbach began his investigation with Canada. Testimony was taken
from customs and immigration inspectors in Port Townsend, Washington,
and in the California port cities of San Diego and San Francisco. When
questioned about the illegal entry of Chinese originating from Canada,
James M. Buckley, an unemployed former assistant manager for the
Northern Pacific Railroad Company, insisted that exclusion laws sharply
diminished illicit movement of Chinese into northern Washington. "While
a good many people think [the Chinese] are coming in by the wholesale,
I do not think so . . . but as to their importation by ship loads . . . that
is done away with now," noted Buckley. "There are some, I think; but I
don't think there are so many as is generally supposed. I don't believe there
is such an amount being smuggled in as some people think."[13] Buckley
believed that the exclusion laws were working at the northern U.S. border.

Lehlbach seemed less convinced, knowing that Chinese migrants were with growing frequency seeking admission through the Canadian border.

When Lehlbach and his committee turned to investigating illicit crossings from Mexico, it soon became clear that the few hundred Chinese entering the United States annually through Canada paled when compared with the few thousand Chinese from Mexico. Lehlbach's investigation revealed that from 1888 to 1890, 3,274 Chinese crossed into the United States from Mexico via San Francisco; of these, 400 headed for Honolulu and 250 to 300 advanced to Canada and the rest supposedly headed to Mexico.[14] But most Chinese destined for Mexico never arrived there; instead, they simply remained in the United States illegally. Traveling through the United States was the problem, but managing it seemed simple enough. The "in-transit transportation" status granted to travelers by immigration officials gave them permission either to disembark from one ship and board a different one or to land in and travel through the United States on their way from one country to another. If in-transit transportation to Mexico via the port of San Francisco was barred, most Chinese would find it a rather challenging and circuitous task to enter the United States. At the urging of Lehlbach's report, in 1891 the secretary of the treasury prohibited the landing of Chinese intending to travel to Mexico via San Francisco.[15] After 1891, Chinese traveling in-transit were ordered to return to China on the same ship on which they had arrived.

If Lehlbach and other American politicians believed that this legislative action would help prohibit Chinese migrants from arriving in the United States, they were partially correct. Under the Chinese Exclusion Act of 1882, Chinese laborers already living in the United States were allowed to return after traveling abroad. They were required to enter through the same port from which they had departed and presented certificates of identification to the collector of customs. In 1888, however, the Scott Act invalidated these certificates and barred Chinese laborers who had been traveling or visiting abroad from returning to the United States.[16] Although an earlier agreement between China and the United States guaranteed laborers freedom of international travel, the Scott Act prevailed. According to census tabulations, the Scott Act had the effect of reducing the Chinese population in the United States by 15,000, from 105,000 in 1890 to 90,000 in 1900.[17]

But as the Scott Act reduced the Chinese population in the United States, it had the unintended consequence of increasing the Chinese population in Mexico and intensifying smuggling activity through northern Mexico. The extraordinary burden of identification placed on Chinese laborers who wanted to reenter the United States from abroad resulted in many settling in Mexico, especially in Sonora and Baja California. In 1895, only 71 Chinese resided in Baja California and about 310 lived in neighboring Sonora.[18] Things had changed considerably five years later. In Sonora, the population rose to 850, and in Baja California, it increased to 188.[19] In the same period, Chinese migrants arriving in Mexico favored landing in Pacific port cities over landing in Gulf port cities. In 1895, 77 landed on the Pacific side and 271 landed in the Gulf ports of Veracruz, Progreso, or Tampico, but six years later, 909 Chinese migrants landed at Pacific ports and thirteen landed in Veracruz.[20]

By 1900, American exclusionists had yet another reason to fear a "Chinese invasion" from the southern border. Mexico's treaty with China had just been ratified, and many in the United States believed that this diplomacy would severely undermine Chinese exclusion laws. American newspapers characterized the Chinese presence in Mexico as a direct threat to exclusion laws and warned their southern neighbor about open immigration policies that might come to burden its nation and its people. Still others exaggerated Mexican immigration policy, reporting that each "Chinaman [received] twenty acres of land" upon entry, and that 600,000 Chinese were expected to arrive in Mexico within a year. Such an influx, it was concluded, would surely result in illegal entry of Chinese into the United States. Although allegations that firms sought to recruit 600,000 Chinese remained unsubstantiated and the hundreds of thousands of immigrants never arrived in Mexico, stories of this type continued. At the same time, Mexican politicians were accused by American officials of falsely promising the Chinese resources when they could not provide adequate employment for their own people.[21]

Before adding more manpower at the border, American politicians tried to broker a treaty with Canada and Mexico to exclude Chinese laborers from North America on the basis of mutual interests. Mexico and Canada shared long stretches of unguarded coastline and frontier line with the United States—lines that were already beset by efficient smuggling rings and understaffed customs offices.[22] In Canada, the case was made on the basis of mutual racial interests. According to historian Kornel Chang, a commitment to white supremacy between the Anglo-American governments of the United States and Canada encouraged bilateral cooperation and constructed the U.S.-Canadian border as impenetrable to Chinese, Japanese, and South Asian migrants.[23] By 1903, American and British diplomacy had carved out an accord, commonly known as the Canadian Agreement, which extended American enforcement of its Chinese exclusion laws beyond its own national borders and into Canada. The goal of the agreement was to preempt illegal border crossings by directing all U.S.-bound Chinese migrants to designated ports along the Canadian border. There, border crossers would be subject to an inspection of their person, and if they met certain health standards for entering immigrants, they received a certificate of admission to the United States.[24]

The U.S. diplomatic relationship with Mexico was nowhere near as harmonious as the amity the United States enjoyed with Canada. For Mexico, a treaty with the United States would work in direct opposition to its colonization, immigration, and development goals. To join in an all-North American alliance with Canada and the United States to exclude the Chinese was simply not plausible for Mexico. Although U.S. diplomats expressed concern that an influx of Chinese into Mexico would mark the end of "Caucasian dominance in this section of the world," apprehensions about racial impurity were not prevailing enough to sway Mexican politicians away from encouraging Chinese immigration, even though many Mexicans had misgivings about the Chinese both culturally and racially.[25] In defending the Mexican position, an unwavering Matías Romero reminded American officials that the Mexican Constitution and its immigration and colonization laws guaranteed freedom of entry, exit, and movement for all people.[26] The American legation in Mexico contradicted Romero's stance and urged an agreement between Mexico and the United States, but Romero and other Mexican officials steadfastly maintained their position in favor of open immigration. Some members of the U.S. Senate were aggravated by Mexico's stance to continue open immigration policies; still others considered it "an almost unfriendly act towards the United States."[27]

The conditions of illegal immigration from Mexico were firmly set by the turn of the twentieth century. Border crossings by Chinese were a product of Mexican and American diplomacy as much as they were an outcome of local specialization in international migration. Mexico's diplomacy with China, not the United States, was in keeping with its liberal immigration and naturalization laws and its constitutional traditions. The Scott Act and the Canadian Agreement linked the United States and its northern neighbor as partners in the exclusion of Chinese and in the maintenance of racially white nation-states. Within a landscape that simultaneously included and excluded, Chinese migrants mapped the borderlands terrain with fluid and transnational movement. The constant presence in the U.S.-Mexico borderlands of American immigration inspectors and their ever-growing power reveal just how perilous cross-border movements were for the Chinese. Yet although transnational migration networks operated in the shadows of people's lives, they certainly wrought profound consequences.

## Overland and Overseas in the United States

The effect of Chinese migration to Mexico on the United States was felt almost immediately at the U.S.-Mexico border, where proximity to open coasts and durable smuggling rings made crossing into the United States by land far more appealing than risking prolonged detention at the port of San Francisco. Several hundred Chinese arrived at the Mexican port cities, specifically Guaymas and Ensenada, intent on crossing into the United States by way of San Diego or Nogales, Arizona. Overland and overseas cross-border networks blazed a trail into the United States. The Baja California-Sonora-United States routes began at the port of San Francisco, where Chinese remained on steamers and did not touch land. The steamers then proceeded in earnest to Mexican Pacific coastal cities, including Salina Cruz, Acapulco, Manzanillo, Mazatlán, Guaymas, La Paz, San José, Cabo San Lucas, Magdalena Bay, or Ensenada (see Map 3.1).[28] If Chinese migrants disembarked in Guaymas, they headed east to Hermosillo, the capital city of Sonora, and settled there or connected with smuggling cartels on the first leg of the illicit trip north. From Hermosillo, Chinese trekked overland to Magdalena, Naco, or Cananea, from where they traveled clandestinely to Fairbank, Benson, and then Tucson, and then traveled by train to Los Angeles, Sacramento, or San Francisco as a final destination. If they landed in Baja California by means of a second boat or smaller steamer, they could travel overland or overseas with the intent to enter the United States. From Ensenada, Chinese trekked directly north to Tijuana and then San Diego. The easterly route from Ensenada to Carrizo or Real del Castillo, then finally north to Campo, California, was more circuitous but, in the

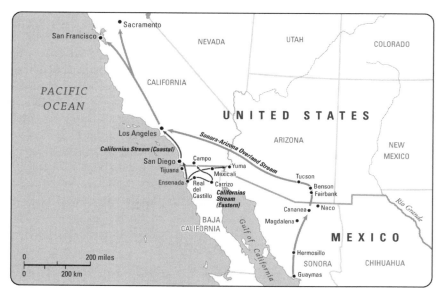

MAP 3.1  Overseas and Overland Routes of Illegal Entry Through the Pacific Borderlands. Drawn by Erin Greb.

estimation of San Diego immigration inspectors, gleaned positive results for border crossers. Still other Chinese would continue northeast to Mexicali, Baja California, or cross into Yuma, Arizona.[29]

Migration networks primarily accommodated men originating from South China, but they also obliged women and children who lived along the Pacific Coast of the United States. When Lai Ngan, for example, left San Francisco for Sonora under extreme duress, she accessed the migration network for Mexico. She boarded a steamer for Guaymas, Sonora, with her daughters, Carmen and Aurelia, to track down her estranged husband, Lee Kwong, and their son, Percy, after two years of separation. Leaving home was not a decision that Ngan made easily, but it may have been softened by childhood experiences. She was born and raised in San Francisco. After her father retired from the Chinese opera in 1883 and returned to Hong Kong, and until her marriage to Kwong, Ngan was cared for by maternal aunts. Before her father's retirement, she had accompanied her father to Chinese theaters in Hong Kong and had become familiar with, and perhaps confident about, the tempo of transnational travel. These experiences as a young traveler came in handy for Ngan as a married adult. When she married Kwong, she was fifteen years old and he was thirty-five. For a while the bond of shared family experiences kept the marriage whole, but in the face of hardship and a twenty-year age difference, Kwong left San Francisco with Percy for the fabled mines of Sonora, abandoning his wife and two daughters. Although she withstood the separation for a while, Ngan was ultimately undeterred by her unfamiliarity with the Spanish language and her lack of knowledge of the specific whereabouts of her husband and son in Sonora. The three intrepid travelers eventually found Kwong and Percy in La Colorada, a small mining town south of Hermosillo. The couple reunited and over the next ten years or so Ngan worked in a Chinese-owned shoe factory, conceived four more children with Kwong, and witnessed the futility of her husband's mining scheme. In 1903, not wanting her children to become Mexican citizens, Ngan moved her family to Nogales, Arizona, where she tended a small store. There, in the store, her husband sold Chinese lottery tickets.[30]

The trials of Ngan's family life provide a poignant example of the durability and complexity of the transnational migration networks that operated along the American and Mexican Pacific coast and the two countries' common national border. These networks lessened some of the burdens of Ngan's challenging family life, in the search for and discovery of Kwong and her son in Sonora, and when she, her husband, and their seven children crossed into southern Arizona undetected. Once they were in Nogales, local webs of support absorbed Ngan and her family into a small but heedful Chinese community. There she and Kwong were never without jobs or without the help of neighbors. When Ngan and her family crossed back into the United States, several hundred Chinese had already traversed the line between Arizona and Sonora, although few had stopped for long stretches of time in Arizona border towns.

Obliging the needs of complex lives like Ngan's ran at cross-purposes with American immigration inspectors' pursuit to enforce Chinese exclusion laws. At the U.S.-Mexico border adjacent to the Pacific coast, such enforcement fell to customs collectors operating in stations in San Diego, Tucson, and Nogales.[31] The then-normal duties incumbent on customs officers—searching all incoming vessels, determining the appropriate duties for taxable items, and tracking and fining smugglers of cigars, *mezcal*, sheep, and opium—were complicated by understaffed and ill-equipped immigration inspectors charged with the overwhelming task of stopping illegal immigration of Chinese from Mexico.[32] In San Diego, five permanent-status customs officials ran the entire customs station, although several temporary inspectors assisted when matters warranted more manpower. The customs stations in Tucson and Nogales were equally understaffed. To guard the three-hundred-mile border with Sonora, the Nogales and Tucson stations shared two collectors, two Chinese inspectors, and one mounted inspector.[33] Although congressional appropriations were made to secure "a special force of inspectors [and] guards . . . to effectively enforce the act," the allotments were of little help because most money was funneled to immigration offices in San Francisco and Los Angeles.[34]

As Chinese migrants increasingly crossed into the United States at the California and Arizona lines, San Diego customs collector John R. Berry employed stop-gap measures. Berry, who occupied the post of San Diego's collector from 1890 to 1894, attempted to lease extra offices to accommodate a growing need for space and worked for a time with local constables offering extra pay for information, but was unsuccessful. In 1890, when eighty Chinese landed in Ensenada, the fear of a Chinese invasion was aroused. "It looks as if the experiment had been tried of entering Chinamen in this round-about way and in small numbers," Berry reported, "and having proved successful an attempt is being made to operate the plan on a larger scale."[35] Aided by the meandrous coastline of the Mexico-California border, the eighty Chinese migrants entered the United States in one of two ways: by means of a second boat that landed at San Diego's unguarded harbor, or overland from Ensenada to San Diego. The San Diego harbor's seven miles of open expanse occasioned the landing of small boats and steamers, and once these had docked, the Chinese migrants went ashore, dispersed into several smaller groups, and headed north for Tijuana or east to Campo. Open coastline and an unguarded boundary made San Diego into a veritable gateway for Chinese entry into the United States.

Berry stood undaunted, but drastic situations required drastic measures. With some appreciable results, Berry and the San Diego Chinese inspector, Datus Coon, first enlisted local constables to do the work of immigration inspectors. The constables monitored the eighty Chinese from Mexico, and when they landed in Ensenada, dispersed, and crossed into the United States, they were arrested. Fortune also played a role. Happenstance had placed the local constables, who had been on duty for no more than thirty minutes, in the path of thirteen border crossers. Once they had arrested them, the constables turned in the migrants to Berry for deportation. The practice of paying local constables for assistance, insisted Berry, had to continue if vigorous enforcement of exclusion laws was to prevail over smuggling rings. "But vigor is impossible without a sufficient force to guard the proper points," Berry argued, "and a sufficient force cannot be obtained without the means and method to compensate local State officials."[36] When Berry's request to pay the local constables was turned down, the San Diego collector went on a hiring spree of sorts, employing for a short time three temporary inspectors, a Chinese inspector, and a mounted inspector to help guard the line.[37] But the hiring of temporary inspectors was no panacea.

Taking on short-term inspectors was problematic because it fostered rifts between the permanent staff and the temporary staff. As it was, permanent inspectors had the benefit of official training and the advantage of some experience enforcing exclusion laws, but because immigration inspectors often resorted to local logic in interpreting wholly extraneous exclusion laws, they left themselves wide open for criticism by San Francisco, Los Angeles, and Washington, DC, officials. Unremitting derision from these outside offices compromised local authority, and at times emboldened temporary inspectors to transgress lines of command and seniority. As Chinese continued to cross and as Berry's patience with rifts among staff wore thin, the San Diego collector resorted to more aggressive and direct methods of enforcement, methods that would have been considered unconventional and inappropriate in other areas but at the San Diego line were reasonable considering the time, place, and predicament.

Berry looked toward the Mexican government to help enforce the law. The collector at San Diego sought to formalize the implementation of exclusion laws, seeking among other things to expand the power of his inspectors south into Mexico. Negotiations began in earnest when Berry made his case to M. G. Montaño, collector of customs at Tijuana, to allow San Diego immigration inspectors to pursue Chinese into Mexican territory. Sounding more like a wary diplomat than an immigration official, Berry appealed to Montaño: "It is the desire of the Government of the United States to scrupulously respect the desire of the Government of

Mexico, and I have no doubt it is equally the desire of the Mexican Government to extend to the Government of the United States such international courtesies as may be practical and that may be necessary," he wrote. "If it is consistent with your wishes and within the scope of your official authority, I would respectfully request that you issue a permit for the Chinese inspectors . . . to cross."[38]

Baja California governor Luis E. Torres responded to Berry's request by authorizing limited power to U.S. customs officials to cross the border into Mexico.[39] His hesitation to offer full border-crossing privileges was not surprising considering that just two months earlier, Baja California Norte had been subject to filibustering attempts by a marauding band of Americans. But in a spirit that harkened back to the early and mid-1880s, when the two nations opened their borders to one another in an attempt to quell Apache raids occurring in southern Arizona and northern Sonora, cross-border privileges were observed.[40] Not wanting to disrupt economic and political relations with the United States, Torres sought a balance between maintaining friendly ties between the two republics and reasserting Mexican sovereignty.[41] Inspectors could enter as private citizens, he explained, but could "do nothing as a United States official" once they were in Mexico.[42] Left with neither the capacity to detain nor the power to arrest, mounted inspectors decided to monitor the movements of Chinese from the ports of Ensenada and La Paz as private citizens of the United States. There they engaged in a regular habit of paying a Mr. Hyde, an American living near Tijuana, for information that Chinese were coming north.[43] The ability of inspectors to warn agents at the border about potential Chinese movements from the coast yielded good results in that inspectors arrested fifteen Chinese border crossers on the basis of the information proffered by Hyde. But using informants in Mexico did not solve the problem of what to do with the Chinese once they crossed into southern Arizona or southern California.[44]

When Berry left his post as collector in 1894, the San Diego customs office was beset more than ever with illegal Chinese immigrants from Mexico. Under the watch of John Fisher, Chinese migrants continued to encroach, but immigration officers pushed back, gaining a firmer hand on the somewhat irrelevant exclusion laws while steadying their staff and their relationship with San Francisco and Los Angeles immigration officials. Some of Fisher's practices, like those of Berry, were aggressive. Fisher was a firm believer in and employer of witnesses in Chinese smuggling cases. The government's case against alleged smuggling leader Captain James E. Wright of the *Nereid* would have been for naught had Fisher not secured witnesses Smith, Lonsdale, and "the Swede Assmussen."[45] All three witnesses contradicted Wright's testimony, and the captain was sentenced in the case. Fisher settled up with his witnesses, except for Smith, who demanded compensation for fourteen, not ten, days' service. Smith, a rancher from Santo Tomás, Mexico, and Fisher finally agreed to extra compensation, because he believed that Smith was the linchpin in getting Wright convicted.[46]

The role of collector of customs was certainly challenging, but Fisher's successor, William W. Bowers, seemed well-poised to take over the busy post. Bowers adopted and expanded upon many of Fisher's practices, and needed to do so, given that the San Diego customs office would come under intense scrutiny both from within and from outside.

As a second-term appointee to the position of collector of customs and a former state senator, Bowers came to San Diego as a seasoned Republican politician who was quite familiar with the exclusionist politics that weighed heavily in California throughout the 1870s and 1880s. Bowers' first challenge as customs collector at the San Diego line (a position he held from 1874 to 1882) occurred when the inspector's time was devoted to assessing fees and penalties on contraband goods, not chasing down Chinese border crossers. Bowers was sympathetic neither to the anti-Chinese movement nor to Chinese migrants. His dispassionate political outlook seemed suitable, and probably necessary, for any high-ranking immigration official to possess. The fair-minded Bowers' complex and challenging task as collector was assisted by the Chinese Bureau, which had been created by the Bureau of Immigration in 1895.[47] In theory, the Chinese Bureau was to share with customs collectors in San Diego, Tucson, and Nogales the responsibility of enforcing exclusion laws. This was not the case for Los Angeles immigration inspectors, who worked alongside the San Francisco office of the Bureau of Immigration and San Diego customs office to ensure consistent application of the Chinese exclusion laws. The Chinese Bureau would come to have a profound effect on the enforcement of these laws. This effect, however, was born out of reaction to, not a vision for, the complexities of Chinese crossing illicitly into the United States at the U.S.-Mexico border.

As chief Chinese inspector for the Los Angeles branch of the Bureau of Immigration, John D. Putnam seemed to have adopted a reflexive prejudice against the Chinese, and he used his capacities as top man in the Los Angeles office of the Chinese Bureau. To test out his suspicions that most Chinese coming from Mexico into the United States arrived illegally, either masquerading as merchants or falsely claiming American citizenship. At the core of Putnam's suspicions was a strongly held belief that an international conspiracy was being conducted in which smuggling rings originating in Hong Kong and San Francisco bribed officials in Mexico with the sole purpose of landing Chinese illegally in the United States. Putnam believed that

Mexican immigration officials and American consular agents in Baja California falsely certified Chinese laborers as merchants.[48] In reporting to the Industrial Commission on Immigration in 1901, Putnam noted that "there is not 1 out of 10 Chinese styling themselves as merchants and so registered who are genuine merchants. . . ."[49] At the border, Putnam believed that the farce continued as Chinese posing as merchants entered illegally because of lapses in judgment or lack of due diligence on the part of San Diego customs collectors.[50] But regardless of how frustrated Putnam was about the efficiency of smuggling rings and the lax practices of the San Diego office, his decision to arrest five Chinese merchants indicated that decisions to deport them would be made under harsh terms and from outside the borderlands landscape.

Putnam put his biases into play when in 1899 he apprehended five Chinese merchants: Lo Fook Chow, Lui Kim Lung (aka Lue Chin Lung), Wong Sin Chune (aka Wong Sing Chung), Wong Lung Shew, and Tom Kim Poy. The five men had arrived in Los Angeles from San Diego when Putnam, guided by his belief that Chinese laborers typically entered the United States without authorization, arrested them for illegal entry at La Grande train depot in Los Angeles. Putnam was convinced that with coaching from smugglers the five Chinese men had cleverly deceived Bowers into certifying documentation verifying their status as merchants and then crossed into California via San Diego under official authorization. In describing the arrest, Putnam assumed that the five Chinese men were taking part in what he believed was an international smuggling conspiracy: "I am convinced that Chinese are passed through the United States in bond to Mexico, where they lie around a Chinese joint for a short time and secure a merchant's certificate and get viseed [sic] by Mexican authorities."[51] Once they were across the border, the firm of Yuen Wo & Company, "who were doing the crooked work in this city," planned to turn the men over to the last leg of the smuggling ring, where they would have been directed to San Francisco or to Port Townsend, Washington.

Putnam's arrest of the five Chinese men was unfounded. When the Los Angeles Chinese inspector searched the men, he all but ignored the documentation for legal entry that Bowers in San Diego and Louis Kaiser, an American consular agent in Mazatlán, Mexico, had certified.[52] Putnam accused Bowers of carelessness for admitting the men without an official investigation into their claims to be merchants. The five Chinese men, Bowers countered, met the burden of proof by obtaining a certificate from the Mexican government, which was then authorized by a U.S. diplomatic or consular representative in Sinaloa, Mexico.[53] Moreover, each man could produce additional verification, whether certification of merchant status, of legal residence, or of place of birth. Despite these particulars, of which

Bowers had been well aware, Putnam proceeded to conduct a two-month-long investigation into the men's claims to be merchants and Mexican and American citizens.

While Putnam conducted his investigation, Bowers objected to what he believed was Putnam's arbitrary brand of enforcing Chinese exclusion laws. Bowers was not a Chinese sympathizer, but he did not want to persecute "the low down Chinese" unjustly.[54] Bowers' duty, as he saw it, was to enforce the exclusion laws and not to find extralegal means to apprehend and deport Chinese border crossers. He defended his judgment to Kaiser and went as far as to question the legitimacy of Putnam's arrest and position, claiming that "these Chinese Inspectors are unmitigated nuisances and frauds." In the same letter to Kaiser, Bowers stated that evidence produced by the five Chinese men met the standard of the law, and that both he and Kaiser were correct in allowing the men to cross the border.

Bowers furthered his criticism of Putnam to Kaiser and to A. H. Butler, president of the California and Oriental Steamship Company, which ran a line of ships that transported Chinese from China to Mexico. To Kaiser Bowers wrote, "If you consider it your duty to certify papers, of course you must do it but inform every Chinaman, that no matter what papers they may have, complying in every respect with every condition of the Laws of the United States, that the Chinese inspectors will arrest them upon landing and put them in prison." He issued a similar warning to Butler and advised the steamship company's president that his company's agents "should notify all Chinamen who intend to come to [San Diego], the probable fate that awaits them."[55]

The five Chinese border crossers were ultimately found to be in the United States illegally.[56] Putnam's decision to detain the men was vindicated because it was eventually revealed that all five had acquired verification under false pretenses. After taking the depositions of more than fifty witnesses, including Kaiser, the findings indicated that the five Chinese border crossers "failed to establish by affirmative proof . . . that [they] are subject[s] or citizen[s] of any . . . country other than China."[57] The evidence that confirmed these men's guilt was not unearthed until after Putnam made the arrest in Los Angeles. It was only because of Putnam's ensuing investigation that knowledge emerged to indicate that the men had gained entry into the United States fraudulently. Putnam's suspicions were confirmed solely by means of his dubious investigation. Putnam's actions exposed the extent to which exclusionist impulses would drive Chinese inspectors and customs agents at major American entry ports to expel the Chinese.

Putnam's actions and the fate of the five Chinese border crossers reveal something much more pernicious at work, however. After the ruling in

*Fong Yue Ting v. the United States* (1893), deportation decisions were treated like admissions decisions.[58] Both cases characterized admission to the United States as conditional and as a revocable license that the government could withdraw at any time despite legal entry. The burdens to admit and deport were removed from court review and placed squarely on immigration authorities, whose approach to enforcing Chinese exclusion was driven by the anti-Chinese politics of the time and a deep-seated anti-Chinese bias. Under the direction of San Francisco collector of customs John H. Wise (who served from 1892 to 1898), immigration inspectors mandated that to gain legal entry Chinese migrants must supply evidence above that which was required by the exclusion laws. The abuses of Wise's brand of enforcement were met with little official opposition, in part because the ideology of exclusion was in keeping with that of most politicians and the majority of the American public, and in part because the U.S. Supreme Court had given unprecedented power to immigration officials in decisions of admission and deportation. Without the benefit of judicial review, admissions decisions were left to the discretion of immigration officials.

Wise's policies had far-reaching consequences because immigration inspectors at the San Francisco offices had long led the charge to enforce Chinese exclusion laws. San Francisco's customs office had a particularly strong influence on Chinese inspectors in satellite offices whose sole role was to enforce exclusion laws. Following the lead of men like Wise and Putnam, Chinese inspectors sought to exclude as many Chinese as possible. "Chinese inspectors," observed historian Lucy Salyer, "approached [Chinese immigration] cases with skepticism, expecting the testimony to be fraudulent. . . . [They] believed that Chinese felt no obligation to tell the truth . . . and could easily obtain witnesses to substantiate their fraudulent stories."[59]

As the century turned, Mexico-based Chinese continued to try to make their way into the United States on their own. In one instance, two Chinese nationals attempting to cross the border from Cananea passed through Douglas, Arizona, with "no papers . . . and disguised [themselves] as Mexican boys." One immigration agent, upon his seizure of the two men, reported that the Chinese nationals "dressed as Mexicans . . . and wore American clothes over their celestial attire and their pig tails had been cut off."[60] But by the early 1900s, the importance of Mexican residency, nationality, and citizenship lessened significantly, and smuggling emerged as a mechanism for challenging the final decisions of immigrant inspectors. The actions that had once ensured deportation of laborers to Mexico and the travel of merchants to the United States became relics of the past.

Rather than maintain immigration procedures based on the preservation of the transnational lives of Chinese laborers and merchants, American officials began applying closer enforcement of the Chinese exclusion laws. This meant that laborers were routinely deported to China, and that merchants' petitions to travel into the United States were received with intense scrutiny.[61] In 1902, responding in part to the high numbers of Chinese entering the United States across its southern border, exclusionists suspended the immigration of Chinese laborers for another ten years. These laws made it nearly impossible for any Chinese person originating from Mexico to enter the United States. Even extraordinary diplomatic efforts by Mexican and American officials who advocated admission for Chinese Mexicans were no match for the enforcement of exclusion laws. The bureaucratic machinery also increased at the border when in 1903 the Bureau of Immigration was placed under the authority of the Department of Commerce and Labor in order to strengthen controls at the Mexican border. Exclusion laws then cast a wide net over Chinese Mexican merchants and over many hundreds of laborers caught at the southern U. S. border.[62] Consequently, crossing into the United States from Mexico necessitated greater organization. No longer were Chinese traversing the border without the assistance of vast smuggling operations. *Coyotes* (smugglers) came to prominence as links in a transnational network of human trafficking responsible for substantially increasing illegal entries from Mexico.[63] Their activities, a direct response to the grip of Chinese exclusion laws, would plague the U.S.-Mexico border over the next few years, and in 1904 the U. S. Congress extended the laws indefinitely, quashing any hope for a flexible solution.

## A Nest of Corruption:
## Chinese Smugglers and the Underground Railroad

At the turn of the twentieth century, smuggling Chinese into the United States intensified dramatically. During this time, the sparsely populated region around the twin border cities of Nogales, Arizona, and Nogales, Sonora, became one of the principal thoroughfares by which smugglers channeled Chinese from the Mexican port cities of Salina Cruz, Manzanillo, Mazatlán, and Guaymas into the United States.[64] Once they had crossed the international boundary, smugglers moved "contraband" Chinese to Los Angeles and San Francisco via southern Arizona. For those seeking to profit from the geographic convenience and economic demand of smuggling Chinese into the United States through the Arizona-Sonora corridor, the clandestine activity proved lucrative and reasonably easy to facilitate. With the exception of an occasional Southern Pacific train route or patrol by customs line riders on horseback, the barren Sonoran desert seemed an open field for Chinese traveling north.

One of the most notorious ringleaders hired by the Chinese Six Companies was Yung Ham, a resident of Nogales, Sonora. Reportedly Ham smuggled more than three thousand Chinese who had landed in Mexico into the United States. Ham's customary technique involved escorting waiting Chinese across the isolated Sonoran desert. On occasion, the smuggler facilitated the quick transport of his clients by loading them into empty freight cars on the Southern Pacific line heading for Los Angeles and San Francisco. Others crossed the desert in small groups and were transported north by other smugglers of the Chinese Six Companies. Groups of laborers destined for mining camps or urban areas in Arizona and California waited in deserted areas until a company agent arrived to lead them to their destination. Before departing, agents of the Six Companies made sure their customers had memorized detailed descriptions of the houses in the United States where they supposedly had been born, and descriptions of their parents, neighbors, teachers, and schools.[65] Frustrating immigration inspectors even more, agents of the Six Companies smuggling ring had little difficulty bribing railroad employees to permit the transport of Chinese in boxcars originating from Guaymas and headed for Nogales, Tucson, and Yuma in Arizona. One account describes the illicit exchange:

I was an engineer on the railroad and the brakeman would signal for me to stop on a curve east of Tucson. The brakeman would say he was checking for a hotbox, but I couldn't see the back end of the train. . . . I would know he was filling the empty boxcar with Chinamen.[66]

As efficient as Yung Ham and the Chinese Six Companies were at smuggling Chinese, American customs officials themselves proved to be among the most infamous and successful traffickers of Chinese into the United States. By the late 1890s, customs collectors in Arizona exercised the power to decide whether to exclude or admit Chinese. Two cases of corruption plagued the Nogales customs house at the turn of the century. In 1899, collector Harry K. Chenoweth, the head of customs at Nogales and a prominent Republican politician of Santa Cruz County in Arizona, was charged with corruption and fraud. His accusers, principal among them Republican politician Allen T. Bird, asserted that Chenoweth was not only smuggling Chinese into southern Arizona, but was also bribing customs inspectors to allow Chinese girls to ride the Nogales train to Tucson.[67] Disguised as Mexicans, the Chinese girls, according to Bird, were able to travel north, where they would be sold to gambling and opium den operators for as much as $2,900 each.[68] Bird, acting on a hunch, relentlessly pursued the Nogales customs collector and his agents. Such clamor caught the attention of Bureau of Immigration and Treasury Department officials, who initiated a full-scale investigation of the customs office and Chenoweth.

The inquiry revealed that Chenoweth had colluded with a ringleader from the Chinese Six Companies in the trafficking of Chinese girls through Nogales. At his trial in Tucson, evidence submitted by officials confirmed Chenoweth's role. The embattled customs collector at Nogales was replaced by William M. Hoey of Muncie, Indiana.[69] The case of Chenoweth turned the quiet border town into a place of contested national political debate over Chinese smuggling. In the ensuing years, Nogales would earn the reputation among Treasury Department officials as a "border town with more hot political contentions than any other community on earth."[70]

The appointment of Hoey raised hopes that by selecting a non-resident of Arizona, scandals of corruption and greed would no longer plague the customs office. New line riders and agents made up the force at Nogales, with Hoey at the helm. Impressed by the scandal involving Chenoweth, Hoey seemed to shun the temptations of the position. In 1900, the Nogales customs collector substantially strengthened the reputation of the Nogales office by weeding out corrupt agents and making several smuggling arrests. Hoey's efforts were praised by Democrats and Republicans alike. Thorough and meticulous in their search for illicit Chinese afoot or on rail, Hoey's men were able to detect and apprehend two women hiding cleverly in the berth of a train. Attempting to conceal themselves behind the drawn curtains of the sleeping compartment, the two Chinese women adorned themselves in the customary dark veils worn by Mexican women of the time.[71] By late 1899, Hoey's remarkable accomplishments earned him the reputation of a diligent and tireless collector—a reputation that seemed beyond reproach.

Less than a year into his term, however, two fellow customs agents in Tucson and Nogales, George W. Webb and J. L. Hathaway, suspected that Hoey and his men were involved in smuggling rings. Webb and Hathaway, agents turned self-appointed detectives, designed a scheme to gather evidence against the customs inspectors.[72] To confirm such corruption, Treasury Department officials set up a secret operative along the Nogales border. Part of the elaborate scheme to catch Hoey included hiring Chinese "secret service men" to bribe customs officials into ensuring safe and unobstructed passage for smugglers. Hoey's men, it was reputed, usually asked between $50 and $200 to guarantee entry into southern Arizona. With few exceptions, it was asserted, the entire customs office and immigration department at Nogales was involved in the conspiracy in one way or another.[73]

Frank Ho (aka Frank Hno and Frank How) and Ye Kim, residents of Sonora, were alleged by Webb and Hathaway's account to be participants in Hoey's cabal, and essential witnesses against their bosses (see Figure 3.1). Ho and Kim had not committed any offenses that warranted official extradi-

FIGURE 3.1 Frank How's U.S. Consular Photo and Seal. Courtesy of the Arizona Historical Society/Tucson. Photo no. B3102. http://www.arizonahistoricalsociety.org

tion, however; thus Webb and Hathaway were unable to garner the cooperation of Mexican officials to extradite the two men. But aided by a strongman by the name of Dickey, Webb and Hathaway used other methods. Webb, Hathaway, and Dickey quickly sped across the border into Nogales, Sonora, and forcibly took both Frank Ho and Ye Kim at gunpoint. Ho, unlike Kim, was permitted legal entry into the United States by virtue of his registration with the U.S. consul at Nogales, Sonora, but this immunity provided no protection against kidnapping by U.S. immigration officials. Later, federal officials justified their illegal action as a necessary expedient, asserting that court review would have been too time-consuming.[74] Ho, by either coercion or sharp persuasion, begrudgingly confessed to paying Hoey nearly $1,000 for allowances of easy passage into southern Arizona. Under similar pressure, Kim suborned perjury when he could no longer fend off the threats and intimidation of Dickey:

[Dickey] say: If you want to go back to Sonora, you tell a lie that you give money to Mr. Hoey. I say: How much you want me to tell that I give him. He say: Suit yourself, one time give 50 and one time give him a 100, and one time give 200. . . . I say I did not send one chinaman [sic] to Mr. Wm. Hoey, I not want you to put that on the book. And Hathaway then pulled a pistol, and he say: you don't do that, I kill you right away, he then take the iron and he scared me. . . . And I say all right, I put it down, how many chinaman [sic] at one time, and he say: suit yourself, one time three, and second time five, and another time five and another time four. And I say allright [sic]."[75]

On August 24, Hoey was arrested. The Treasury Department indicted the Nogales collector on three accounts of bribery, conspiracy, and corruption for smuggling Chinese into the United States.[76] In addition to Hoey, those arrested included the Tucson customs collector, Benjamin F. Jossey, Frank Ho, and Quong Wing of the Chinese Six Companies. Each man was charged with participating in a smuggling arrangement allegedly made profitable to the Nogales collector. Jossey, Hoey's colleague in the Tucson customs house, lacked the personal fortitude to stand trial and face public humiliation. Rather than confront possible criminal prosecution, he shot and killed himself. Although the local coroner's jury ruled Jossey's death an accident, others, including the Nogales jurors, concluded that Jossey's "suicide" was an admission of his guilt and a testament to Hoey's innocence. Hoey's acquittal was no less secured by his attorney, Charles Blenman, who was successful in exposing the unlawful manner in which the government had tried to secure witnesses against his client. Hoey was subsequently acquitted.[77]

After the Hoey affair, aggressive efforts were made to increase surveillance of the Arizona line. The Treasury Department, pressured by national coverage of corruption and illegal immigration, added seventy-five mounted inspectors to patrol its southern border with Mexico, and conducted comprehensive investigations exposing several "Chinese in-transit" conspiracies, that is, ruses of migrants passing through the United States, allegedly bound for other destinations, who nonetheless remained in the United States.[78] So extensive was the organized system of passage that several investigators were mystified as to why the scheme had not been detected sooner.

Chinese smuggling continued to plague the Arizona-Sonora border-lands throughout the early 1900s. The Pacific Mail Steamship Company (PMSC, discussed in Chapter One) persisted in its supply of an "endless chain-manner of coolie labor" into Mexico.[79] In 1903, the China Commercial Steamship Company (CCSC) triggered a price war with the PMSC. With four large boats, the CCSC intensified competition in the transportation of Chinese labor into the Americas via Mexico by cutting the cost of migration from fifty dollars per person to fifteen dollars per person. Chinese immigration doubled, from 1,900 in 1903 to 3,800 in 1904.[80] Moreover, immigration officials confirmed the long-held notion that most Chinese who disembarked in Mexican ports planned to move furtively into the United States. To thwart such activities, border line riders and immigrant inspectors attempted to measure and expose the extensive trafficking lines along the border. Special agent and U.S. marshal of Arizona M. H. McCord uncovered evidence from scores of Chinese headed to the United States. The federal agent reported that several Chinese possessed papers in their travel bags that outlined directions and routes to enter the United States. Soon after the first raid occurred on a Pacific Mail steamship, the border crossers no longer carried paper instructions but continued to enter the United States through Mexico. McCord captured the perceptive action of the Chinese Six Companies: "The ringleaders appeared very alert, for, after the first series of raids, officials in this country were informed that nothing more of an incriminating character could be found on the immigrants."[81]

Chinese migrants employed other strategies to gain entry, even without the benefit of experienced smugglers. The majority of efforts to smuggle Chinese into the United States continued through systematic trafficking schemes. But contrary to these efforts and to claims by border agents that illicit activity was low, the most complicated and successful scheme to smuggle Chinese into the United States was yet to be uncovered.

The systematic practice of trafficking Chinese into the United States from Mexico intensified in the early 1900s along the Arizona-Sonora corridor. When a plot to smuggle twenty thousand Chinese "coolies" from Guaymas was discovered in 1903, Arizona immigration authorities were already in the midst of exposing the so-called underground railroad (see Figure 3.2). The stealthy movements of smugglers and their clients brought in thousands of Chinese by way of covert transportation on stagecoaches, boxcars, and burros. This method allowed for both the evasion of exclusion laws and the avoidance of deportation. Jim Bennett, a notorious trafficker of Chinese in British Columbia, Canada, moved his operations to Mexico after narrowly escaping capture by Canadian police. Bennett, the mastermind of the Sonora-to-Arizona smuggling scheme that

FIGURE 3.2 "Wrecking of the 'Chinese Underground Route.'" San Francisco Bulletin, August 21, 1904. From the Connell Family Scrapbook, folder 2, Charles T. Connell Papers, MS 0166. Courtesy of the Arizona Historical Society/Tucson. Note that the photograph used in Frank How's consular documentation is the same one used in this broadsheet. http://www.arizonahistoricalsociety.org

began in 1901, had controlled operations so meticulously that it took immigration officials more than three years to uncover the plot. The clandestine route, originating in the Sonoran port city of Guaymas, meandered through Hermosillo, Cananea, Magdalena, and Naco. In Arizona, the underground route twisted through the Santa Cruz and Santa Rita Mountains, where border crossers took a respite in the railroad town of Fairbank. Making Fairbank the main terminal of activity, Bennett was able to maintain a constant flow of Chinese border crossers from Sonora into southern Arizona.

Bennett's operation proved to be remarkably resilient even in the face of vigilant Chinese inspectors who were well aware of the existence of smuggling rings in the area. Rather than err on the side of haste, the success of the operation depended on time-tested relationships forged between the ringleader and his assistants. Relying entirely on his own careful discernment of character and temperament, Bennett hired men to generate business in Sonora, to monitor the routines of immigration agents, and to harbor Chinese border crossers. Bennett's approach proved quite successful. His shrewd manner of selecting smugglers engendered such a high degree of confidence among fellow guides that the Fairbank gang was reputed to have netted thousands of dollars a month for their efforts. Without fear of detection, Bennett and his crew escorted Chinese laborers into the United States for a fee that ranged from $50 to $200.[82] Usually the collection of the full fare for passage occurred in the city of final destination. In other instances, the smugglers required a good-faith payment at Fairbank. As a long-standing rule, Chinese border crossers needed to prove to the smugglers that they possessed the full fee for passage before proceeding to California.[83]

The illicit activity that facilitated the passage of hundreds of Chinese into the United States relied on clever techniques of forgery and deception. Bennett's ring seemed heavily dependent on the efforts of four men: Frank How, Lee Quong, Louis Greenwaldt, and B. C. Springstein.[84] While Quong escorted Chinese along the underground route, Greenwaldt and Springstein forged certificates of residence to ensure the safe passage of border crossers once they arrived in the United States. Greenwaldt was a former San Quentin convict who had served a term of six years for Chinese smuggling in 1892. He joined Springstein in Cananea, Sonora, to complete the forgery ring.[85] Armed with a metal plate for printing documents, rubber stamps, and a seal maker that impressed "O.M. Welburn Internal Revenue Collector, First District of California" onto the documents, the Fairbank gang produced replicas of certificates of residence.[86] The team of Springstein and Greenwaldt duplicated more than three hundred certificates, and for $100 they filled in the appropriate information for passage.[87]

As soon as Chinese nationals secured a certificate, they sojourned north with Lee Quong and one of his assistants. Quong was nicknamed "The Jew" and "Sheeney John" because he allegedly resembled someone of the "Hebrew race." Fluent in English, Quong was a part-time truck farmer who sold his produce in nearby Bisbee and Tombstone. Quong's principal occupation, however, was that of Chinese smuggler. He employed Frank How, a smuggler whose notoriety came to light in the Hoey case, and Wonk Tunk and Charley Lee to aid him in the efforts to escort and harbor Chinese.[88] Taking advantage of the long-distance patrolling techniques of immigration inspectors, Quong and Tunk loaded Chinese posing as Mexicans into boxcars destined for northern Sonora. To blur the line between Chinese and Mexican border crossers, Quong, How, and Tuck had their Chinese patrons "cut off their queues and dressed as Mexicans" to escape detection.[89] Once their customers were safely inside the boxcars, Quong quickly refastened the door seals as if they had not been broken. In northern Sonora, the Chinese would travel to their destination, Fairbank, on a road not recently patrolled by inspectors. By closely monitoring the routines of Chinese inspectors, Quong could usually easily determine the routes that he and his clients would take into Fairbank. Bennett's guides and their patrons traveled without fear of detection and were relatively successful in gaining passage without incident.

Chinese inspector Charles Connell was one of the men who cracked this smuggling ring after months of trailing the Fairbank gang. On a visit to Naco, Sonora, with Special Immigration Agent V. M. Clark, Inspector Connell encountered two Chinese men who had in their possession blank certificates of residence. The two border crossers stated that they had secured their documents from Springstein. In an attempt to confirm their account, Connell queried federal immigration authorities who had supposedly issued the official certificates of residence. Numbers located in the upper left corner of the documents in question seemingly confirmed their authenticity. As it turned out, Connell's watchful eye caught an inconsistency not found in official certificates of residence: an additional letter *m*.[90] Even though Connell and Clark were acting outside their jurisdiction, they pursued the case into Sonora, arrested Springstein, and confiscated mounds of evidence against the ringleader.[91] Springstein confessed to his illegal activity soon after agents interrogated the smuggler in their "sweat box."[92] Among those implicated were How, Quong, Greenwaldt, and Bennett. Moreover, written evidence recounting the particulars of the smuggling cast doubt on Quong's innocence. Connell came upon a letter written by Quong to his friend Ho Kwong (who also could be Frank How):

Yesterday I received a letter from you acknowledging the receipt of $25 sent for urgent use and speaking of your having five pieces of merchandise [sic] there are white men who would take a hand if there should be customers to be smuggled over right along. . . . A few days ago they got Wong Shai In, Wong Chun Yick, Yee Tuk Wai, and several others . . . you cannot smuggle anybody out by the fast trains. . . . There are boats now coming from China to Guaymas, which will no doubt bring over a great many customers. Just as soon as you receive any let me know immediately without fail.[93]

With the arrests of Quong and Springstein, inspectors concentrated their efforts on apprehending the elusive Greenwaldt and Bennett. Greenwaldt, who possessed the original metal plate used to manufacture fraudulent certificates, managed to evade Connell. Before his escape to Vancouver, British Columbia, Greenwaldt left Springstein holding six hundred unused certificates of residence. Once Greenwaldt arrived in Canada, he immediately established a regular line of ships for transporting Chinese nationals headed toward the port of Guaymas. Bennett, the founder of the overland smuggling route, also escaped Connell's grip and lived in "princely fashion as an American capitalist in Mexico."[94]

Before his deportation, Quong revealed several critical aspects of the smuggling ring. He testified that he had witnessed Chinese being routinely packed into boxcars and provided with food and water on their trek toward San Francisco, the principal destination of most crossers. In one tragic incident, Quong described the capture of five Chinese crossers traveling in a Southern Pacific boxcar on their way to San Francisco. One man died of thirst along the way, and others suffered severe dehydration. Despite his detailed description of incidents of Chinese smuggling, Quong denied all participation in the ring and tried to preserve his status in the United States by producing a seemingly authentic certificate of residence issued out of San Francisco. After hearing the testimony of Arizona residents Frank Meyer, Gus Klein, and George McDonald, authorities deported Quong to China.[95] With the conviction and deportation of Quong in June 1904, many believed that Arizona and Sonora's "underground railroad" would cease operation.

In fact, Quong's arrest merely slowed the scheme until William Wright, collector of customs in Naco, Arizona, discovered the Mexican link to the operation. Wright came upon a forged certificate in the pocket of a Chinese border crosser that was similar to the ones produced by Quong, Greenwaldt, and Springstein. As the border crosser relayed his story to Wright, the collector began to notice more parallels with the scheme of Quong, Bennett Greenwaldt, and Springstein. Chinese disembarked at Mazatlán and were escorted to Cananea, where they were coached by smugglers on the questions to which American immigration or customs inspectors would expect sharp answers. Responses were prepared, rehearsed, and mastered. Chinese clients were then transported to Guaymas to board a small boat to the Colorado River region, and there they paid approximately $100 for the fraudulent certificates. With the permission of Sonoran governor Rafael Izábel, Wright and Mexican and American police raided the Palace Saloon in Cananea, Sonora, and confiscated more than three hundred forged blank certificates of residence that contained the additional letter *m*.[96]

At the turn of the twentieth century, the smuggling of Chinese into the United States exposed the weakness of Mexican and American immigration law at their common border. Clearly national laws did little to deter smuggling of Chinese into the United States through the Arizona-Sonora borderlands. In one such case, acting Chinese inspector Frank W. Heath of the Tucson Chinese division of the Bureau of Immigration interrogated Law Yoke Who, a miner arrested in Naco, Arizona, for illegal entry. The statements, which were filtered through Chinese interpreter Lee Park Lin, revealed that Who had inadvertently entered the United States from just outside Cananea, Sonora. Putting up no front, Who admitted that he had crossed "with no intention of coming into the United States, but [was] arrested on [his] way to Pilares, Mexico, to work in the mines."[97] But the miner's story of naiveté suffered when Inspector Heath discovered that Who had been carrying a paper with instructions on how to proceed to certain places in the United States. Who had received the paper from Lee Choong Quai in Cananea. "He just gave me that paper," proclaimed Who, "and I never had any intention of going to the United States, but somehow it was with some of my papers when arrested."[98] To ensure that Who did not again attempt entry into the United States, border officials kept consistent with the practice of deporting alien Chinese to China, regardless of alleged residency in Mexico, and Who was subsequently expelled from the United States.

Sophisticated smuggling rings stymied the efforts of immigration agents to enforce exclusion at the border. Instead, complex systems of illicit passage sustained the vibrant and lucrative economy of smuggling for both Chinese and American agents. In 1907, W. Iberry, a Guaymas businessman, indicated to immigration inspector Marcus Braun the magnitude of Chinese immigration to the north. He stated, "About 20,000 Chinese had entered the state of Sonora in the past year and [I am] willing to wager any man that not 4,000 could be found there now.[99] With this insight, Iberry summed up what Chinese inspectors, private citizens, and government officials had been witnessing for the past eight years or so—the resilience of Chinese smuggling rings that effectively altered the social landscape of the borderlands. Although no accurate figure exists for the total number of Chinese who made their way into the United States, the vast majority of criminal cases brought before the territorial courts of Nogales, Yuma, and Tucson were suits filed against Chinese for violating exclusion laws (see Figures 3.3 and 3.4).[100]

FIGURE 3.3  Sam Kee, Deported January 11, 1904, Tucson, Arizona. From the John Murphy Scrapbook, Charles T. Connell Papers, MS 0166. Courtesy of the Arizona Historical Society/Tucson. http://www.arizonahistoricalsociety.org

FIGURE 3.4  Gee Bow, Deported October 3, 1904, Tucson, Arizona. From the John Murphy Scrapbook, Charles T. Connell Papers, MS 0166. Courtesy of the Arizona Historical Society/Tucson. http://www.arizonahistoricalsociety.org

## Sonoran Chinese and the Future of Immigration to Mexico

By the turn of the twentieth century, Porfirian economic development projects had flourished into real results for Mexico's elite class and a cohort of mostly American and British investors. European and American capitalists responded to investment opportunities that made foreigners the majority owners of Mexican mining and railroad industries. Transportation networks were oriented northward and facilitated the transport of coffee, tobacco, silver, copper, and oil out of Mexico and into the United States and Europe. China and Mexico continued to trade with one another, but when compared with the United States and Britain, the promising eastern power was no match either as a destination for Mexican goods or as an investor in Porfirian progress.

Before the turn of the century, Mexico was receptive to Chinese immigration in accordance with Porfirian ideals. The principles of the Díaz regime held that liberal immigration policies would foster economic development. In a climate thus favorable to foreigners, Chinese merchants prospered. After 1900, however, the Mexican government grew more sympathetic to grievances that Chinese immigration should not occur without oversight or restriction. Criticism of the lack of sanitary regulation, for example, resulted in new demands for admissions criteria and, in 1903, new codes were adopted to regulate sanitary conditions on ships arriving in Mexico. Each Chinese migrant was required to present a medical affidavit confirming a clean bill of health, and steamship companies were required to have a disinfecting apparatus to sterilize baggage and clothing. Each immigrant was to be bathed before landing. Although the China Commercial Steamship Company was not the only carrier of Chinese migrants into Mexico, Mexico's Health Council ordered it to construct an observation zone and a quarantine barracks in Manzanillo, the only port permitted to land Chinese after 1903, for immigrants with contagious diseases.[101]

Concerns over Chinese migration continued. That same year, more federal-level action in Mexico indicated a growing official anti-Chinese sentiment. The Mexican national government undertook measures to study Chinese immigration and attempted to regulate its scope and dispersal. Under the direction of the secretary of the interior, a presidential committee convened in 1903 to explore the status of Chinese immigration. The committee of Genera Raigosa, Eduardo Liceaga, Rafael Rebollar, José Covarrubias, and José M. Romero tackled the public health issues first. They produced two questionnaires that were circulated in each state. Each questionnaire was designed to capture basic demographic information, as well as the most dreadful aspects of each population, including the frequency of crimes committed, the number of beggars, and the number of insane. The Immigration Commission concluded that Asian immigration posed no threat to Mexican society. To stay the course with Chinese immigration was an especially important decision in light of concerns over public health and the spread of disease. To proponents of eugenics, criminality, poverty, and insanity were public health traits thought to be transmittable through close contact. The commissioners concluded that the Chinese would never assimilate into Mexican society but were economically important. Free immigration was a necessity, the Commission affirmed, and Chinese immigration should continue, but it would require regulation.[102]

Committee member José Covarrubias, an engineer by training, concluded that the Chinese who came to Mexico constituted the dregs of Chinese society. They arrived with no capital and only the ability to labor in the most menial jobs or to farm as peons. Covarrubias' report warned of the arrival of waves of single men who could jeopardize the future of the Mexican race through intermarriage. Their concern with monetary gain and financial trickery would squeeze out most Mexican businesses, and profits earned in Mexico would be remitted to China. For all his criticism, Covarrubias did concede that as laborers, especially in the *tierra caliente*, the Chinese were of great benefit. Importantly, Covarrubias believed the Chinese to be temporary laborers, not permanent settlers.[103] The remaining committee members reached a similar conclusion. Although they loathed the Chinese, they believed that the Chinese posed no real, long-term danger to Mexican society. As workers in regions that were historically uninhabitable or not arable, the Chinese, as temporary immigrants, served Mexican development well. Regulation of Chinese immigration was a necessity, but restricting free immigration was not.[104]

From 1903 to 1909, the National Sanitary Service oversaw immigration from China until it proved inadequate to the task. In 1909 the responsibility of immigration regulation for all migrants was handed over to the newly created Mexican Immigration Service, a national agency designed to enforce Mexico's new immigration laws, which were in keeping with earlier attempts to restrict entry on the basis of public hygiene concerns.[105] Immigrants with plague, cholera, yellow fever, typhoid fever, tuberculosis, leprosy, beriberi, and trachoma were prohibited. At the same time, by order of the government, shipping companies assumed greater responsibility for the welfare of immigrants, including guaranteeing a cost-free return trip if the immigrant failed to land successfully. The new immigration law in Mexico also mirrored some aspects of the U.S. Chinese exclusion laws, particularly the Geary Act, which required immigrants to register with the state—in effect requiring that immigrants carry a passport-like form of identification on their person.

On the eve of Mexico's revolution, this burgeoning population of Chinese would come to symbolize Mexico's rejection of Porfirian modernization schemes that had brought forth foreign immigration and foreign investment. Securing immigration from China had been but one factor in Diaz's scheme, albeit a very successful one. The third national census, in 1910—the year before Diaz's ouster—indicated that 13,203 Chinese lived in Mexico, principally in the northern states of Sinaloa, Baja California, Coahuila, and Sonora.[106] The success of Chinese immigrants, who by now had become a vital part of Mexico's economic reality, was a source of first unease and then indignation to native Mexicans. Even though the Chinese were not accumulators of wealth on the scale of multinational corporations, they endured the hatred of Mexicans who wanted desperately to break from dependence on foreigners, including those who had made themselves into Mexicans, as had the Chinese. When in 1911 Díaz was ousted from the presidency and exiled to France, Mexico was no longer even a semblance of its former self. Racked with factionalism and violence, Mexico would endure a seven-year revolution that was to change the landscape of its Chinese community. With American attention now on Mexican rebels and the thousands of Mexicans who crossed to escape revolutionary violence, the smuggling of Chinese drew only slight attention. At the same time, Mexican immigration restriction narrowed opportunities for Chinese, although not on the same scale as in the United States. The Revolution in Mexico drove a formidable wedge between Chinese communities in Mexico, which after 1910 engaged in little cross-border exchange due to the unfettered violence of the Revolution.

# 4 The First Anti-Chinese Campaign in the Time of Revolution

It was only a matter of months after the outbreak of the Mexican Revolution (1911–1917) that Sonoran Chinese flocked to Arizona border towns. Southern Arizona newspapers headlined the exodus: "Chinamen in Sonora, Feel Effect of Race Hatred" and "Fear for Their Lives."[1] Six Chinese, two captured in Lochiel and four near Nogales, Arizona, escaped the grip of Mexican rebels occupying Sonora, but after crossing into the United States, they were detained by local immigration inspectors. Deportation was inevitable for Sonoran Chinese because there was no official alternative to exclusion laws. A few months before this incident, seven Chinese who feared they would be embroiled in a revolutionary insurrection fled into the American border towns of Naco and Lewis Springs. Tucson immigration inspectors Frank W. Heath and Jeff Milton questioned the men. One of the seven, who seemed to have spoken for the group, expressed his fear that if they had stayed on the Mexican side of the border "[our] lives would be taken as a reward for [our] temerity."[2]

These were not exaggerated words. Only one month before the seven Chinese men were caught on the Arizona line by Heath and Milton, revolutionary violence claimed the lives of 303 Chinese and five Japanese in Torreón. Located in southern Chihuahua, a Mexican state that shares its northern border with Texas, Torreón was an essential and strategic port of transportation and commerce that linked central and southern Mexico to the northern region of the country. On May 15, 1911, followers of revolutionary leader Francisco Madero (*maderistas*) claimed Torreón, but as they did, they committed one of the most savage atrocities against the Chinese in Mexican history. Within a span of two days, the *maderistas* slaughtered half of the city's Chinese community in a chaotic orgy of brutality. Chinese minister to Mexico Chang Yin Tang chronicled in Washington the heinous actions of the rebels, and the law firm of Wilfley and Bassett, which was hired by Chinese and Americans officials to investigate, described the massacre as an "act of race hatred . . . executed with savage ferocity."[3]

Wilfley and Bassett detailed the manner in which soldiers of the revolutionary army murdered unsuspecting Chinese: "In one instance the head of a Chinaman was severed from his body and thrown from the window into the street. In another instance a soldier took a little boy by the heels and battered his brains out against a lamp post. In many instances ropes were tied to the bodies of the Chinamen and they were dragged through the streets by men on horseback. In another instance a Chinaman was pulled to pieces in the street by horses hitched to his arms and legs." Just before the massacre, witnesses observed, speeches riddled with xenophobic references incited the crowds of revolutionary supporters against all foreigners. The Chinese, however, were of particular focus. Violence against the Chinese ensued, as did wanton vandalism. When Wilfley and Bassett completed their report, they estimated property damage at Torreón to be near $1 million.[4] The human cost—loss of fathers, mothers, children, siblings—was beyond quantification.

Far from provoking moral outrage, the massacre at Torreón sparked more anti-Chinese violence throughout Mexico.[5] In the first year of the revolution, Mexican rebels and unknown individuals killed 324 Chinese residents. Murders of Chinese in Mexico continued throughout the nation, especially in large cities. By 1919, anti-Chinese fervor had contributed to the deaths of 129 Chinese in Mexico City and 373 in Piedras Negras, Coahuila.[6] These deaths did not occur in isolation; they resulted from the culmination of a nationalistic campaign that played on anxieties that Mexicans harbored about their own economic security, their racial integrity, and their role in the revolutionary project. That the rhetoric of this Sinophobia-inspired nationalism would ultimately lead to bloodshed should have come as no surprise to anyone observing it. In Sonora, the cauldron of revolutionary violence was stirred most vehemently by José María Arana, a Magdalena schoolteacher and businessman. Arana and his followers shared a commitment to imposing and sustaining an anti-Chinese rhetoric based on racial ideals that subsumed, insidiously, women's political equality. The *antichinistas* spurred the passage of draconian labor, public hygiene, and marriage laws and enforced them with brutal vigilantism. The anti-Chinese ferocity in Sonora came to violent fruition under unrelenting political pressure from these *antichinistas* and their supporters.[7]

## The Commercial and Businessmen's Junta and the Rise of the Anti-Chinese Campaign

In retrospect, it might seem inevitable that efforts to marginalize Chinese economic power would lead to bloodshed. Its earliest progenitors, however, would stoutly deny that their goals had ever included the loss of life. Their intention, they would insist, had merely been to restore Mexicans to their social and economic prominence. In February 1916, the Mexican businessmen of Magdalena, Sonora, took the first steps in organizing a campaign to oust the Chinese from the state. They established the Commercial and Businessmen's Junta, with Francisco C. López as its first president. Among the aims of the Junta was to uplift the Mexican merchant from competition with Chinese businessmen. The hope was that other Mexicans in Sonora would soon follow suit. To rid Sonora of the Chinese, the organization planned to use legal means. Supporters were certainly urged to carry out the imperatives of the anti-Chinese campaign, but to do so within the dictates of law, reason, and morality. The Junta deplored Chinese economic success and blamed the exodus of young unemployed Mexican men into the United States on the good fortunes of the Chinese. Mexican youth, they contended, were prepared for careers in business, but found themselves without work because of the Chinese.[8]

As the Chinese established themselves in business, the Junta condemned them for their success. Mexican merchants, they charged, could not compete with the pernicious, inexorable tentacles of the "yellow plague." Chinese merchants, the Junta claimed, outcompeted Mexican merchants because they sold inferior products at lower prices and had access to cohesive business networks that reached into the United States, the Caribbean, and Central America.[9] This simple prescription to realize high profits was further reinforced by the lifestyles of Chinese merchants. It was assumed that the Chinese had no families; therefore, the Junta charged, they lived frugally, either in the back of their stores or together in large numbers in small houses. Mexicans, on the other hand, supported large families in homes that they either rented or owned. Merchants had the additional burden of renting a separate space in which to conduct business.[10] Ignacio Burgos, a businessman from Pilares de Nacozari, drew irreconcilable divisions between Chinese and Mexican merchants in keeping with the Junta's perception: "The Chinese succeed while we are forced to close our doors, and our families starve."[11] If these factors were not enough to give the Chinese the competitive edge over Mexican merchants, tax evasion and graft were.[12] Chinese merchants were formidable competitors, but it was their portrayal by the Junta as unscrupulous businessmen that made them appear to be unworthy Mexicans.

The Commercial and Businessmen's Junta rapidly gained adherents. They appealed to a Sonoran sense of nationalism that was expressed through violent Sinophobia, both implied and executed. In the face of uncertainty, nationalism provided a sense of social cohesion made possible through steadfast patronage of Mexican-owned businesses and a common disdain for the Chinese. As nationalism and anti-Chinese sentiment began to envelop Sonora, the armed conflict of the Revolution fostered violence against the Chinese, who were largely viewed as stalwarts of the Porfirian regime. Each tenet of the Junta's nativist platform insinuated that the Chinese had bribed Sonora's governors under the Porfiriato: Ramón Corral, Luis Torres, and Rafael Izábel.[13] Each proposal attempted to reduce the influence of the Chinese, who had benefited from free immigration and lax tax codes for foreign businesses during Díaz's rule.

When the Junta presented its formal organizational structure to Governor Plutarco Elías Calles, who supported the campaign, the Sonoran economy was in shambles. The costs of the Revolution were steep and dear in terms of both money and mortality. Communication systems were destroyed and disastrous floods had disrupted agricultural and industrial projects. But according to the *antichinistas*, it was the presence and activities of Chinese merchants that had hurt Mexican commerce and industry more than any other force. "The [Chinese merchant] has no conscience and doesn't care if his customers are poisoned from his dirty merchandise," José Barnal, a Moctezuma merchant, maintained. "He buys field crops for practically nothing from Mexican farmers who are forced to sell in order to pay their most pressing bills. Then these Chinese bastards sell these crops back at 500 percent profit."[14] In times of crisis, Chinese businesses closed their doors and accepted only gold in payment for goods. Chinese were good businessmen, but according to the Junta, they were bad Sonorans.[15]

The Junta asked for the immediate expulsion of the Chinese. They realized, though, that ridding the state of the Chinese would be met with intense resistance from Chinese and Mexican officials alike. Mexican officials might publically support anti-Chinese policy, but privately they would recognize the economic importance of Chinese-owned businesses. The Junta proposed several measures to address numerous complaints about the lifestyle of Chinese, a turn that expanded their original platform to include social and cultural grievances. One major objection was the marriage of Mexican women to Chinese men. To prohibit such unions, as well as to curtail the prevalence of prostitution and concubinage, the Junta proposed that the naturalization of Chinese be abolished and that Chinese-Mexican marriages be outlawed. Junta leaders also advocated that contact between Chinese men and Mexican girls and women in stores and other public places should be banned.[16]

The Junta's expanded platform appealed to José María Arana. From 1916 until his death in 1921, Arana infused the Junta's substantive but rather staid agenda with a populist expression that played to the fears of the working class, the middle class, and women. His anti-Chinese exhortations were rife with metaphor and contempt (see Figure 4.1). Almost

FIGURE 4.1 José María Arana Warns a Crowd of Supporters, "Whomever does not hear my words, tomorrow they will lament the suffering of the mother country which we were not able to defend." Arana's sign reads, "Mexican: For each dollar you spend at a Chinese store, fifty cents goes to Shanghai and the other fifty cents is used to enslave you and to prostitute the women of your race." Source: José Ángel Espinoza, *El ejemplo de Sonora,* Mexico City: n.p., 1932, p. 33. Courtesy of the Arizona Historical Society/Tucson. http://www.arizonahistoricalsociety.org

immediately his hate-rhetoric took hold. His substance and style appealed to workers in Cananea, a mining town where anti-foreigner sentiment had been running high since before the Revolution. There Arana delivered a colorful diatribe against the Chinese, who he said had the "tentacles of an octopus, the immunity of Mithridates, the talons of a bird of prey, and the venom of a serpent."[17] In the ensuing months Arana traveled throughout Sonora and pushed the Junta's program. He portrayed the Chinese as privileged, and condemned their immunity from compliance with commercial laws, which the Chinese enjoyed under Porfirian governors Corral, Torres, and Izábel.

As Arana's campaign gathered momentum, he widened the scope of grievances against the Chinese. Along with his devoted acolyte Serapio Dávila, he reiterated all previous complaints and, in addition, stressed the need to abrogate Mexico's treaty with China. With greater urgency, however, Arana advocated for a more direct course of action. He exhorted all Mexicans to confront and eradicate the "Chinese plague": prostitution, opium, business monopolies, diseases, and corruption. Arana saw the governorship of Sonora as the main vehicle by which to destroy the Chinese, even though the tenure of Sonora's governors tended to be rather brief.[18] Governors Adolfo de la Huerta, Cesareo Soriano, Plutarco Elías Calles, and Francisco Elías all supported the anti-Chinese campaign at various times in their successive administrations between 1916 and 1921. Each leader, no matter how tenuous and brief his reign, brought his own animus and agenda to the issue of "the Chinese problem."

Arana saturated the governor's office with missives, complaints, and demands. The state legislature, Arana insisted, needed to appoint inspectors to monitor frequently the business ledgers of Chinese merchants.[19] Because one of the complaints charged that the Chinese refused to employ Sonorans, the Junta found an 1875 law stipulating that 50 percent of all workers of any business enterprise must be Mexicans. In addition, the Junta demanded that all business transactions be conducted in Spanish and that only a small number of Chinese be permitted to live in the same house. At Arana's urging, Mexican merchants branded the Chinese a health hazard and requested that Chinese immigration cease or that they be placed in special barrios.[20] The merchants filed the usual charges against the Chinese: moral corruption, economic perfidy, and general untrustworthiness.[21] As the pressure and stridency of anti-Chinese propaganda increased, Sonoran governors consistently took action to restrict immigration.[22]

In addition to his near-constant travel on behalf of the anti-Chinese crusade, Arana also founded and published *Pro-Patria* (pro-fatherland). Under the banner "Either them or us," Arana articulated the anti-Chinese campaign to readers throughout the state.[23] He used this broadsheet to "point out the evils and vices of the Chinese . . . and called on our Mexican patriotism to arouse the spirit of solidarity to counter the Chinese plague."[24] Slanderous jokes and derogatory remarks were prime fare in the paper. Arana printed a sample question from a school examination and answered it in his own vein. In response to the query, "What are the most intractable of animals?" he depicted a classroom of students who replied, "Flies, chickens, *cochis* [small fish with vicious teeth] and Chinese."[25]

*Pro Patria* waged a constant campaign to reveal Chinese abuses, to oust the Chinese from positions of economic power, and finally to uplift Mexican business, agriculture, and industry. The dangerous element of the Chinese stood in the way of this last goal. Arana believed that Mexican hospitality, indolence, and indifference allowed the Chinese to enter the country and to prosper to the point that they menaced the economic and cultural strength of Mexico. He asserted that Mexicans and Chinese were simply culturally irreconcilable: "Together we [Chinese and Mexicans] cannot be, because of an absolute incompatibility in race, social customs, and economy."[26]

That all of the actors described to this point have been men should not be misconstrued to mean that Mexican women were invisible in the anti-Chinese campaign. One of the most devout of the *antichinistas* was María de Jesús Váldez, a university-educated Magdalena schoolteacher. Váldez was so enamored of Arana's campaign that she took up the banner herself, lecturing frequently and fervently about the evils of Chinese influence and the absolute imperative of Mexican women doing their part to counter this influence. Váldez, who began delivering her own speeches in 1917, declared with certitude that the Chinese were the lone source of Mexican degeneracy and economic stagnation. That Váldez likened them to a swarming weed that was stifling Mexican prosperity was met with little surprise and even less disagreement, for the Chinese had long been the object of public scorn, especially among Sonora's middle class. Audiences listened raptly as Váldez advocated the physical separation of Chinese from Mexicans, which she said would remove the most formidable obstacle to Sonoran progress. "The people of Sonora need to rid themselves of these noxious weeds—the Chinamen. These people have become the master of our progress . . . [They] cultivate our soil like a vampire squeezing out the blood of our people. [They] must be removed to a place where [they] no longer will hinder our society."[27]

The resolution to remove the Chinese from centers of commerce or to rid Sonora entirely of its so-called "yellow menace," less original than perhaps was suggested, was initially the inspiration of José María Arana, whom Váldez referenced throughout her speeches. Yet Váldez knew well that following through required not only advocacy, but also electing politicians determined to exhaust every legal, political, and economic maneuver to do so. In Váldez's view, the ultimate power of the resolve lay in the hands of women; though they could neither vote nor seek office, they still boasted a brand of patriotism honed in the fervor of the Revolution. Mexican women held the key to restoring Mexico to its "greatness, power, and invincibility" (see Figure 4.2). As the solution to the travesty in which the Chinese dominated Sonora's economy and seduced its women, Váldez sup-

FIGURE 4.2 Postcard to Arana from the Junta Femenil Nacionalista de Sinaloa (Nationalist Women's Group of Sinaloa). José María Arana Papers, folder 5. Courtesy of University of Arizona Libraries, Special Collections. Váldez and Arana's exhortations resonated with women in Sinaloa, Sonora's southern neighbor.

ported Arana's proposal that no Mexican woman enter their stores and no Mexican person do business with them.

Another of the regulations jointly pushed by Arana and Váldez was the notice that "Chinese merchants . . . are strictly forbidden to joke in any way with their clients or customers, especially with little girls or women, as to do so is improper and detrimental to morality." Váldez's audience recoiled in horror when confronted with the example of Chinese in Sinaloa, where, she claimed, they ran the economy and married the most *blanca* (fairest-skinned) women, all with the approval of the people, the society, and the government.[28] If, as Váldez reasoned, women could not protect the *patria* with the ballot as could their enfranchised male counterparts, then to exhort the cause of the people in support of revolutionary leaders was equally worthy.

In her late-1917 address, Váldez outlined many of the tenets of Sonora's anti-Chinese campaign while elevating its leader, Arana, to demigod-like status. What may have attracted Váldez and many others to this xenophobe was that even in the midst of revolutionary chaos, Arana lucidly identified an "other," a people with whom all Mexican social classes had some complaint. Cast as ruthless business competitors, tax evaders, lecherous bachelors, and race contaminators, the Chinese came to symbolize the most ruinous consequences of Porfirian liberalism. Into this cauldron Váldez added an element that she was singularly equipped to address: women as the moral guardians of Mexican racial purity. A true Mexican woman would scorn the advances of a licentious Chinese man, preserving her virtue for one who deserved it. In so doing she would further the Mexican cause and enhance its national identity. By contrast, a Mexican woman who gave her body to a conniving Chinese predator—a man who in all likelihood carried numerous diseases and who actively worked to undermine the very country of her birth—such a woman had effectively given herself to whoredom. Her children would be racial contaminants, her womanhood wasted, and her nation soiled. Váldez's rhetoric, filled with dire warnings about Mexican-Chinese unions, was accompanied by the very real consequences of laws that made a married woman's citizenship dependent on that of her husband. Within the specific confines of Mexican law, dependent citizenship allowed for the immediate naturalization of a foreign woman married to a male Mexican citizen, but also for the *loss* of citizenship for a woman married to a foreigner.[29] In Sonora, dependent citizenship applied mostly to Mexican female citizens who chose to marry Chinese men. In accordance with the law, these women were stripped of their Mexican citizenship and lost any claim to transfer property to heirs—even if their foreign (read Chinese) husband was a Mexican citizen by naturalization. Thus, when a Mexican woman married a non-natal Mexican citizen, she became foreign and was left without financial means of her own. Women married to foreigners in fact became legal foreigners in the land of their birth. Furthermore, if she left Mexico with her foreign husband and their children and later desired to return, she could not, because upon her marriage the right of repatriation was forfeited.[30] However, the status and rights of children born to Mexican women and foreign men were unclear.

The breathtaking irony of all this was that Mexican women who were enticed and enjoined to do their part for the revolution would in fact gain no discernible benefits. They had much to lose and little to gain. For Váldez, however, such matters were inconsequential. All that mattered was ridding the nation of its Chinese pestilence, and women must do their part. Largely focusing on sexual and romantic ties between Chinese men and Mexican women, *antichinistas*—both male and female—became especially agitated when Chinese men formed unions with socially prominent and beautiful women. For example, in 1917, Francisco Ibáñez wrote to Arana in order to communicate a "disgraceful accident" that had occurred in his hometown. According to Ibáñez, some time ago Miguel Moo, an apothecary doctor, had settled in Nacozari. Moo attracted many clients and ostensibly had a reputation not for curing but for killing his patients. Local authorities in Nacozari and other areas, Ibáñez wrote, did not interfere with this activity. Worse than Moo's routine poisoning of Chinese patients, Ibáñez conveyed, was the doctor's impending marriage to Francisca Acuña, "one of the precious Jewels of this locale." Ibáñez went on to relay another accusation. Moo placed a second young woman, from Tepachi, under the influence of poisonous substances and narcotics. Adding that he knew the Chinese man, Ibáñez said he had always seen Moo very high on opium and the doctor had been incarcerated for his drug abuse and for the poisoning of others. Ibáñez reported that Moo had not yet married Acuña and remained in jail.[31]

The overzealous followers of Arana, inflamed by anti-Chinese rhetoric, resorted to violence. Several unknown individuals bombed two Chinese stores in La Esperanza and wounded three Chinese. The owners estimated losses at two thousand pesos. On the same evening, bombs wracked three Chinese stores in Pilares de Nacozari, causing minor damage. And the next afternoon, in the midst of an Independence Day celebration, rioters tore down and destroyed the Chinese flag that was on the Fraternal Union building in Nacozari.[32]

Conditions worsened for the Chinese in the fall of 1917 as the Sino-phobic-inspired campaign intensified. Under the tacit approval of Governor Plutarco Elías Calles, who loathed the Chinese, Arana's campaign gradually bore fruit as several towns passed new regulations against them. Calles supported a special taxation of Chinese farmers and merchants in the agricultural towns around the capital.[33] To further reinforce his backing of the working class, Calles denied reentry permits to Chinese who had left Mexico for China and desired to return through the border town of Nogales, Sonora. The governor also maintained a consistent pro-working-class stance when he rejected a request by American and Chinese officials to resettle in Sonora a few dozen of Pershing's Chinese Mexicans who were awaiting relocation in Columbus, New Mexico.

Cesareo G. Soriano, interim governor from 1917 to 1918, suggested that the Mexicans compete with the Chinese and have the townspeople refuse to buy anything from them.[34] In Guaymas, Juan Lung Tain and Company and Fon Qui, the two largest Chinese firms in the state, protested the increase in their taxes while others continued to pay at the old tax rate. The municipal president of Guaymas retorted that the taxes were not discriminatory but were levied on all importers, and that beyond this the new taxes were not harsh because the Chinese were wealthy and monopolized commerce and the import trade. Again, higher taxes aimed almost exclusively at Chinese remained in effect despite protests. In reality, there were insufficient numbers of Mexican merchants to provide a real comparison to substantiate the Chinese claim of discrimination.[35]

## Opposition to Arana's Campaign

Both public and official opposition to the Chinese spread in 1917, and although Calles and Soriano favored the campaign, Soriano attempted to oppose its more blatant and illegal tactics.[36] As attacks on the Chinese increased, so did Chinese complaints. Finally, Soriano issued a circular to all municipal presidents and ordered them to give Chinese the protection guaranteed to all foreigners by the Constitution. He also cautioned them to prevent violence and anti-Chinese disturbances. Consistent with his policy of favoring a diminution of Chinese influence but maintaining legality, Soriano conceded that anti-Chinese activity could continue, but municipal authorities must control it and maintain order.[37]

In November, Juan Lung Tain protested vigorously to the governor that Arana's campaign was nothing short of incendiary. In addition to the charges of false statements and deliberate lies, Tain accused Arana of inciting the violence against the Chinese in Sonora and of using his campaign as a means of furthering his candidacy for municipal president in the forthcoming elections. The Chinese condemned Arana because he played on public sentiment and ignorance to promise their expulsion if he were elected. They noted that even if he won the post, he could not oust them, relegate them to a separate barrio, or close their stores. The federal and state constitutions, the penal code, and the 1899 treaty with China guaranteed their rights. No local officials had the power to supersede these provisions.[38]

Tain then proceeded to refute the main lines of Arana's arguments against the Chinese. To the charge that they monopolized commerce and tried to prevent the growth of the Mexican merchant, he argued that the Mexicans preferred to shop at Chinese stores because the prices were lower. He also noted that the families of the leaders of the anti-Chinese crusade bought from the Chinese in order to save money. In response to Arana's promise that conditions would improve once the Chinese left, Tain asked why Mexicans had not already lowered their prices. He charged that Arana did not really care about Mexicans and the local economy but wanted instead to destroy the Chinese. Tain stressed that the Chinese were honest, hardworking people who paid their taxes punctually. He also refuted the charge that they bribed local officials. As to Arana's obsession with the idea that the Chinese prostituted Mexican women, Tain responded with bitter contempt that Arana seemed intent on sullying the reputation of Mexican women to further his campaign. After a long discourse on the anti-Chinese campaign, the Chinese defense against these abuses, and the legal rights that Arana had violated, Tain concluded that if Chinese immigration was prejudicial and their businesses detrimental to

Mexico, then the legislature could decree they must leave. But until then, the laws protected them from Arana's campaign.[39]

Arana replied with utter certainty that his crusade was morally just and that his sixteen national juntas with more than five thousand members had an obligation to broadcast the vices of the Chinese in order to halt a further increase in both their numbers and their economic power. Among his followers Arana numbered several newspapers and the majority of the people of Sonora and other states.[40] He continued that the Chinese were a dangerous group because of their economic monopolies and social corruption. For these reasons, they must go and Mexico must take steps to amend the treaty with China.[41]

Concurrent with Tain's eloquent refutation of Arana's tactics, some Chinese resorted to vulgar and threatening methods of retaliation. Two postcards were sent to Arana and Dávila, ostensibly from two love-struck female relatives of Sonoran Chinese. In reality, the adorations of these two "female admirers," including a short message from "Sister Hing Lung," contained cordial but explicit warnings to the *antichinistas* that were actually written by male members of various Chinese underground organizations.[42] Members of the Chinese mafia, or the Black Hand (see below), claimed responsibility for this series of correspondences to Arana and Dávila. Their follow-up letter to Arana from "Fu Fon Culong" was even less cordial and more explicit than those from his "female" correspondents (see Figure 4.3). Fu Fon Culong wrote to Arana in a familiar, mocking Chinese-Spanish idiom:

Very Dear Little Potbelly: I send to you from the honorable Chinese Colony of Cananea two photographs, one for you, the other for Serapio [Dávila]. The [photographs] are from my little sisters who have fallen in love with you from your pictures. Within the next few days you are going to see some *paisanos* [fellow countrymen] of the Black Hand who are on their way to castrate you because you harm us Chinese badly while we do nothing against you. Now I tell you little potbelly be very careful with your little balls, because they are going to be cut off all at once. So in that way little *capón* [eunuch] you will be more pleasing to my little sisters.

Yours from here to the land of Confucius, Fu Fon Culong[43]

At a certain point, even Sonorans found Arana's vitriol unpalatable. Although Sonoran governors supported Arana's anti-Chinese campaign publically, they were also keen to preserve Sonora's national image and Mexico's international reputation. Soriano further criticized Arana for his failure to hold to certain standards of political and civic decorum. In a letter to the Sinophobe, Soriano conveyed his criticism of Arana's tactics regarding the "Chinese problem" in Sonora. He agreed with Arana's theories about Chinese economic dominance and the need to uplift Mexicans

FIGURE 4.3  Postcard from Senorita Hing Lung: Image of an Asian Bride. Reverse side of postcard reads, "This is for you, you chubby peddler, and for those who worship you and commit frenzy on your behalf: stand on your feet; I implore your compassion and your heart, or you will all go to hell." José María Arana Papers. Courtesy of University of Arizona Library, Special Collections.

as a modern and progressive people, but he rebuked the brand of propaganda used in *Pro-Patria*. Soriano believed that Arana's anti-Chinese campaign "left much to be desired, not only in matters of gentlemanly and noble conduct, but also in the most trivial rules of the education of men."[44] Soriano charged that Arana misused the press, a medium intended to further Mexico's aspirations as an open and democratic nation. In Soriano's estimation, the press bore the responsibility to instill in the masses the doctrines of universal fraternity, harmony, and brotherhood. *Pro-Patria* was quite remiss in this aspect and instead spewed vulgar responses by diatribe, insults, and parochialism. "If *Pro-Patria* wants to do anything patriotic," Soriano urged, "it should be toned down. It is presented in the language of a barroom." Soriano expressed concern that Arana's approach took advantage of hard-working Mexicans. "Far from being for the public welfare," continued Soriano, "[*Pro-Patria*] exploited the little intelligence of our popular masses."[45] Soriano stressed the constitutional guarantees of free speech, association and assembly, and cautioned Arana against abusing these rights by reviling the Chinese. Soriano also instructed all municipal officials to see that no anti-Chinese rallies occurred, but if any did, officials were to punish all the participants.[46]

Soriano was not the only Sonoran governor to object to *Pro-Patria* and Arana's tactics. Governor Calles also refused to accept Arana's excessive gift: ownership of the Soledad and Arana Brothers mining companies. "Truthfully, I cannot accept your gift . . . since I am a simple man without adequate capital to manage [the mines]."[47] When Calles left the governorship of Sonora and retreated to Agua Prieta, he tried other avenues to persuade Arana to end his campaign against the Chinese. He drew on Guadalupe de Pradeau, a confidant of Calles's, to appeal to Arana's wife, Tacha, to end the action against the Chinese. "To continue the campaign," implored Pradeau to Tacha, "would spell disaster for you and your children."[48] Pradeau's appeals fell on deaf ears: the couple continued to participate in the elections in Magdalena city, where José María was a candidate for mayor and where he repeatedly incited local crowds to anti-Chinese violence. Arana subsequently was arrested by Sonoran officials four days before the ballots were drawn and therefore was prevented from seeing his candidacy through. Arana spent eighteen days in the Hermosillo penitentiary and laid blame for his arrest squarely on the Chinese who, he said, "prevented [his] success by pouring out money and influencing persons of power to press their claims against [him] before the election." Arana concluded, "These charges were endorsed by the wealthiest men in Sonora: Juan Lung Tung [and] Juan Tam Chee."[49] After Arana's imprisonment, *Pro-Patria* folded, but the flames of his animus for the Chinese continued to burn in *El Sol, Orientación, La Palabra, El Macriado, Nuevos Horizontes,* and *El Machete.*[50]

Despite Soriano's warnings, Arana refined his attacks on the Chinese in 1919 as more and more legal impediments were imposed.[51] After his imprisonment in the latter days of his 1918 mayoral campaign, Arana turned his sights to the position of Magdalena's municipal president. Campaigning once again on an anti-Chinese platform, he emerged victorious from this election. After his triumph, he immediately increased the monthly taxes of Juan Lung Tain from 250 pesos to 400 pesos. He thought the precarious economic situation and the dire straits of the poor dictated drastic measures. Sonoran Chinese in Hermosillo complained about the continuous slanderous attacks that the authorities never punished. They charged that the attacks were only for Arana's personal gain, not part of any patriotic crusade. Arana attacked the editor of *El Tiempo* in a public letter after the publication charged that the anti-Chinese campaign was unconstitutional. Arana countered that all his activities were legal under the state and federal constitutions.[52] Arana's propaganda campaign was partially effective in March 1919 with the passage of the state's Organic Law of Internal Administration. Article 60 of this law ordered that all municipal councils, for reasons of hygiene and health, would relegate all Chinese houses and stores to special barrios; and Article 61 allowed each municipal council to establish its own procedures to carry out the law.[53]

In a lengthy defense of the state legislature's action, Calles told the secretary of the interior that the deputies, after long debate, had passed the law for the good of the state. Among the major considerations were the deputies' experiences in their own districts, and they thought the new articles accurately reflected public sentiment. Calles added that Sonora suffered more than any other state from the errors of the Porfiriato, especially from the influx of Chinese immigrants. Chinese dominated commerce and ran the largest businesses. Even more alarming was the increase in their numbers from 859 in 1900 to 4,486 in 1910 to an alleged ten to fifteen thousand in 1919.[54] For these reasons, Calles noted, harsher anti-Chinese measures had to be instituted.

## The Squeeze: 1919 Labor Law and the Cananea Expulsion

Unable to defeat the law that created barrios, the Chinese soon faced another and more serious threat to their businesses. In 1919, the Sonoran legislature passed the Labor and Social Provision Law, or Article 106, commonly referred to as the 80 Percent Law, which mandated that Mexicans must constitute at least 80 percent of the workforce of foreign-owned businesses.[55] Whereas some cities, such as Magdalena and Hermosillo, threatened Chinese establishments with severe punishments if they did not comply with the new law, others, such as Guaymas, delayed enforcing the decree, instead relying on stringent tax measures against Chinese merchants. Around the same time, the leadership in Hermosillo also appointed a group of doctors to report on the health of Chinese merchants and laborers as well as on the sanitary quality of their buildings. For the Chinese, Article 106 was to impinge on their economic power over the course of the next twelve years. The article stated that in "every business, workshop, or industrial or mercantile establishment, the owners were obliged to employ eighty percent Mexican workers."[56]

Cananea would prove to be the most enthusiastic enforcer of the Labor and Social Provision Law. In July of that year, R. R González, municipal president of Cananea, emphasized in a circular that he would actively pursue execution of the law. He granted all Chinese businessmen two weeks to comply. A commission was to investigate all houses and businesses on that date.[57] In an attempt to circumvent the law, the Chinese created societies in which all members were made partners and thus, they argued, there were no employees and Article 106 would not apply. Calles, however, hastily intervened. These partnership societies, he asserted, did not qualify for exemption from the law.[58]

The Chinese did not bear these injustices in silence. Outside of Cananea, the greatest number of complaints emanated from the political climate in Magdalena. Benjamin Ungson, president of the Unión Fraternal China, or UFC, a mutual aid organization in Nogales of which most Chinese (see Chapter 6) were also members, objected strenuously to Article 106. Ungson asserted that it violated the protection of individual guarantees that were in Article 1 and the employers' rights that were in Article 4 of the Mexican Constitution. In voicing his objections, the Nogales merchant pointed out that Article 106 would give an unfair competitive advantage to Mexican merchants. "Why," Ungson asked, "should any Mexican, whether he was able or honest or not, have an advantage over a Chinese?" Ungson pointed out that the law was primitive and suggested that Mexico should place itself within the scope of "civilized nations who had long ago, abolished such discrimination."[59] Besides, he concluded, the labor law made no business sense:

Immediately we have the case of the employer who already has foreigners in his establishment. It is practically impossible for him to discharge his employees, for they are his co-workers for the success of his business and they are possessed of the professional secrets upon which depend his trade, his commerce, his products. The employer who should do so would have to train anew the employees that would come to him by the law's decree, and he would have to begin again the drudgery that he had commenced long before. . . . [60]

In Guaymas, no attempts were made to enforce Article 106, even though the Chinese owned 75 percent of the grocery trade there. Chinese merchants nonetheless feared this type of oppressive legislation. They also worried that Guaymas would witness race riots similar to the ones in 1915 that cost Chinese considerable losses in merchandise. Appalled at the callous injustices the Chinese faced, the Chinese legation in Mexico blamed Arana's personal greed as the motivation behind the decree of expulsion. In defense of the Chinese and at the urging of the Chinese consul general in Mexico City, President Venustiano Carranza instructed Sonoran governor Adolfo de la Huerta to prevent local officials from expelling the Chinese and to order their protection.[61]

Protests against Chinese noncompliance immediately ensued against those Chinese who did not capitulate to Article 106. De la Huerta sent a telegram to the Sonoran House of Deputies that cited "intense antagonism" between Mexicans and Chinese. The source of tension, de la Huerta explained, was the Chinese business monopoly and the tendency of Chinese residents to spread diseases. De la Huerta urged that all violence cease, fearing that this animosity would have fatal consequences, especially in Cananea, where anti-Chinese sentiment ran especially high. Cananean residents in fact violated the governor's request to voice their sentiments peacefully and instigated some of the earliest and most intense anti-Chinese violence in the 1920s. The discriminatory attitudes that had led to the passage of the Labor and Social Provision Law further became a tangible part of state policy as de la Huerta proceeded to recommend that the Chinese merchants in Cananea be expelled as of January 1, 1920. On November 25, 1919, the council notified the Chinese that they could not import any more merchandise and must sell their entire stocks by the end of the year, and that any unsold items would revert to the council. For the convenience of the Chinese, the council was willing to provide a train to take them to the border on New Year's Day.[62]

Ungson condemned the action as an intrigue of Mexican storeowners. Merchants vociferously protested the latest action against them. Hum Fook, representing 125 Cananea Chinese merchants, and José Chang, representing another 38, argued that expulsion would spell the economic ruin of the Chinese in the state. Fook and Chang then asked the Nogales district judge for a *writ of amparo*, a course of legal action intended as an effective and inexpensive instrument to protect an individual's constitutional rights.[63] After they conveyed the injustices of the labor law, Fook and Chang reiterated that the expulsion decree was illegal. It violated not only constitutional guarantees of liberty and freedom to engage in business, but also Mexico's 1899 treaty with China. Ironically, it also violated Article 1 of the labor law itself, which prohibited interference in anyone's business.[64]

As the date neared for the expulsion of the Chinese, Augustín Centeno Barcena (a jurist whom Arana had maligned as an *abogado chinero*, or Chinese lawyer) presented the Chinese case to the court. Attacking the council's statement of unfair Chinese competition as a subterfuge, Barcena accused the council of being a front for a few speculators who, unable to compete with the Chinese, desired their expulsion. Recalling de la Huerta's inaugural address of September 1919—a mere two months prior—in which he promised to end violence against the Chinese because it gave Sonora a bad name, the Chinese lawyer suggested that it was time for de la Huerta to fulfill his commitment.[65] In his defense, de la Huerta charged that the Chinese had violated Article 106 of the labor law and therefore he and the Cananea council were correct in closing stores and allowing no new ones to open. In addition, de la Huerta stressed his strict adherence to the law while he catered to public interest and the national conscience. He foresaw serious consequences for Sonorans if the judge suspended the Cananea ordinance.

Facing impending expulsion, Chinese merchants appealed both to their own advocates and to those Mexicans who were in various positions of power. In an overwhelming majority of cases, their entreaties were ignored or dismissed. For instance, in 1919 the Chinese *chargé d'affaires* sent a note to the Mexican Foreign Affairs Office protesting Sonora's Labor and Social Provision Law. In the note, this diplomat claimed that the law ignored Article 127 of the Mexican Constitution by failing to create boards of conciliation and arbitration through which the law might have been mediated. The Chinese official also argued that the law was impractical because of the lack of qualified Mexicans to fill positions vacated by foreigners, and because of a contradictory amendment within the law itself that limited the firing of foreigners.[66] In addition to the protests of Chinese merchants themselves, the Chinese legation in Mexico City voiced its outrage at the callous injustices inherent within the labor law. The legation also appealed to Mexican President Carranza. It was only at this highest level that Chinese protests were granted an audience and a response. Carranza instructed de la Huerta to prevent the Chinese expulsion from Cananea. Moreover, Carranza ordered the protection of the Chinese.[67]

In two separate decisions on the cases of Hum Fook and José Chang, the court suspended Cananea's act to expel the Chinese. The Chinese may have been spared expulsion for the time being, but despite Carranza's directive and the court's orders, many observers believed that de la Huerta would not comply with the decision. Francisco Chiyoc of the UFC in Cananea believed that de la Huerta did not consider Carranza's promises of protection to the Chinese to be binding. The *writ of amparo* suspended the Cananea decree and the Chinese remained, although not without ongoing harassment and brutality.[68]

At the beginning of 1920, then, the Chinese remained in Sonora and anti-Chinese legislation was in a state of limbo, because of either *writs of amparo*, presidential restrictions, or the lucrative practice of accepting graft or donations from the Chinese.[69] Although fifty Chinese left Sonora in December of 1919, and an average of thirty more left each month until the end of 1920, an influx of new arrivals from Sinaloa stabilized the Chinese population in Sonora at an estimated five thousand. De la Huerta suggested that the Chinese forsake business and go into agriculture as a compromise in order to forestall drastic measures. The Chinese rejected this latest proposal because they would have no protection in the outlying areas. A second suggestion, that a number of Chinese leave Sonora monthly until all or most had departed, was deemed to be equally distasteful and was summarily rejected.[70]

Upon his ascension to the governorship of Sonora, de la Huerta actively pursued an anti-Chinese agenda, with the added power of his new office, despite President Carranza's reprobation. He consistently supported the efforts of Arana and others against the Chinese, from his election campaign to the end of his term in 1923. De la Huerta supported the Cananea expulsion decree, resisted efforts from Mexico City to protect the Chinese, and enforced his choice of an anti-Chinese municipal council in Guaymas. He also advocated amendments to Mexico's 1899 treaty with China to limit Chinese immigration and their rights in Mexico. The treaty and the subject of its renewal introduced a new phase in the anti-Chinese campaign.[71] Magdalena citizens circulated a petition to abrogate the treaty and reinforce the governor's plans. De la Huerta intimated to Consul Dyer that repeal of the treaty was his next goal because the Chinese population in Sonora had stabilized after the failure of the Cananea expulsion decree. When de la Huerta submitted his petition to annul the treaty, he told Dyer that "very soon the Chinese problem . . . will be solved."[72]

Although Chinese suffered attacks throughout the state of Sonora, the Arizpe district was the scene of continuous violence. In 1921, Fronteras and Agua Prieta rivaled Cananea for outbreaks against the Chinese. In November, Felipe González Cortés, a Hermosillo-based sanitation inspector who had attempted to stir up the Guaymas populace against the Chinese, appeared in Agua Prieta. In a large demonstration he stressed the need to stop Chinese immigration.[73] The Chinese of the Arizpe district in turn charged Mexicans with harboring malice toward them and deliberately harassing them with the intent to force their exodus. Benjamín Ungson indicated to the governor that two political parties in the election in Fronteras were prejudiced against the Chinese there. One party supported Francisco Blanco and circulated flyers indicating that the Chinese supported his rival, Felipe Luna. The flyer, in pidgin Spanish, imitated the way the Chinese spoke and stressed the benefits the Chinese would get if Luna won: "We like Mesians cuz they vely dumb."[74]

By late 1921, Arana's campaign, begun in 1916, had reached its peak, with constant harassment of the Chinese through both legal and extralegal means. Although Arana himself had died early in 1921 (allegedly the victim of a Chinese scheme to poison him), a new publication, *La Pulga,* advanced the anti-Chinese campaign. The newspaper asserted first that government officials aided Chinese interests because they wanted Chinese tax dollars and wanted to present an appealing face to the international community; and second that poverty-stricken Mexicans allowed the Chinese to prosper by patronizing their grocery stores and other businesses.

Finally, the editor foresaw in the not-so-distant future the possibility of a Chinese governor of Sonora if the Sonorans failed to take decisive punitive action. The editor of *La Pulga* claimed that gold, the Chinese "religion," lured Mexican women to Chinese beds. Thus the "bestial Quasimodos" gradually ruined the Mexican race.[75] In his second article, the *La Pulga* editor turned from the question of the prostitution of Mexican women to the exodus of unemployed Mexicans from Sonora. He charged that Chinese in the state enriched themselves and returned to China while Mexicans starved at home and faced discrimination in the United States. Unable to outpace Chinese competition, Mexicans witnessed the appearance of Chinese stores on every corner. Even worse, Chinese businessmen employed no Mexicans despite Article 106.[76]

In its third issue, *La Pulga* looked with horror on Chinese merchants who dominated the central market while there were only a few Mexican vendors. He charged that they invaded every business until the Mexican enterprise was a mere tributary to them.[77] *La Pulga*'s editor called for a grandiose meeting of protest against the Chinese to promote the idea of a designated Chinese barrio. He also suggested that a special plea to the state legislature be made to prohibit the immigration of Chinese into Sonora unless they brought a thousand pesos with them. The editor proposed a plan to create an anti-Chinese police force, to be supported by a head tax levied on every Chinese resident. Surveillance of Chinese men and the prevention of concubinage with Mexican women would stand as the most important tasks of the police. Another proposal, citing the Chinese tendency to spread disease, called for a designated sanitary inspector to visit all Chinese residences and stores. If these proposals were not enough to marginalize the Chinese, *La Pulga* urged Mexicans to break up Chinese neighborhoods through extra legal means.[78]

Venustiano Carranza, who decreed a return to constitutional rule, had begun his tenure as president of Mexico (1917–1920) at the height of anti-Chinese sentiment. Relative to some of the leaders who preceded and followed him, Carranza at least gave the appearance of being less profoundly Sinophobic. In the last two years of his tenure, he faced considerable obstacles in enforcing Mexico's new Constitution. Although Article 123 of the Constitution outlined agrarian and labor rights, Carranza did little to fulfill the aspirations of the working and agrarian classes, leaving the eight-hour work day, the abolishment of debt peonage, and the national minimum wage salary unevenly enforced throughout Mexico. Carranza was also unable to adequately implement subsoil rights to protect Mexico's natural resources. According to historian Linda Hall, when Carranza requested that foreign-owned oil companies register their land holdings with the government and apply for new drilling permits, American companies refused. Carranza insisted that the companies register their holdings, but backed down from previous demands for drilling permits.[79] As difficult as things were internationally, domestic crises actually posed the most serious challenge. Poor climatic conditions and uncertain markets forced agricultural production to new lows, as unemployment reached new highs. Beset by these dire economic conditions, Carranza faced renewed opposition within his ranks, including from some, such as Álvaro Obregón, who had previously numbered among his allies.

In June of 1919 Obregón announced his candidacy for the presidency. His ascendancy to this office occurred at a time when Chinese immigration had increased considerably. The Chinese immigrant population, which had declined to 3,300 from 1914 to 1918, surged to 6,100 between 1919 and 1921.[80] Faced with both opposition to immigration and growing demands for nullification of the treaty with China, Obregón's government chose to seek a compromise with the Chinese. Although Obregón desired Chinese laborers, he did not want to afford them rights. After long diplomatic negotiations and strident debate among the legislators, Alberto J. Pani, Mexico's secretary of foreign relations, and Quang Ki Tseng, China's diplomatic envoy, signed an amendment to the treaty on November 21, 1921, prohibiting the immigration of Chinese laborers to Mexico. With the exception of this amendment, the 1899 treaty with China remained unchanged.[81] Chinese immigration declined after 1921, not only in total numbers but also in relation to other nationalities. Chinese, who comprised 12.49 percent of all immigrants from 1911 to 1915, and 6.69 from 1916 to 1920, fell to only 2.61 percent of all entrants from 1921 to 1924.[82]

Despite official harassment, immigration restrictions, and an organized anti-Chinese campaign in Sonora, the Chinese survived into 1922 and continued to dominate the retail trade in most goods and in wholesale and retail grocery businesses. Passive resistance, complaints to the authorities in Sonora, Mexico, and Washington, DC, and the willingness of officials to accept bribes and to look the other way all combined to mitigate the pressures of Arana and his cohorts. A tightly knit organization of cooperative societies also aided the Chinese to resist the Cananea expulsion and to fend off financial ruin.[83] But Arana had established the organization of juntas, groups of merchants, and virulent press campaigns that subsequent crusaders were to use with more effect against the hated Chinese. Arana had also implemented the procedures of legal impediments and official harassment that later anti-Chinese leaders refined and extended. But despite Arana's best efforts, the Chinese remained in Mexico, with as much if not more financial wherewithal as before 1916.

The end of the violent phase of the Revolution in Sonora and the appearance of the new Constitution transformed anti-Chinese campaigns in the state. The violent attacks diminished in number and intensity, but simultaneously legal restrictions proliferated. Calles and de la Huerta, barred from political power during the Porfiriato, rose from the middle class to dominance in Sonora during the Carranza years. Both were imbued with a dislike of foreign interest, especially from the United States and China. Armed with Mexico's new constitution and an emergent nationalism, Calles and de la Huerta supported Arana's campaign of "Mexico for the Mexicans, China for the Chinese." Despite Arana's death, the anti-Chinese forces continued to advocate expulsion of the Chinese well into the 1920s. As these forces gained strength and support, the consequences would reach across the border into a nation that had already made its stance on the Chinese abundantly clear.

## The View from Across the Line

As the newest and youngest appointee of the Chinese Bureau, Clifford Alan Perkins learned quickly to manage the myriad complexities of the position of Chinese inspector for Tucson. As a former postal worker in El Paso, Texas, Perkins had originally despaired of gaining the employment he would come to loathe. As he later commented, "Nobody seemed to be interested in hiring an inexperienced, nineteen-year-old semi-invalid, at least until I applied at the post office." Perkins soon grew tired of his routine. Despite his suspected tuberculosis, he longed for excitement and frequently vented his dissatisfaction to his coworker May Brick. As Perkins later recalled, Brick looked him up and down and said, "If I were a young man your age . . . I'd get a job with the Immigration Service." Perkins ruefully admitted to never having heard of the Immigration Service, whereupon Brick informed him that the Service dealt with mounted surveillance of the southern U.S. border and the expulsion of aliens. As if the excitement were not enticement enough, Immigration Service work paid twice his current wage. "That was enough for me," proclaimed an eager Perkins, and fourteen months later he found himself stationed in Tucson—a town he later described as "some sort of jumping-off spot to oblivion."[84]

What Perkins had in fact jumped off into was a borderlands in the midst of intense and chaotic social rupture. Beginning in 1910, the devastation of ongoing revolution drove more than 350,000 Mexicans across the border into the United States.[85] So constant was the stream of Mexican immigrants entering border cities from the interior states of Jalisco, Guanajuato, and Michoacán that the total border population increased by 2 million residents between 1910 and 1920.[86] As the Chinese population in Sonora decreased from 4,486 to 3,639 during the ten years after the Revolution began, the numbers of Chinese entering the United States from Mexico increased.[87]

Instead of actively seeking to curb the influx of Mexicans as they did the Chinese, U.S. employers welcomed Mexicans as a source of cheap, tractable labor for burgeoning agribusiness and industrialization in the American Southwest and Midwest.[88] Mexican labor continued to travel north even as the considerable bureaucratic machinery of the Bureau of Immigration restricted the passage of Chinese into the United States. As smuggling persisted, state controls to reestablish national sovereignty along the U.S.-Mexico border intensified with the purpose of closing the border to transnational crossings of Chinese immigrants from Sonora into Arizona. Regardless of the large influx of Mexicans into the American Southwest in the first half of the twentieth century, nativist movements continued to seek an end to Chinese immigration into the United States.

This was the fractious setting in which the small-town Wisconsin native began his new career. Now twenty-two, Perkins had come to Tucson in search of an "exciting, possibly dangerous job [that could] eventually prove an open sesame to the mysteries of the Orient." Some of Perkins' initial expectations were fulfilled. He was a critical cog in a mounted guard patrolling the southern Arizona border with Mexico under immigration inspector Alfred E. Burnett. With growing frequency, the team of nine immigration agents apprehended and deported Chinese who were in the United States illegally. Most of the time, though, Perkins monitored the surrounding countryside for fifty miles, in twelve- to fifteen-hour shifts, seven days a week, alternating days and nights. He ensured that all westbound Southern Pacific Railroad passenger and freight trains originating in Sonora were inspected for smuggled Chinese.

If Perkins' youth helped him to sustain the regimen of inspecting trains and cargo boxes and monitoring large swathes of land, then it also worked against him. With no seniority in the Tucson office, Perkins was often called up for horseback duty with very little notice or on very little sleep. With a watchful eye on the Chinese communities in southern Arizona, immigration inspectors paid particular attention to the activities of Chinese in Tucson and made routine stops at Chinese-owned businesses and gathering places. Throughout the 1910s, Perkins and his colleagues frequented long-suspected sanctuaries for contraband Chinese in Tucson and its environs— the vegetable gardens at Fort Lowell, for example—because of their remote locations. Checking on the truck farmers required a thorough inspection of their *chock chees* (certificates of residence) and verification of the information contained in their papers. "They looked very much alike in the harsh glare," commented Perkins, "and unless we knew them, we had to examine their papers and check them against a loose-leaf record we took with us showing the names and types of documents carried by Chinese residing or working in every establishment in town."[89]

Information was essential to the success of border patrol surveillance of the Tucson Chinese community, and the Bureau had collected a great deal on the daily activities and interactions of these individuals. The record books of the Chinese Bureau catalogued this information not as a function of bureaucratic policy but rather as "logical lists to maintain of persons with whom we were in continuous contact."[90] Inspectors, however, went beyond the "logic" of their lists as they hired Mexicans living in Nogales, Sonora, to take photographs of suspected Chinese border crossers. These photographs circulated not only within Tucson but also among other immigration offices throughout southern Arizona, presumably to help distinguish between aliens and residents. Even as Perkins and his inspection colleagues extended the use of photographs beyond their initial intent, U.S. immigration officials increasingly recognized the limitations of those photographs. After the passage of the Immigration Act of 1917, surveillance moved from photographs to the body. According to historian Anna Pegler-Gordon, immigration inspectors were granted license to demand that border crossers submit to a newly instituted disinfection process to check for diseases, especially typhus.[91] Immigrants were instructed to strip naked and were given a sanitary bath of soap, water, and kerosene. Their clothes and baggage were also fumigated. In El Paso, Texas, this process included a delousing station. Medical inspections were increased, experienced immigrant officers were transferred from Ellis Island to southern border stations, and further documentation was added to an already unwieldy immigration regime. These procedures would prove to constitute new grounds on which to exclude hopeful immigrants.

The 1917 Immigration Act also marked a critical moment with regard to surveillance of Mexicans at the border. Habitual border crossers were issued border-crossing identification cards, a precursor to the modern-day passport. The identification cards allowed immigration inspectors to track and monitor the trans-border movements of local residents; they also afforded *fronterizos* unfettered crossings without constant examination by border officials. For others, entering the United States was quite costly. Customs collectors were instructed to impose an eight-dollar "head tax" on all first-time border crossers. (To give some perspective on the severity of this provision for entry, the 1917 eight-dollar lien, when translated into 2012 terms, approximates $150 in purchasing power.) The act also extended myriad prohibitions against immigrants who were "liable to become a public charge," as well as against contract laborers, but it was relatively generous when it came to agricultural workers from Mexico. This generosity hardly represented a spirit of beneficence; rather, the lenience arose in response to the vociferous and financially powerful voice of agricultural growers who needed—and demanded—unrestricted access to Mexican fieldworkers. In acquiescence, William Wilson, the U.S. secretary of labor, exempted Mexican agricultural workers from the head tax, contract labor prohibitions, and the literacy requirement, asserting that Mexicans represented an easily managed, inexpensive labor force. As aliens, they could press no claim to permanent residency, unlike Filipinos, who were viewed as a potential source of tractable labor but were U.S. nationals. Wilson stated, "The temporary admission . . . of Mexicans . . . is much preferable to the permanent establishment . . . of unskilled workers from the Philippines."[92] Once Mexican workers had served their purpose, their whereabouts could be easily identified and they could therefore be removed from the United States without delay.

As the Act of 1917 placed more prohibitions on Mexicans, it also widened the scope of Asian immigration restriction. Immigrants permanently excluded from countries of the "barred Asiatic zone" included native inhabitants from Afghanistan to the Asian-Pacific region. Inspectors at the southern U.S. border, then, were tasked with fitting even harsher immigration polices into their already exhausting regimen of border surveillance strategies. Moreover, Chinese in southern Arizona were themselves required to exercise even greater vigilance. Already among the targets of stringent exclusion laws, they now needed to be mindful of these additional efforts to circumscribe their numbers and their influence. The result was an ever-heightening tension between three groups: one sworn to make the U.S. border impenetrable, another attempting to safeguard its status as American without the stigma affixed to alienage, and a third believing that breaching the border might well prove the only means of its survival.

As the Chinese established permanence in Tucson, border officials sharpened their surveillance skills and honed their knowledge of bureaucratic procedures. The Chinese Bureau set forth early, influential guidelines that served as the basis for enforcing immigration law over the next few decades. The training of inspectors was of primary concern to chief border officials and, consequently, agents underwent rigorous examination regarding the legal intricacies of exclusion laws. Forty-six questions tested agents' ability to filter the many complex scenarios that arose at the border. Questions ranged from queries about the seven excluded classes to the points of entry on the Canadian-U.S. border. More stringent testing, designed to prevent the entry of Chinese, was captured in the following scenarios:

A Chinese woman marries an [American]-born Chinaman, in Mexico. Should she be examined under the Immigration Laws?

A father comes to the U.S. and is naturalized. Has wife and minor child in country from whence he came, the latter having been born before the father's naturalization. Are the children citizens of the U.S. at the time of their arrival here?

What facts are to be included in the report of Commissioners of Immigration, or Inspectors-in-Charge [sic], to the Collector of Customs when a U.S. Attorney is requested to institute proceedings for the recovery of prescribed penalties, or to undertake criminal prosecution of an alleged offender against the Immigration Laws?[93]

To clarify such complexities, the Chinese Bureau in Tucson adopted severe measures and methods of questioning suspected aliens that at times involved material evidence. Clifford Perkins was but one of a few hundred men who patrolled the southern border of the United States in this turbulent, unpredictable era. The early guardians of the U.S. border proved to be inadequate in the face of desperate Chinese who were driven into the United States by both Mexican law and Mexican hatred, even at the risk of capture. To cross the border into the United States was to risk deportation; to stay in Mexico was to risk death. Although these Chinese *fronterizo* communities were divided by only one hundred miles, the mix of virulent Sinophobia in Mexico and immigration restriction in the United States drew a permanent wedge between them.

In little more than a decade, anti-Chinese sentiment had grown from a chorus of disaffected businessmen to a campaign of fevered rhetoric of race hatred that culminated in a succession of progressively more draconian laws. In the short term, Arana's campaign served most Sonorans well, but in the long run it destabilized the state economically and socially. Sonora was economically anemic without the Chinese, and the violence against them drew harsh criticism from the international community and from many Mexicans. Arana's tactics nonetheless proved durable even as they were loathed by some, like Soriano, whose personal enmity for the Chinese was exceeded only by his vision of a liberal, democratic Mexico. When the national political leadership took up the Sonoran cause against the Chinese, they too would be caught in the tension between their own Sinophobia on the one hand and the push to develop the postrevolutionary Mexican economy on the other. For Sonoran Chinese, relief from Sinophobic rhetoric would not be gained by crossing the border into Arizona. There they would be met by a growing American immigration bureaucracy that had benefited from earlier experiences enforcing Chinese exclusion laws. Sonoran Chinese faced an untenable choice: remain in Mexico and fight it out with nationalist Sonorans, or cross into the United States and risk deportation. But the same revolutionary fervor that spurred on an anti-Chinese dynamic in Sonora created, although through much trial and tribulation, avenues of legal migration and long-term settlement in the United States for some Chinese who had lived in Mexico. Within the relatively short span of a few hundred miles there occurred an intricate convergence of international, regional, and local forces that would come to bear on the Chinese in the next few years.

# 5 Myriad Pathways and Common Bonds

Chinese borderlanders, like other *fronterizos*, learned a good deal about the Mexican Revolution. They heard tales of horror and heroics from neighbors and relatives who themselves may have heard the stories second- or thirdhand. Some probably steered clear of news about mass executions and forced expulsions, given that the memory of large-scale massacres of Chinese, Mexicans, and other populations was still fresh. Others had the unfortunate fate of having the violence repeatedly come to them. In Torreón, Chihuahua, six years after the 303 mostly Chinese residents were massacred, Francisco "Pancho" Villa and his militia returned to the town and murdered five Arabs; eighty Mexicans sympathetic to his rival, Venustiano Carranza; and sixty Chinese.[1] As revolutionary violence drew closer, Lebanese, Spanish, and American residents increased protection of their person and their property upon any sign of a raid. Once the rebels had made their exit, the residents permitted themselves a measure of relief. Chinese, however, remained vigilant long after the last combatant had left town, their focus on ensuring the safety of neighbors, family, and stores.

As might well be imagined, such continuous violence did not engender feelings of loyalty to the Mexican cause among Chinese residents. They were understandably reluctant to risk their lives in battle for this new, emerging Mexico that held them in such contempt. Few Chinese participated directly, as soldiers, in the Mexican Revolution, but those who did assisted the United States in its undeclared war against Villa, under the watch of General John J. Pershing. More than five hundred Chinese in Mexico attached themselves to Pershing's "Punitive Expedition," a military force ordered by President Woodrow Wilson to track and capture Villa, who had raided the border town of Columbus, New Mexico, in March of 1916.[2] Villa's raid had no rhyme or reason, except that it was in keeping with the Mexican rebel's reputation as a pillager. The constancy of gunfire during Villa's mid-March foray into Columbus terrorized the town's thirteen hundred residents and caught off guard an American battalion of six hundred men stationed at the border town. Although Columbus sat three miles from Chihuahua, Mexico, it seemed an unusual choice of a place to exact revenge on American support for the existing Mexican regime, to which Villa stood firmly opposed. In the words of historian Friedrich Katz, the town "had no glitter to attract a raiding party."[3] Columbus, though, stood as an easy mark for gathering support for Villa's larger campaign to unseat Carranza as Mexico's president. Villa's four hundred to five hundred men looted for guns, food, women, horses, and Springfield rifles while townspeople—especially Anglo Americans—became human fodder for Villa's new approach to prisoners of war: immediate execution.[4]

Pershing answered President Wilson's call for retribution. With 4,800 American troops and an additional 2,500 Mexican cavalry under the command of General Luis Gutiérrez, Pershing chased Villa and his insurgents throughout the blistering Chihuahua desert for nine months.[5] Pershing might well have succeeded in his mission had he not been circumscribed by an agreement brokered between Wilson and Carranza that limited the range within Mexico that the U.S. Cavalry could track Villa. While garrisoned outside Colonia Dublán, a Mormon colony of more than a thousand Latter Day Saints, Pershing had much time to contemplate the human landscape around him. Mormon exiles and American and Mexican cavalry, infantry, and artillery troops dominated the scene, but Chinese sutlers and laborers received much of Pershing's attention. Obtaining supplies had proved difficult and local help was hard to come by. Mexicans refused, because of either nationalistic pride or fear of retribution from Villa's men, to sell hungry soldiers anything to eat. If not for the Chinese, who initially encamped at Colonia Dublán seeking protection from Mexican revolutionaries, the general's troops would have had a tougher go.[6]

In a harsh climate of rebellion and revolution, the Chinese relieved the hardship of Pershing's battalion. The general looked to Chinese laborers to help dig trenches and set up tents, while Chinese sutlers delighted the needy troops with doughnuts, pies, tobacco, and fruit. And many soldiers, long overdue for a bath, "obtained [their] first good wash by buying a cake of soap from a Chinaman."[7] In Colonia Dublán, both merchants and laborers aided the expeditionary forces in whatever manner was necessary, until January 1917, when Wilson ordered Pershing out of Chihuahua without the capture of Villa. As Pershing evacuated his troops, and a caravan of approximately one thousand Mexicans and Mormons who had previously been encamped at Colonia Dublán, there was considerable consternation about the Chinese. If they remained in Chihuahua, "[the] ignorant coolies," Pershing feared, "would likely be robbed . . . by the

Villistas."[8] If they crossed into the United States, they would invariably face deportation as illegal immigrants. Despite the risk, Pershing escorted 524 Chinese sutlers and laborers into Columbus, the border town origi- nally invaded by Villa, where the refugees would spend the next few months awaiting their fate.[9] Pershing's highly organized evacuations of the American and Mexican refugees were relatively straightforward affairs— orderly, and not terribly dangerous or tense. The Americans moved on to other parts of the United States, and the Mexicans either returned to Mexico or accepted employment in Arizona, New Mexico, or Colorado.[10] Evacuation of the Chinese, however, was a different matter. Pershing's cav- alry surrounded the group, knowing that they were at risk of capture and deportation as they crossed into the United States.

Pershing undertook the endeavor not, one suspects, out of any deep affiliation with or respect for the Chinese. The general's statement about "ignorant coolies" belies such an assumption. Compelled more by a sense of honor and gratitude, Pershing felt that the U.S. government owed a great debt to the Chinese who had assisted him in Colonia Dublán. This outlook was shared by others, among them Major John W. Parker, to whom Pershing assigned general command of the Columbus refu- gees. Parker made a similar plea, but with more urgency and without the oblique condescension of Pershing: "A little thing, merely the honor of the Punitive Expedition and of the United States, requires that protection be given to these faithful [Chinese] camp followers."[11] But Pershing's and Parker's view had its detractors. Labor union leaders objected to the Chi- nese presence in Columbus because they stood as potential competitors of the working class. "Charity begins at home," asserted Ed Beasley of the Missouri Laundry Owners' Association. "We should see that these refu- gees are . . . deported from this country."[12] Nativist sentiment against the Chinese refugees was strong, and many more, especially U.S. immigration officials, advocated for the deportation of the refugees. But the view of Pershing and Parker held sway, and the Chinese refugees were permitted to remain in Columbus, albeit under the supervision of the Department of War, until a workable solution was brokered.[13]

Of the original 524 Chinese sutlers and laborers who came out of Chihuahua with Pershing's expedition, a few voluntarily returned to China. Most of the refugees nevertheless endured five years in Columbus, sup- ported by the fundraising efforts of the San Francisco-based Chinese Six Companies and the diplomatic advocacy of T. K. Fong, consul-general at San Francisco. Eventually, in late 1921, Congress passed a joint reso- lution, Public Law No. 29, permitting the remaining Chinese laborers to become legal residents of the United States.[14] As the Chinese laborers pre- pared to leave Columbus, General Pershing returned to bid them to "learn the American language" after being released from military custody and to become good citizens.[15]

Not all Chinese, however, went through the protracted ordeal in Columbus. Some forty of the refugees met the definition of merchant as defined in the Chinese exclusion laws and were thus allowed immediate legal entry into the United States as an exempted class of Chinese immigrants. Li Weikun was among those few fortunate Chinese who gained such legal entry into the United States as a merchant (see Figure 5.1). In a decision that contravened prevailing nativist attitudes, Weikun and a handful of other Chinese were granted Section Six status by the U.S. Immigration Service. The status

FIGURE 5.1  Li Weikun as Pershing Soldier. Courtesy of the Arizona Historical Society/Tucson. Photo no. B52028, MS 1242. http://www.arizonahistoricalsociety.org

was extended to those individuals among the 524 remaining Chinese refugees who could offer evidence that they were members of the merchant class according to standards previously established by exclusion laws.[16]

Weikun and the other Chinese who had served with Pershing were almost certainly mindful of the political intricacies of immigration exclusion. The distinction of merchant status set in motion a life-changing series of events for the former sutler, who in 1917 decided to move to Tucson where, he had heard, things were better for the Chinese.[17] As he crossed into the Old Pueblo, Weikun might well have considered the particular privileges of his merchant status: relative freedom from deportation, certainly, as well as other options of which he might avail himself in the future, including ease of travel to China, and permission to sponsor the admission of immediate family and clan members. But as merchant privileges distinguished Weikun from many Chinese in Tucson, ethnic and regional differences existing between Chinese residents and newcomers such as Weikun were also sources of tension that overlapped the intensification of American immigration laws. A native of the *Siyi* district of China's Guangdong Province, Weikun settled on the outskirts of Tucson to avoid conflict with immigrants from the rival *Sanyi* district. Although Guangdong Province was a hemisphere removed from Arizona, the hostilities between Chinese from *Siyi* (meaning Four Districts—Enping, Taishan, Xinhui, and Kaiping) and Chinese from *Sanyi* (meaning Three Districts—Panyu, Nanhai, and Shunde) that had their nascence there were so strong that Chinese from the two areas settled physically apart from one another in Tucson. Tensions between the two *huigan* (district-based associations) could also have lingered from the failure of the *Sanyi*, who were largely controlled by the Six Companies, to lead a successful boycott of the Geary Act.[18]

Regional and ethnic differences divided the Tucson Chinese community, and as these existing conflicts wrought meaningful tensions between neighbors, immigration restrictionism cleaved new divisions among the Chinese themselves and between Chinese and Mexicans. Kith relations gave way to ties based on revised understandings of social belonging that consisted of a constellation of categories based on newly inscribed racial classifications and class hierarchies. As immigrants from Mexico and China continued to arrive in Tucson in the 1920s, differences in legal status and disparate economic resources drew distinctions between immigrants and first-generation Tucsonans, whether Chinese or Mexican. Chinese' relationships with Mexicans held less importance, but were not altogether severed. Arrangements between working-class Chinese and Mexicans continued even though both groups made everyday choices about social and economic exchange more on the basis of ethnic loyalties than on kith bonds.

By the 1920s, connections between Chinese and Mexicans in Tucson were already guarded, but an additional element would emerge with the influx of Chinese and Mexican laborers into southern Arizona, a development that would intensify the growing wariness between the two groups. Moreover, the manner in which immigration laws inscribed these newcomers as impossible subjects—an illegal but necessary source of American labor without the rights of citizenship—widened the divide between Chinese Americans and Mexican Americans. The recent surge of immigrants wrought myriad changes between the two groups—some of which served to bring them closer and others that created new divisions. Both Chinese and Mexicans navigated this new racial terrain, although not always in ways that strengthened relationships between the two communities. Li Weikun's odyssey from Pershing auxiliary solider to *Siyi* outcast surrounded by *Sanyi* rivals to successful merchant and family man illustrates the regional, local, and international forces that came to weigh heavily on the settlement of Tucson Chinese.

## *"A Mecca for Chinese": Tucson in the 1920s*

The Tucson that promised Li Weikun and other Chinese economic stability and relative personal safety was experiencing considerable social and cultural change. The 224 Chinese residents, mostly small-scale grocers, restaurateurs, and truck farmers, continued to make the Old Pubelo a place of rightful permanence, although class divisions between the Chinese and Mexicans began to emerge.[19] But when compared to the heightened race hatred against Chinese in Mexico, Tucson's Chinese community created modest economic and social ties through a constellation of kith relations. In the 1920s, Tucson Chinese rewove the web of their community under relatively favorable social conditions, and at a time when restrictive land laws and insular Chinatowns sharply limited occupational and geographic mobility elsewhere. For instance, California's 1913 Alien Land Law, the first of its kind, barred "any alien ineligible for citizenship" from purchasing land or from leasing it for more than three years. A harsher 1920 amendment to the California law prohibited the transfer of land, by sale or lease, to noncitizens. In 1921, a year after California amended the original land law, the Arizona state legislature enacted a similar law barring all "aliens ineligible to citizenship from owning land."[20] Although these legal maneuvers constrained the lives of Chinese in California and Arizona, well-established kin and kith ties in Tucson seemed to have attenuated the impact of restricted land ownership. The continuation of land leasing among neighbors in El Barrio acted as a keystone in the lives of Tucson Chinese. By the mid-1920s, Tucson enjoyed a reputation as "a Mecca for . . . Chinese refugees."[21]

Given Tucson's reputation as a relatively safe harbor for Chinese, Wei-kun's decision to move to the Old Pueblo was an easy one. Weikun maintained a modest existence at Tucson's periphery before relocating to the center of town when there was an influx of Siyi kith who began settling in the area. The merchant promptly opened a grocery store and meat market with kin from his village in China: Lee Kan, Lee How, and Lee Hing.[22] With $3,000, Weikun sponsored the legal entry of his two merchant partners from China and notarized his new business with them as partners. Their store on North Main Street, officially called the Yan Lee Hing Company but known throughout Tucson as Pay 'n Save, prospered.[23] Weikun's relationship with Steinfeld and Company, a well-established merchant firm owned by Albert Steinfeld, kept his shelves stocked with wholesale and retail dry goods and meat for local customers. But like some businesses in El Barrio, Weikun's store was occasionally robbed by marauding locals. Alberto M. Flores and Aurelio B. Navarro pled guilty to charges of assaulting Weikun and robbing his store. Navarro, because he was a minor, drew a five-year suspended sentence, while the older Flores earned a two-to-three-year term in state prison.[24]

In the midst of these enterprises, family became a priority to Weikun. Long-standing Arizona marriage codes typically narrowed a grocer's choices, because these laws prohibited Chinese men from taking a Mexican or white bride. Weikun, however, already had a family: the wife and son he had left behind in China sixteen years ago. The grocer took advantage of his merchant status and sponsored the admission of his wife and son to Tucson. With virtually no obstacles in the territorial courts, Weikun's wife, Huang, and their son, Li Huaying, landed in Tucson only twenty days before the passage of the National Origins Act in May 1924.[25]

The National Origins Act decreased the total number of admissible immigrants to 150,000 per year, barred the admission of Italians, Jews, and Poles, and permanently prohibited all Asian migration. Had Weikun waited to bring his wife to the United States until the National Origins Act became law—less than three weeks after her actual departure from China—Arizona judicial officials would have deliberated and possibly denied the entry of Huang and Li Huaying. Instead, the admission of Weikun's wife and son was practically anticlimactic. It involved merely the confirmation of his merchant status and verification that Weikun had performed no manual labor except that which was necessary to conduct his grocery business.

In addition, Weikun's priority to establish business relations when he sponsored the admission of kin member Li Yeming before that of his wife and son underscored the crucial place of *guanxi* relations in Tucson. Merchant status in effect hastened the use of *guanxi* practices that underpinned family structure. Weikun's impressive success with his Pay 'n Save store not only served to secure his own financial well-being but also added to an extensive *guanxi* network that encompassed fictive kin in Tucson and biological kin in China and the Philippines. As the eldest of three brothers and the most well-to-do, Weikun assumed the responsibility of maintaining familial order and presiding over disputes among kin. When Meihe, Weikun's younger brother, died in the Philippines in 1934, Weikun assumed the responsibility of his modest estate. Handling Meihe's affairs was more complicated than Weikun had initially anticipated. Meihe had incurred debt from a business colleague, Weize, and at the time of his death he was still in arrears. Getting at the truth of the matter required several exchanges between Weikun and another younger brother, Hongjing. "Recently I received the letters from Weize's family," Hongjing relayed to Weikun. "The letter said that Meihe once borrowed money from Weize. Weize himself also wrote to me about the money matter and mentioned that Meihe himself didn't returned the money last September. . . . I thought, brother, that you might know the truth."[26] The matter of Meihe's unpaid debt highlighted the burden of Weikun's position as head of his family. As the primary financial gatekeeper, it fell to Weikun to ascertain the veracity and extent of his late brother's debt.

Weikun's familial responsibilities did not end with the disentangling of Meihe's financial obligations. The Tucsonan storeowner was the arbiter of any and all disputes, financial and otherwise, that arose among kin, no matter how distant the relation. Not only did his brother Hongjing ask Weikun to serve as intermediary, but so too did Weikun's nephew, grand-nephew, and nephew-in-law. None of these requests for help were small matters. In the space of a month, for example, Qu Xijun, Weikun's nephew-in-law, wrote frequently and urgently about the desperate predicament of his bamboo ginger and Huai flour business. Qu noted, "I assume you have received [all my letters]. I am very concerned that we did not receive your letters since then. . . ." Qu beseeched his uncle-in-law to loan him ten thousand yuan to stock his store and keep his business afloat. With tax liabilities looming that stood to cripple his business, Qu's desperation left him no easy alternative. "I felt shameful and beg you to lend me Hong Kong cash," Qu pleaded. "It is very hard for me to ask for the money, but times are harsh. Please help me and send the money back as soon as you can." When several weeks had passed and Qu had not heard from Weikun, he wrote again, imploring his uncle-in-law. Mounting financial liabilities and the shifting winds of China's political landscape made Qu feel as if he were "soaked in deep water and roasted in hot fire." Qu closed his last letter to Weikun with impending resignation while at the same time, given a new tax debt, placed his future in the hands of his uncle-in-law. "We have no hope," submitted Qu in a postscript. "I received notice of my business tax totaling 300 yuan . . . . I shall report to you if I have further information."[27]

The time and energy that Weikun spent as familial overseer at times competed with the demands of maintaining his business affairs in Tucson. While Weikun mediated the financial entanglements of kin in China and the Philippines, the Tucson merchant was also trying to manage his Pay 'n Save, which in 1932 had moved to larger quarters on South Meyer Street. Weikun leased from Leandro and Lucy Ruiz a large corner building suitable for a store and living quarters. For this space he paid the Ruizes $55 a month while agreeing to keep the property free from nuisances, trash, and neglect.[28] Although Weikun's profits were modest, he cemented his status as successful merchant with the purchase of a 1930 Chevrolet half-ton pickup.[29] Fiscal prudence, though, dictated that he buy a used truck even though the enterprising merchant could have probably afforded a new vehicle.

Against the backdrop of Weikun's activities, first-generation Chinese continued to reside mostly in El Barrio, where family businesses and modest wealth accumulation portended financial stability but not affluence. Their alliances with Mexicans held less importance when *tucsonenses* declined in status, influence, and wealth. As the Chinese population increased in southern Arizona, Mexicans lost significant land holdings and had few avenues by which to access such large-scale economic enterprises as mercantilism, commercial agriculture, and mining. In the words of anthropologist Thomas Sheridan, in the 1920s, opportunities for Mexicans "simply were not equal for the majority of [*tucsonenses*], either in the marketplace, the political arena, or the public schools."[30] Immigration also exacerbated social inequality as Mexicans, who were left untouched by National Origins Act quotas, arrived in the United States in unprecedented numbers, increasing their population from 486,418 in 1920 to 1,422,533 in 1930.[31] This influx, however, created divisions not only between Chinese and Mexicans, but also between *hispanos* who had established themselves in the region by the late-nineteenth century and the new Mexican immigrants.

An additional facet of this tension arose from the risk, incurred by immigrant Mexicans, of both detection and deportation as a function of the newly formed Border Patrol, one outgrowth of the National Origins Act. Although Mexicans were ostensibly exempt from the quotas established by the act, their apprehension and accompanying rejection increased with the imperative of visas. In 1926, when 60,620 Mexicans were admitted legally into the United States, 726 were prohibited from entering due to lack of visas. This was almost twice as many as were debarred (329) because they did not posses sufficient financial wherewithal to guarantee that they would not become "a public charge."[32] The following year this discrepancy grew even more pronounced, with a roughly 7 to 1 ratio between prohibition based on visa reasons (1,326) and prohibition based on insufficient economic status (206).[33] With this heightened focus on apprehension and deportation, Mexicans had joined the Chinese as aliens within the United States. Both may have aspired to be U.S. citizens; both may have in fact *been* U.S. citizens. But both would now be the targets of ever-tightening border controls.

## Miscegenation and Chinese-Mexican Marriage

After 1924, the coupling of Chinese men—whether with Chinese women or Mexican women—continued to be the most challenging experience of daily life. Extended separation, the norm for both merchants and laborers living in the United States, not only created tremendous strain on marriages but also continually forced the Chinese to reconstruct their families in response to immigration and anti-miscegenation laws. Li Weikun's circumstances were favorable and quite unusual. Most Chinese men faced formidable barriers in bringing their Chinese wives into the United States. Newly arrived Chinese women confronted the challenge of a mandated court appearance to prove they were married to a "lawfully domiciled Chinese merchant." Although Chinese females constituted 12.6 percent of the U.S. Chinese population in 1920, less than 10 percent of all Chinese living in Tucson were women.[34] Chinese men in Tucson faced legal barriers in their attempts to facilitate the lawful entry of their Chinese wives, as well as in their efforts to marry Mexican women in Arizona. Residential proximity with Mexicans, considered racially "white" by Arizona legislators, complicated day-to-day relations between residents in El Barrio. In 1901, Arizona lawmakers passed a second and harsher anti-miscegenation law that prohibited "all marriages of persons of Caucasian blood, or their descendants, with negroes [sic], Mongolians or Indians, and their descendants."[35] According to territorial law, all marriages of such nature were declared "null and void," and those solemnizing racially mixed marriages were subject to fines up to $300 dollars and imprisonment up to six months.[36] Although the number of Chinese merchants increased from forty in 1900 to sixty-three in 1910, their relative economic power did not constitute any political challenge to the decision of the court.[37]

In the face of legal prohibition, the incidence of Chinese marrying Mexican women remained rare in the first two decades of the twentieth century.[38] In 1900, two Mexican females married two Chinese men and between them had three children of mixed heritage.[39] Ten years later, the territorial census listed three women—two Mexican and one French— living with Chinese men. Between the three families there were eleven children of mixed-race parentage. It seems likely that although there was an increase in the number of Chinese children, the two Mexicans originally listed in the 1900 census were the same women listed in the 1910 census.[40] Despite their attractiveness as good providers, most Chinese men in Tucson remained unmarried. For laborers—who made up the vast majority of Chinese in Tucson—the prospect of marriage was even less likely. Combined with a highly skewed gender ratio, harsh anti-miscegenation laws forced most Chinese men in Tucson to live a bachelor's life.[41] Rather than pursue social integration through marriage ties with whites, the Chinese continued to assert themselves in Tucson through daily interactions with Mexican residents.

Legal obstacles did not hinder the marriage of Lily Liu to Frank Valenzuela. Liu, a first-generation Chinese American woman and an engine cleaner for the Southern Pacific Railroad Company, married Frank Valenzuela, a Mexican man, in 1923.[42] Although Arizona laws prohibited their marriage in the state, the couple legally sanctioned their union in Lordsburg, New Mexico. Liu and Valenzuela lived with his parents in Tucson until Valenzuela abandoned his wife, who was pregnant with Stella, and their first child, Sylvia. In addition, Liu also experienced considerable hostility from Valenzuela's parents. She suggested that the hostility derived not from her race but from Liu and Valenzuela not being married before she become pregnant with Sylvia. Liu married Valenzuela after she gave birth to Sylvia and lamented, "It was not my wish for it to be this way." When Liu later married her second husband, Raymond Liu, her two daughters born to Valenzuela retained their biological father's surname. Raymond Liu raised Sylvia and Stella Valenzuela from the time they were infants, despite his wife's past relationship. "That's the only papa they know," proclaimed Lily Liu about her children's relationship with Raymond Liu.[43] The complexities of daily life often shaped the identities of first-generation Chinese Americans, and at times were outside the parameters of Arizona law.

The making of ethnicity for first-generation Chinese, then, hardly remained calcified in a fixed set of customs and practices passed on from the immigrant generation; rather, a blended ethnic identity emerged that was Mexican, American, and Chinese. During the 1920s, this multi-faceted ethnic identity characterized most first-generation Tucson Chinese even as the middle-class status of Mexicans began to erode. According to anthropologists Florence and Robert Lister, most "American-born Chinese moved into the Hispanic barrio, where the majority of [the immigrant-generation Chinese] had also moved."[44] As Tucson's Mexican population gradually shifted to the southern part of the Old Pueblo, the Chinese merchants and their families followed.[45] Although first-generation Chinese in Tucson forged an economic niche for themselves as small-scale merchants or service workers, and although the number of Chinese-owned businesses did increase during the 1920s, the wealth generated by this small community was by no means sizable.

The experiences of Don Wah were emblematic of the early Chinese merchants in this neighborhood.[46] Before his arrival in Tucson in May 1899, Don Wah was employed as a cook for the Southern Pacific Railroad, but he quickly moved from that occupation to business ownership. When Don Wah was thirty, he traveled to China to marry an eighteen-year-old woman named Fok Yut Ngan (Silver Moon).[47] Yut Ngan was the youngest daughter of a wealthy family, and before she married Wah and came to Tucson, she learned embroidery and a few housekeeping skills. As a newlywed, Wah established a bakery and then a grocery store in the Mexican and Chinese section of Tucson, between Convent and Main Street. Wah, a fluent speaker of Cantonese but with some rudimentary English and Spanish skills, was also a popular member of the Tucson Chamber of Commerce.[48] Yut Ngan's parents had assumed their daughter would be entering a life of ease comparable to what she had always known in Fujian, China. Little did they know that Fok Yut would not only take to domestic chores but also would work in her husband's first business enterprise, a Mexican bakery at the corner of Convent and Simpson Streets.[49] Devotion and duty drew her from sleep at three o'clock in the morning, when she would carry their daughter Esther to the bakery papoose-style to wrap the day's bread. Don Wah was equally dedicated to his businesses and his community. For him, civic participation extended beyond mere appearance. One story recounts that Wah, while in the middle of receiving a haircut, broke himself away and headed to the voting polls to break a tie over where the Drachman School should be built.[50] The school was not a segregated place of Chinese education. It served all children in Tucson. A U.S. citizen by virtue of his birth in San Francisco, Don Wah involved himself in the full breadth of local issues, unlike the majority of Tucson Chinese, whose civic participation was largely restricted to informal neighborhood matters because they were ineligible for naturalization.[51] As his daughter Esther— Wah's third child and a first-generation Chinese Tucsonan born in 1917— recalled, Wah was fond of reminding his family, "The community is the extension of your home."[52] Wah's activity contrasted sharply with the far more segregated experiences of Chinese in cities such as San Francisco and Los Angeles.

Chinese enterprises like Wah's tended to be quite modest. Wah's grocery store was small and a walled curtain often separated the Don family's living space from its working space. "The store itself . . . was perhaps twelve feet by twelve feet and immediately at the back of the store there was a cloth curtain and as you went in, there was a bedroom," Esther recalled. "We didn't have many rooms and there were about three of us, I remember, in one bed, and my oldest sister, Rose, she had some sort of boxes with a plank board and a mattress on top of that."[53] Despite the compromises that Esther and her siblings bore because of the lack of space, she nonetheless recalled her childhood with fondness. Every day, Esther and her siblings took in all of El Barrio's particular childhood conventions, such as savoring the refreshing treat of an ice chip from "Vaca" Urquides' truck wagon while hitching herself to its rear for a short ride (see Figure 5.2). The Don children dug up "dirt rubies" after monsoon rains and made the best of Chinaberry trees by fashioning bows and arrows from their branches. The hot summer months saw the Don children seek respite by swimming in the irrigation canals, because the public pools were closed to the Chinese. They picnicked at the San Xavier Mission Church and there

FIGURE 5.2 Picture of Esther Don and Her Siblings Taken on the Southeast Corner of Convent and Jackson Streets, 1927. The Don Wah family had a grocery store and living quarters on the northwest corner. Pictured in the Mexican sombreros are Esther Don and Luella Don. Between Esther and Luella are Phillip and Dorothy Don. Courtesy of Esther Don.

played "Ron Cheif [sic] Flon" with Mexican children, only to realize later as adults that their favorite game was actually called "Run, Sheep, Run."[54]

Alongside childhood frolicking, the expectation remained that children from modest backgrounds would contribute to the family's economic well-being. The Don family, whose second business was a grocery store at the corner of Convent and Jackson Streets, depended in large part on their children, especially the eldest sons and daughters, not only to help with basic chores but also to facilitate customer interactions when more fluency in English was required. Esther Don Tang recalled the early years of settlement in Tucson as a time when "everybody . . . worked hard."[55] Describing her childhood years, Tang vividly remembered the early days in the little barrio grocery. "We were a big family—nine girls and one boy—and we all had to help. . . . It didn't matter how young you were. When we started school we also stocked the shelves, we dusted them and when we got a little older we would make change."[56] They also depended on the trustworthiness of their customers. With such practices and relationships, Chinese grocers flourished. Tang recalled customers buying their groceries: her mother would mark the amounts they owed in the *cartera* (payment notebook) and return the *cartera* to the customer. As Tang remembered, on payday everyone would return to the store to settle their accounts. "That was really trust!" she reminisced fondly.[57]

Gradually many proprietors expanded their businesses by hiring nonfamily labor and purchasing trucks with an icebox in the cab to ensure fresh and cool produce. As in the rest of Tucson, the affluence of Chinese and Mexicans were closely interconnected. This would take on particular poignancy as the fortunes of one group rose and the other fell. The Don family transported groceries to, among many other places, outlying Marana, where Mexican migrant workers labored in cotton fields. Tang recalled the routine of trucking produce and food to the farmworkers with her father at dawn's break: "We'd get there, it'd be cold, and . . . these workers would evidently jump out of their bed, already clothed—I think they wore their clothes, you know—so it must have been real cold. . . . And I recall vividly how sometimes they wouldn't be able to pay and they'd say, 'Oh, Chopo . . .' because my dad wasn't very tall . . . they'd say 'no te puedemos pagar,' or 'no tenemos dinero esta semana' ['We cannot pay you; we don't have money this week']." Tang recalled the compassion of her father toward migrant farmers: "My dad would say, 'Oh, take some groceries anyway,' and he'd give them groceries because they had children. And my dad, he probably would starve us to death [laughs] before he'd allow anybody else, any customer's children, to starve."[58]

Mexican migrant families hung between the uncertainties of subsistence and abject poverty, and Chinese grocers and merchants at times absorbed

unpaid debts left by these families. Regardless, Chinese and Mexican families both large and small faced economic hardships from their position in
the labor market—as migrant farmers, small-scale merchants, or consumers. Seasonal demands for labor to pick cotton (or "white gold"), wheat,
barley, or alfalfa prompted the legal migration of more than 72,000 Mexicans into the American Southwest between 1917 and 1922. In the same
period, labor contractors provided Arizona growers with about thirty
thousand Mexican workers to work the cotton fields. The poverty of the
farmworkers in Marana, recognized by grocer Don Wah and his daughter Esther, underscored that a common wage of an entire migrant family
was less than eighteen dollars a week. And often, according to anthropologist Thomas E. Sheridan, growers withheld half of the workers' wages to
defray the cost of transportation, or took it as repayment of debt incurred
in company stores.[59] Knowing that the migrant farmers had little money,
Wah nonetheless continued to truck groceries into Marana, never com-
plaining about unpaid debts. Other Chinese grocers and merchants in
Tucson also continued to serve Mexican migrant farmers in the nearby
agricultural areas, as well as other working-class *hispanos* who lived in the
neighborhood.

With its occupationally and ethnically diverse population of business
proprietors, farmworkers, sales clerks, and vendors, El Barrio expanded
south and west of downtown even as commercial and cultural activities
between Chinese and Mexican residents continued to thrive on and near
South Meyer Street.[60] "On Meyer Street there was a Chinese store carrying
Oriental food staples, next door was the White House department store,
Kaufman's, Tito Flores' drug store, [and] a pool hall owned by a Japanese
family, the Oyamas," recalled Tang. "Within the complex were cubicles
for bachelors. At the west end facing Main Street was the community club
house, Kuo Ming Tang, with a gold ornate carved temple for worship."[61]
Next to Mexican merchants offering staple items, Chinese venders also
sold rice, beans, tea, and silks. El Cortez Market at the center of El Barrio was the home of a Chinese-Mexican deli.[62] It would be a matter of
only a few years before first-generation Chinese Americans began learning
Spanish and cultivating friendships with neighboring Mexicans. According
to one account, most first-generation Chinese Americans learned to speak
Spanish quite young, as workers in the family store. "I learned to speak
Spanish at a very young age, because of the business relations we had. The
stores were in the . . . Mexican-American neighborhood and for the most
part those of my generation and then of the generation ahead of me allied
themselves mostly with the Mexicans-Americans."[63]

Chinese and Mexican children were treated similarly in the public
schools, especially in the primary grades. Given their proficiency in Span-

ish and Chinese, respectively, Mexican and Chinese children were often assumed to have no fluency in the English language. Although Chinese and Mexican children spoke English routinely to their parents, schoolteachers often placed their young pupils in classes aimed at helping them to acquire English. Tang recalled that during the first grade at Mansfeld Elementary School (now called Safford), she was placed into 1-C, a class reserved for children who had little command of the English language. "I think most of the Mexican children were put in 1-C too . . . but they never tested me . . . but by golly, the worst thing was that I had an ugly little old shriveled up old lady for 1-C, and I cried and I wept." Tang remembered that in the first grade, she "didn't want to go to school." Soon the Mansfeld schoolteachers realized the error of their ways and placed the youngster in 1-A. To the first-grader, her new teacher, Miss Penney, was "an angel," a very good teacher among some teachers who were "awfully bad."[64] Unaware that Chinese was not actually the primary language spoken by Tang and some of her school-age peers, teachers often made assumptions about their ability to learn English and thus excel academically.[65] Mexican children, in Tang's estimation, had little recourse to challenge inadequate instruction.

Although Chinese and Mexicans shared similar educational experiences, the stability of homelife afforded Chinese children an advantage that Mexican migrant children did not enjoy. By the mid-1930s, Tucson's Chinese population of approximately five hundred reflected a more even gender balance, and the children of these families attended public schools as a matter of course, with most matriculating in elementary school. Ten attended junior high and fourteen went to senior high. Nine Chinese from Tucson were enrolled at the University of Arizona; two of these were graduate students. Among the seven undergraduates, two majored in mining engineering and five studied letters, arts, and sciences.

Public education, however, did not engender a strident assimilationist perspective. Several University of Arizona alumni made use of their degrees to establish professional success in China. Tin P. Kwok, for example, received a master's degree and a juris doctorate from Columbia University. He practiced law in Canton, China. Yu Hsueh Ting earned a bachelor's degree and a master's degree at the University of Arizona and went to work for the Ministry of Finance in Nanking. Maude Don, the first American-born Chinese at the University of Arizona to earn the prestigious Marian L. Heard Scholarship, pursued a master's degree in business and administration. Her master's thesis, interestingly, focused on the history of the Chinese in Arizona. May Nelda Don, who bore no relation to Maude Don, received her bachelor's degree in education and pursued a master's degree in the same discipline.[66]

Education not only provided an opportunity for intellectual development but, more important, was also a vehicle that transmitted the qualities of being both Chinese and American (see Figure 5.3). But American-born Chinese in Tucson were particular about which attributes of each culture they would esteem. George Lim, writing for the *Arizona Citizen* in 1935, captured the essence of first-generation Chinese Tucson identity by lauding the "inherent thrift and industry of the Chinese race and the go-gettiveness of the American-born Chinese." Lim and others of his generation assimilated and bore the material markers of Americanism. "You would be surprised to know the number of luxurious automobiles owned by the various Chinese in this city, and other luxuries of life which we now possess." Lim saw endless horizons of opportunities, asserting that the world, figuratively, "[was] their apple."[67]

Lim and other first-generation Chinese in Tucson certainly enjoyed the fruits of their own and their predecessors' efforts. Their tone was somewhat congratulatory, and their chosen narrative for the most part cast them in direct opposition to immigrant Chinese (described in the Chinese section of the eleventh annual rodeo edition of *the Arizona Citizen* as "uneducated; their culture was entirely Chinese"). They also distanced themselves from newly arriving Chinese and Mexican immigrants, who occupied jobs at the bottom rung of the economic ladder. By contrast, they saw themselves as the exemplars of commerce and ingenuity. When the grocery stores of their parents were turned over to the "sons and daughters . . . great changes began to come about. . . . The new Chinese grocery in those cases is a Phoenix standing triumphantly in its own ashes, as genuine and graphic a rebirth as may be found anywhere."[68]

Educational success, then, was a critical element of first-generation Tucson Chinese life. Even as Chinese assumed their role as university-educated individuals in their community, they remained tied to Chinese culture and traditions as part of an American identity. English proficiency was an

---

FIGURE 5.3 (OPPOSITE) School Board of the Chinese School. Throughout the 1920s and 1930s, Chinese school classes were held in both the original and the 1931 church buildings, and later in the Chinese Chamber of Commerce building. The first Chinese school in Tucson was established in 1900 by W. L. Black at the corner of Mesilla and Meyer Streets. Today the Chinese school operates from the Tucson Chinese Community Center. Front row, left to right: Gin King Wong, Soleng Tom, Mr. Gee, Frank Wong, unidentified man, Paul Don, unidentified girl, unidentified woman; back row, left to right: Joe Tang, Mr. Low, Lim Shiu, unidentified man, Mr. Lim Yuen, George Lee. Courtesy of the Arizona Historical Society. Photo no. 59749. http://www.arizonahistoricalsociety.org

imperative feature of academic success in the American school system, yet the parents of the immigrant generation often lamented that their children were losing the use of the Chinese language. When the Chinese Evangelical Church—a nondenominational institution—was established in Tucson in 1926 by Minister Frank Wong and his wife, Pauline, one of its main objectives was to offer language classes, in the hope that the "Chinese children educated here in the Christian faith and the Chinese language would wish to go back to China and do something for the country"[69] (see Figure 5.4). Harry Gin recalled that children routinely attended classes at night, beginning at 6:00 PM and ending at 8:00 PM. Because of the many demands of school and family responsibilities, many first-generation Chinese Americans bemoaned their "regimen of American school, school activities, Chinese school, working at the family store, and then doing homework before going to bed."[70] If the routine of these activities was not enough, wedding banquets, red egg ceremonies marking the one-month birthday of infants, and New Year's celebrations infused first-generation Chinese American Tucsonans with the culture of their parents.

With each generation of Tucson Chinese, close-knit relations—whether through *guanxi* practice or through the reliance on family labor—marked out a clear sense of place and identity, even though exclusion laws shadowed their daily lives. Changes in kith and kin, like those adopted by Li Weikun and Don Wah's family, demonstrated the flexibility of close relations and their importance in daily life. Successful transition also involved *guanxi* practices when, in the mid-1920s, San Francisco Chinese began to make Tucson their new home in increasing numbers.

## Transnational Ties and Guanxi

Bonds of kinship, *guanxi*, and friendship reunited Tucson resident Ji Xianxing with his youngest son, Zhenran, in the Old Pueblo, and these ties sustained Ji Xianxing through a personal crisis that would otherwise have left him destitute. Preparations had long been in the making to rejoin Ji Xianxing with his youngest son. Before arriving in the Old Pueblo in 1910, the fifty-one-year-old Ji Xianxing had resided in San Francisco for fifteen years in the company of his eldest son, Ban, and members of his

---

FIGURE 5.4 (OPPOSITE) Chinese Evangelical Church, Established 1926. After raising $6,000 for a new building, the Chinese Evangelical Church was reopened on Christmas day, 1931. Courtesy of the Arizona Historical Society. Photo no. 59747. http://www.arizonahistoricalsociety.org

hometown, Le Chong village in Guangdong, China. There, as later in Tucson, he had kept in step with a father's role; for example, he made and sustained a network of support that would aid in the landing of his sons in the United States and their return trips to China. When times were flush, Ji Xianxing sent money to his wife and his mother, but more often the Tucson resident received financial support from his middle son, Binglun. These transnational networks not only sustained Ji Xianxing during financially trying times, they also sustained familial bonds across the Pacific Ocean.[71]

Binglun, the brother between Ban (who died in China in 1920) and Zhenran, was Ji Xianxing's most intrepid son. Over the span of ten years, Binglun traveled from San Francisco to Le Chong village four times to visit his family.[72] Long stays in China garnered Binglun a wife and four sons, and secured his place as the most important son in his family, despite being a middle child. At his late-1926 homecoming to China, Binglun greeted his family with gifts and money, sharing American-made cookies with his nephews. Although his sojourn home was a festive affair, the middle son had returned to China with the purpose of escorting his younger brother Zhenran to the United States. From Le Chong village the brothers traveled to Hong Kong, where they stayed for a few months in Gongyi Yuan, a hostel for sojourners awaiting their transportation to the United States. There, in April of 1927, the brothers embarked on a ship en route to San Francisco, with the assurance that their father, although he was living in Tucson, had drawn on his connections in the California port city to make certain that his sons landed safely. Not only was information filtered thorough Ji Xianxing's San Francisco network, but money sent by the Tucson resident was also fanned out to his sons and to those aiding in their landing.[73] Money was certainly significant, but it was not the only factor at play. A two-to-three-month detention was commonplace for those Chinese who landed in San Francisco seeking legal entry into the United States. The dissemination of information between Ji Xianxing, his middle son in San Francisco, and his youngest son in the barracks at Angel Island was equally critical. Without the constant flow of accurate information, Ji Xianxing believed, his youngest son stood to face harsh scrutiny when he was confronted with pointed questioning by Angel Island immigration inspectors.

Ji Xianxing's concern was not unfounded. He knew well enough that the reception of Chinese migrants was often unpredictable, and at times ended in death. His friend and former neighbor in Le Chong village, Ji Guo, had lost both of his sons, Zhen Da and Zhen Ji, during their attempt to enter the United States. The two had sojourned to San Francisco, apparently without the assistance of Le Chong villagers or *guanxi* connections in the United States. Unfortunately, when they landed in 1910, Zhen Da and Zhen Ji found themselves detained at Angel Island. Zhen Ji died in a wooden barrack shortly after landing, and five years later Zhen Da died on the streets of San Francisco. To avoid the misfortunes of his friend Ji Guo, Ji Xianxing drew on his relations with fictive kin Lunwei, Qianxin, and Liangxiu, all of whom lived in San Francisco. His *guanxi* ties to "Uncles" Lunwei and Qianxin and "Brother" Liangxiu involved, among other things, the safe harboring of monies for Ji Xianxing's sons once they landed in San Francisco. Relations with fictive kin also afforded Ji Xianxing contingency plans if his sons by chance could not land at Angel Island. Brother Liangxiu, who was sent to greet the sons in the absence of their father, was supposed to supply the brothers with enough money to enter the United States in another manner.[74]

In advance of their travel, Ji Xianxing had sent his middle son a series of letters to share with his younger brother. The last of these was so filled with copious details that he closed by noting, "I have to stop writing because the paper is running out."[75] Ji Xianxing's letters contained lengthy narratives about various experiences and objects, such as the dimensions of the god shrines in both their home and their village, the distances between neighboring villages and the number of houses therein, and the materials used to build local roads.[76] Constant communication and absolute attention to even the most seemingly minor details carried the weight of entry or exclusion. The youngest son's admission was certainly less worrisome from a legal standpoint as he came from a family with a well-established history of legal entry and lawful residency in the United States. His burden, nonetheless, was great. The task of entry charged Zhenran with memorizing nearly twenty years of family comings and goings between the United States and China. In interviews with U.S. immigration officials he was held accountable for the details about each time any member of the family had left the United States. Purpose of travel, port of entry information, and length of stay were among the routine questions asked by immigration officials. Queries often went beyond the prescribed domain and crossed a line into the personal. Answers about gifts and their intended recipients, and plans for procreation during a visit home were also included in the scope of officials' questions. In addition to the sheer amount of information that Zhenran was responsible for understanding, Ji Xianxing's youngest son was also expected to know whose story was whose. Zhenran had to match the travel particulars of his father, his eldest brother, and his second-eldest brother to their sojourns, because they occurred independently from one another. To make matters even more complicated, Zhenran also needed to provide all of this information—and to answer any trick questions that immigration officials might also pose—without appearing to have been coached.

Ji Xianxing's missives, then, were hardly exercises in minutiae. To pre-
pare his youngest son for the arduous trial awaiting him and his midddle
son for the grueling tutelage he would need to provide, Ji Xianxing first
described in exacting detail the god shrines that sat within his home in
China, and the god shrine that stood at the center of Le Chong village. The
house god shrine, which sat in the back living room, was inscribed with
golden words in calligraphy style etched on a green background. The name
of every ancestor was recorded on the shrine in parallel order.[77] Moreover,
the home god shrine had approximately the same dimensions as the village god shrine. Near the village shrine stood a wooden security shed in
which the night watchman used to store his personal belongings and the
materials needed to clean and maintain the shrine. If he was asked about
the condition and style of the security shed, Zhenran was to say that it
was modern in design because it had been renovated during Republican-
era China. Ji Xianxing recalled having been asked to sketch the shrine
itself during his initial immigration interview.[78] At that moment, the Le
Chong village resident had apparently reached the end of his patience. "I
am not able to draw," he had replied stubbornly. "I never learned how to
draw. I was never involved with a drawing job, and I do not know how to
start drawing."[79] Although Ji Xianxing had been obdurate during his own
immigration interview, he encouraged his sons to adopt a far more accommodating attitude about such details. "You should draw these pictures,
Binglun," Ji Xianxing exhorted his son, "and send them to me as soon as
possible, because I will check it for you."[80]

Ji Xianxing then turned to the conditions of various roads in and around
his village. He could certainly have anticipated this line of inquiry. It was
an almost customary domain of interrogation for immigration inspectors.
Chinese wishing to land successfully were routinely asked to describe their
village of origin, including its layout, its population, and the styles of its
roads and houses. This system of intense inquiry, based on unearthing the
minutest elements of one's life, served as a particular method of interrogation. Because Ji Xianxing had not been born a U.S. citizen, immigration
authorities had not pressed their inquiries into the realm of the birth order
of his sons or the activity of his children, but their questioning had reached
into the configuration of daily life in Le Chong village.

Ji Xianxing thus knew that this realm of information would need to be
made particularly explicit. In a barrage of staccato-like questions during
his own immigration interview, Ji Xianxing's interrogators had pressed
him into a recitation about the quality of roads in and near Le Chong
village. Asked if they were made of stone or soil, he had replied that
although there were highways of both types, most were made of stone.
The roads near the mountain, by contrast, were made of soil. He elabo-

rated that the road to Le Chong village was made of both mud and stone, but the road to the right of the village had been laid over with stone. Ji Xianxing had gone on to recall a stone road leading directly to the neighboring village of Xinchang. This remembrance in turn led to a discussion of the proximity and population of neighboring villages. Ji Xianxing had been asked how many villages were located near Xinchang, a town approximately two-thirds of a mile from Le Chong. Unsure of exactly how many villages neighbored Xinchang, he could only reply that "there are many villages . . . but I cannot recall exactly the names of the villages." Upon reflection, however, Ji Xianxing was able to summon that the village nearest to Xinchang had been Shanglin, a town of approximately 120 houses. When immigration officials, perhaps taken aback at the specificity of Ji Xianxing's testimony about Shanglin, had pressed him about why he was able to remember such a detail about that village in particular, Ji Xianxing had recollected that Shanglin had been built on a road near the top of a mountain.[81]

As it turned out, the safe and successful landing of Zhenran did not require extraordinary actions by Ji Xianxing or his fictive kin. Zhenran not only landed safely and successfully, but he was also confident that any financial or personal hardship he would encounter could be weathered by his father and his kin network.

*Guanxi* relationships would prove to be equally malleable and responsive to Ji Xianxing's own crisis. In July of 1928, misfortune struck the Le Chong native. The house he shared in Tucson with his friends Shengzhao and Lisheng caught fire, and in his attempt to grab his passport and money, Ji Xianxing's neck and right arm were severely burned. He missed work at the Richelieu Café for more than a month, yet Ji Xianxing's fictive kin not only worked his restaurant shifts but also cared for him on a daily basis. He wrote in a letter to Binglun, "I felt so lucky. I did not die in the fire."[82] His letter went on to discuss the ongoing severity of his injury, saying, "About my burn wound, I cannot tell you how much pain I was in two weeks ago when the weather was very hot every day. I hope that the weather becomes cooler so that people in Tucson can feel a bit more comfortable. . . . I went to Garden Lan last Monday morning, and the next day, I felt better."[83] Several times Ji Xianxing implored his son not to worry, because others suffered much worse.

If circumstances were trying for Ji Xianxing, they paled in comparison to the hardships of the Liangbans. For two and a half months, misfortune shadowed this husband and wife. After two weeks of unemployment and financial setback, they were forced to live a transient life, rooming for two months at the home of Yashou, a mutual friend, and two weeks somewhere else. While sleeping in their most recent place of refuge, the couple was awakened at midnight and apprehended by "foreign officials." Ji Xianxing was silent about the reason for the couple's arrest, but he conveyed to Binglun that two kinsmen stood bail, ending the Liangban couple's ordeal in prison.[84] Ji Xianxing was acutely aware of his good fortune and his friends, and the safety net afforded by both.

Ji Xianxing's letters in the midst of this crisis make clear the extent to which he relied on his fictive kin for support. Despite Ji Xianxing's injuries and financial setback, *guanxi* relationships sustained him during this ordeal. He suffered other types of consequences because of his injury. Although *guanxi* relationships were critical in his recovery, Ji Xianxing's ailing status also shifted much of the family's financial burden onto Binglun. In a letter to his middle son, Ji Xianxing revealed that although his health had improved, his financial situation was quite dire: "I received [your] remittance [of] $100. It was nice of Shengzhao to put that money toward our living expenses." For the time being, Binglun's father may have been relieved and even grateful for his son's generosity, but Ji Xianxing knew that caring for his injury would be long-term and would require a constant commitment of financial support from his son. Ji Xianxing warned Binglun, "You better have some more money in hand, because . . . my situation is truly out of control like a huge mountain."[85]

Binglun's subsequent financial help, although meager, engendered the gratitude of his father, but the responsibility of daily care fell on Ji Xianxing's housemates, Shengzhao and Lisheng. While Shengzhao cared for the household, Lisheng provided financial support, and at times even paid Ji Xianxing's medical expenses. Doctor visits, which tallied to more than $300, filled Ji Xianxing with angst, but the timely gifts of money, tea, and a much-desired Chinese-English dictionary seemed to ease the worried Tucsonan.[86] In considering the connections between the three men—Ji Xianxing, Lisheng, and Shengzhao—what emerged was a sense of commitment and interdependence that extended beyond what might be considered the purview of common friendship or amity. Ji Xianxing's housemates were deeply and consistently proactive in anticipating and responding to his needs. When Binglun remitted money to his father, Shengzhao applied it to the household expenses, reflecting the trust and license given over to him.

Even though the household of Ji Xianxing consisted exclusively of men, gender roles gave order to the operation of the home. By the 1920s, in Tucson Chinese men outnumbered Chinese women by approximately 3 to 1.[87] Many Chinese men had wives who had remained in China; others were bachelors whose marriage prospects were dim given the gender ratio in the Chinese community. Chinese men created meaningful emotional attachments with their housemates. Households such as that created by

Ji Xianxing, Lisheng, and Shengzhao had roles like any other home. One person was primarily in charge of cooking and cleaning; another might be principally responsible for financial matters; but it was probable that all men participated in both activities.

The deep attachment and devotion among Ji Xianxing, Lisheng, and Shengzhao underscored the affective dimension of *guanxi*, which reached well beyond utilitarianism. Although Ji Xianxing's earlier connections with San Francisco fictive kin were critical in facilitating the successful migration of his sons, it was *guanxi* combined with *ganqing* (affection) that illustrated the depth of fellowship among Tucson Chinese. Such relationships comprised not only affection but also obligation. Ji Xianxing's reliance on his son Binglun, illustrated how entrenched these bonds were, and the cost of abjuring them. His oldest son, Ban, returned to Le Chong village in June of 1910 after living in San Francisco for less than six months. In 1911 he returned to San Francisco and made the city his home until 1921. At that time, and for reasons unknown, Ban returned permanently to China. Letters never illuminated the source of the estrangement. Ji Xianxing's correspondence made clear that once Ban left the United States, the father-son bond was severed and there could be no reparation. Writing to Binglun, Ji Xianxing lamented, "We haven't corresponded with one another or exchanged money since then. Yes, it is true."[88] Whatever happened between the father and his oldest son, Ban's ten-year sojourn in San Francisco after his initial return to China apparently did nothing to bridge the estrangement. With this rupture, Binglun assumed the primary financial responsibility for his family's well-being, an obligation ordinarily assigned to the eldest son. This responsibility was not negotiated or offered; it was assumed on the part of both father and son. Those of Ji Xianxing's letters that addressed pragmatic matters such as money or Zhenran's preparation for his immigration interview were invariably sent to Binglun, who was now presumed to be the oldest son.

Just as Ji Xianxing's connections with his fictive kin had facilitated his sons' successful migration to San Francisco, the combination of *guanxi* and *ganqing* that eased the burden of his injury illustrated the depth of fellowship among Tucson's Chinese. Kin and kith relations between Chinese and Mexicans were equally important in this period of hardening immigration restrictionism. These linkages would open up myriad opportunities for *fronterizos* to engage in economic activities and social exchanges that were otherwise prohibited by the law or by custom. The connections sustained by Don Wah, Li Weikun, and Ji Xianxing anchored first-generation and immigrant Chinese to Tucson while preserving ties to China. Tucson Chinese such as Don Wah, moreover, continued neighborly ties to Mexicans in El Barrio through everyday activities, even as Wah and his wife fostered linkages abroad. In Tucson, daily interaction and transactions between truck farmers, grocers, and merchants and their diverse clientele nurtured friendship and kinship—relations engendered because of social integration, not isolation. These strong ties, nourished for decades in Tucson despite the immigration restrictionism that weighed heavily on Chinese American communities, were noticeably and ominously absent just across the border. Sonoran Chinese would find no such safety net in post-revolutionary Mexico.

# 6 Por la Patria y por la Raza
## (For the Fatherland and for the Race)

SINOPHOBIA AND THE RISE OF

POSTREVOLUTIONARY MEXICAN NATIONALISM

Hip Lee and Lung Yink Han were not alone in objecting to the creation of *barrios chinos* (Chinese neighborhoods), but they served as powerful examples of Chinese resistance. The decree, known as Law 27, gave Sonoran municipal officials the authority to relocate Chinese, their families, and their businesses into designated areas throughout the state beginning in late December 1923.[1] No doubt Law 27 conveyed the hatred of many Sonorans for their Chinese neighbors. To counter the segregation decree, members of the Chinese community flooded local courts with petitions objecting to Law 27. Amid the barrage, Lee and Han's appeal stood out. Their words, sharp and shrewd, drew out the capriciousness of the barrioization decree. They presented themselves not as isolated individuals but as Mexicans who were entitled to the civil rights guaranteed to all. These two Nogales residents, by invoking Mexican constitutional tradition, outlined the breadth of national belonging, as embedded not only in political rights but also in the "full enjoyment of social and private rights." After leveling further charges and accusing state authorities of devising a law so cruel it defied common notions of human decency, Lee and Han affirmed simply and directly that no political body could constrain individual liberties, no matter what the rationale.[2]

Without question, Lee and Han and the other petitioners were standing on firm ground. In an unrelenting effort to crush Sonoran Chinese, local lawmakers violated constitutional guarantees when the barrioization decree was created. With the assistance of a Nogales-based attorney, Arsenio Espinoza, who drafted appeals on behalf of Chinese clients, Lee and Han also made it clear that the motivation behind Law 27 was bigotry against the Chinese and their families. Lee and Han's appeals struck a nerve, and in 1925, shortly after Chinese petitioners drew out their legal arguments against barrioization, Sonorans ended all courtroom pursuits of mandatory relocation. But when lawmakers passed the barrioization decree in late 1923, most lawmakers believed it was within their legal bounds to do so. A sizable cadre of local officials hinged the legality of Law 27 on Article 40 of the Mexican Constitution, which recognized that "states are free and sovereign in all internal matters, and on that basis, can legislate on any subject."[3] Such understanding of legislative jurisdiction was in keeping with a long-standing governing tradition in Sonora that favored localism over federal powers. The barrioization decree represented this governance preference, as did other anti-Chinese labor, sanitation, and marriage legislation. Although these prohibitive laws went unenforced for a while, the tension between local and federal control did bring into sharp relief the manner in which *antichinistas* pursued discourses of racial exclusion and, conversely, how Sonoran Chinese reasserted claims of civic inclusion over the course of the next decade.

It was clear from the nature of anti-Chinese legislation that the struggle over civic belonging in postrevolutionary Sonora would be fought on both public and private grounds. Grocery stores, bedrooms, and the streets transformed into front lines of incendiary Sinophobia and violence, and in every instance Chinese compelled officials at the local, state, and national levels to guarantee political protections and ensure personal freedoms. Upholding constitutional values in order to shield Sonoran Chinese from attack widened the political divide between ordinary Sonorans and Presidents Álvaro Obregón and Plutarco Elías Calles, both natives of the state. Although Obregón and Calles loathed the Chinese, their overarching concerns for the economic future of Mexico, its international reputation, and its constitutional traditions gave currency to the claims of Chinese that they were rightful Mexicans, even though they were not *mestizos*. This was particularly the case with Calles, who had safeguarded the constitutional rights of Sonoran Chinese even as he undid Mexico's rather liberal immigration laws.

If the assertion of political rights reinforced a sense of civic belonging among Sonoran Chinese and created a small opening for debating alternative notions of *mestizaje* in the early 1920s, then by 1931 that opportunity had vanished.[4] Behind these struggles lay a deep, consuming drive on the part of Mexicans to fulfill their understanding of the revolution's racial agenda, which by then had attached itself to the national eugenics and social hygiene movements. By the mid-1920s, the most powerful anti-Chinese crusade since the campaign of the late 1910s convinced the majority of Mexicans that avoiding "the injection of sickly yellow blood . . . into [their] families" was a necessary element of postrevolutionary Sonoran society.[5] José Ángel Espinoza, one of the most notorious *antichinistas* of the postrevolutionary era, stated the gravity of what was at stake: "This is a life or death situation. If we continue with little interest toward the depressing action of foreigners, our race will be lost quickly and this catastrophe will be our own responsibility."[6] The anti-Chinese movement convinced others of its purpose, derided those Sonorans who did not agree, and ensured that anti-Chinese codes would be enforced. In speeches and writings on barrioization, public health, and Chinese-Mexican marriage, *antichinistas* cast Chinese as repugnant and racially unfit for the new nation. The Chinese became the prevailing object of hatred, a common foe, one that was formidable, yet like many ethnic minorities, profoundly vulnerable to the vicious politics of racism and nationalism. In the end, Sonoran Chinese learned that the basis of the postrevolutionary project was Sinophobia and not the Constitution.

## Race, Rights, and the First Tong War

More than two years before Lee and Han contested the barrioization law in the Nogales municipal court, a string of violent skirmishes had broken out between Mexico's rival tongs, or gangs.[7] The street warfare was sporadic but protracted, and lasted for more than three months. Few Chinese escaped the weighty costs of the melee, which brought about both immediate and long-term consequences. Initially the street violence among tongs looked liked direct attacks on the governing regime, and some Sonorans feared an eruption of violence similar to that experienced during the Revolution. When it turned out to be Chinese-on-Chinese violence, Sonorans then worried that children playing on the street would get caught up in the crossfire. No such incidents occurred, but the fears did feed into portrayals of Chinese as fantastically barbaric and violent. What endured from the first tong war, however, was far more unsettling for Sonoran Chinese: it ignited a new round of prohibitive anti-Chinese codes.

Until the 1920s, the Sociedad Masónica Chee Kung Tong (CKT) and the Kuomintang Partido Nacionalista China de la República Mexicana (KMT) in Sonora were rival tongs, but not bitter ones. They had competed for a few years over a sparse pool of potential members and for control of underground gambling houses, prostitution rings, and opium houses, as well as legitimate commercial projects. By the spring of 1922, however, rivalries had hardened. The main source of tension lay in the controversy over China's new leadership under Sun Yat-sen, the founder of the Nationalist Party, which became the Kuomintang in 1919.[8] Sun's KMT was ardently opposed by the Sonora CKT, which had shifted its support to the Manchu emperor.[9] The tongs clashed after the UFC decided to contribute funds to Sun's nationalist cause despite objections from CKT members.[10] Fighting peaked before Sonoran municipal authorities could quell the melee, and by then more than twenty-five Chinese lay dead.[11]

In June 1922 an informal truce set in and street fighting among the rival factions ceased. Peace, however, was short-lived, giving way to other types of disorder that would plague Sonora over the next few years. Without any warning or legal basis, local policemen arrested tong members suspected of participating in the internecine fighting. All were imprisoned in the state penitentiary in Hermosillo and awaited deportation, without courtroom trial. In the aftermath of this first tong war, the Chinese were obliged to wage political battles in Sonora courtrooms. One consequence of these courtroom battles was that Chinese merchants, upon whom local residents depended for produce and dry goods, closed their stores. Both attention and money had to be diverted to their legal struggles.

CKT members bore the brunt of incarceration and legal harassment, because they opposed and subverted the KMT and Sun's Republican government, which Mexico recognized as the legitimate governing body of China. Of the 250 Chinese prisoners held in the Hermosillo penitentiary, 10 percent were KMT members and 60 to 70 percent were CKT members.[12] Protesters, labor unions, and town council members throughout Sonora called for the expulsion of the *extranjeros perniciosos* (pernicious foreigners). Not only did these appeals remain in step with the sentiments of *antichinistas* and Sonoran governor Francisco Elías, but they also caught the attention of a known critic of the Chinese, Mexican president Álvaro Obregón.[13]

Obregón, also a former governor of the state, called on Article 33 of the Mexican Constitution, which conveniently afforded the president power to expel any foreigner deemed harmful to the nation (see Figure 6.1).[14] Without the burden of due process, Obregón had the authority to deal swiftly with the tong prisoners, and no doubt he would have done so but for the objections of Chinese, the most vigorous coming from the CKT and its working class constituency. Obregón was certainly not sympathetic to the Chinese, but as president he wanted to maintain at least a semblance of constitutional adherence for the sake of international appearances.

Juan Lin Fu, the interim president of the CKT, expressed his association's complaints against the governor of Sonora to President Obregón and outlined the dubious circumstances in which the prisoners were held. "Without making known the motive for apprehension or permitting them a defense," Fu asserted, "Governor Elías did not extend rights [to imprisoned Chinese] that even the most hardened criminals obtain."[15] In his reply to Fu, Obregón not only condemned the assassination of rival tong members as deplorable and against the morality and laws of Mexico, but also revealed to Fu his plans to deport all Chinese currently imprisoned in Hermosillo.[16] Immediately, Fu and other prominent members of the Chinese community decried Obregón's decision as politically impetuous and criticized the president for not conducting a thorough investigation to determine exact culpability. Fu continued to press for mediation and a different result while Mexican allies lobbied for the release of prisoners whom they believed were falsely charged. By aligning with Elías, Obregón not only legitimized *antichinistas'* worst assumptions about tong members, but also unwittingly strengthened the resolve of Sonoran Chinese to continue fighting for their rights.

Fu's final appeal to President Obregón was less cordial but persuasive, if no less underhanded. Fu alerted Obregón of the status of seventeen members of the rival KMT who remained free and without charges, even though "reliable facts" indicated that they were among the "principal intellectual leaders" of the bloody tong war. Fu assured Obregón of his organization's willingness to accept any consequence of guilt, but in almost the same breath Fu assigned blame to his rivals.[17]

By this time, others joined the support of Fu's protests. Wealthy merchant Juan Lung Tain, CKT members Lin Mo Poing and Alfonso Hoy, and the newly elected representative of Sonoran and Sinaloan Chinese to the president, Guadalupe Kung, pressed Obregón for a more moderate solution. Kung requested a federal investigation of the tong crisis and a temporary stay of Obregón's deportation order.[18] Although passionately waged, the appeals of Tain, Lin, Hoy, Kung, and Fu fell on deaf ears as far as Obregón was concerned, but they did manage to persuade Obregón's politically astute secretary of the interior, Plutarco Elías Calles, to consider a more restrained course of action, one consistent with ensuring the political rights of Sonoran Chinese. Calles, also former governor of the state and a future successor to Obregón as president, granted Kung's request for an official investigation. Under Calles's watch, Interior Ministers Antonio Pozzi and Martín F. Bárcenas traveled to Sonora in August to determine the origins of the internecine conflict. They concluded that the KMT, not the CKT, bore responsibility for causing the outbreak of tong violence. Pozzi and Bárcenas not only confirmed by their investigation the account of events originally conveyed to Obregón by Chinese officials and CKT witnesses at the outset of tong violence, but they also determined that most of the Chinese imprisoned in Hermosillo did not participate in the conflict.[19] By December the crisis had broken, ending the imprisonment of most of the Sonoran Chinese. As it turned out, the only decree Obregón could order was one to deport forty-three tong members, the majority of whom were from the KMT.[20]

What came, then, of the first tong war was that the Chinese began to figure out how to counter *mestizaje* on their own terms, which often meant harnessing political and economic resources to challenge claims that they were not rightful Mexicans.

The first tong war also exposed many contradictions, and the first of these lay squarely with local consumers. Before the tong war, Sonorans had been accustomed to patronizing well-stocked Chinese-owned grocery stores and merchandise shops. As the fallout from the street violence ensued, Chinese businessmen were drawn away from attending to their stores, and Sonorans were consequently faced with widespread scarcities of produce and wares, and higher costs for staple goods. In Nogales, tempers flared between federal troops guarding Chinese-owned groceries and angry Sonorans who threatened to bomb the stores if they remained closed.[21] Yet when Chinese entrepreneurs did return to their places of business—only after police authorities guaranteed their safety—*antichinistas* took action, casting store owners as embodying the "horror and the blood of the morbid traditions of the Orient."[22] They were accused of having strong tentacles in the trafficking of cocaine, opium, and prostitutes. President Obregón chimed in, adding that merchants were significantly "harmful to public health" and "weak, vicious, ugly, criminal, and germy."[23] Few Sonorans, however, outwardly recognized their reliance on Chinese-owned businesses, or the irony—if not outright hypocrisy—in railing against the insidious, treacherous Chinese as they unloaded their grocery-store stock. Magdalena's municipal president, Eduardo Arias, nonetheless did acknowledge that without Chinese merchants, local residents would have to go without vegetables, and city coffers would greatly suffer from the loss of tax revenue.[24]

In such an uncertain environment, one of the vital lessons taken from the illegal detainment and deportation of Sonoran Chinese was that Mexican citizenship through naturalization provided a shield of protection against the ferocity of attacks and the capriciousness of anti-Chinese politicians. The process was clear and simple enough. At least six months before he actually petitioned the federal government for naturalization, the aspiring citizen was to declare to his local *ayunatamiento* (town council) his intention to become a Mexican citizen and that he was willing to renounce his foreign nationality. To be eligible for citizenship, one had to have a trade or profession to support oneself, no criminal record, and proof of at least two years' residency in Mexico.[25] In the winter months following the tong war, more than 120 Chinese were naturalized, making up more than 63 percent of all foreigners granted citizenship that year. In 1923, 160 Chinese became citizens. When Nogales merchants Alfonso J. Ben and George On asserted, "We are Mexican citizens in full possession of our rights, and therefore, enjoy the full extent of all laws accorded to us just as they are enjoyed by other Mexicans," they did so to remind those in power of their full and legal rights.[26]

FIGURE 6.1  Anti-Chinese Protest Advocating Article 33. Source: Espinoza, *El Ejemplo de Sonora*, 145. Courtesy of the Arizona Historical Society/Tucson. http://www.arizonahistoricalsociety.org

Despite high rates of naturalization, the privileges of citizenship and the rhetoric of civic belonging fit imperfectly alongside the experiences of national membership (see Table 6.1). *Antichinistas* decried the naturalization of Chinese, and some, like José Ángel Espinoza, explicitly stated that "every naturalization certificate our government extends to a Chinese citizen is like a rattlesnake placed at the bosom of the motherland."[27] No

TABLE 6.1
*Naturalization of Chinese in Mexico: 1922–1932*

| Year | Naturalized Chinese | Other Naturalized Foreigners | Percent Chinese |
| --- | --- | --- | --- |
| 1922 | 122 | 197 | 63.0 |
| 1923 | 160 | 371 | 43.0 |
| 1924 | 98 | 205 | 48.0 |
| 1925 | 122 | 322 | 38.0 |
| 1926 | 23 | 95 | 24.0 |
| 1927 | 21 | 305 | 7.0 |
| 1928 | 13 | 323 | 4.0 |
| 1929 | 6 | 366 | 1.7 |
| 1930 | 11 | 540 | 2.0 |
| 1931 | 3 | 1,106 | 0.3 |
| 1932 | 6 | 1,278 | 0.5 |

Source: *Boletín Oficial*, Secretaría de Relaciones Exteriores, vols. 39–59, Mexico City.

one, however, argued that Chinese could not exercise rights as Mexican citizens, and Sonoran Chinese certainly did not act like or consider themselves to be outsiders. Many described themselves as "chinos de origen y mexicanos por naturalización" (Chinese by origin and Mexican by naturalization).[28] Even Chinese who chose not to naturalize believed they were entitled to make claims on those in power. Sonoran municipal officials and Mexican federal authorities knew this well. Whereas those at the national level somewhat reluctantly guaranteed political rights for Sonoran Chinese, those at the local level turned to a discourse of eugenics and direct political attack to assail marriage rights and impinge on business practices.

It was during the Calles administration and the subsequent six-year period known as the *Maximato* (1928–1934) that Sonorans found meaning in the postrevolutionary project and a solution to the so-called Chinese problem. After 1924, common ground emerged as an outlet for Sonorans' anxiety about the Chinese community and for national concerns over the racial makeup of Mexico. The rhetoric of degeneration and regeneration took hold and provided a shorthand for who belonged and who did not in postrevolutionary Mexico. Degeneration and regeneration and the dramatic racialized inversions the latter entailed was one of the most significant tropes of Mexican culture during the twentieth century, surfacing in images from film, theater, public art, and political satire. The discourse of degeneration portrayed subjects as racialized inferiors, better suited than *mestizos* to simple, repetitive work and life. It warned against the debilitation of the *mestizo* through improper miscegenation, just as much as it encouraged separation between racially incompatible groups. To a great degree, the rhetoric of degeneration referred directly to the debilitated nature of Chinese, whom Sonorans associated with bachelorhood, opium smoking, and tong violence, and in turn with perceptions of moral and physical depravity. Degeneration corresponded with its opposite, regeneration, to attach the *mestizo* firmly at the center of the new nation and the new order of modernization. Groups able to adapt to complex situations thrived, regenerated, and took on higher expressions of intellect and humanity.[29] The Chinese, this trope suggested, were hardly fit applicants for such progress. By the mid-1920s, the trope of degeneration and regeneration gave *antichinistas* a rhetorical device with which to distinguish themselves as worthy citizens and the Chinese as unsuitable and degraded, even despicable, members of the Mexican nation. The postrevolutionary mission, from the establishment of new political institutions to the configuration of new cultural projects, involved the *mestizo* as the architect of social renewal and social unity.

The discourse of degeneration and regeneration was not easily separated from postrevolutionary understandings of *mestizaje*, the blending of

Indian and Spanish peoples, and *indigenismo*, an approach invented by Mexican elites and scholars to managing the so-called "Indian problem."[30] Oaxacan educator and philosopher José Vasconcelos drew together the connections in his popularization of *la raza cósmica* (the cosmic race) as a mystical symbol of Hispanic civilization. Vasconcelos believed that *mestizaje* could homogenize Mexicans racially and hasten Mexico into a new age of universalism, unity, and modernization.[31] As a "fifth race," the Mexican *mestizo* was "the bridge to the future" and could take his or her proper place alongside four great contemporary races—the white, the red, the black, and the yellow.[32] The *mestizo* became the new regime's metaphor for national regeneration and, importantly, was in keeping with the goals of *indigenismo*—to educate, to homogenize, and to integrate Indians into Mexican society.[33] The nationalization of indigenous peoples was a critical project of the new Mexican state. Although similar projects had been undertaken prior to 1910, revolutionary *indigenistas* claimed a more enlightened approach than the Porfirian practices of expulsion or forced integration of Mexico's indigenous populations.[34]

Sonorans outwardly embraced the national agenda aimed at regenerating the race and furthering the Mexican revolutionary project by accepting that the nationalist prescriptions of *mestizaje* and *indigenismo* could homogenize Mexicans and unite Mexico racially. Sonorans, however, had their own established understandings of race and social unity and drew very clear distinctions between themselves as *blanco-criollos* (white Creoles) and indigenous peoples, whom they considered *indios bárbaros* (savage Indians) and the most significant barriers to progress. The deportation of Apaches in 1886 and Yaquis in 1908 from Sonora attested to the long-standing enmity that *blanco-criollos* held toward native peoples. The *blanco-criollo* favored Porfirian-inspired approaches over the assimilationist philosophy of postrevolutionary elites and scholars. Sonorans' own beliefs about race mixture were applied to the Chinese, who, like the Apaches and Yaquis before them, laid out what they believed were legal and rightful claims to civic belonging. Porfirian tactics died hard in Sonora.

The discourse of degeneration and regeneration penetrated almost every aspect of daily life, permitting *antichinistas* to begin constructing the architecture of virulent nationalism in which the expulsion of Chinese was the goal. To *antichinistas*, one evil dominated all others, for it threatened Sonorans and the nation directly: the marriages of Mexican women and Chinese men. Hostility toward Chinese-Mexican matrimony loomed large in newspapers, the constitutions of anti-Chinese committees, and the minutes of town-council meetings. In late December 1923, Sonora banned such nuptials by passing Law 31.[35] Although the status of existing Chinese-Mexican marriages went unchallenged, lawmakers authorized fines of $100 to $500 against individuals performing wedding ceremonies for Mexican-Chinese couples.

While lawmakers warned local judges and the clergy against performing Chinese-Mexican marriages, they also made the gender and racial framework of Mexican nationalism clear by identifying the law's only potential violators: "Mexican women and individuals of the Chinese race, even those obtaining Mexican naturalization."[36] Nothing in Law 31 addressed the status of marriages between Chinese women and Mexican men. This inconsistency went unnoticed, but suggested two scenarios: that the dearth of Chinese women posed only a remote possibility of their marriage to Mexican men, and that a Mexican man dared not betray the revolutionary racial code by marrying a Chinese woman. Within a political climate suffused with gendered and racialized prescriptions for appropriate partnerships, Law 31 placed degeneration squarely at the feet of Mexican women by imposing on them certain consequences for choosing Chinese men as marital partners. For Mexican women, marriages to Chinese continued to exclude them from Mexican citizenship; the 1886 Law of Alienage and Naturalization continued to govern women's nationality despite greater constitutional reforms in 1917.[37] *Antichinistas* clearly preferred to portray the root causes of degeneration as the marriage choices of Mexican women rather than the suitability of Chinese men. Scorning Mexican women gave *antichinistas* greater influence throughout Sonora, especially after the passage of Law 31, and they expressed no hesitation in using it to cast children of Mexican-Chinese couples as being equally as debilitated as their parents, and as a warning to others.

The obligation of a Mexican woman to forsake marriage to a Chinese man profoundly prescribed the racial boundaries of marriage and social belonging in postrevolutionary Sonora. To challenge *mestizaje* by marrying a Chinese man was to threaten the nation by injecting degeneracy and sexual impurity into the race. *El Nacionalista*, a well-known source of Chinese enmity in Cananea, helped inflame local imaginations about the actions of "traitorous elements" that assisted in the contamination of the race. With much intrigue, *El Nacionalista* reported that Apolonio and Clara Escalante sold their daughter, María, to Luis Chan for an undisclosed amount of money. Chan, a produce grower, lived with María, a minor, for more than a year as a married couple. Chan, depicted as "thin, sickly, malodorous, and showing the symptoms of tuberculosis," represented Sonorans' worst mental image of degeneration, and the fact that Apolonio and Clara Escalante colluded in their daughter's ruin deepened fears about the sexual motives of fantastically unhealthy Chinese men and the lengths to which some went to satisfy their greed.[38] In adopting the rhetoric of degeneration, the newspaper assured its mostly working-class readership in vivid language of the day that Chinese risked public ridicule, ostracism, and legal action for coveting, living with, or marrying Mexican women or girls.

The actions and rhetoric of *antichinistas* impressed Sonorans with the social decay of Chinese-Mexican marriages and the need for a ban. They were similarly struck by proposals for the forced relocation of Chinese businesses, organizations, and families to designated *barrios* throughout Sonora. Before the Chinese could muster up their resources to challenge Law 27, circulars disseminated throughout Sonora triumphantly announced the locations of their own *barrio chino*. Predictably, *barrios chinos* were designated in remote municipal areas on expropriated land, a sacrifice all previous owners were to make out of "high patriotism and common good."[39] Law 27 made no reference to compensating former land or property owners, but made clear that within four months after the passage of the barrioization decree, state authorities were to have completed the task of concentrating Chinese into designated areas throughout Sonora. From January to April of 1924, each municipality was charged with establishing the physical parameters of its *barrio chino*. Guaymas's *barrio chino*, for example, would begin at "Street 12 until the sidewalk of Avenue 10; from there until the west sidewalk of Avenue 17; from there until the north sidewalk of Avenue 8; from there until the west sidewalk of Street 16 and south until one reaches the southern city limits."[40]

The motivation to install *barrios chinos* had more to do with isolating Chinese businesses and families and containing the spread of Chinese marriage or free unions (defined as a couple living together in a marriage-like state) than with real concerns over public health and sanitation. Some municipal presidents worked hand in glove with *antichinistas* to force Chinese into *barrios* and to dissolve their romantic partnerships or marriages, even if it meant slandering the character of Mexican women. The municipal president of Cumpas, Florencio Frisby, was one such individual; he not only falsely accused Pacifica Morales and Adela Barrios de Hong of "living in a house of prostitution or in concubinage," but also ordered the two Mexican women to live in the residential area of Cumpas reserved for prostitutes (*zonas de tolerancia*).[41] Morales and Barrios de Hong vigorously countered Frisby's charges by publically affirming their partnerships with Luis Sujo and Juan Hong as "clean, honest, and lawful."[42] Free unions were legitimate partnerships and were often the arrangement preferred by Mexican women over marriage; in Cumpas, one-quarter of Chinese men lived in free unions with Mexican women.[43] Barrioization thus served as a device for controlling Mexican-Chinese unions, whether free or legal; for isolating Chinese-owned businesses; and for limiting Chinese

political influence. Those who challenged the anti-marriage and barrioization decrees chanced public derision, hatred, and the full reckoning of
anti-Chinese fervor.

The ties between Chinese and Sonorans would be further challenged,
and strained, by the renewal of tong violence and increased economic
competition, which in the mid-to-late 1920s fueled *antichinistas* in
ways that Sonoran Chinese had barely anticipated. The schemes of *antichinistas* came into sharp focus again in September 1924, when the CKT
and KMT renewed their rivalry with the assassination of Francisco Yuen,
a prominent Agua Prieta merchant, KMT member, and esteemed member of the Sonoran Chinese community.[44] Yuen's assassination prompted
the second tong war, and legal maneuvers dealing with the fallout of this
war commenced, just as they did two years earlier when the CKT and
KMT first clashed in Nogales. Local police rounded up 240 tong members, listed another 106 as fugitives, ordered the confiscation of weap-
ons, and tried to determine the responsible parties.[45] President Obregón
heeded the advice of the Chinese minister, G. Hsiang Hu, and limited his
expulsion order to tong members who were not citizens of Mexico and to
those proven guilty by official investigation of internecine conflict. Tong
violence waned after Obregón applied Article 33 to CKT leaders, but few
fully understood the Pandora's box that was opened following the order
to expel some tong members. Whereas Sonoran Chinese imagined that
the scorn of anti-Chinese agitators had now ended, most ardent critics of
the Chinese were hardly satisfied with a few dozen expulsions. The very
success of Chinese in fending off attacks through local and international
advocacy and by petitioning President Obregón directly in fact emboldened *antichinistas* to employ progressively harsher tactics. During the
mid-to-late 1920s, anti-Chinese agitators sketched the boundaries of full
civic belonging by constructing a discourse of xenophobic nationalism
that worked alongside pro-race, pro-fatherland crusades. Speeches and
newspaper circulars depicted the Chinese, in explicit language and graphic
imagery, as a common foe who "absorbed all our wealth and degenerated
our race," and as one made formidable because of "the complacency of
some judges and the disregard of morality and highly questionable inter-
pretations of the Constitution by some lawyers."[46] Most Sonorans could
not agree on whether this conflict was between economic competitors or
could be traced to an increasingly rancorous and exclusionary nationalistic movement. Those who believed that marriages between Chinese men
and Mexican women were manageable or that nationalism was merely
a sentiment among enthusiastic patriots overlooked a highly capricious
ideological undercurrent that some Sonorans would harness as the basis
for a new social order.

## The Great Convention and Constitutionalism

By 1925, the most famous people in Sonora were Carlos González Tijerina, a lawyer from Nogales; José Ángel Espinoza, a state representative from Cananea; and Juan Calderón, a physician. These three Sonorans gained notoriety by mounting the most brutal campaign against Sonoran Chinese to date. Espinoza, the owner and editor of *El Nacionalista* and author of two derisive tomes on Sonoran Chinese, *El problema Chino en México* (The Chinese problem in Mexico) and *El ejemplo de Sonora* (The example of Sonora), was by far the most vociferous and cruelest critic of the three.[47] Espinoza put his creative skills to effective use as artist and rhetorician of several caricatures of Chinese. His images fed and sustained nightmarish fantasies about merchant monopolies, racial contamination, and tong violence. His vitriolic rhetoric nourished the appetite for direct violence of fellow Sonorans Calderón and González Tijerina. Together the three *antichinistas* took full advantage of an opportunity to refashion an anti-Chinese discourse to reverse the Mexicanization of Chinese that had been occurring progressively over the preceding decades, and which egalitarian immigration and colonization laws had accelerated. Their 1925 campaign was impressive, less so for the violence they fomented than for their success in inextricably branding Sonoran Chinese as both irredeemable carriers of degeneracy and formidable business competitors, and thereby linking Chinese to larger discourses of postrevolutionary nationalism. In renewing and applying an older, Porfirian approach to the Chinese issue, the campaigns of Espinoza, Calderón, and González Tijerina molded Sinophobia into a coherent racist ideology, one that terrorized Chinese by custom and by law, and one in which the parameters of civic belonging were made explicit.

Until the mid-1920s, there were few signs that Sonoran Chinese would soon suffer the fate of official expulsion. From the time of José María Arana's crusade through the second tong war, Sonoran Chinese galvanized every resource and political strategy available to fend off unjust laws and to counter racism. In a February 1925 meeting at Nogales's Karam Hall, this all began to change.[48] *Antichinistas* in Cananea, Hermosillo, and Nogales, who in the previous month had organized their energies in groups called *Comités de Salud Pública* (public health committees), united their efforts to incite another anti-Chinese campaign.[49] In a missive to Calles, González Tijerina alerted the president about a "Great Anti-Chinese Convention" to commence organizing workers, *campesinos* (farm laborers), and delegates from Sonora and neighboring states, and to exploit generalized fears of the Chinese as fierce competitors and as race contaminators. The platform of the Great Convention gave no indication of a nationally informed, cohesive agenda; the anti-Chinese movement remained a locally and regionally derived cause.[50] The president of the new campaign, Salvador Múñoz Tostado, however, did organize a special meeting in Nogales for "all wives of the dedicated working class so that the campaign may take in mind the propaganda Mexican women may develop."[51] The "greatness" of the convention lay in its organizational originality; for the first time, Sonorans coordinated previously discrete efforts into a regionally coherent political movement that crossed class and gender lines, however gratuitously.

Autonomy was encouraged. Satellite committees took up their own names and mottos. Sonorans evoked the slogan "por la patria y por la raza" (for the fatherland and for the race) to signal their engagement in and support for the campaign aimed at ridding the state of its Chinese population. Other committees throughout northern Mexico named themselves similarly—the Junta Nacionalista (Nationalist Youth Group), the Liga Nacional Pro-Raza (Pro-Race National League), and El Club del Pueblo (The People's Club). Each committee was free to adopt secondary principles governing their local operations.[52] The program of the Great Convention, however, was set. All auxiliary committees were to drum up support for Mexican merchants and wholesalers, to organize new women's committees, and to alert authorities about public health violations on the part of Chinese.[53] These efforts of course required money. When González Tijerina petitioned President Calles for assistance in securing a thirty-thousand-peso credit for the Nogales committee, the *antichinista* appealed to the president's Sonoran roots and his adherence to economic nationalism.[54] Calles quickly agreed, and although assisting González Tijerina may be interpreted as a digression from the president's usual pragmatism, Calles, who was undoubtedly supportive of the committee's similar economic ideology, was probably more keen to reward *antichinistas* for their legal and peaceful approach to organizing than to endorse the full agenda of the Great Convention.

Mobilization activities of *antichinistas* began in earnest, and for a time Mexicans did organize themselves peacefully and legally. Pro-raza, pro-patria leagues sent missives to one another in support of local anti-Chinese laws, while state leaders expressed solidarity by forwarding letters to federal officials urging reform of national immigration and trade laws. The State Congress of Zacatecas, Mexico, for example, supported a host of reforms that almost all anti-Chinese leagues previously and continuously advocated for, from abrogating Mexico's 1899 Treaty of Amity, Commerce, and Navigation, to commissioning a census on illegal Chinese immigration, to prohibiting the reentry of Chinese into the country regardless of citizenship status.[55]

*Antichinistas* also galvanized the political energies of women into separate anti-Chinese subcommittees in Nogales, Cananea, and Hermosillo. Women's moral authority, given their role as keepers of the home and the race, compelled many Mexican men into action and strengthened arguments for economic and racial solidarity, especially among the working class. Emélida Carrillo led one of two women's anti-Chinese subcommittees in Nogales, writing copiously and reproachfully to Governor Bay and President Calles. "It is intolerable to see Asians exercising so much power in our State," admonished Carrillo. "[They] are no longer content with owning all of our industries, [they] are now trying to dominate politically. . . . sadly we have seen how Asian gold influences politics."[56]

The idea that Sonoran Chinese were strenuous economic and political competitors was a commonly held view among *antichinistas,* one that both women and men had regularly infused into anti-Chinese discourse as early as 1917. At the Great Convention, ordinary Sonorans heard firsthand that among the most significant threats to postrevolutionary Mexico were not only racial contamination but also Chinese economic dominance. With a large measure of certainty, Sonorans accepted as valid the charges that Chinese monopolized commerce at the expense of Mexicans, that they employed too few non-Chinese workers, and that they took advantage of a captive market of consumers by overcharging for staple goods. It was a point of view reflexively embraced by union members, women, and the middle and professional classes.[57]

There was some basis for this view. Although the Chinese were not barred from any areas of employment, they gravitated toward mercantilism. Chinese dominated manufacturing firms, but when Mexican merchants began to stiffen, they moved from clothing and shoe production to wholesale grocery and retail stores. Chinese merchants and grocers thus began to compete intensely with and at times to outnumber Mexican-owned grocery and mercantile shops throughout Sonora. In Cananea, out of 355 Chinese residents, 232 were merchants; in Pilares de Nacozari, 40 of the 64 Chinese residents owned retail stores or groceries.[58] By 1919, in Nogales, the Chinese dominated local commerce, owning ten more mercantile stores and twenty-nine more groceries than Mexicans did. Francisco Chiyoc, secretary of the Nogales UFC, confirmed that the Chinese owned nearly all the businesses in town, especially those dealing in groceries, piece goods, notions, household articles, and tobacco.[59] Chinese competition outpaced Mexican-owned businesses. This was dramatically the case in Hermosillo, the capital city of Sonora. Chinese-owned stores, especially concentrated in the sale of apparel and shoes, surpassed Mexican-owned stores 116 to 27. By the mid-1920s, Chinese owned 40 percent of manufacturing firms and small-scale dry-goods shops while controlling 65 percent of all grocery stores in Sonora.[60]

Competition, however, was a fundamental reality of the business world, and nothing about it could justify the course of action consistently and fervently taken by *antichinistas* after meetings and protests. Clearly commerce in Sonora involved the participation of many Chinese businessmen, and their success was quite evident to their Mexican competitors. The most heated calls for barrioization occurred in Tampico, Tamaulipas, when the Unión de Comerciantes de Abarrotes por Menor (Union of Small Grocers) petitioned the governor to create a Chinese quarter to protect the interests of small merchants. Two years later, a Sonora-style anti-Chinese campaign was in full force.[61]

In Sonora, during the spring and summer months of 1925, peace was but a chimera. The relationship between Sonoran Chinese and *antichinistas* descended into a vortex of hatred and fury. After uncontrolled violence had effectively negated the original program of the Great Convention, *antichinistas* found common ground in pursuing an agenda of brutality that many local officials tacitly supported. In Fronteras, five Chinese merchants were murdered after rejecting legislation requiring the purchase of permits to transport goods out of town. Four gunmen were caught near Agua Prieta, one of whom was Julio Martínez, the nephew of Fronteras' municipal president and renowned *antichinista* Miguel Durón.[62]

The mayhem in Fronteras signaled things to come. In July alone, Chinese-owned stores in the Nogales, Arizpe, and Navajo districts were burned and looted, and three Chinese were killed. Those who escaped bodily injury did so only after they paid off extorters.[63] At every step, Chinese Minister Wang and Chinese vice consul T. T. Lee made clear the complicity among municipal presidents, police officials, and high-level politicians in perpetuating anti-Chinese violence. As Chinese officials tried to counter fears of increasing Mexican-on-Chinese violence, Sonoran authorities ignored rumors of growing disorder.

Juan Calderón, perhaps the most gifted orator among the *antichinistas*, instigated a group of protestors into action in Moctezuma by reminding them that the sovereignty of the nation resided in the will of the people.[64] "If leaders cannot lead," Calderón warned, "then it will be up to the people to enforce laws upon the Chinese."[65] The proving ground of Calderón's violent Sinophobia was Nacozari, a small mining town where leaders did not yield to *antichinista* threats. On a late August night, Calderón and his cronies raided stores, set some on fire, and kidnapped several Chinese, some of whom were murdered. As the threat of more violence loomed, federal troops were marshaled to nearby Pilares to protect against further mayhem, although assaults on Chinese persons and property continued until the raiders were captured and imprisoned in early September.[66]

Ferocious measures were put in place as part of the *antichinistas'* political action. As unsettling as this was to *fronterizos*, few were powerful enough to stem the tide of anti-Chinese legislation and violence. Many Sonoran Chinese contemplated the closure or relocation of stores, but it was one thing to mull over a change of venue or a change in occupation, and quite another to carry out these actions. Few Chinese actually left their stores for another means of livelihood, even though tensions again increased when the Second National Anti-Chinese Convention took place in Hermosillo in mid-October. The Sonora state legislature buttressed the Convention by contributing 200 pesos to the cause and by subsidizing *El Nacionalista*, the official broadsheet of the anti-Chinese movement, with 250 pesos.[67] For three days, local and regional *antichinistas* reveled in the emotionalism of González Tijerina's and Calderón's speeches. But the images of debauched and pestilent Chinese put forth by the recently elected director of the National Anti-Chinese Committee, José Ángel Espinoza, were the most impressive.[68] In the mid-1920s, Espinoza's portraits of Sonora Chinese were direct attacks on their racial unsuitability that appealed both to those harboring subtle anti-Sinitic impulses and to those proclaiming rabid Sinophobic ideologies. The transmogrification of Chinese into pestilent merchants and heroine-injecting, opium-smoking tongs resonated, but the images and rhetoric of intermarriage and offenses to public hygiene provided the vehicle in which the anti-Chinese campaign rode to its apex. Espinoza's hatred of the Chinese was in step with the Sonoran enmity for native peoples and non-European foreigners, and his caricatures of Chinese nourished an anti-Chinese vitriol that fed on fear and racism (see Figure 6.2). Most Sonorans objected to the marriages or free unions of Chinese men and Mexican women. Through Espinoza's images they could see the dire social and racial hazards of such unions.

Espinoza's women were cast as untrustworthy and physically and morally weakened by race mixture. By virtue of marriage, *chineras* (Mexican women who married Chinese men) carried race poisons: they were unkempt, diseased, and saddled with half-clothed, mongrelized children. Degeneracy was clear, but Espinoza suggested a worse outcome: the fate of the "wretched one" awaited any woman crossing into the mysterious and closed world of Chinese men. Instead of material comfort and abundant leisure, *chineras* reaped the misfortune of their miscalculated decision and surrendered meekly to a life of coercion, ridicule, and shame (see Figure 6.2). Yet there was a hint of optimism in Espinoza's portrayals. The wives or partners of Chinese men were perhaps redeemable if they were willing to choose a different life path. Regeneration was always part of the

¡Ah infeliz!.... Creíste disfrutar de una vida barata al entregarte a un chino y eres
una esclava y el fruto de tu error es un escupitajo de la naturaleza....

FIGURE 6.2 "Oh wretched one! You thought you would enjoy an easy life by
giving yourself to a Chinaman, but you are a slave and the fruit of your error is a
freak of nature!" Source: Espinoza, *El Ejemplo de Sonora*, p. 172. Courtesy of the
Arizona Historical Society/Tucson. http://www.arizonahistoricalsociety.org

architecture of race in Sonora, and the representations of women held this
promise even for race traitors. By contrast, Espinoza's drawings of men
and children were grotesque. They were racially unredeemable. They were
also reminders of failed laws (anti-miscegenation, barrioization) aimed at
discouraging racially "unfit" Chinese from biological and social reproduction with racially "fit" *mestizos*.

Espinoza's caricaturing energized the anti-Chinese movement in powerful ways, both seen and unseen. In creating stark contrasts between the
appearance of Mexican women at "the time of the wedding night and
five years later," Espinoza made visible the intersection of Sinophobia and
Mexican nationalism (see Figure 6.3). *Antichinistas* gaped at the contrasts
in shock and disbelief, quickly reckoning the horrific misfortunes of race
mixing for women, their offspring, and the nation. Images of the *chineras*

transported the Sinophobic audience into the duality of regeneration and degeneration and became what Susan Bordo calls a "medium of culture."[69] The bride, whose body was striking in its anatomical representation of the nation as young, modern, energetic, and voluptuous, unwittingly assisted in her own ruin through intercourse with a licentious Chinaman. Five years later, these qualities were shrunken away. The breasts of the *chinera* carried the metaphor of the Mexican nation and the choices of the *mestizo* people either to reject or to accept suckling Chinese, knowing that weakened offspring suffering from the neglect and preoccupations of both parents were the consequences to bear. Espinoza also succeeded in succinctly designating the Chinese "other" as already degenerate, insatiably lustful in the first vignette, and disengaged and prattling on in the latter.

Espinoza's representations in *El ejemplo de Sonora* helped to solidify a racial boundary that in years past was imagined but not yet fully formed in the consciousness of Sonorans or fully realized in the actions of *anti-chinistas*. What had competed with Espinoza's horrific images was the reality of the everyday lives of Chinese. Intermarriage was commonplace, naturalization rates were higher among Chinese nationals than any other

La noche de bodas.....

y cinco años después

FIGURE 6.3 "The Wedding Night . . . and Five Years Later." Source: Espinoza, *El Ejemplo de Sonora*, 36. Courtesy of the Arizona Historical Society/Tucson. http://www.arizonahistoricalsociety.org

group of foreigners, and merchants and grocers had long dominated the ownership and operation of small-scale commerce throughout Sonora. The images of *chineras*, Chinese men, and mongrelized children helped to fix Chinese-Mexican families as race degenerates emblematic of a decaying nation. In fixing the "other," Espinoza laid bare two choices for Sonorans: to compromise the revolutionary project by integrating the Chinese fully (and racially) into Mexican society, or to embrace *mestizaje* as a critical cultural-social feature of the new state. By 1931, Sonorans chose the latter, and in doing so not only articulated the rationale of their anti-Chinese sentiment, but also alluded to the means by which *antichinistas* were to fulfill their nationalistic aspirations. Stirred by Espinoza's fantastically horrific images of Chinese, *antichinistas* entered the most public and private realms of Sonoran Chinese—families, businesses, and fraternal organizations—to show to all that "the Chinese, by mere fact of their savagely brutal lifestyles have been unworthy of living under the protection of the laws and civilized towns."[70] In rhetoric and then in action, crusading *antichinistas* bombarded the public with their message. Their efforts bore deeply into Sonoran society as well as into those other parts of northern Mexico with substantial numbers of Chinese.

Throughout the mid- to late 1920s, attacks against Chinese ebbed and flowed in Sonora and the Mexican north. As the postrevolutionary project unfolded and the presidency passed from the hands of Obregón to Calles (who served from 1924 to 1928), various groups competed intensely to define the revolution's meaning at the local and national levels. In Sonora, exploiting the so-called Chinese problem continued to curry political favor among workers, professionals, and peasants, and it involved no radical revision of class relations. At stake were the loyalties of Mexicans, including, ironically, Sonoran Chinese, whose allegiance Calles had sought to gain. Having prospered politically from prior anti-Chinese campaigns, Sonoran middle and working classes garnered a strong local following through renewed anti-Chinese crusades after 1924. The movement took on an almost-exclusively racialized and gendered form, one that played a dramatic and often violent role in reinforcing *mestizaje* as the new Mexican identity, and Mexican women as guardians of the race. Calles, although an ardent *antichinista*, was often caught between constitutional mandates to ensure the civil rights of naturalized Chinese, and the stridency of anti-Chinese campaigns in Sonora. To be sure, Calles manipulated the Sinophobia of Sonorans to achieve political ends, but until the end of his presidential term he pursued a rather conciliatory line toward Sonoran Chinese as part of a patchwork political strategy beholden to *caciques* (political bosses), workers, *campesinos*, Chinese ministers, and Washington, DC, officials. The president's approach to Sonoran Chinese and *antichinistas* demonstrated what historian Jürgen Buchenau has astutely observed about Calles and the character of the Mexican revolution: "Calles . . . therefore displayed the revolution's contradictions between popular aspirations and elite rule, between promises and betrayal, and between nationalist visions and capitalist reality."[71] At the constant prodding of Chinese and their supporters, Calles managed each political predicament with pragmatism, even though at times his decisions were at odds with *antichinistas* and they tested his own contempt for Chinese.

Calles's displeasure with local Sonora officials was palpable. Just as he had dealt with numerous complaints from Sonoran Chinese as Obregón's secretary of the interior during the governorship of Francisco Elías in the early 1920s, he also dealt with similar predicaments that arose during the governorship of Alejo Bay (1923–1927). What grieved Calles most was the charge that local Sonoran officials encouraged attacks, participated in anti-Chinese leagues and protests, and worked outside the law to achieve their ends.[72] With the encouragement and support of Governor Bay and the regional press, officials such as Felipe González Cortés, a Hermosillo-based sanitation inspector, felt no compunction declaring that "all municipal and state authorities . . . were in accord" with the leaders of the anti-Chinese crusade.[73] Calles, ever-conscious of his political reputation, warned *antichinistas* against pursuing illegal tactics against Chinese, especially any line of attack that would draw international criticism and sully the reputation of the presidency and the nation. In a starkly worded missive to the governors in Sonora, Baja California, Sinaloa, Nayarit, Coahuila, Chihuahua, Tamaulipas, Chiapas, and Yucatán, Calles minced no words for their allowing *antichinistas* to run amuck and for their failure to protect the rights of all citizens and residents. "In [your] states, anti-Chinese groups . . . have committed countless atrocities against the Chinese people and their interests," admonished Calles. "Chinese nationals living in this country are entitled to the same principles set forth in our Constitution—to enjoy the same individual guarantees as Mexicans."[74]

The president, however, left the governors with a guide for future action. In his rebuke, Calles recalled the 1921 amendment to the Treaty of Amity, Commerce, and Navigation prohibiting the immigration of Chinese laborers into Mexico. He asserted that "the Executive will continue to own such a stance . . . but with respect to Chinese citizens who entered the country and reside here under the protection of our Constitution and the Treaty prior to the respective measures, the federal government and the [s]tates have the inescapable duty to accord [them] guarantees established in the Constitution."[75] The president perhaps alleviated some *antichinista* anxiety when he supported 1926 federal legislation to further restrict immigration. But as it turned out, this legislation's greatest impact was to deter American tourists from visiting Mexico and to substantially increase the bureaucracy of Mexico's immigration agency. The Mexican Immigration Law of 1926, which took effect on November 1 of that year, placed a six-month limit on visiting tourists, scientists, transients, and foreign merchants. All foreign persons entering Mexico, including short-term tourists, were photographed and required to be placed in a "Book of Aliens." Only after foreigners replied to an "immigrant questionnaire," underwent a health examination, and proved they were well-behaved persons who held an "office, profession, or honorable livelihood" would an immigrant identification card be issued, for a fee of one dollar.[76]

Harry L. Walsh, an American consul in Nuevo Laredo, lashed out at Mexico's "disastrous" and xenophobic immigration law. "This law has driven away American tourists . . . leaving their money in Mexico and taking away nothing which belongs to the Mexicans. The tourist is, in fact, the best visitor, the best foreigner if such an expression may be used. . . . For these reasons, even countries touched with xenophobia make efforts to attract and entertain him."[77] Restrictions also applied to "working immigrants," who were admitted only if they were under a labor contract or if they could show sufficient "pecuniary resources . . . to meet personal and family needs" for three months without a job. The Departamento de Gobierno (Department of the Government) also held out special authority to temporarily prohibit the entry of foreign laborers "when . . . work in the country is scarce."[78]

In 1927, Calles continued to tether his commitment to the working class and small merchants by restricting Middle Eastern immigration. Calles effectively prohibited most Syrians, Lebanese, Armenians, Palestinians, Arabs, and Turks from entering Mexico on the basis that these groups participated in "trading in the smallest way" and "money lending . . . in the form of street peddling."[79] It was unclear how such prohibitions would increase opportunities for working-class Mexicans, because most of these immigrants were listed as farmers and, according to Calles, much of their work activity "did not constitute a useful economic factor in the development of public wealth, nor can be considered a productive contingent."[80]

As Calles solidified his reputation as an advocate of the working class and as an immigration exclusionist, for a time he took no direct action to destabilize Mexico's Chinese population through reform. The 1926 immigration laws allowed naturalized citizens to continue bringing into the country "ascendants and descendants, and brothers and sisters under age."[81] Likewise, when Sonoran *antichinistas* complained to federal authorities that state measures on intermarriage, immigration, and barrioization went unenforced, they received little support. In keeping with Calles's stance, the attorney representing the national government concluded that such prohibitions either violated the Mexican Constitution or were sufficiently accounted for in new immigration laws.[82] In their advocacy for civil rights, Calles and his cadre of officials placed themselves in a small minority of postrevolutionary politicians who insisted on maintaining constitutional guarantees for naturalized Chinese Mexicans and Chinese nationals.

There had been vociferous demands from *antichinistas* and others that Mexico repeal its Treaty of Amity, Commerce, and Navigation with China until the United States officially recognized Mexico's revolutionary government.[83] Since 1899, the treaty had conferred protective status as subjects from a most favored nation upon Chinese nationals in Mexico. Sonoran Chinese frequently evoked the treaty asserting their "right to travel and conduct business in all parts of Mexico under the same conditions as nationals from other nations."[84] In July 1927, Calles finally yielded to overwhelming *antichinista* fervor and abrogated the treaty with China.[85] But even without the protection of the Treaty of Amity, Commerce, and Navigation the Chinese community was socially and politically entrenched in Sonora and continued to defend itself with the shield of the Constitution. Calls for barrioization went unheeded, labor laws went unenforced, and in 1928 the U.S. vice consul in Mexico City, John E. Jones, observed that "despite the [Sonora] State law, there is considerable intermarriage between Chinese and natives."[86] These outcomes deeply troubled *antichinistas*.

## El Maximato: Mexico for Mexicans

The turning point for *antichinistas* came at a moment of political volatility. By late 1928, Calles had vacated the presidency in preparation for Obregón's second presidential term, but Obregón was assassinated, presumably by order of Calles. During the *Maximato*, Calles wielded immense power behind the scenes, selecting three presidents and controlling local officials, political organizations, and state governors.[87] When, for example, General José Gonzalo Escobar led a rebellion against Calles in Sonora, the former president acted decisively to unseat Escobar's supporters and fellow *obregonistas*, Alejo Bay, and the current Sonora governor, Fausto Topete (1927–1929). After order was restored under the military leadership of General Lázaro Cárdenas in 1929, Calles handed local authority to an old ally and distant relative, former governor Francisco Elías. Elías's return to the governorship effectively extended the scope of Calles's power in Sonora while firmly orienting the state's interests in the direction of workers, *campesinos*, petty merchants, and *antichinistas*. To earn the trust of workers, Calles supported a temporary prohibition of foreign workers entering into Mexico. More important, he permitted

Elías to resurrect the tactics of rabid *antichinistas*—arson, thuggery, and legal harassment—that worked in tandem with a heightened anti-Sinitic discourse.[88] Their revised politics reinvigorated the anti-Chinese platform and harnessed support for Calles's newly created National Revolutionary Party (*Partido Nacional Revolucionario*, or PNR) in 1929.

Under Elías, a common ground emerged in Sonora that united local and national concerns over the racial makeup of Mexico with local anxiety about the Chinese community. The locus of this anti-Chinese campaign resided in a Sinophobic propaganda that emerged during the earlier years of the eugenics and social hygiene movement in Mexico. Sonora was one of the earliest states in Mexico to politicize eugenics as a social movement that, according to historian Alexandra Minna Stern, began in earnest nationally after 1917. Stern points out that "after the revolution of 1910, an energetic cohort of professionals and leaders, emboldened by the egalitarian promises of the 1917 constitution, embarked on a plan of reconstruction and regeneration. . . . These men and women fashioned their blueprint for national cohesion and societal fortification . . . by linking these to eugenic notions of biosocial vigor."[89]

To bolster public sanitation reforms, Mexican eugenicists and Sonoran public health officials alike drew on French naturalist Jean Baptiste de Lamarck's theory of the inheritance of acquired characteristics. The significance of the Lamarckian outlook was that it assumed that traits passed along through generations were subject to change depending on the environment in which the offspring were raised. In other words, a good environment promoted good genes. Lamarck not only posited a gradual process by which genetic fitness emerged over generations, but also believed, for example, that changes to a parent's morphology would appear in that parent's progeny. Thus a lizard that had had its tail removed would give birth to offspring without tails. *Antichinistas* were eager to embrace this idea, despite the fact that it was so readily disproved. (The next generation of lizards actually emerged tail intact.) This perspective allowed the *antichinistas* to assert a pseudo-scientific rationale for what amounted to racial cleansing. Mexican eugenists, although well acquainted with Gregor Mendel's and August Weismann's theories of biology confirming that hereditary material was typically transmitted from generation to generation without any alteration, nonetheless remained loyal Lamarckians. In the theory of acquired characteristics Mexican reformers grounded a social movement that blurred the distinction between nature and nurture, a belief consistent with an optimistic expectation that reforms of the social environment would result in permanent racial improvement. By adopting a Lamarckian stance, *antichinistas* could reconcile the paradoxes of creating a racially homogenous national body from *mestizos* and indigenous peoples.[90] Yet as reformers encouraged the procreation of racially "fit" hybrids, they fervently discouraged "unfit" Chinese from biological and social reproduction. But this racial cleansing came at a very high price. It helped to solidify a racial boundary between Sonoran *blanco-criollos* and racial "others" that, ironically, compromised the revolutionary project in the state: the emergence of new, modern Mexico.

At almost every turn, Elías, aided by *antichinistas* and public health officials, filtered his legal and extralegal attacks through a scientific-medicalized lens in which the entry requirements for being a true Mexican were made clear (see Figure 6.4). The term *racial poisons*, coined by British neo-Lamarckian and eugenicist Caleb William Saleeby, was attached to the discourse of degeneration-regeneration and worked in tandem with that discourse to force the Chinese out of Sonora and other northern states.[91] Alcohol, drugs, and sexually transmitted diseases were the most pernicious "racial poisons" that emerged alongside immigration and intermarriage as key regulative norms in which Sonoran public health officials and *antichinistas* sought reform.

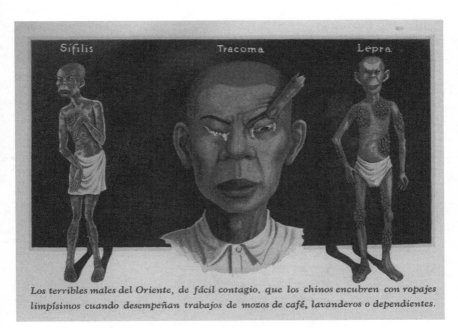

*Los terribles males del Oriente, de fácil contagio, que los chinos encubren con ropajes limpísimos cuando desempeñan trabajos de mozos de café, lavanderos o dependientes.*

FIGURE 6.4 The Horrific Evils of the East, Which Easily Spread as the Chinese, Masking Spotless Clothes, Perform Work as Waiters, Launderers, or Sales Clerks. Source: Espinoza, *El Ejemplo de Sonora*, 92. Courtesy of the Arizona Historical Society/Tucson. http://www.arizonahistoricalsociety.org

By 1930, several milestones marked the Arizona-Sonora borderlands as an intensely racially contested landscape in the process of social rupture. Regulating grocery stores was among the harshest, most insidious interventions that officials made into the lives of Sonoran Chinese—and one of the most effective as well. The identification of Chinese merchants as carriers of "racial poisons" allowed public health officials to sanction Sinophobia through draconian laws and penalties. Grocers and merchants were shackled by the steely reforms of a newly created Directorate General of Public Health, led by Dr. Antonio Quiroga. "The stores are stacked floor-to-roof which impedes the entry of light and air," Quiroga complained. "Darkened aisles present a danger to health, while living and sleeping in uncomfortable and unsafe places evidence the feebleness of the Chinese race."[92] Restrictions on warehousing goods in stores and living in and sleeping on the premises made staying in business more difficult, especially after grocers were prohibited from selling fresh meats or vegetables, bread, and medicine.[93] Unsealed items that came in contact with diseased Chinese, it was widely believed, posed a serious public health hazard, especially for children and pregnant women. Every Chinese-owned grocery store, through restrictionist public health codes, symbolized racially contested terrain, and this inscribed the contours of public health and sanitation reform. Such reform went hand in hand with another agenda: to restrain competition. Constraints on wholesaling staple items in bulk, selling a myriad of goods, and keeping long hours—strategies that kept Chinese grocers more competitive than Mexicans—also helped to justify wide-ranging reforms.

Fears of a depraved, parasitic, and dysgenic "Chinese hydra" crept into immigration reform. Less than a year after Quiroga began instituting biosocial reforms, the Mexican government acted to exclude all Chinese immigration following a 1930 report by Andrés Landa y Piña, director of population and head of the Servicio de Migración (Migration Service). Landa y Piña detailed for federal authorities the causes of emigration and placed the onus squarely on Chinese immigration. "Asian immigration has invaded our Pacific coastal towns," the director affirmed, "where they *have* settled themselves as foreign invaders, without requirements of any kind [and] in places most convenient for their purposes."[94]

Since 1926, the Mexican government had worked diligently to quell Chinese immigration and the racial poisons it supposedly carried. Immigrants were routinely deloused and vaccinated against syphilis, bubonic plague, and beriberi by agents working for the Servicio de Migración and the newly created Servicio de Inspección de Inmigrantes (Immigration Inspection Service). Despite sanitation baths, Chinese were still believed to carry leprosy and trachoma, ailments that prophylactics could not prevent.

Border controls wound their way into the interior. Maintaining vigorous health standards through immigration sweeps reached hysterical levels as municipal officials in Guaymas and Hermosillo routinely arrested Chinese residents not in possession of an immigrant identification card. Officials also routinely raided well-known opium dens and gambling halls, and extorted merchants for money or goods.[95] Many arrested in these raids were summarily deported.

Eugenics and social hygiene rules instituted in all Chinese-owned markets and groceries and immigration reform aimed at pathologizing Chinese were two extreme measures introduced alongside a far more familiar response aimed at ridding Sonora of its Chinese population: the continuation and intensification of efforts to suppress or overturn interracial marriage. It is difficult to comprehend the legislative undoing of marriage vows, yet in reviving Law 31, Sonorans consented to the "complete and absolute dissolution" of all Chinese-Mexican marriages.[96] Such treatment hardly seems surprising when we consider that Mexican-Chinese miscegenation had long been the bane of *antichinistas*. The belief that Chinese-Mexican marriages were threats to racial integrity pervaded a broad spectrum of social classes and political interests. When the Supreme Court in Mexico City rejected Francisco Hing's appeal to overturn Sonora's Law 31, anti-Chinese zealots throughout Mexico realized that they could safely pursue anti-miscegenation legislation and apply violence against those who would not comply. Racial purists were encouraged by Elías's orders and circulars to report cases of Chinese men living with or married to Mexican women. At times *antichinistas* apprehended the head-of-household. Under Elías's regime, anti-miscegenation laws intensified to such an extreme that officials working for the Sonoran Civil Registry were obliged to report "any women soliciting a birth certificate of any infant appearing to be Chinese."[97] Such activity caused enormous disruption to families and placed the children of Mexican-Chinese unions in jeopardy. After public outcry from Chinese and Mexicans alike, Elías retreated slightly from his harsh stance and targeted Chinese-Mexican unions without children.[98]

Undaunted by this minor setback, Elías continued his assault on Chinese by reviving the 1919 Labor and Social Provision Law (Article 106), which mandated that all businesses ensure that 80 percent of their employees be Mexican.[99] Initially, Chinese defied the law by claiming they had no employees, just family members who worked to maintain the business without pay. Chinese merchants considered family members to be co-owners or associates, not employees. When Elías began fining Chinese who did not comply with the new labor law, merchants began employing Mexican women to run their stores. Outmaneuvered but not outdone, Elías banned the employ of women in all Chinese-owned businesses, believing simultaneously that close proximity fostered romance *and* that the "Mongolians tended to assault girls and inexperienced maidens attending [their] businesses."[100] In either case, the outcome, in Elias's view, could not be good.

By September 1931, Chinese looked at Sonoran society with a clear view for their safety and future, and what they saw told them that no new powers were stirring. Rodolfo Elías Calles, the son of the *jefe maximato*, (political boss) assumed the governorship of Sonora, in time to witness the mass exodus of Chinese. As they caucused about the last wave of attacks under Elías Calles, the Chinese arrived at the conclusion that leaving Sonora was an unavoidable reality. Some stayed, but most began liquidating their stores, settling old accounts, and packing up what goods they could carry across the Arizona border or into Sinaloa.[101] The exodus was a capitulation to the *antichinistas*, but it was also a decision arrived at by consensus on the part of Sonoran Chinese on the basis of the violence of the past and a concern for what brutality loomed if more challenges were waged.

Harsh economics lessons followed as the remaining *sonorenses*—pure Mexicans, untainted by Chinese poisons—faced the long-term costs of a racially cleansed, postrevolutionary society. When all was said and done, food shortages, forced liquidations, and losses in revenue saddled *sonorenses*. It is difficult to discern the degree to which the global economic depression hastened the expulsion. Some Chinese hoped that the economic squeeze might reverse their fortune. No such thing transpired. As a steady stream of Chinese made their way out of Sonora from late 1929 to early 1933, more than eight million pesos ($3,200,000) were withdrawn from Mexican banks, forcing permanent closures.[102] Personal losses assumed much more complication and perhaps more injury. In Agua Prieta, Chinese farmers abandoned their land on the assumption that farm equipment would be wholesaled to Mexican farmers; no one purchased the equipment. These Chinese farmers left Sonora with what personal property they could carry into nearby Douglas, Arizona.[103] The wholesale firm of Juan Lung Tain, long considered the wealthiest merchant in Sonora, lost one million pesos in the expulsion, while the Fon Qui Company suffered a similar loss in retail goods and groceries.[104] Ng Wo of Nogales left behind a store valued at 250,000 pesos when he left Sonora for Arizona; and further south in Navojoa, the Ching Chong Company abandoned an enterprise valued at 500,000 pesos.[105] Operating in conjunction with mine closings, high rates of unemployment, social dislocation, and an influx of repatriated Mexicans and Mexican Americans into border towns, the expulsion of Chinese was disastrous for Sonora and Sonoran officials. Sonoran Chinese had garnered substantial wealth and property during their stay in Mexico, and when they departed, so did their resources.

Leaving their homeland was devastating. Few probably entertained thoughts of returning to Sonora or recovering what property or capital two or more generations of hard work had accumulated. Governor Elías's official expulsion order of September 1931 turned out to be an anticlimactic occurrence, as the message of unwelcome had been a long and constant one. Most Chinese began leaving Sonora in August of 1931, and they continued to do so in their greatest numbers through September of 1933, aided somewhat by Sino-American diplomacy, the cooperation of American officials at the border, and eager steamship companies. A few pledged to stay, but most were in fact weighing the safety and efficiency of the northern route through Arizona against the conveniences of the southern route through Sinaloa to Central and South America, Hong Kong, or Shanghai. Either way, Sonoran Chinese and the many thousands of Chinese who soon followed from neighboring Chihuahua, Sinaloa, Coahuila, Tamaulipas, and Baja California faced the agony and humiliation of exiles victimized by Mexico's postrevolutionary nationalist campaigns. They left Mexico having been drawn together in relations of kinship, work, sociability, and marriage. At the Arizona border, the treatment of the exiles varied from the "uncommon good sense of [U. S. border patrol officers who] allowed them every consideration" to the cruelty of Mexican immigrant agents extorting costly exit fees. Chinese who wanted to avoid detention could purchase a permit of temporary residency. Those who refused or simply could not afford the permits were stripped of most of their clothing. The Chinese Six Companies arranged for ships to leave from San Marcos Island off the eastern coast of Baja California. According to historian Julía María Schiavone Camacho, the Shanghai steamer offered little convenience and comfort for the exiles.[106] Stops in La Paz, Manzanillo, Mazatlán, and finally Guaymas were made worse by the load of gypsum, with its acrid, gaseous odor, mined from Baja California caves, that would be hauled along with them to the port of Shanghai.[107]

Prompted solely by fear, the exodus had no internal logic or strategy. Sonoran Chinese left, in whatever way they could (see Figure 6.5). Days before Elías's expulsion decree, American newspapers reported forty-nine Chinese arriving at Nogales, Arizona, while a Chihuahua-based source and the *New York Times* corroborated the flight of one thousand Chinese to Nogales and Mazatlán the next day.[108] Heading north overland through Arizona, some traveled "in-transit," a status permitting Chinese to enter the United States legally and under a $500 bond en route to China via San Francisco.[109] Most of the 180 exiles embarking from the port of San Francisco on the *President Monroe* were unable to come up with the bond and were detained; only twelve children and fifteen women could afford the fee.[110] In another account, forty-seven Chinese crossed into Nogales.

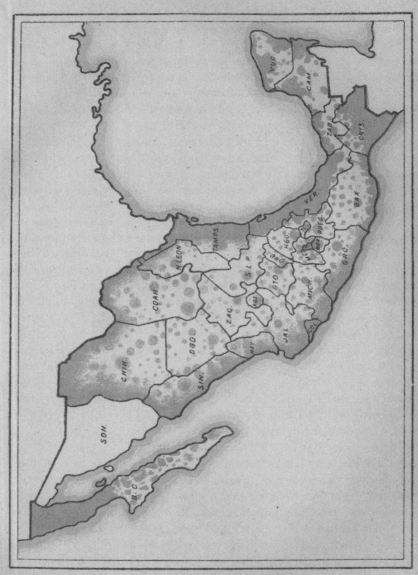

Mexicano: El color amarillo que ves en la carta geográfica de tu patria, es la demostración del dominio mongol. Ves a Sonora limpio de la mancha asiática, pues sigue el ejemplo de este pueblo batallador y pronto harás de tu patria chica una entidad que podrás llamar tuya y de los tuyos.

Among this group were a woman and her seven children, who were all stripped of their personal items before leaving Sonora. Without money for bond or transportation expenses, Chinese such as these were charged with illegal entry, as stipulated by U.S. law, and were held in southern Arizona jails awaiting deportation hearings. Sino-American diplomacy persuaded Calles to delay his official order, but postponing the inevitable did little to slow the exodus of Chinese. Most were either dispossessed of their capital and belongings in Sonora or by thugs or immigrant inspectors looting them along the way to China. Dr. David Trembly MacDougal observed the Sonora exodus from the Carnegie Institute in Nogales, Arizona. The following month, in mid-October 1931, MacDougal noted that "many of these departing Chinese have married Mexican women, some of whom with their children accompany them into exile." The refugees, added Mac-Dougal, had once been prosperous, but would return to China destitute despite "a lifetime of skillful and honest work."[111]

Throughout the Mexican north, where comparable race struggles ensued, Chinese left en masse. To further an anti-Chinese agenda at the national level, Sonorans José Ángel Espinoza, Miguel Salazar, Walterio Pesqueira, and José María Davila founded the Comité Directivo de la Campaña Nacionalista Antichina (Steering Committee of the National Anti-Chinese Campaign), which was a branch of Calles's PNR. This committee was critical in convincing the national congress to enact new legislation based on Sonora's labor law. The new national Mexican labor law required that all Mexican businesses retain a workforce that was 90 percent Mexican.[112] The law drew many American workers out of Mexico, and also proved to be the death knell for Chinese outside of Sonora. In Sinaloa, the Chinese population plummeted when widespread calls to obey that state's Ninety-Percent Labor Law led the governor to expel the Chinese in 1933. Sinaloa's Chinese population dropped from 2,123 in 1930 to 283 in 1940. In Coahuila, the Chinese population fell from 918 to 256.[113] By 1932, 60 percent of Chihuahua's Chinese population had departed, and by 1940 only 681 Chinese from Mexicali, Baja California, remained from a 1927 population of 5,889.[114] In Sonora, where the anti-Chinese campaign began and where the movement was most vicious, only 92 Chinese remained in 1940, down from 3,571 in 1930.[115]

<hr />

FIGURE 6.5 (OPPOSITE) "Mexicano: The yellow you see in the map of your country is proof of Mongolian domination. Look at Sonora free of Chinese; then follow the example of this embattled people and soon you will have a region that you can call yours all your own." Source: Espinoza, *El Ejemplo de Sonora*, p. 187. Courtesy of the Arizona Historical Society/Tucson. http://www.arizonahistorical society.org

By most measures, historians have agreed, Sonorans had eradicated the so-called yellow hydra when, in late 1931, Chinese were officially ousted from the state and the racial landscape was transformed. So thorough was the racial cleansing that José Ángel Espinoza urged the same course of action for the entire nation, so that other regions could enjoy the same outcome as Sonora. "If the entire Republic has the courage to continue Sonora's example, we will soon be able to enjoy the satisfaction of a promising future by getting the [political] organization necessary so that our country can become strong, respectable, and happy."[116] Sonorans did get the governing body they wanted, but they did not get the desired economic outcome. Mexicans, unexpectedly, did not take over vacant Chinese-owned businesses, and the lack of dry goods and produce left many, especially those living in small towns, bartering for such items.[117] At the national level, the anti-Chinese campaign won over some adherents, but never inspired the same virulence as was demonstrated in the north. Not long thereafter, rabid Sonoran *antichinistas* transferred their Sinophobia onto the Jewish community. Expulsion was considered, but not implemented. Sonorans' hatred for others was reserved for the expulsion of Chinese, and for indigenous peoples before them.

A critical flaw lay in the expulsion order. After 1934, as Lázaro Cárdenas ascended to the presidency, *sonorenses* believed that by expelling Chinese they had helped to bring down one of the strongest bulwarks of pre-revolutionary Mexico. But as this story has shown, Sonorans got it wrong. In ousting the Chinese, just as they did the Yaquis and Apaches before them, Sonorans failed to comprehend the fullness of the revolutionary project laid out in democratic, constitutional traditions. Sonorans embraced postrevolutionary *indigenismo* and *mestizaje*, but when they did, they also employed their own understanding of race and social belonging, an understanding that was more in keeping with old-regime policies of expulsion or forced integration than with the new regime approach favoring cultural assimilation. Their treatment of Chinese, especially when stirred into a toxic mix of virulent Sinophobia and Porfirian-inspired *indigenismo*, weakened any claim of civic belonging made by Sonoran Chinese. Yet until the rise of the *Maximato*, Sonoran Chinese had not given in to demands for expulsion, nor had *antichinistas* claimed full victory. The Chinese hoped that the economic impact of the Great Depression would help Sonorans reconsider their importance to the state. That expulsion followed shortly thereafter had little to do with sound economic forecasting or the actual presidency of Calles, and more to do with the political expediency of the PNR, in its efforts finally to consolidate the national revolutionary project. And in Sonora this meant placing the power of the nation-state behind the local agenda: the anti-Chinese movement.

The expulsion of Sonora Chinese has endured among the revolution's many fateful cornerstones. Espinoza's "example of Sonora" prevailed and racial cleansing, which confined civic belonging to narrow concepts of *mestizaje*, replaced the revolutionary project. Despite their insistence on political and constitutional rights—egalitarianism, naturalization, and meaningful citizenship—the Chinese were unmade as Mexicans by campaigns waged mostly in northern Mexico, and in Sonora in particular. They were portrayed as parasitic and unfit for modernization, even though claims of civic belonging repeatedly demonstrated that *mestizaje* was also malleable and situational. Calles realized this too, if only temporarily. Had constitutionalism continued during the *Maximato* as it did during Calles' presidency, the revolution would have charted a different course, especially among Chinese, women, *campesinos*, and the working class. That the *jefe máximo* allowed the most brutal and violent forms of *mestizaje* to hold sway over political rights was further testament to the gulf between what the Revolution could have been and what it ultimately proved to be.

# Epilogue

*Making the Chinese Mexican* is not an excavation of a lost world or an attempt to rewrite a neglected people back into the record of history. In many respects, this story of Chinese *fronterizos* has confounded our view of the region because nation-centered narratives had previously divided the borderlands into neat conceptual categories. The imposition of specious space-time boundaries of American and Mexican national histories obscured the experiences of Chinese *fronterizos* even though they constituted vibrant communities and were critical protagonists in the development of U.S. and Mexican immigration policies. Recovering these stories has involved unfolding multiple layers of imperial, colonial, and national histories, all of which worked in conflicting ways on those who lived between nations.

Exclusionary nationalisms proved to be the most powerful forces of identity making and social belonging on both sides of the border. When Chinese immigrants initially arrived in the United States and Mexico, they faced the pressure to adapt to their new home, even as they kept prior allegiances and family ties intact. The imperatives of nationalism, however, demanded that certain concessions be made among Chinese *fronterizos*, the most powerful of which was a kind of selective amnesia that encouraged an abiding loyalty to the nation. On both sides of the border, nationalism helped immigrants to accommodate their place within a new homeland, even as they recalled the past in ways that often eschewed painful family histories.

In 1970, Joe Wong, a native of Sonora, sat down to share the story of his family's history. With an air of pride that imparted more self-respect than arrogance, Wong relayed the account of his father, a Mexican citizen who had resisted the 1931 expulsion decree along with forty-seven other Chinese in the state. The basic fact of his father's Mexican citizenship,

Wong insisted, stood between exile and inclusion. "My father was a Mexican citizen," Wong asserted, "so they couldn't touch him." Wong's father was among a few Chinese in Guaymas who withstood the intimidation of police and soldiers so that he could remain in the place he considered home. Wong's tone in recalling this story was noticeably bereft of resentment and recrimination. He acknowledged that his family, by remaining in Sonora, endured the sting of Sinophobia, while at the same time emphasizing that through the years "better feeling developed between [his family] and the Mexicans." In appraising the climate of the 1970s, Wong concluded that there remained "hardly . . . any prejudice" between the two groups.[1] It's striking to note, however, that even as Wong asserted himself and his family as rightful Mexican citizens, he cast Chinese as outsiders. Throughout his reminiscences, Wong alluded to "us and the Mexicans" and, in so doing, tacitly denied himself as an ethnic Mexican. In spite of his self-exclusion and decades of Sinophobia waged against Sonoran Chinese like his father, Wong viewed his family's trial as a short-term departure from an inclusive national narrative.

If selective recollection was the manner in which Sonoran Chinese made sense of state-sponsored expulsion, then a similar process was at work just across the border in Tucson. Most reflexively, Chinese success in the Old Pueblo was almost universally attributed to the exceptional qualities of Arizona pioneers and not to the struggles and perseverance of the Chinese themselves. In a story that appeared on the front page of a 1935 special edition of the *Arizona Citizen*, Tucsonan George Lim wrote, "Without this sympathy and understanding, and yes, even patience, the Chinese could not attain any measure of success. The early Arizona pioneers, who had conquered this new desert land . . . made this wonderful city in which we now live. The Chinese in this community owe much to the early pioneer."[2] In Arizona, the pioneer came to symbolize a deep sense of common history among European settlers, and later this distinction was incorporated by some Tucson Chinese to mark their common destiny with the majority population even as immigration restrictionism and unabashed racism were still in play.

Both Joe Wong and George Lim emphasized their inclusion as members of the modern nation-state in which they lived. The recollections of their past burnished the mantle of national belonging. For Joe Wong, the 1931 expulsion decree and the tensions it engendered over the next four decades were events best left to the past. For George Lim, the ability of Tucson Chinese to assimilate and imitate their pioneering European-origin brethren constructed an unchanging core of the American nation at the Arizona borderlands. Although it seems counterintuitive that Sonoran Chinese and Tucson Chinese would erase or recast the more regrettable episodes of their nations' past, one need only consider the power of national belonging. To advance into modernity with a common destiny, affiliation with and loyalty to one's country must be unwavering. To look backward with objectivity is to risk ambivalence and alienation—sentiments and experiences that may cast doubt on one's full commitment to the adopted nation. Joe Wong and George Lim made compromises in the telling of history to accommodate national narratives, and in so doing they buried the most painful aspects of their families' and communities' experiences. Although such compromises may have been necessary in their view, selective amnesia and historical revision were constitutive bonds on which Mexican and American exclusionary nationalisms relied.

Historical recasting such as that of Joe Wong and George Lim would have offered little solace to those who were actually expelled from Sonora or to those who were deported from the United States. Despite Wong's assertion decades later that his family's Mexican citizenship afforded security from expulsion, many Sonoran Chinese had found the protection of official national membership woefully inadequate during a period of intense nativism. In the same vein, George Lim, by aligning Tucson Chinese closer to pioneering Arizonans than to the earliest Chinese settlers in El Barrio, eschewed Chinese heritage for Americanism. Lim's perspective, however, seemed more reasonable, if no less ironic given that Mexicans and Mexican Americans would begin bearing the stigma of alienage alongside Chinese and Chinese Americans. The Great Depression provided the whetstone on which American and Mexican nationalism was further sharpened. Within national economic climates in which jobs and money were scarce, the United States and Mexico looked for new and convenient scapegoats. In both nations, deportation and its euphemistic complement, repatriation, emerged as concomitant strategies to deal with immigration and national belonging (see Figure E.1). Even as some 3,500 Sonoran Chinese were expelled from Mexico, approximately 500,000 Mexicans and Mexican Americans were forcibly repatriated to Mexico from the United States. Such simultaneous exoduses, regardless of the niceties in which they were cloaked ("repatriation" versus "deportation") marked an entrenchment of restrictionist immigration policy as official state practice in both the United States and Mexico. Whereas previously Mexicans in the United States and Chinese in Mexico had been loathed but tolerated, they were now active targets for expulsion, despite high rates of citizenship by naturalization and a clear commitment to the national project as established merchants, workers, and families.

Using the repatriation of Mexicans from its northern neighbor as both impetus and panacea, Nogales, Arizona, resident Francisco Martínez wrote to Mexican President Calles about the activities occurring in the United States: "If the Americans can do this to a neighboring country,

FIGURE E.1 Picture of unidentified Chinese man expelled from Sonora. Courtesy of the Arizona Historical Society. Photo no. 58643. http://www.arizonahistorical society.org

to Mexicans, why don't we take advantage of this idea—using it against Chinese?" (It is interesting to note that Martínez was a U.S. citizen living in Arizona, a fact that obviously did not preclude his deep investment in Mexico's treatment of its Chinese denizens.) The expulsion of Chinese, *antichininstas* hoped, would open up hundreds of jobs that would go to Mexicans and simultaneously rid the nation of what Martinez called "this *peste* [plague]." The shortage of Mexican men in certain Sonoran towns, which had concerned anti-Chinese activists since the 1910s, began to be filled, although to a limited degree: when Mexicans returned to Mexico upon their repatriation, they often resettled in states other than Sonora, and many did not have the skills or capital of merchants.

Even as Mexican officials welcomed the return of their citizens from the United States and the new arrival of Mexican Americans, they extended a similar but perhaps more poignant invitation to a group they had previously scorned: Mexican women who had married Chinese men. They had been stripped of their citizenship because of that union. Moreover, those who left Mexico for China with their husbands and Mexican-Chinese children were denied the right of repatriation under Plutarco Elías Calles in the event they wished to return to their homeland. In 1938, rebuking Calles's expulsion of the Chinese, Lázaro Cárdenas rescinded that denial, to the great relief of many Mexican women who had found their lives in China to be miserable. They reported frequent physical abuse at the hands of their Chinese husbands. Further, both the wives and their children were often abandoned in China with no means of survival.[3]

Distinctions between legality and illegality, outsider and rightful resident, encompassed numerous statuses among Mexicans and Chinese in Mexico and the United States. Such subtleties and their arbitrary contradictions emerged directly from anti-immigrant movements and restrictionist laws designed to quell nativist fears and to earn the loyalties of allies in a time of global or national urgency. The Chinese exclusion laws, the Sonoran expulsion decree, the repatriation of Mexicans and Mexican Americans, and the campaign to reunite Mexican women previously expelled from Mexico contained both elements in their genesis and in their closing stages. Repatriating Mexican women and their Chinese Mexican children from Macao and greater China in 1938 was one way in which the Cárdenas presidency repudiated the nationalistic politics of the Calles regime. The administration of Adolfo López Mateos (1958–1964) ostensibly completed the repatriation of Mexicans from China, an effort that also helped to establish Mexico as a modern, democratic, and internationally accountable nation. Nonetheless, the repatriation movement of formerly expelled Mexicans was neither entirely complete nor fully inclusive. Chinese men who held Mexican citizenship were more often refused readmission on the basis that they were not fully Mexican and that they would pose—once again—a threat to Mexico's economy.[4]

After the late 1930s, immigration from Mexico ebbed and flowed depending on the whims and needs of the United States and the economic climate of Mexico. The Second World War gave rise to the Bracero Program (1942–1964), a bi-national agreement between the U.S. Farm Security Administration of the Department of Agriculture and Mexico's Ministry of Foreign Affairs. The program provided U.S. growers, who were facing severe wartime workforce shortages, the labor of approximately five million Mexican men. But when Americans feared an invasion of so-called illegal aliens from Mexico after the war had ended, Operation Wetback, a state-sponsored deportation campaign, was put into play in 1954. Modeled on the 1930s repatriation drive, Operation Wetback likewise was responsible for more than one million Mexicans and Mexican Americans leaving the United States, voluntarily and not.

American immigration policy continued to be contradictory and politi-cally opportunistic when it abolished the Chinese exclusion laws. In 1943, the signing of the Magnuson Immigration Act in the U.S. Congress ended the sixty-one-year regime of exclusion and made Chinese eligible for U.S. citizenship through naturalization. Although the repeal mandated that Chinese no longer be excluded on the basis of race and class qualifica-tions, and made them eligible for naturalization, the Magnuson Act should not be construed as equalizing immigration practice. Indeed, it was mostly a political gesture to China, a World War II collaborator with the Allied Forces. After all, only 105 Chinese—the lowest number for any immigrant group—were admissible into the United States per year until 1965, when Lyndon Johnson, in a comparable gesture to international reputation, signed the Hart-Celler Act, abolishing the National Origins quotas (1924) altogether. "[This bill] repairs a very deep and painful flaw in the fabric of American justice. It corrects a cruel and enduring wrong in the con-duct of the American Nation."[5] The Hart-Celler Act, commonly known as the Family Reunification Act, was ostensibly designed to renounce the discriminatory practices of former U.S. immigration policies. Although this immigration act was designed to showcase egalitarianism and universal inclusion, the families most intended for reunification were actually those of European descent; unexpectedly, however, families of Asian and Latin American origin constituted the vast majority of new immigrants, both legal and illegal.[6]

Against a backdrop of such complexities and contradictions, the most basic of human structures—the family—would face myriad challenges in the countries they either had chosen or were forced to call home. Through-out this history, women and their children suffered immensely for violat-ing the norms and dictates of the nation, even as they stood as the most powerful witnesses to that nation's past. As a teenager living in Magdalena, my grandmother observed firsthand the Chinese expulsion and recounted it vividly for me decades later, her regret regarding the forced exodus undi-minished by the passage of time. Far from disparaging Chinese influences in Mexico, my grandmother is probably best described and remembered as a Sinophile. One of her greatest laments about the expulsion had been the loss of what she considered the singular ambition of Sonoran Chinese. Her long-standing admiration for Chinese culture was evident in the stories she relayed to me and in some of her affinities, including her preference for Chi-nese cuisine, a source of some disappointment for me as child who wanted nothing more than her delicious rice and beans. But beyond her admiration for the Chinese and her distress regarding their treatment as outcasts in Sonora, my grandmother would nonetheless share in some of their expe-riences as an adult immigrant who arrived in southern Arizona with five children in tow in 1944 (see Figure E.2). That a better life awaited María Peña and her family would eventually prove to be the case, but only after enduring far more adversity than they must have anticipated. And like Joe Wong and George Lim, she also would suppress painful memories of hard times that would later emerge, although begrudgingly, from her children.

Hardship met them at almost every corner. Juan Peña, my grandfather, labored for Arizona's Copper King, Phelps Dodge, first as a miner and then as a foundry hand. But the work in Bisbee was brutal and dangerous, and the family did not reunite immediately. After their passage across the border, my grandmother and her children spent one month by themselves in a hotel in Douglas, Arizona, living off what my grandfather would send them. They left Douglas for Tucson, and after a stint with relatives in the Old Pueblo, they reunited with my grandfather in Bisbee, but this settling proved to be short-lived. The Peña family soon left southern Arizona for work in the fields of California, where commercial agriculture demanded

FIGURE E.2 María Ochoa Durán de Peña and children. From top left: Santos, the author's mother; María; and Lydia. From bottom left: Guillermina; Gerardo (newborn); and José. Peña family photograph.

a seemingly endless supply of farmworkers. The reality of children working to help support their families was also the case with my mother and
the older siblings. Once they were in Fresno, a central California agriculture stronghold, the two oldest girls, Lydia and Santos, and their oldest
brother, Joe, worked long hours picking grapes. Over the years, in a kind
of migratory circuit, the family moved next to nearby Kingsburg to harvest
the same fruit, then to neighboring Merced to pick bell peppers, and then
to Planada to harvest figs and tomatoes. As young teenagers they trekked
north for the cherry and peach seasons in Napa and Sonoma.

The injustice of young children and teenagers working so hard for so
many hours a day was only heightened by their reaping so few rewards
for that labor. As was the practice of the time, the head of the household
received their children's earnings, but those wages rarely went toward the
family's support. Other aspects of their lives suffered as well. Agricultural
work typically received greater emphasis than school. My mother recalled
the disappointment of routinely enrolling in high school in late September
or early October, too late to take the typing and secretarial classes she
yearned to study. Her family's story is emblematic of borderlands immigrants, both Chinese and Mexican, who struggled in the everyday, endeav-
oring to find a place of permanence amid unpredictable and often harsh
circumstances.

The story at the center of this text—that myriad and complex forces
can produce unpredictable, sometimes perplexing outcomes—is also the
enduring story of this nation's present in Arizona. The southern border
region of that state has emerged as a modern-day flashpoint of American nativism even as neo-liberalism binds the United States economically
closer to Mexico. Concomitantly, immigration complexities have vexed
national leaders to a condition of near paralysis while hundreds of border
crossers arrive daily from Mexico. In frustration over the lack of comprehensive immigration reform at the national level, American state and local
authorities have wrested control over the immigration debate from the
federal government and set its tenor. In 2010, the Arizona state legislature
passed the one of the harshest immigration policies in the nation: SB 1070,
also known as the Support Our Law Enforcement and Safe Neighborhoods Act, which gives local law enforcement officials in Arizona the
authority to inquire about any individual's legal status and to detain and
hand over to U.S. Immigration and Customs Enforcement those persons
who are suspected of being illegal.

Now, as in exclusion-era U.S. and postrevolutionary Mexico, immigrants
and individuals who are racially, ethnically, and phenotypically similar to
those people deemed illegal are subject to the scrutiny of neighbors, border
officials, and local authorities. Mexicans in early twenty-first-century Ari-

zona, like the Chinese before them who were asked for their *chock chees* and considered illegal until proven otherwise, must now face almost comparable scrutiny and derision. Within the anti-immigrant movement emerging in Arizona in the early part of the twenty-first century, the subtleties of neighborhood relations, bonds of trust, and the expectation of reciprocity have given way to suspicion and polarizing rhetoric among Arizonans. In the midst of such exclusionary inclinations, those persons suspected to be not "real" Americans are vulnerable to the talons of a police state.

Immigration and its attendant tensions present the U.S.-Mexico borderlands with a continuing dilemma, the solution to which is no more apparent now than it was when virtually all Chinese were barred from entering the United States and when they were officially expelled from Sonora in the early 1930s. This work has examined the overlapping contexts of Chinese settlement at the U.S.-Mexico borderlands that laid bare racial structures and immigration bureaucracies by which the United States and Mexico defined who would and would not become part of their nations. As Chinese *fronterizos* and countless other borderlanders have demonstrated, national boundaries are fluid, created from relationships as much as etched by global forces.

REFERENCE MATTER

# Abbreviations

ACES   El Archivo del Congreso del Estado de Sonora, Hermosillo

AGES   Archivo General del Estado de Sonora, Hermosillo, Sonora

AGN   Archivo General de la Nación, México, D. F.

AGN-DGG   Archivo General de la Nación, México, D. F., Secretaría de Gobernación, Dirección General del Gobierno, México, D. F.

AGPJ   Archivo General del Poder Judicial (Supremo Tribunal de Justicia), Hermosillo, Sonora

AHF   Arizona Historical Foundation, Hayden Library, Tempe, Arizona

AHS   Arizona Historical Society, Tucson, Arizona

AHSRE   Archivo Histórico de la Secretaría de Relaciones Exteriores, México, D. F.

AR-CGI   *Annual Report of the Commissioner-General of Immigration*

ASLAPR   Arizona State Library, Archives and Public Records, Phoenix, Arizona

AZ-CCF   National Archives and Records Administration Pacific Region, Laguna Niguel, California, Records of the District Court of the United States for the Territory of Arizona, First Judicial District, "Criminal Case Files, 1882–1912," RG 21

AZ-CD   National Archives and Records Administration Pacific Region, Laguna Niguel, California, Records of the District Court of the United States for the Territory of Arizona, First Judicial District, "Commissioners' Dockets," RG 21

AZ-CEC   National Archives and Records Administration Pacific Region, Laguna Niguel, California, Records of the District Court of the United States for the Territory of Arizona, First Judicial District, "Chinese Exclusion Cases, 1886–1906," RG 21

AZ-CECF   National Archives and Records Administration Pacific Region, Laguna Niguel, California, Records of the District Court of the United States for the Territory of Arizona, First Judicial District, "Commissioners' Early Case Files," RG 21

AZ-CMCF   National Archives and Records Administration Pacific Region, Laguna Niguel, California, Records of the District Court of the United States for the Territory of Arizona, First Judicial District, "Commissioners' Case Files, 1882–1912," RG 21

AZ-ECFCD   National Archives and Records Administration Pacific Region, Laguna Niguel, California, Records of the District Court of the United States for the Territory of Arizona, First Judicial District Court, "Early Case Files Commissioners' Dockets," RG 21

AZ-SDCEC   National Archives and Records Administration Pacific Region, Laguna Niguel, California, Records of the District Court of the United States for the Territory of Arizona, Second Judicial District, 1886–1911, "Civil and Chinese Exclusion Cases," RG 21

BCDS   *Boletín de la Cámara de Diputados del Estado de Sonora*

BC-LACD   National Archives and Records Administration Pacific Region, Laguna Niguel, California, Bureau of Customs, Los Angeles Collection District, "Incoming Letters: 1883–1908," RG 36

BCM   Biblioteca de El Colegio de México, México, D. F.

BDGM   Biblioteca Dirección General de Estadística, México, D. F.

BFO-BL   Britain, Foreign Office, Bancroft Library

BPPC   British Parliamentary Papers, China

CCP   Charles T. Connell Papers

CECN   National Archives and Records Administration Washington, DC, Department of Justice, Records of the Immigration and Naturalization Service, Chinese Exclusion Act Case Files of the Nogales Office, RG 85

CEDAZCA   Database complied by the author of all Chinese immigrants caught for illegal entry at the Sonora-Arizona border, 1882–1912

CMCUALSC   University of Arizona Library, Special Collections, Tucson, Arizona, Chinese Manuscript Collection, AZ 375

CQM   National Archives and Records Administration Washington, DC, Records of the Department of the State Relating to the Chinese Question in Mexico, 1910–1929

DWCBF   Don Chun Wo, Biographical File

EDTC   Esther Don Tang Collection

EDTTOHP   Esther Don Tang, Tucson Oral History Project

FRUSMX   United States Department of State, *Papers Relating to the Foreign Relations of the United States with Mexico*

IAMEX   National Archives and Records Administration Washington, DC, Records of the Department of the State Relating to Internal Affairs of Mexico, 1910–1929, RG 59

JMAP   José María Arana Papers

LM-PCRO   Pima County Recorder's Office: Leases and Mortgages, 1880–1902

NARA-CP   National Archives of the United States, College Park, Maryland

NARA-DC   National Archives of the United States, Washington, DC

NARA-PR   National Archives of the United States, Pacific Region, Laguna Niguel, California

RDC-SDC   National Archives and Records Administration Pacific Region, Laguna Niguel, California, Records of District Courts of the United States, Southern District of California, RG 21

RG   Record Group

RINS   National Archives and Records Administration, Records of the Immigration and Naturalization Service, RG 85

SDCD-IGC   National Archives and Records Administration Pacific Region, Laguna Niguel, California, Records of the U.S. Customs Service, San Diego Collection District, "Incoming General Correspondence" (9L-43), 1901–1909, RG 36

SDCD-LRTD   National Archives and Records Administration Pacific Region, Laguna Niguel, California, Records of the U.S. Customs Service, San Diego Collection District, "Letters Received from the Treasury Department" (9L-44), 1880–1909, RG 36

SDCD-LSST   National Archives and Records Administration Pacific Region, Laguna Niguel, California, Records of the U.S. Customs Service, San Diego Collection District, "Letters Sent to the Secretary of the Treasury" (9L-39), 1882–1908, RG 36

SDCD-OGC   National Archives and Records Administration Pacific Region, Laguna Niguel, California, Records of the U.S. Customs Service, San Diego Collection District, "Outgoing General Correspondence" (9L-38), 1885–1909, RG 36

SDCD-SALR   National Archives and Records Administration Pacific Region, Laguna Niguel, California, Records of the U.S. Customs Service, San Diego Collection District, "Special Agents Letters Received" (9L-46), 1894–1909, RG 36

SDCD-SALS   National Archives and Records Administration Pacific Region, Laguna Niguel, California, Records of the U.S. Customs Service, San Diego Collection District, "Special Agents Letters Sent to the Secretary of the Treasury" (9L-40), 1885–1909, RG 36

TJCO-LRSDLA   National Archives and Records Administration Pacific Region, Laguna Niguel, California, Records of the U.S. Customs Service, Tia Juana Customs Office, "Letters Received from the Offices of the San Diego and Los Angeles Customs Collectors" (9L-62), 1894–1922, RG 36

UALSC   University of Arizona Library, Special Collections, Tucson, Arizona

USCAMEX   National Archives and Records Administration Washington, DC, General Records of the Department of State, Dispatches from United States Consuls in Acapulco, Mexico, 1823–1906, RG 59

USCEMEX   National Archives and Records Administration Washington, DC, General Records of the Department of State, Dispatches from United States Consuls in Ensenada, Mexico, 1832–1896, RG 59

USCGMEX   National Archives and Records Administration Washington, DC, General Records of the Department of State, Dispatches from United States Consuls in Guaymas, Sonora, Mexico, 1832–1896, RG 59

USCHMEX   National Archives and Records Administration Washington, DC, General Records of the Department of State, Dispatches from United States Consuls in Hermosillo, Sonora, Mexico, 1905–1906, RG 59

USCMMEX   National Archives and Records Administration Washington, DC, General Records of the United States Department of State, Dispatches from United States Consuls in Mazatlan, Mexico, 1826–1906, RG 59

USCNMEX   National Archives and Records Administration, Washington, DC, General Records of the Department of State, Dispatches from United States Consuls in Nogales, Sonora, Mexico 1889–1906, RG 59

# Notes

INTRODUCTION

1. Keefe, Patrick Radden, "The Snakehead: The Criminal Odyssey of China-town's Sister Ping," *New Yorker* 82, no. 10 (April 24, 2006): 68; originally cited in Chinese *World Journal*, New York, May 23, 2005.

2. Julie Preston, "Prosecutors Say Defendant in Immigrant Smuggling Case Ran an Underground Empire," *New York Times*, May 23, 2005, p. B1; Alan Feuer, "U.S. Tells of Ocean Transfer in Smuggling of Immigrants," *New York Times*, June 14, 2005, p. B3; and Niona Bernstein, " Making It Ashore, but Still Chasing U.S. Dream," *New York Times*, April 9, 2006, p. 1.

3. Lee Lamothe and Richard Dickens, "Big Sister Is 'One of Us,'" *National Post*, June 16, 2003, p. A1; "The End of the Road for 'Big Sister,'" *South China Morning News*, June 12, 2003; Julia Preston, "Trial Starts with Details of Immi-grant Smuggling," *New York Times*, May 17, 2005, p. B1; and Alan Feuer, "Busi-nesswoman Known as Sister Ping Is Found Guilty of Federal Conspiracy Charges," *New York Times*, June 23, 2005, p. B3.

4. For more on Sister Ping and similar immigrant-smuggling accounts, see Pat-rick Radden Keefe, *The Snakehead: An Epic Tale of the Chinatown Underworld and the American Dream* (New York: Doubleday, 2009); Sheldon Zhang, *Chinese Human Smuggling: Families, Social Networks, and Cultural Imperatives* (Stanford, CA: Stanford University Press, 2009); and Ko-lin Chin, *Smuggled Chinese: Clandes-tine Immigration to the United States* (Philadelphia: Temple University Press, 1999).

5. The most recent strand of this borderlands historiography includes the work of Cynthia Radding, *Wandering Peoples: Colonialism, Ethnic Spaces, and Ecologi-cal Frontiers in Northwestern Mexico, 1700–1850* (Durham, NC: Duke University Press, 1997); Linda Gordon, *The Great Arizona Orphan Abduction* (Cambridge, MA: Harvard University Press, 1999); Juan Flores Mora, *The Making of the Mexican Border: The State, Capitalism, and Society in Nuevo Leon, 1848–1910* (Austin: University of Texas Press, 2001); Benjamin Heber Johnson, *Revolution in Texas: How a Forgotten Rebellion and Its Bloody Suppression Turned Mexicans into Americans* (New Haven, CT: Yale University Press, 2003); Andrés Reséndez, *Changing National Identities at the Frontier: Texas and New Mexico, 1800–1850* (Cambridge, UK: Cambridge University Press, 2005); Samuel Truett, *Fugitive Landscapes: The Forgotten History of the U.S.-Mexico Borderlands* (New Haven, CT: Yale University Press, 2006); Pekka Hämäläinen, *The Comanche Empire* (New Haven, CT: Yale University Press, 2008); Brian DeLay, *War of a Thousand Deserts: Indian Raids and the U.S.-Mexican War* (New Haven, CT: Yale University Press, 2008); Karl Jacoby, *Shadows at Dawn: A Borderlands Massacre and the Violence of History* (New York: Penguin Press, 2008); Katherine Benton-Cohen, *Border-*

*line Americans: Racial Division and Labor War in the Arizona Borderlands* (Cambridge, MA: Harvard University Press, 2009); Patrick Ettinger, *Imaginary Lines: Border Enforcement and the Origins of Undocumented Immigration, 1882–1930* (Austin: University of Texas Press, 2009); and Kelly Lytle Hernández, *Migra! A History of the U.S. Border Patrol* (Berkeley: University of California Press, 2010).

6. This early work on Chinese in Mexico includes Charles C. Cumberland, "The Sonoran Chinese and the Mexican Revolution," *Hispanic American Historical Review* 40, (1960): 191–211; Leo Michael Jacques Dambourges, "The Anti-Chinese Campaigns in Sonora, 1900–1931" (PhD diss., University of Arizona, 1974); Dambourges, "Have Quick More Money Than Mandarins: The Chinese in Sonora," *Journal of Arizona History* 17, no. 3 (1976): 201–218; Philip Dennis, "The Anti-Chinese Campaigns in Sonora, Mexico," *Ethnohistory* 26, no. 1 (1979): 65–80; Dambourges, "Chinese Merchants in Sonora, 1900–1931," in *Asiatic Migrations in Latin America*, ed. Luz M. Martínez Montiel (Mexico City: 1981), 13–20; Evelyn Hu-DeHart, "Immigrants to a Developing Society: The Chinese in Northern Mexico, 1875–1932," *Journal of Arizona History* 21, no. 1 (1980): 49–86; Hu-DeHart, "Racism and Anti-Chinese Persecution in Sonora, Mexico, 1876–1932," *Amerasia Journal* 9, no. 4 (1982): 1–28; Hu-DeHart, "The Chinese of Baja California Norte, 1910–1934," *Proceedings of the Pacific Coast Council on Latin American Studies* 12, (1985–1986): 9–30; Hu-DeHart, "Coolies, Shopkeepers, Pioneers: The Chinese of Mexico and Peru (1849–1930)," *Amerasia Journal* 15, no. 2 (1989): 91–116. For a lesser known work, see Patricia Irma Figueroa Barkow, "El movimiento antichino en México de 1916–1935: Un caso de 'racismo económico'" (master's thesis, Universidad Nacional Autónoma de México, 1976).

7. José Jorge Gómez Izquierdo, *El movimiento antichino en México (1871–1934): Problemas de racismo del nacionalismo durante la Revolución Mexicana* (Mexico City: Instituto Nacional Antropología e Historia, 1991); Juan Puig, *Entre el río Perla y el Nazas: la China decimonónica y sus braceros emigrantes, la colonia China de Torreón y la matanza de 1911* (Mexico City: Consejo Nacional para la Cultura y las Artes, 1993); Raymond B. Craib, "Chinese Immigrants in Porfirian Mexico: A Preliminary Study of Settlement, Economic Activity, and Anti-Chinese Sentiment," Latin American Institute Research Paper Series, no. 28 (Albuquerque: University of New Mexico, 1996), pp. 1–33; Robert H. Duncan, "The Chinese and the Economic Development of Northern Baja California," *Hispanic American Historical Review* 74, no. 4 (1994): 615–647; Gerardo Rénique, "Anti-Chinese Racism, Nationalism and State Formation in Post-Revolutionary Mexico, 1920s–1930s," *Political Power and Social Theory* 14 (2000): 91–140; Rénique, "Race, Region, and Nation: Sonora's Anti-Chinese Racism and Mexico's Postrevolutionary Nationalism, 1920s–1930s," in *Race and Nation in Modern Latin America*, eds. Nancy P. Appelbaum, Anne S. Macpherson, and Karin Alejandra Rosemblatt (Chapel Hill: University of North Carolina Press, 2003), pp. 211–236; Moisés González González Navarro and Delia Salazar Anaya, *Xenofobia y xenofilia en la historia de México, siglos XIX y XX: homenaje a Moisés González Navarro* (Mexico City: SEGOB, Instituto Nacional de Migración, Centro de Estudios Migratorios, 2006); Julía María Schiavone Camacho, "Traversing Boundaries: Chinese, Mexicans, and Chinese Mexicans in the Formation of Gender, Race, and Nation in

the Twentieth-Century U.S.-Mexican Borderlands" (PhD diss., University of Texas at El Paso, 2006); and Robert Chao Romero, *The Chinese in Mexico, 1882–1940* (Tucson: University of Arizona Press, 2010).

8. For scholarship on Latin American Studies, see Humberto Monteón González and José Luís Trueba Lara, *Chinos y antichinos en México: Documentos para su estudio* (Guadalajara, Jalisco: Gobierno de Jalisco, Secretaría General, Unidad Editorial, 1988); Félix, *El proceso de aculturación de la población de origen chino en la ciudad de Mexicali* (Mexicali: Universidad Autónoma de Baja California, Instituto de Investigaciones Sociales, 1990); Eduardo Auyón Gerardo, *El dragón en el desierto: los pioneros chinos en Mexicali* (Mexico City: Instituto de Cultura de Baja California, 1991); José Luis Trueba Lara, *Los chinos en Sonora: Una historia olvidada* (Hermosillo: Instituto de Investigaciones Históricas, Universidad de Sonora, 1990); James R. Curtis, "Mexicali's Chinatown," *Geographical Review* 85, no. 3 (1995): 335–348; María Elena Ota Mishima, Moisés González Navarro, Sergio Camposortega Cruz, and Javier Rodríguez Chávez, eds. *Destino México: Un estudio de las migraciones asiáticas a México, siglos XIX y XX* (Mexico City: El Colegio de México, Centro de Estudios de Asia y África, 1997). For scholarship on Asian American Studies, see Hu-DeHart, "*Huagong and Huashang*: The Chinese as Laborers and Merchants in Latin America and the Caribbean," *Amerasia Journal* 28, no. 2 (2002): 64–90; Robert Chao Romero, "Transnational Chinese Immigrant Smuggling to the United States via Mexico and Cuba, 1882–1916," *Amerasia Journal* 30, no. 3 (2004/2005): 1–16; Hu-Dehart, "Voluntary Associations in a Predominantly Male Immigrant Community: The Chinese on the Northern Mexican Frontier, 1880–1930," in *Voluntary Associations in the Chinese Diaspora*, ed. Khun Eng Kuah-Pearce and Evelyn Hu-Dehart (Hong Kong: Hong Kong University Press, 2006), pp. 141–168. It is important to note that scholarship on the Asian diaspora has burgeoned alongside the work on Asians in Latin America: Adam McKeown, *Chinese Migrant Networks and Cultural Change: Peru, Chicago, Hawaii, 1900–1936* (Chicago: University of Chicago Press, 2001); Andrew R. Wilson, *Ambition and Identity: Chinese Merchant Elites in Colonial Manila, 1880–1916* (Honolulu: University of Hawai'i Press, 2004); Daniel M. Masterson with Sayaka Funada-Classen, *The Japanese in Latin America* (Champaign: University of Illinois Press, 2004); Jeffrey Lesser, *Searching for Home Abroad: Japanese-Brazilians and Transnationalism* (Durham, NC: Duke University Press, 2003); Lok Siu, *Memories of a Future Home: Diasporic Citizenship of Chinese in Panama* (Stanford, CA: Stanford University Press, 2005); Moon-Ho Jung, *Coolies and Cane: Race, Labor, and Sugar in the Age of Emancipation* (Baltimore, MD: Johns Hopkins University Press, 2006); and Lisa Yun, *The Coolie Speaks: Chinese Indentured Laborers and African Slaves of Cuba* (Philadelphia: Temple University Press, 2007).

9. Over the past few years, scholars have explored new questions about the Chinese at the U.S.-Mexico border. See, for example, Grace Peña Delgado, "In the Age of Exclusion: Race, Region, and Chinese Identity in the Making of the Arizona-Sonora Borderlands, 1863–1943," (PhD diss., University of California, Los Angeles, 2000); Erika Lee, "Enforcing the Borders: Chinese Exclusion Along the U.S. Borders with Canada and Mexico, 1882–1924," *Journal of American His-*

*tory* 89, no. 1 (2002): 54–86; Delgado, "At Exclusion's Southern Gate: Changing Categories of Race and Class Among Chinese *Fronterizos*, 1882–1904," in *Continental Crossroads: Remapping U.S.-Mexico Borderlands History*, ed. Samuel Truett and Elliott Young (Durham, NC: Duke University Press, 2004), pp. 183–207; Erika Lee, "Orientalisms in the Americas: A Hemispheric Approach to Asian American History," *Journal of Asian American Studies* 8, no. 3 (2005): 235–256; Lawrence Douglas Taylor Hansen, "The Chinese Six Companies of San Francisco and the Smuggling of Chinese Immigrants Across the U.S.-Mexico Border, 1882–1930," *Journal of the Southwest* 48, no. 1 (2006): 37–61; Camacho, "Crossing Boundaries, Claiming a Homeland: The Mexican Chinese Transpacific Journey to Becoming Mexican, 1930s-1960s," *Pacific Historical Review* 78, no. 4 (2009); Julian Lim, "Chinese and *Paisanos*: Chinese Mexican Relations in the Borderlands," *Pacific Historical Review* 78, no. 1 (2010): 50–85; and Romero, *The Chinese in Mexico*.

10. Michel-Rolph Trouillot, *Silencing the Past: Power and the Production of History* (Boston: Beacon Press, 1995), p. 26.

11. Vasconcelos was one among several other important Mexican scholars who wrote about *mestizaje*. See especially *La Raza Cósmica: Misión de la raza Iberoamericana y Notas de viajes a la América del sur*. Barcelona: Agencia de Liberia, 1925. See also Manuel Gamio, *Forjando Patria (pro nacionalismo)* (Mexico City: Porrúa Hermanos, 1916), pp. 93–96. Compare A. F. Basave Benítez and Andrés Molina Enríquez, *México mestizo: análisis del nacionalismo mexicano en torno a la mestizofilia de Andrés Molina Enríquez. Sección de obras de historia* (Mexico City: Fondo de Cultura Económica, 1992) and Molina Enríquez, *Los grandes problemas nacionales* (Mexico City: Imprenta de A. Carranza e hijos, 1909), pp. 312–313, 345–346, 357–360.

12. Ben Vinson III and Matthew Restall, eds. *Black Mexico: Race and Society from Colonial to Modern Times* (Albuquerque: University of New Mexico Press, 2009), pp. 4–9. See also Alfonso Toro, "Influencia de la raza negra en las formación del pueblo mexicanos," *Ethnos. Revista para la vulgarización de Estudios Antropológicos sobre México y Centro América* 1, no. 8–12 (1920–1921): 215–218; Gonzalo Aguirre Beltrán, *La población negra de México: Estudio etnohistórico* (Mexico City: Fondo de Cultura Económica, 1989); and Germán LaTorre, *Relaciones geográficas de Indias (contenidas en el Archivo General de Indias de Sevilla: La Hispanoamérica del siglo XVI): Virreinato de Nueva España*, vol. 4, no. 4 (Mexico City: Censos de población, 1920).

13. Izquierdo, *El movimiento antichino en México;* Dambourges, "The Anti-Chinese Campaigns"; Puig, *Entre el río Perla y el Nazas*; Craib, "Chinese Immigrants in Porfirian Mexico"; Barkow, "El movimiento antichino en México de 1916–1935"; Diego L. Chou, "The Chinese in Mexico (1876–1931)." *Cuadernos americanos* 15, no. 89 (2001): 73–85; Cumberland, "The Sonoran Chinese and the Mexican Revolution"; Rénique, "Anti-Chinese Racism, Nationalism, and State Formation"; Félix, *El proceso de aculturación*; Catalina Velázquez Morales, "Diferencias Políticas entre los Inmigrantes Chinos del Noroeste de México (1920–1930): El Caso de Francisco L. Yuen," *Historia Mexicana* 55 (October-December 2005): 461–512; Rénique, "Race, Region, and Nation"; and González Navarro and Salazar Anaya, *Xenofobia y xenofilia en la historia de México*.

14. Prasenjit Duara, *Rescuing History from the Nation: Questioning Narratives of Modern China* (Chicago: University of Chicago Press, 1997), p. 4. Duara elaborates on his notions of authenticity and nationalism in *Sovereignty and Authenticity: Manchukuo and the East Asian Modern* (New York: Rowman & Littlefield, 2004); "Transnationalism and the Challenge to National Histories," in *Rethinking American History in a Global Age*, ed. Thomas Bender (Berkeley: University of California, 2002), pp. 25–46; "Civilizations and Nations in a Globalizing World," in *Reflections on Multiple Modernities*, ed. Dominic Sachsenmeier, Jens Reidel, and Shmuel Eisenstadt (Berlin: Brill Academic, 2002), pp. 79–99; and "The Regime of Authenticity: Timelessness, Gender, and National History in Modern China," *History and Theory* 37, (October 1998): 287–308.

15. Duara, *Rescuing History from the Nation*, pp. 8–9.

16. Ernest Gellner, *Nations and Nationalism* (Ithaca, NY: Cornell University Press, 1983); Karl Deutsch, *Nationalism and Social Communication: An Inquiry into the Foundations of Nationality*, 2nd ed. (Boston: MIT Press, 1966); and Benedict Anderson, *Imagined Communities: Reflections on the Origin and Spread of Nationalism* (London: Verso, 1983).

17. Compare the uses of *frontier*, *borderlands*, and *bordered lands* in Jeremy Adelman and Stephen Aron, "From Borderlands to Borders: Empires, Nation-States, and the Peoples in Between in North American History, *The American Historical Review* 104, no.3 (1999): 814–841. For analyses of Bolton's work, see David J. Weber, "Turner, the Boltonians, and the Borderlands," *American Historical Review* 91, no. 2 (1986): 66–81; Albert L. Hurtado, "Parkmanizing the Spanish Borderlands: Bolton, Turner, and the Historians' World," *Western Historical Quarterly* 26 (Summer 1995): 149–167; Donald E. Worster, "Herbert Eugene Bolton: The Making of a Western Historian," in *Writing Western History: Essays on Major Western Historians*, ed. Richard W. Etulain, pp. 193–214 (Albuquerque: University of New Mexico Press, 1991); and Samuel Truett, "Epics of Greater America: Herbert Eugene Bolton and the Quest for a Transnational American History," in *Interpreting Spanish Colonialism: Empires, Nations, and Legends*, ed. Christopher Schmidt-Nowara and John M. Nieto Phillips, pp. 213–247 (Albuquerque: University of New Mexico Press, 2005).

18. For readings on empire-national crossroads of the American West and Southwest, see William Cronon, George Miles, and Jay Gitlin, "Becoming West: Toward a New Meaning for Western History," in *Under an Open Sky: Rethinking America's Western Past*, ed. William Cronon, George Miles, and Jay Gitlin (New York: Norton, 1992), pp. 10–11. For a discussion of Spanish colonialism as a means to examine nation building, see Christopher Schmidt-Nowara and John M. Nieto-Philips, eds. *Interpreting Spanish Colonialism: Empires, Nations, and Legends* (Albuquerque: University of New Mexico Press, 2005), pp. 4–9; Jay Gitlin, "On the Boundaries of Empire: Connecting the West to Its Imperial Past," in *Under an Open Sky: Rethinking America's Western Past*, ed. William Cronon, George Miles, and Jay Gitlin, pp. 71–89 (New York: Norton, 1992); Howard Lamar, *The Far Southwest, 1846–1912: A Territorial History* (Albuquerque: University of New Mexico Press, 1991); James F. Brooks, *Captives and Cousins: Slavery, Kinship, and Community in the Southwest Borderlands* (Chapel Hill: University of North

Carolina Press, 2002); Hämäläinen, *The Comanche Empire;* and DeLay, *War of a Thousand Deserts.*

19. Thomas Bender, *A Nation Among Nations: America's Place in World History* (New York: Hill and Wang, 2006). For comment on Bender's work, see Sven Beckert's featured review in *American Historical Review* 112, no. 4 (2007): 1123–1125. Although in *A Nation Among Nations* Bender narrates American history as viewed through a transnational lens, several scholars critique nation-based history in this work. For nearly three decades, American historians have written about the virtues of transnationalism, but not without debate about the place of American "exceptionalism," comparative history, and the drawbacks of nation-centered writing. For a deft discussion of this topic, see Ian Tyrell, "American Exceptionalism in an Age of International History," *American Historical Review* 96, no. 4 (1991): 1031–1055; Michael McGerr, "The Price of the 'New Transnational History,'" *American Historical Review* 96, no 4 (1991): 1056–1067; Ian Tyrell, "Ian Tyrell Responds," *American Historical Review* 96, no. 4 (1991): 1068–1072; David Thelen, "Audiences, Borderlands, and Comparisons: Toward the Internationalization of American History," *Journal of American History* 79, no. 2 (1992): 432–462; Thelen, "Rethinking History and the Nation-State: Mexico and the United States as a Case Study: A Special Issue (September 1999): 439–452; Thelen, "The National and Beyond: Transnational Perspectives on United States History: A Special Issue," *Journal of American History* 86, no. 3 (1999); 965–975: George M. Fredrickson, "From Exceptionalism to Variability: Recent Developments in Cross-National Comparative History," *Journal of American History* 82, no. 2 (1995): 587–604; Daniel T. Rodgers, "Exceptionalism," in *Imagined Histories: American Historians Interpret the Past,* ed. Anthony Molho and Gordon S. Wood (Princeton, NJ: Princeton University Press, 1998), pp. 21–40; Patricia Nelson Limerick, "Going West and Ending Up Global," *Western Historical Quarterly* 32, no. 1 (2001): 5–23. For seminal essays on transnationalism in the American historical context see Laurence Veysey, "The Autonomy of American History Reconsidered," *American Quarterly* 31, no. 4 (1979): 455–477; Akira Iriye, "The Internationalization of History," *American Historical Review* 94, no. 1 (1989): 1–10; and "AHR Conversation: On Transnational History," *American Historical Review* 111, no. 5 (2006): 1141–1165.

20. Several scholars have reached beyond conventional national histories and stories. See Madeline Y. Hsu, *Dreaming of Gold, Dreaming of Home: Transnationalism and Migration Between the United States and South China, 1882–1943* (Stanford, CA: Stanford University Press, 2000); Yong Chen, *Chinese San Francisco, 1850–1943—A Transpacific Community* (Stanford, CA: Stanford University Press, 2002); Erika Lee, *At America's Gates: Chinese Immigration During the Exclusion Era, 1882–1943* (Chapel Hill: University of North Carolina Press, 2003); Adam McKeown, *Melancholy Order: Asian Migration and the Globalization of Borders* (New York: Columbia University Press, 2008); Jung, *Coolies and Cane;* McKeown, *Chinese Migrant Networks and Cultural Change;* Lisa Yun, *The Coolie Speaks;* and L. Eve Armentrout Ma, *Revolutionaries, Monarchists, and Chinatowns: Chinese Politics in the Americas and the 1911 Revolution* (Honolulu: University of Hawaii Press, 1990).

21. Transpacific travel linking the centers of imperial Spanish America with its farthest colony, the Philippines, occurred during the Manila Galleon shipping trade (1571–1815) and corresponded somewhat with nineteenth-century movements of Chinese into the Americas. Spain's coveted oceanic system of exchange shuttled the first Chinese into the Americas, although the few who arrived remained almost entirely in Lima and Mexico City. Some Chinese came to Mexico as servants of Spanish officials, but most were barbers. By 1635, the municipal council (*cabildo*) in Mexico City agreed with complaints that Chinese barbers out-competed their Spanish counterparts. The *cabildo* therefore sought to limit the number of Chinese barbershops to twelve. It was decades after Mexico's independence from Spain, when goods that came from Asia via Acapulco hit frontier markets, that Chinese began to traverse into what became the Arizona-Sonora borderlands. See Homer H. Dubs and Robert S. Smith, "The Chinese in Mexico City in 1635," *Far Eastern Quarterly* 1, no. 4 (1942): 387–389; and Peter Boyd-Bowman, "Two Country Stores in XVIIth Century Mexico." *Americas* 28, no. 3 (1972): 237–251. "Two Country Stores in XVIIth Century Mexico," *Americas* 28, no. 3 (1972): 237–251. For more on the dynamics of Catholicism and Chinese middlemen in the Philippines, see Alberto Santamaría, O. P., "The Chinese Parian (El Parian de Los Sangeleyes)," in *The Chinese in the Philippines: 1570–1770*, ed. Alfonso Felíx Jr. (Manila: Solidaridad, 1966), pp. 76–81; and William Lytle Schurz, *The Manila Galleon* (New York: E. P. Dutton, 1939). Galleon trade wares circulated among missionaries and Spanish elites in Sonora, but by no means were they staple or even intermittently circulating items. Sonorans instead relied heavily on the bounties harvested by local indigenous labor, as well as on regional markets near Parral, Chihuahua. Father Eusebio Kino, a Jesuit missionary in the Pimería Alta from 1678 to 1711, often marveled at the bounty of the Sonoran desert and the region's lack of dependence on long-distance trade by the viceroyalties. See Eusebio Kino, *Kino's Plan for the Development of Pimería Alta, Arizona and Upper California: A Report to the Mexican Viceroy*, trans., Ernest J. Burrus (Tucson: Arizona Pioneers' Historical Society, 1961), p. 32; and Eusebio Kino, *Kino's Historical Memoir of Pimería Alta*, trans. Herbert Eugene Bolton (Cleveland, OH: Arthur H. Clark, 1919). For a discussion about Mexican silver in the Philippines and China, see Katharine Bjork, "The Link That Kept the Philippines Spanish: Mexican Merchant Interests and the Manila Trade, 1571–1815, *Journal of World History* 9, no. 1 (1998): 25–50.

22. See Nicholas Van Hear, *New Diasporas: The Mass Exodus, Dispersal and Regrouping of Migrant Communities* (Seattle: University of Washington Press, 1998), pp. 15–16; Douglas Massey, "Theories of International Migration: A Review and Appraisal," *Population and Development Review* 19, no. 3 (1993): 431–466; Alejandro Portes and Julia Sensenbrenner, "Embeddedness and Immigration: Notes on the Social Determination of Economic Action," *American Journal of Sociology* 98, no. 6 (1993): 1320–1350.

23. Chicano, Asian American, and labor historians have greatly influenced this book. In particular, the groundbreaking essay of James Barrett, David Roediger, and Klaus Unger, and the sweeping works of Karen Isaksen Leonard, Sucheng Chan, and George J. Sánchez inform my discussion of work patterns and the formation of American ethnic identities in southern Arizona. See James Barrett, David

Roediger, and Klaus Unger, "In-Between Peoples: Race, Nationality, and the 'New Immigrant' Working Class in the United States," *Werkstatt Geschichte*, 14, no. 39 (2005): 7–34; Karen Isaksen Leonard, *Making Ethnic Choices: California's Punjabi Mexican Americans* (Philadelphia: Temple University Press, 1992); Sucheng Chan, *This Bittersweet Soil: The Chinese in California* (Berkeley: University of California Press, 1989); and George J. Sánchez, *Becoming Mexican American: Ethnicity, Culture, and Identity in Chicano Los Angeles, 1900–1945* (New York: Oxford University Press, 1993).

24. I borrow Mae Ngai's concept of "impossible subjects" for my discussion of Chinese and Mexican *fronterizos*. See Ngai, "The Strange Career of the Illegal Alien: Immigration Restriction and Deportation Policy in the United States, 1921–1965, *Law and History Review* 21, no. 1 (2003): 69–107; and *Impossible Subjects: Illegal Aliens and the Making of Modern America* (Princeton, NJ: Princeton University Press, 2004).

25. See several articles in the *Tucson Daily Citizen*: "China Fights Sonora Order," August 29, 1931; "Chinese Envoy Seeks to End Exile Orders," September 2, 1931, p. 4; "U.S. to Aid Chinese in Sonora Case," September 3, 1931; "Gung'l Asks Orders in Handling Influx of Expelled Chinese," August 31, 1931, pp. 1, 6; "Canton Irate with Mexico," September 9, 1931; and "U.S. Asked to Aid Expelled Chinese," September 1, 1931, p. 1.

26. "China Fights Order," *Tucson Daily Citizen*, August 29, 1931, p. 1; "Expulsion of Chinese from Sonora Is Denied," *Arizona Daily Star*, September 6, 1931, p. 1; and "Employment, Sonora and the Chinese," *Arizona Daily Star*, September 6, 1931, p. 8.

27. "Mexican Wives Leaving Sonora," *Arizona Daily Star*, September 5, 1931, p. 1. "Exiles Start Journey to Land of Birth," *Tucson Daily Citizen*, September 8, 1931, p. 1.

28. Camacho, "Traversing Boundaries," p. 144.

29. Secretaría de la Economía de la Nacional, Dirección General de Estadística, Mexico, *Sexto censo de población, 1940: resúmen general* (Mexico City: Talleres Gráficos de la Nación, 1943), pp. 9–10, 47–48. Of the 155 Chinese remaining in Sonora, 148 were men and sixty were naturalized Mexican citizens, and only seven were women, three of whom were naturalized Mexican citizens.

CHAPTER 1

1. Matías Romero, *Mexico and the United States: A Study of Subjects Affecting Their Political, Commercial, and Social Relations, Made with a View to Their Promotion* (New York: Knickerbocker Press, 1898), pp. iii–iv.

2. Matías Romero, ed., *Correspondencia de la legación mexicana durante la intervención extranjera, 1860–1868*, 10 vols. (Mexico City: Imprenta de Gobierno, 1870–1892), pp. 44–45.

3. "Inmigración china en México," *Revista Universal*, August 20, 1875, p. 1.

4. "Conveniencia de enviar una legación mexicana a China y al Japón," *El Correo del Comercio*, July 18, 1876, p. 1.

5. Letter from Matías Romero to A. Ignacio Mariscal, Secretary of Foreign Relations, September 14, 1882, 44:6:47, Secretaría de Relaciones Exteriores, Direc-

ción General del Acervo Histórico Diplomático Mexico City; from here on referred to as AHSRE.

6. Instituto Matías Romero (Mexico) and Rosario Green, *Instituto Matías Romero: XXV aniversario* (Mexico City: Secretaría de Relaciones Exteriores, 1999), pp. 135–140. Also consult Matías Romero, *Diario personal, 1855–1865*, ed. Emma Cosío Villegas (Mexico City: El Colegio de México, 1960), pp. 56–63; and Felipe Pardinas, *Relaciones diplomáticas entre China y México, 1898–1948*, vol. 1 (Mexico City: Secretaría de Relaciones Exteriores, 1982).

7. General R. Alexander, *British Opium Smuggling: The Illegality of the East India Company's Monopoly of the Drug; and Its Injurious Effects upon India, China, and the Commerce of Great Britain* (London: Judd and Glass Printers, 1856), pp. 23–26.

8. Algernon Sydney Thelwall, *The Iniquities of the Opium Trade with China; Being a Development of the Main Causes Which Exclude the Merchants of Great Britain from the Advantages of an Unrestricted Commercial Intercourse with That Vast Empire* (London: William H. Allen, 1839), pp. 47, 86.

9. Donald Matheson, *What Is the Opium Trade?* (Edinburgh, Scotland: Thomas Constable, 1857), pp. 9–11; and Ellen N. La Motte, *The Opium Monopoly* (New York: Macmillan, 1920), pp. 65–66.

10. Thelwall, *The Iniquities of the Opium Trade with China*, 73. The original text was in capital letters for Thelwall's emphasis, but I have chosen not to do so here.

11. Westel W. Willoughby, *Foreign Rights and Interests in China* (Baltimore, MD: Johns Hopkins University Press, 1920), pp. 102–103, 106–107. The Nanking Treaty (1842) stipulated other demands. The Qing government paid $6 million in indemnities to *hong* and British opium merchants for losses in trade, and they compensated the British government $12 million in war expenses. After 1861, Russian, French British, and American legations in Beijing were established and foreign ships were permitted to navigate the Yangtze River. For more on the decline of the so-called Canton system and the rise of Western markets in China, see Paul Arthur Van Dyke, *The Canton Trade: Life and Enterprise on the China Coast, 1700–1845* (Hong Kong: Hong Kong University Press, 2005).

12. Adam McKeown, "Conceptualizing Chinese Diasporas, 1842–1949," *Journal of Asian Studies* 58, no. 2 (1999): 306–337; esp. 313, 315. Until the mid-1840s, the Qing society and economy organized markets to meet local and regional needs; farming and industry in the northern regions were vital in this endeavor. For the importance of Shanghai and Hangzhou as crucial port cities before 1842, see Robert Fortune, *Two Visits to the Tea Countries of China and the British Tea Plantations in the Himalaya with a Narrative of Adventures, and a Full Description of the Culture of the Tea Plant, the Agriculture, Horticulture, and Botany of China* (London: W. Clowes, 1852), pp. 43–44, 83–86.

13. Ernest John Eitel, *Europe in China: The History of Hongkong from the Beginning to the Year 1882* (London: Luzac, 1895), pp. 171–172. The Qing government officially ceded Hong Kong to the British Empire on September 9, 1842, as part of the Nanking Treaty agreement, but activities of the British free-trade colony began in early 1840.

14. John Francis Davis, *The Chinese: A General Description of the Empire of China and Its Inhabitants* (New York: Harper, 1836), 31. For a more thorough discussion of trade in Canton, see John King Fairbank, *Trade and Diplomacy on the China Coast: The Opening of the Treaty Ports, 1842–1854* (Cambridge, MA: Harvard University Press, 1964), pp. 39–56; and for more on the relationship between Europeans and *hong* merchants, see Weng Eang Cheong, *The Hong Merchants of Canton: Chinese Merchants in Sino-Western Trade, 1684–1798* (New York: Routledge, 1997).

15. David Scott, *China and the International System, 1840–1949: Power, Presence, and Perceptions in a Century of Humiliation* (Albany: State University of New York Press, 2008), pp. 26–35; Yen-p'ing Hao, *The Commercial Revolution in Nineteenth-Century China: The Rise of Sino-Western Mercantile Capitalism* (Berkeley: University of California Press, 1986), pp. 12, 71–86; Peter Ward Fay, *The Opium War, 1840–1842: Barbarians in the Celestial Empire in the Early Part of the Nineteenth Century and the War by Which They Forced Her Gates* (Chapel Hill: University of North Carolina Press, 1997), pp. 29–45.

16. For accounts of the Taiping Rebellion, see Thomas H. Reilly, *The Taiping Heavenly Kingdom: Rebellion and the Blasphemy of Empire* (Seattle: University of Washington Press, 2004); and Jonathan D. Spence, *God's Chinese Son: The Taiping Heavenly Kingdom of Hong Xiuquan* (New York: Norton: 1996).

17. Triad organizations were Chinese secret societies, originally formed in the late seventeenth century to overthrow the *Qing* dynasty and restore its Chinese Ming predecessor. They had similar rituals and acted as both fraternal and criminal organizations. They grew in strength after the Red Turban Rebellion and played an erratic and violent role in China. For more on Chinese triads, see Floyd Chueng, "Performing Exclusion and Resistance: Anti-Chinese League and Chee Kung Tong Parades in Territorial Arizona," *Drama Review* 46, no. 1 (2002): 39–59; and L. Eve Armentrout Ma, "Urban Chinese at the Sinitic Frontier: Social Organizations in United States' Chinatowns, 1849–1898," *Modern Asian Studies* 17, no. 1 (1983): 107–135.

18. Hsu, *Dreaming of Gold, Dreaming of Home*, pp. 24–27; and Jaeyoon Kim, "The Heaven and Earth Society and the Red Turban Rebellion in Late Qing China," *Journal of Humanities and Social Sciences* 3, no. 1 (2009): 1–35.

19. Persia Crawford Campbell, *Chinese Coolie Emigration to Countries with the British Empire* (Charleston, SC: BiblioLife, 2009); esp. pp. 86–135. For comparative studies of Chinese and Indian migrant labor and sugar production in the British Caribbean, see Walton Look Lai, *Indentured Labor, Caribbean Sugar: Chinese and Indian Migrants to the British West Indies, 1838–1918* (Baltimore, MD: Johns Hopkins University Press, 1993); Andrew Wilson, ed., *The Chinese in the Caribbean* (Princeton, NJ: Markus Weiner, 2004); and Martin Edward Peck's work comparing the Spanish and British West Indies indenture systems, "Chinese Coolie Emigration to Latin America," (master's thesis, Ohio State University, 1934).

20. Jung, "Outlawing "Coolies," p. 679.

21. Arnold Meagher, *The Coolie Trade: The Traffic in Chinese Labors to Latin America 1847–1874* (Bloomington, IN: Xlibris, 2008), pp. 34–39; Rebecca Scott, *Slave Emancipation in Cuba: The Transition to Free Labor, 1860–1899* (Princeton, NJ: Princeton University Press, 1985), pp. 29–35, 88–110; Matthew Guterl, "After

Slavery: Asian Labor, the American South, and the Age of Emancipation, *Journal of World History* 14, no. 2 (2003): 209–242; Lucy M. Cohen, *The Chinese in the Post-Civil War South: A People Without History* (Baton Rouge: Louisiana State University Press, 1984), pp. 41–54.

22. There are several hundred newspaper accounts of the coolie trade into Latin America and the Caribbean. See, for example, "The Chinese Labor Question: Coolie Emigration and Stream of Industrials from Asia," *New York Herald*, July 27, 1869, p. 5.

23. Juan Pérez de la Riva, *Los culíes chinos en Cuba* (La Habana: Editorial de Ciencias Sociales, 2000), esp. pp. 19–25, 111–124; Lisa Yun and Ricardo René Laremont, "Chinese Coolies and African Slaves in Cuba, 1847–1874," *Journal of Asian American Studies* 4, no. 2 (2001): 99–122; Lisa Yun, *The Coolie Speaks*, pp. 16–17, 28–35.

24. "Lord Edward to West India Committee," Enclosure 530, British Parliamentary Papers, China, Irish University Press Area Studies Series, vol. 2 (Dublin: Irish Academic Press, 1971); from here on referred to as BPPC.

25. *Ta Tsing Leu Lee: Being the Fundamental Laws, and a Selection from the Supplementary Statutes, of the Penal Code of China*, trans. George Thomas Staunton (London: Cadell and Davis, 1810), pp. 543–544. One such statute reads, "All . . . private citizens who clandestinely proceeded to sea or trade, or who remove to a foreign island . . . shall be punished according to the law against communicating with rebels and enemies, and consequently suffer death by being beheaded." For a deft discussion of the Ming and Qing immigration laws, see Robert L. Irick, *Ch'ing Policy Toward the Coolie Trade, 1847–1878* (Taipei, Taiwan: Chinese Material Center, 1982), pp. 6–15; and Ching Yen Hwang, *Coolies and Mandarins: China's Protection of Overseas Chinese in the Late Ch'ing Period, 1851–1911* (Singapore: University of Singapore Press, 1985).

26. Letter from Dr. John Bowring to the Earl of Malmsbury, December 27, 1852, vol. 2, no 14, *BPPC*.

27. "Mr. Harvey to Dr. Bowing," Enclosure 7 in vol. 3, no. 14, December 22, 1852, *BPPC*.

28. Hubert Howe Bancroft, *The New Pacific* (New York: Bancroft, 1915), pp. 413–414.

29. U.S. Census Bureau. "Sex, General Nativity, and Color: Chinese Population by Counties," *Population Census of the United States, 1870* (Washington, DC: U.S. Government Printing Office, 1872), p. 345. For the history of Chinese in Idaho, Oregon, Utah, and Nevada, respectively, see Leiping Zhu, *A Chinaman's Chance: The Chinese on the Rocky Mountain Mining Frontier* (Boulder: University of Colorado, 1997); Marie Rose Wong, *Sweet Cakes, Long Journey: The Chinatowns of Portland, Oregon* (Seattle: University of Washington Press, 2004); Andrew Taylor Kirk, "Radical Labor, Racism, and the Preservation of Hegemony in Ogden, Territorial Utah, 1885–1886," *American Journalism* 24, no. 4 (2007): 149–173; and Leiping Zhu and Rose Estep Fosha, *Ethnic Oasis: The Chinese in the Black Hills* (Pierre: South Dakota State Historical Society Press, 2004).

30. Letter from Lieutenant Governor W. Caine to his Grace the Duke of Newcastle, enclosure in vol. 4, no. 6, May 4, 1854, BPPC.

31. Letter from Dr. John Bowring to the Earl of Malmesbury, May 17, 1852, enclosure in vol. 3, no. 2, BPPC.

32. "Memorandum of the Coolie Ships on Board of Which Mutinies Have Occurred, or in Which Vessels or Passengers Have Met with Disaster, from the Year 1845 up to the Year 1872," n. d., enclosure 3, vol. 4, no. 6, *BPPC*.

33. Letter from Dr. John Bowring to the Earl of Malmesbury, August 3, 1852, enclosure 5, vol. 3, BPPC.

34. "Depositions of Kidnapped Coolies Brought from Whampoa," January 12, 1860, enclosure 26, vol. 4, no. 13, deposition no. 68, BPPC.

35. Letter from Sin Hoon to Robert J. Nelson, enclosure 4, vol. 3, no. 5, August 30, 1852, in "Papers Relating to Chinese Immigrants Recently Introduced into British Guiana and Trinidad," vol. 3, BPPC. On Spanish salaries, see letter from James T. White to Messrs. Tait and Co., December 9, 1853, enclosure 3, vol. 3, no. 3, BPPC.

36. Guano not only contained the nitrates of fish-eating birds but also was uniquely constituted from weather patterns that prevented rainfall and its dilution. For more on the guano trade, Chinese labor, and Peru's economy, see Juan de Arona, *La Inmigración en el Perú: Monografía Histórico-Crítica* (Lima, Peru: Imprenta del Universo, de Carlos Prince, 1891), pp. 39–81; Watt Stewart, *La servidumbre china en el Perú: una historia de los culíes chinos en el Perú, 1849–1874* (Lima, Peru: Mosca Azul Editores, 1976); and Paul Gootenberg, *Imagining Development: Economic Ideas in Peru's "Fictitious Prosperity" of Guano, 1840–1880* (Berkeley: University of California Press, 1993).

37. Various sources were consulted in listing the Chinese populations in Cuba, Peru, and the British Caribbean. For Cuba, see Denise Helly, *The Cuba Commission Report: A Hidden History of the Chinese in Cuba* (Baltimore, MD: Johns Hopkins University Press, 1993), p. 21; Yun, *The Coolie Speaks*, 19–20; Yun and Laremont, "Chinese Coolies and African Slaves," p. 113; Eugenio Chang-Rodríguez, "Chinese Labor Migration into Latin America in the Nineteenth Century," *Revista de Historia de America* 46 (December 1958): 379–381. Yun and Laremont use figures from British Consulate reports of 1873, citing that 138,156 Chinese embarked on ships headed for Cuba from 1847 to 1873, whereas Eugenio Chang-Rodríguez references 140,000.

38. Yun, *The Coolie Speaks*, pp. 16–17, 28–35. See also Evelyn Hu-Dehart, "Chinese Coolie Labor in Cuba and Peru in the Nineteenth Century: Free Labor or Neoslavery?" *Journal of Overseas Chinese Studies* 2, no. 2 (1992): 149–181; and Hu-Dehart, "Chinese Coolie Labour in Cuba in the Nineteenth Century: Free Labour or Neo-Slavery?," *Slavery and Abolition: A Journal of Slave and Post-Slave Studies* 14, no. 1 (1993): 67–83.

39. Anita Bradley, *Trans-Pacific Relations of Latin America: An Introductory Essay and Selected Bibliography* (New York: Institute of Pacific Relations, 1942), p. 48. See also Ma. Isabel Chong Martínez, *La migración china hacia Cuba 1850–1930* (Mexico City: Facultad de Ciencias Políticas y Sociales-UNAM, 1986), pp. 120–140.

40. Yun, *The Coolie Speaks*, 12–13; and Herbert S. Klein, *African Slavery in Latin America and the Caribbean* (Oxford, UK: Oxford University Press, 1986), p. 92.

41. Frederic Phillip Maude and Charles Edward Pollock, *A Compendium of the*

*Law of Merchant Shipping: With Appendix Containing All the Statutes, Orders in Council and Forms of Practical Utility*, Vol. 1 (London: Henry Sweet, 1881), p. 721.

42. Jung, *Coolies and Cane*, pp. 9, 11–38.

43. Cong. Rec., 36th Cong., 1st sess., HED 88, p. 1; 37th Cong., 2d sess., HED 16, esp. pp. 1, 3–16, 21–36; Cong. Globe, 37th Cong., 2d sess., pp. 350–352.

44. William McDonald, ed., *Select Statutes and Other Documents Illustrative of the History of the United States, 1861–1898* (New York: Macmillan, 1898), pp. 25–27; and U.S. Congress, *1862 Anti-Coolie Law*, 37th Cong., 2nd sess., 12 Stat. 340, February 19, 1862, pp. 340–341.

45. See the Burlingame Treaty in Frederick Wells Williams, *Anson Burlingame and the First Chinese Mission to Foreign Powers* (New York: Scribner's, 1912), pp. 275–280.

46. Andrew Gyory, *Closing the Gate: Race, Politics, and the Chinese Exclusion Act* (Chapel Hill: University of North Carolina Press, 1998), pp. 76–90.

47. Meagher, *The Coolie Trade*, 106, 127; Yun and Laremont, "Chinese Coolies and African Slaves," pp. 111–112. For a detailed analysis of the human misery and politics of ending the coolie trade, seeHelly, *The Cuba Commission Report*. For an analysis of the report, see Yun, *The Coolie Speaks*.

48. Chang-Rodriguez, "Chinese Labor Migration," p. 383.

49. Thomas W. Chinn, H. Mark Lai, and Philip P. Choy, eds., *A History of the Chinese in California: A Syllabus* (San Francisco: Chinese Historical Society of America, n. d.), p. 265, Table 2.

50. In 1810, Father Miguel Hidalgo called for the end of slavery in Mexico. However, it was not until the final years of the independence movement that the Spanish viceroyalty in Mexico City abolished the slave trade, in 1817. For more than a decade the slave trade into Mexico was suspended, until 1829, when slavery was abolished under the regime of Vicente Guerrero. See Gonzalo Aguirre Beltrán, "The Slave Trade in Mexico," *Hispanic American Review* 24, no. 3 (1994): 412–431; Dennis N. Valdés, "The Decline of Slavery in Mexico," *The Americas* 44, no. 2 (1987): 167–194; and Pierre L. Van Den Berghe, "The African Disapora in Mexico, Brazil, and the United States, *Social Forces* 54, no. 3 (1976): 530–545. For a global perspective on abolitionism see Frederick Cooper, Thomas C. Holt, and Rebecca Scott, eds., *Beyond Slavery: Explorations of Race, Labor, and Citizenship in Postemancipation Societies* (Chapel Hill: University of North Carolina Press, 2000).

51. Jung, *Coolies and Cane*, 19–40; Guterl, "After Slavery; and Cohen, *The Chinese in the Post-Civil War South*, pp. 41–54.

52. *St Louis Globe-Democrat* (St. Louis, MO), February 25, 1879, p. 2.

53. Francis A. Walker, *A Compendium of the Ninth Census* (Washington, DC: U.S. Government Printing Office, 1872), pp. 28–29.

54. B. E. Lloyd, *Lights and Shades in San Francisco* (San Francisco: A. L. Bancroft, 1876), p. 259.

55. Committee of the Senate of the State of California, *Chinese Immigration: The Social, Moral, and Political Effect of Chinese Immigration.* (Sacramento: State Printing Office, 1876), p. 33. See also Lee, *At America's Gates*, pp. 25–27.

56. "Chinese in Tucson, *Arizona Daily Star*, July 9, 1879, p. 1.

57. *Acts, Resolutions, and Memorials Adopted by the Sixth Legislative Assembly of the Territory of Arizona* (Tucson: Office of the Arizona Citizen, 1871), pp. 66–67.

58. *Laws of the Territory of Arizona: Thirteenth Legislative Assembly; Also Memorials and Resolutions* (San Francisco: H. S. Crocker, 1885), p. 73.

59. Walker, *A Compendium of the Ninth Census*, pp. 126–135.

60. See also "Chinese Population by Decades and Geographical Divisions" in the Tucson Chinese Research Collection, MS 1242, Arizona Historical Society, Tucson, p. 595.

61. Correspondence from James Chester Worthington to Dan Worthington, June 21, 1880, James Chester Worthington Papers, MS 0890, folder 1, AHS.

62. Historian Alexander Saxton contends that as an outcome of these rallies, California labor leaders discovered a political issue strong enough to unite labor in California—the expulsion of the Chinese from the state and the ending of free immigration into the United States. For an explanation of "sand lot" influence, see Alexander Saxton in *The Indispensable Enemy: Labor and the Anti-Chinese Movement in California* (Berkeley: University of California Press, 1971), pp. 117–123; and Ronald Takaki, *Strangers from a Different Shore: A History of Asian Americans* (Boston: Little, Brown, 1989). For a convincing challenge to Saxton's thesis, see Gyory, *Closing the Gate*, pp. 109–135.

63. Gyory, *Closing the Gate*, pp. 110–120, 133.

64. Correspondence to Dan Worthington from James Chester Worthington, July 16, 1880, MS 0890, folder 1, AHS.

65. An act to execute certain treaty stipulations relating to the Chinese, May 6, 1882, Enrolled Acts and Resolutions of Congress, 1789–1996, General Records of the United States Government, RG 11, National Archives and Records Administration, Washington, DC; hereafter referred to as NARA-DC.

66. Matías Romero, *Geographical and Statistical Notes on Mexico, 1837–1898* (New York: Putnam's, 1898), p. 242. Many authors have commented on the use of Chinese labor in northern Mexico during the mid-1860s. Ostensibly these workers toiled in construction and mining projects but did not settle permanently in Mexico. See Mexico, *Maximilian's Asiatic Colonization Scheme*, trans. Richard H. Dillon (Chicago: 1952). For accounts of Chinese in Sonora before 1880, see *Boletín Oficial* (Ures), July 14, 1876; *La Era Nueva* (Hermosillo) February 3, 1878; *El Municipio* (Guaymas), March 1, 1878; and *La Constitución* (Hermosillo), June 26, 1879.

67. As quoted in Matías Romero, *Revista Universal* (Mexico City), May 30, 1874, p. 1.

68. *La Libertad* (Mexico City), October 3, 1879, p. 1.

69. Alberto Mertes in *El Monitor Republicano* (Mexico City), March 26, 1884; and "Los Chinos," *El Monitor Republicano*, April 3, 1886, p. 3.

70. Emperor Maximilian von Hapsburg was installed as monarch in Mexico in 1864 by Napoleon III and was the de facto head of state. He experimented with recruiting former confederate soldiers, Turks, Egyptians, and South Asians. He recruited Chinese to work on the Ferrocarril Nacional Central (Central National Railroad) and granted a ten-year royal concession to D. Manuel B. da Cunha Reis

to contract with South Asian and Arab laborers for five to ten years on mining and agricultural projects in Veracruz. Maximilian's project was short-lived; in 1867 Benito Juárez overthrew the French despot. For a discussion on Arab immigration in early republican Mexico, see da Cunha Reis, *Estatutos de la Compañía de Colonización Asiática* (Mexico City: Imprenta de J. M. Lara, 1866), pp. 154–157. For discussion of Middle Eastern immigration into Mexico at the beginning of the late nineteenth century, see Theresa Alfaro-Velcamp, *So Far from Allah: Middle Eastern Immigrants in Modern Mexico* (Austin: University of Texas Press, 2007); and Zidane Zeraoui, "Los arabes en Mexico: el perfil de la migración," in *Destino México: un estudio de las migraciones asiáticas a México siglos XIX y XX*, ed. Maria Elena Ota Mishima (Mexico City: El Colegio de Mexico, 1997), p. 303. For a discussion of Arab immigration in the early republic and general immigration into Mexico, see Dieter George Berninger, *La inmigración en México, 1821–1857* (Mexico City: Secretaría de educación pública, 1974); and Moisés González Navarro, *Los extranjeros en México y los mexicanos en el extranjero, 1821–1970* (Mexico City: Colegio de México, Centro de Estudios Históricos, 1993).

71. Justo Sierra, *The Political Evolution of the Mexican People*, trans. Charles Ramsdell (Austin: University of Texas Press, 1969), p. 368.

72. Mexico, "Corresponde al año trascurrido de diciembre de 1876 a noviembre de 1877," in *Memoria presentada al Congreso de la Unión por el Secretario de Fomento, Colonización, Industria, y Comercio* (Mexico City: 1877), pp. 440–442.

73. Letter to J. Ross Browne, U.S. Minister to China, from the Office of Lower California Company, New York, June 8, 1868, 15:1:6, AHSRE. See also J. Ross Browne, "Explorations in Lower California," *Harpers* 37 (1868): 740–752.

74. Duncan, "The Chinese and the Economic Development of Northern Baja California," pp. 616, 614–647.

75. Arthur F. Corwin, "Historia de la emigración mexicana, 1900–1970: literatura e investigación," *Historia mexicana* 22 (October-December 1972): 188–220; and Moisés González Navarro, *La colonización en Mexico, 1877–1910* (Mexico City: Talleres de Impresión de Estampillas y Valores, 1960), pp. 160–172.

76. Moisés González Navarro, El Porfiriato: La vida social, Vol. 4 (Mexico City: Hermes, 1957), pp. 160, 166.

77. "Articles of Contract Between the Pacific Mail Steamship Company and the Mexican Republic," in correspondence of October 10, 1895, in United States Department of State, dispatches from United States Consuls in Acapulco, Mexico, 1823–1906, National Archives Microfilm Publications, Microcopy 143, reel 7 (Washington, DC: National Archives and Record Service, 1949), RG 59; from here on referred to as USCAMEX.

78. Letter from Spenser St. John, British Envoy to Mexico, to Foreign Minister Lord Granville, March 19, 1884, Great Britain, Public Record Office, Foreign Office, Consular Dispatches from Mexico, 1822–1902, series 50/volume 445/folio 33, reel 178, Britain, Foreign Office, Bancroft Library; from here on referred to as BFO-BL.

79. Letter from Ignacio Mariscal to secretary of state, Mexico, October 8, 1884, in Mexico Foreign Relations Office, *Correspondencia Diplomática Cambiada entre el Gobierno de los Estados Unidos Mexicanos y Los Varias Potencias*

*Extranjeras*, vol. 4 (Mexico City: Tipografía La Luz, 1887), pp. 606–607; and letter to Theodore Schneider from Edward Wingfield, October 21, 1884, 44:6:35, 1884–1888, AHSRE.

80. Letter from Spenser St. John to Foreign Minister Lord Granville, March 19, 1884, 50/445/33, reel 178, BFO-BL.

81. Letter to José Fernández from Spenser St. John, British Special Envoy in Mexico, December 2, 1884–1888, 44:6:35, AHSRE.

82. Ibid.

83. Ibid.

84. Letter from Ignacio Mariscal, minister of foreign affairs, to Lord Edmond Fitzmaurice, undersecretary of British Foreign Affairs, December 3, 1884, 44:6:35, 1884-1888, AHSRE. Mariscal spent months negotiating the resumption of diplomatic relations with Great Britain, and these efforts were on the verge of success. The resumption of diplomatic relations hinged on resolving claims for past losses made by British citizens in Mexico. Mexico feared potential claims by Chinese migrants if they fell under British protection.

85. "Good offices" means the "unofficial, personal and friendly efforts of a diplomatic agent, as distinguished from the official, formal, and governmental support of a diplomatic claim." See Edwin Montefiore Borchard, *The Diplomatic Protection of Citizens Abroad: Or the Law of International Claims* (New York: Banks Law, 1915), p. 440. For discussion of the decision to accept good offices over official diplomatic claim, see letter to Ignacio Mariscal, Minister of Foreign Relations, from Lionel Carden, British Envoy to Mexico, April 8, 1885, 44:6:35, AHSRE. See also Lionel Carden, British Envoy to Mexico, to Ignacio Mariscal, Minister of Foreign Relations in Mexico, May 1, 1885, Romero, *Correspondencia, 1881–1886*, vol. 4, p. 629.

86. Letter to Minister Chang from Matías Romero, May 5, 1886, L:E:1983, H/352 (72:51) "899"/1, AHSRE.

87. Letter to Matías Romero from Minister Chang, December 9, 1887, L:E:1983. /352 (72:51) "899"/1, AHSRE.

88. Ministerio de Fomento, Mexico, *Boletín de la dirección general de estadística de la Republica Mexicana, 1888–1891*, 8 vols. (Mexico City: n.p., 1888–1891), vol. 1, pp. 41–46; vol. 2, pp. 78–84; vol. 3, 4, pp. 88–89; vol. 6, p. 129; vol. 8, p. 130. In the same period, Delia Salazar Anaya cites 3,850 Chinese landing in Mexico. See *La población extranjera en México (1895–1990): Un recuento con base en los censos generales de población* (Mexico City: Instituto Nacional de Antropología e Historia, 1996), pp. 276–278.

89. Mexico, *Colonization and Naturalization Laws of the Republic of Mexico with Amendments* (Mexico City: n. p., 1905), p. 6.

90. Mexico, *Colonization and Naturalization Laws*, pp. 12–18.

91. For more on the Qing immigration law, *hai jin*, see Guanhua Wang, *In Search of Justice: The 1905–1906 Chinese Anti-American Boycott* (Cambridge, MA: Harvard University Asia Center and Harvard University Press, 2001), pp. 19–21.

92. John V. A. MacMurray, *Treaties and Agreements with and Concerning China, 1894–1919* (New York: Oxford University Press, 1921), p. 214; Manuel de Azpiroz and Wu Ting-fang represented Mexico and China, respectively. The

treaty was ratified in Washington, DC, on July 9, 1900. For a thorough history of events before and after treaty negotiations, see Vera Valdéz Lakowsky, "Estudio historicó del tratado sino-mexicano de 1899," (PhD diss., Universidad Nacional Autónoma de México, Mexico City, 1979); and Kennett Cott, "Mexican Diplomacy and the Chinese Issue, 1876–1910," *Hispanic American Historical Review* 67, no. 1 (1987): 63–85.

93. See Articles IV, V, and VIII of the Treaty of Amity, Commerce, and Navigation. The treaty was ratified for a ten-year period, after which Mexican and Chinese officials could review terms. See William Woodville Rockhill, ed., *Treaties and Conventions with or concerning China and Korea, 1894–1904, Together with Various State Papers and Documents Affecting Foreign Interests* (Washington, DC: U.S. Government Printing Office, 1904), pp. 468–475.

94. MacMurray, *Treaties and Agreements*, p. 214.

95. Ibid. Compare Articles 13, 14, and 15 to Article 17.

96. Correspondence, "Petition from over 480 Chinese Workers in Tampico," June 13, 1899, 17:21:55, AHSRE. In 1884, the Mexican Pacific Navigation Company was established to transport Asians (Chinese, Koreans, and Japanese) to Tampico and Veracruz to complete the Tehuantepec railroad under the London firm of contractors S. Pearson & Son. It is unclear how many workers were Korean and how many were Chinese. The Japanese government prevented any emigration to Mexico until 1895, and only then as colonists, despite Mexico and Japan commencing diplomatic relations in 1888.

97. Native Sonorans spoke Tepiman, Opatan, Taracahitan, Tubar, Corachol, and Cahitan, and each of these languages contained several dialects. For an analysis of Uto-Aztecan language groups, see Mario Cortina-Borja and Leopoldo Valiñas C., "Some Remarks on Uto-Aztecan Classification," *International Journal of American Linguistics* 55, no. 2 (1989): 214–239; and Wick R. Miller, "The Classification of the Uto-Aztecan Languages Based on Lexical Evidence," *International Journal of American Linguistics* 50 (January 1984): 1–24.

98. I am greatly indebted to Cynthia Radding's seminal histories on native Sonorans under Spanish rule. Her assertion that Spanish colonialism created overlapping spheres of power illuminates in this work the economic and cultural foundations of national society in the Arizona-Sonora borderlands. See Cynthia Radding Murrieta, *Entre el desierto y la sierra: las naciones o'odham y tegüima de Sonora, 1530–1840* (Mexico City: Centro de Investigaciones y Estudios Superiores en Antropología , 1995); and *Ciclos demográficos, trabajo y comunidad en los pueblos serranos de la Provincia de Sonora, siglo XVIII (Congreso sobre a História da População da América Latina* (Ouro Preto, Brazil: Fundação SEADE, 1990). See also Cynthia Radding, *Wandering Peoples;* and Radding, *Landscapes of Power and Identity: Comparative Histories in the Sonoran Desert and the Forests of Amazonia from Colony to Republic* (Durham, NC: Duke University Press, 2005).

99. When in 1854 officials signed what Americans called the Gadsden Purchase and what Mexicans termed the Mesilla Treaty, Mexico received payment of $10 million for land that eventually coursed the transcontinental railroad through southern Arizona, connecting the American southwest to both Pacific and Southern markets. For more discussion, see Legislative Assembly of the Territory of Arizona,

*The Territory of Arizona: A Brief History and Summary* (Tucson: Citizen Office, 1874). See also B. Sacks, *Be It Enacted: The Creation of the Territory of Arizona* (Phoenix: Arizona Historical Foundation, 1964); Lamar, *The Far Southwest;* and James Officer, *Hispanic Arizona, 1536–1856* (Tucson: University of Arizona Press, 1987).

100. See the definition of kinship in Manuel L. Carlos, "Kinship and Modernization in Mexico: A Comparative Analysis," *Anthropological Quarterly* 46, no. 2 (1973): 75–91; Hugo G. Nutini and Douglas R. White, "Community Variations and Network Structure in the Social Functions of Compadrazgo in Rural Tlaxcala, Mexico," *Ethnology* 16, no. 4 (1977): 353–384.

101. For an examination of kinship networks in Arizona during the late nineteenth century, see Eric Meeks, *Border Citizens: The Making of Indians, Mexicans, and Anglos in Arizona* (Austin: University of Texas Press, 2007).

CHAPTER 2

A portion of this chapter was originally published as Grace Peña Delgado, "Of Kith and Kin: Land, Leases, and Guanxi in Tucson's Chinese and Mexican Communities, 1880s–1920s," *Journal of Arizona History* 46, no. 1 (2005): 33–54; reprinted with permission of the AHS. Another portion of this chapter was originally published as Grace Delgado, "Neighbors by Nature: Relationships, Border Crossings, and Transnational Communities in the Era of Chinese Exclusion," *Pacific Historical Review* 80, no. 3 (2011): 401–429. (c) The Pacific Coast Branch, American Historical Association, published by the University of California Press; it is reprinted here with the permission of the University of California Press. Another portion of this chapter was originally published as Grace Peña Delgado, "At Exclusion's Southern Gate: Changing Categories of Race and Class Among Chinese Fronterizos, 1882–1904," in *Continental Crossroads: Remapping U.S.-Mexico Borderlands History*, ed. Samuel Truett and Elliott Young, pp. 183–207; copyright 2004, Duke University Press, all rights reserved, reprinted by permission of the publisher.

1. I have used the names of Chinese individuals as they have appeared in primary sources. For the most part, Chinese immigrants maintained the traditional ordering of their name once they were in the United States—that is, a surname or "family name" (such as Lee) followed by a given name or "first name" (such as Ding). It was also common for two given names to follow a surname (as in Don San Wo). At times Chinese immigrants in Mexico and the United States adopted a Westernized name by reversing the surname–given-name order to given-name–surname (as in Tim Chong). For the most part, however, the Chinese immigrants in Sonora adopted a Western-style name (such as Juan Lung Tain) more quickly than Chinese immigrants in Arizona did, perhaps in keeping with Spanish-style names and the national culture. This practice was especially common among Chinese merchants in Sonora.

2. "Speeches: Chinese Heritage History," folder 1, box 12, Esther Don Tang Collection, MSS 94, Arizona Historical Foundation (from here on referred to as AHF), Hayden Library, Phoenix, Arizona; from here on referred to as EDTC.

3. Don San Wo and Dolores M. Serón, lease, April 3, 1902, Pima County Re-

corder's Office: Leases and Mortgages, 1880–1902, RG 110, SG 5, Arizona State Library, Archives and Public Records (ASLAPR); from here on referred to as LM-PCRO.

4. By 1910, the majority of Chinese living in Arizona resided in the southern portion of the territory. The same was true for Mexicans, but they were much more dominant than the Chinese. See U.S. Census Bureau, *Thirteenth Census of the United States, 1910* (Washington, DC: U.S. Government Printing Office, 1914), Table 12, "Indian, Chinese, and Japanese Population, by Counties (Washington, DC, 1913), p. 80, and Table 1, "Color, Nativity, and Parentage," p. 77. Compare population statistics for Chinese and Mexicans in U.S. Census Bureau, *Eleventh Census of the United States* (Washington, DC: U.S. Government Printing Office, 1895), Table 33, "Foreign-Born Population Distributed According to Country of Birth, by Counties, 1890," p. 610. A small number of Chinese settled in the Arizona Territory, some joining Chinese railroad workers already in Prescott. In Phoenix, a family of five (three males and two females) operated a laundry business from their home. Twenty more toiled at the Vulture Mine near Wickenburg in 1868, but upon realizing the grave dangers of mining in the middle of Apache lands, they left the region, never to return. For more on the family in Wickenburg, see *Weekly Arizona Miner* 8, no. 10 (1871, March 11), p. 3. For more on the family in Phoenix, see Arizona State Historic Preservation Office, *The Chinese in Arizona, 1870–1950*, prepared by Melissa Keane, A. G. Rogge, and Bradford Luckingham (Phoenix: Arizona State Parks Board, 1992), p. 35.

5. This chapter builds on previous scholarship on Chinese in southern Arizona. See Lawrence Michael Fong, "Sojourners and Settlers: The Chinese Experience in Arizona," *Journal of Arizona History* 21, no. 3 (1980): 1–30; Heather S. Hatch, "The Chinese in the Southwest: A Photographic Record," *Journal of Arizona History* 21, no. 3 (1980): 257–274; Florence C. Lister and Robert H. Lister, *The Chinese of Early Tucson: Historic Archeology from the Tucson Urban Renewal Project* (Tucson: University of Arizona Press, 1989); J. Homer Thiel, *Archaeological Investigations of a Chinese Gardener's Household*, Tucson, Arizona (Tucson: Center for Desert Archaeology, 1997); Wengsheng Wang, "The First Chinese in Tucson: New Evidence on a Puzzling Question," *Journal of Arizona History* 43, no. 3 (2002): 369–380; and Andrea Pugsley, "'As I Kill This Chicken So May I Be Punished If I Tell an Untruth': Chinese Opposition to Legal Discrimination in the Arizona Territory, *Journal of Arizona History* 44, no. 2 (2003): 170–190.

6. Act of May 1882, 22 Stat. 58, Sec. 3. For population numbers, see U.S. Department of Commerce and Labor, Bureau of Immigration and Naturalization, *Annual Report of the Commissioner-General of Immigration* [from here on referred to as AR-CGI]: *1903–1911* (Washington, DC: U.S. Government Printing Office, 1912), p. 32. For more on the 1884 amendment, see *Chinese Treaty Stipulations*, 2254 H.rp.614, particularly Sec. 2; on the Scott Act, see the Act of September 13, 1888 (25 Stat. 476, Sec. 6, at 477), and the Act of May 5, 1892 (27 Stat. 25); on Hawaii, see the Act of July 7, 1898, and the Act of April 30, 1900 (31 Stat. 141); on the Philippines, see the Act of April 29, 1902; and on permanency, see the Act of April 27, 1904 (33 Stat. 428).

7. "Arizona," *Californian* 1, no. 4 (1880): 369.

8. U.S. Census Bureau, Tenth Census of the United States (Washington, DC: U.S. Government Printing Office, 1883), Table V, "Population, by Race and by Counties: 1880, 1870, 1860," p. 380. Not until the dismantling of the Chinese Exclusion Laws in 1943 would the Chinese in Arizona reach numerical heights on par with the population of the 1880s. For a compilation of demographic statistics on Chinese in Arizona, see Arizona State Historic Preservation Office, "The Chinese in Arizona, 1870–1950," prepared by Melissa Keane, A. G. Rogge, and Bradford Luckingham (Phoenix: Arizona State Parks Board, 1992), p. 14.

9. Very little has been written about early *guanxi* relations among Chinese migrants in the United States and Mexico, although much has been written on Chinese fraternal associations and surname organizations. For a discussion of *guanxi* in the modern-day context, see Thomas Gold, Doug Guthrie, and David Wank, *Social Connections in China: Institutions, Culture, and the Changing Nature of Guanxi* (Cambridge, UK: Cambridge University Press, 2002). See also Adam McKeown's ideas on Chinese trans-Pacific networks and P. Steven Sangren's work on Chinese patrilines. For literature addressing the establishment of Chinese relationships other than those that are agnatic, see P. Steven Sangren, "Traditional Chinese Corporations: Beyond Kinship," *Journal of Asian Studies* 43 (1984): 391–415; Lawrence W. Crissman, "The Segmentary Structure of Urban Overseas Chinese Communities," *Man* 1 (1967): 185–204; Gold, Guthrie, and Wank, *Social Connections in China*; and David M. Schneider, "Kinship and Biology," in *Aspects of Analysis of Family Structure*, ed. Ansley J. Coale (Princeton, NJ: Princeton University Press, 1965), pp. 83–101. For an exploration of Chinese kinship systems and their relationship to recreating so-called bachelor communities abroad, see Hsu, *Dreaming of Gold, Dreaming of Home*, pp. 10–11, 13, 60–61, 109–112, and 177–178; G. William Skinner, *Chinese Society in Thailand: An Analytical History* (Ithaca: Cornell University Press, 1957); and Wilson, *Ambition and Identity*.

10. Thomas Sheridan, *Los Tucsonenses: The Mexican Community in Tucson, 1854–1941* (Tucson: University of Arizona Press, 1992), pp. 41–54; and Benton-Cohen, *Borderline Americans*, pp. 33–34. Charles Pomeroy Stone, *Notes on Sonora* (Washington, DC: Henry Polkinhorn, 1861), p. 8; and J. Ross Browne, *Adventures in Apache Country: A Tour Through Arizona and Sonora, with Notes on the Silver Regions of Nevada* (New York: Harper, 1869), p. 245.

11. Estevan Ochoa, Biographical File, p. 2, AHS.

12. Lease 496–7, LM-PCRO. An earlier lease between kinsmen Wong Ty and Wong was chartered in Tombstone in 1879. See Lease 242, LM-PCRO.

13. Lease 496–7, LM-PCRO. Chinese also leased land from European Americans. In 1881, Haw Wang leased from Cornelius Ryan a parcel of land on his 320-acre property. The exact acreage leased was not clear but Haw was free to cut timber on Ryan's property provided the timber was used to improve Ryan's property or Wang's home. See Lease 428, LM-PCRO.

14. Lease 186–7, LM-PCRO.

15. Territory of Arizona, Second Legislative Assembly, *Acts, Resolutions, and Memorials Adopted by the Second Legislative Assembly of the Territory of Arizona* (Prescott: Office of the Arizona Miner, 1866), chap. 30, sec. 3, p. 58. By the late nineteenth century, the relationship between Mexicaness and whiteness was not al-

ways clear. However, by the mid-1920s, Mexicans were considered not white but a race of their own. On the relationship between Mexicans and whiteness, see Ian F. Haney-López, *White by Law: The Legal Construction of Race* (New York: New York University Press, 1997); Neil Foley, "Becoming Hispanic: Mexican Americans and the Faustian Pact with Whiteness," in *Reflexiones 1997: New Directions in Mexican American Studies*, ed. Neil Foley (Austin: University of Texas Press, 1998), pp. 53–70; Foley, *White Scourge: Mexicans, Blacks, and Poor Whites in Texas Cotton Culture* (Berkeley: University of California Press, 1999); Dara Oreenstein, "Void for Vagueness: Mexicans and the Collapse of Miscegenation Law in California," *Pacific Historical Review* 74, no. 3 (2005): 367–407; Carlos K. Blanton, "George I. Sánchez, Ideology, and Whiteness in the Making of the Mexican American Civil Rights Movement, 1930–1960," *Journal of Southern History* 72, no. 3 (2006): 569–604; and Peggy Pascoe, *What Comes Naturally: Miscegenation Law and the Making of Race in America* (Oxford, UK: Oxford University Press, 2009).

16. In 1892, Tucson storeowner Lip Gee's affair with Ms. Jesús Rascón resulted in a legal charge of fornication, not violation of anti-miscegenation laws. Gee was found not guilty of the charges. See case 720 in Records of the District Court of the United States for the Territory of Arizona, First Judicial District, "Criminal Case Files,1882–1912," RG 21, National Archives and Records Administration, Pacific Region (from here on referred to as NARA-PR); from here on referred to as AZ-CCF.

17. Lease 332, LM-PCRO.

18. Lease 688, LM-PCRO.

19. Barrio Viejo ("old neighborhood"), Barrio Libre ("free zone"), and La Calle ("the street") were other neighborhoods that also encompassed parts of South Meyer, Main, Pennington, Pearl, Congress, and Alameda Streets. For the most part, the boundaries of these neighborhoods shifted over time and were never stable. Importantly, all of Tucson's barrios were located south of the Walled City, the Plaza de las Armas. For a deft discussion, see Lydia R. Otero, *La Calle: Spatial Conflicts and Urban Renewal in a Southwest City* (Tucson: University of Arizona Press, 2010), pp. 14–40. See also Thomas Sheridan, *Los Tucsonenses: The Mexican Community in Tucson, 1854-1941* (Tucson: University of Arizona Press, 1986), pp. 237–238.

20. "Long Adobe Building Forms Tucson's Present Chinatown," *Tucson Citizen*, February 22, 1935; and "Long Adobe Is New Chinatown of Old Pueblo," *Arizona Daily Star*, February 20, 1937. Another building in Tucson's first Chinese neighborhood was a wooden structure, formerly the town's zoo. It was located on North Main Street between Pennington and Ott Streets. See "Two Historic Buildings Are Condemned and Order Given to Repair or Destroy," *Tucson Citizen*, February 18, 1925.

21. Lister and Lister, *The Chinese of Early Tucson*, 3; and Arizona State Historic Preservation Office, *The Chinese in Arizona 1870–1950*, pp. 15–17. See also Sheridan, *Los Tucsonenses*, p. 80.

22. *W. A. Dalton et al. v. Leopoldo Carrillo et al.* (1885). See Charles Drake Collection, MS 0228, box 20, folder 13, AHS. Although the court case is first referred to as *W. A. Dalton et al. v. Leopoldo Carrillo et al.*, the court consistently

refers to the case as *W. A. Dalton v. Leopoldo Carrillo* after the first day of testimony. Here I refer to the same case as *Dalton v. Carrillo*. The three defendants were Leopoldo Carrillo, Sam Hughes, and W. C. Davis.

23. I borrow the phrase "hard man with a dollar" from Sheridan's description of Carrillo. See Sheridan, *Los Tucsonenses*, 51. Carrillo went through many occupations. He defined himself as a freighter in the 1850s. See the Leopoldo Carrillo, Biographical File, folder 1. In the 1860s, Carrillo worked as a merchant; see Division of Women's and Professional Projects, Works Progress Administration, *The 1864 Census of the Territory of Arizona* (Phoenix: Historical Records Survey, 1938), line 1077; and U.S. Census Bureau, "Chinese Population by Decades and Geographical Divisions," *Population Census of the United States, 1870* (Washington, DC: U.S. Government Printing Office, 1872), Arizona Territory, Pima County, Tucson, p. 31.

24. Carrillo owned the vast majority of Chinese gardens, but W. C. Davis, Samuel Hughes, Soloman Warner, John Warner, an unidentified Mexican traditional farmer, and the Sisters of St. Joseph occupied small patches of this land as well. See *Dalton v. Carrillo*, pp. 19–20.

25. Donald J. Pisani, "Enterprise and Equity: A Critique of Western Water Law in the Nineteenth Century," *Western Historical Quarterly* 18, no. 1 (1987): 16–21; and Benton-Cohen, *Borderline Americans*, pp. 19, 35–37. See also Samuel C. Weil, *Water Rights in the Western States* (San Francisco: Bancroft-Whitney, 1908), pp. 4–5; and Dean E. Mann, *The Politics of Water in Arizona* (Tucson: University of Arizona Press, 1963).

26. *Dalton v. Carrillo*, p. 19.

27. Ibid., p. 58.

28. Ibid., p. 19–21.

29. Leases 187-7 and 464-5, LM-PCRO. In 1891, a Chinese farmer was fined $10 for stealing water from the Santa Cruz Company. Judge Slater, who fined the farmer, hoped that this punishment would serve "as a warning to others." See *Arizona Daily Star*, March 21, 1891.

30. Interview with Lillian Grossetta Barry, Tucson Oral History Project (AV-0358-05), AHS.

31. Abraham Chanin with Mildred Chanin, *This Land, These Voices: A Different View of Arizona History in the Words of Those Who Lived It* (Tucson, AZ: Midbar Press, 1977), p. 70.

32. Interview with Lillian Grossetta Barry, Tucson Oral History Project (AV-0358-05), AHS.

33. Clera Ferrin Bloom, Biographical File, June 5, 1897. Also cited in "The Orientation of Tucson's Chinese," ephemeral file entitled "Chinese in Tucson," AHS.

34. Compare Wing Wo Yuen's 1893 lease with the information in the *Twelfth Census of the United States, 1900*, for Tucson, where he is listed as a grocer.

35. Sheridan, *Los Tucsonenses*, 67. Sheridan cites an unpublished manuscript by Julio Bentacourt as to the final adjudication of the case, but he does not elaborate on the justification of the final ruling. Water rights laws for Arizona adopted on March 23, 1895, indicate a strong commercial bias in the distribution and use of water. Section I states that "all rivers, creeks, and streams of running water in

the territory of Arizona are hereby declared public, and applicable to the purposes of irrigation and mining, as hereinafter provided." This nonetheless contradicts Section 25: "the laws and customs of Sonora and the usages of the people of Arizona shall remain as they were made and used up to this day." See "Water and Water Rights up to March 23, 1895," Allison Family Papers, MS 0013, folder 16, box 2, pp. 1, 6, AHS.

36. Lister and Lister, *The Chinese of Early Tucson*, 5. The data in Table 1.2 in the Listers' book is derived from the federal censuses of 1880, 1900, and 1910. During the 1880s and 1890s, the Chinese ran many of the laundries in Bisbee and Tombstone as well. See "Arizona Album," *Tucson Citizen*, November 29, 1955.

37. Richard Stokes, "Bisbee No Good for Chinamen," *Cochise Quarterly* 3, no. 4 (1973): 6–9.

38. *Bisbee Daily Review*, April 14, 1904; May 24, 1904; August 13, 1904; December 5, 1903; September 30, 1902; and *Douglas Daily International*, September 30, 1902; August 1, 1903. See also Annie M. Cox, "History of Bisbee, 1877–1937," master's thesis, University of Arizona, 1938, pp. 65–67; Bisbee Research Collection, MS 0189, folder 2; and Truett, *Fugitive Landscapes*, p. 123. On laundry work by Chinese men and competition among women, see Joan S. Wang, "Race, Gender, and Laundry Work: The Roles of Chinese Laundrymen and American Women in the United States, 1850–1950," *Journal of American Ethnic History* 24, no. 1 (2004): 58–99.

39. Tera W. Hunter, *To 'Joy My Freedom: Southern Black Women's Lives and Labors After the Civil War* (Cambridge, MA: Harvard University Press, 1997), p. 78; on competition among black women and Chinese men in Atlanta, Georgia, see pp. 208–209.

40. *Galveston Daily News*, August 7, 1877.

41. "The Little Man from China," *Tombstone Daily Epitaph*, February 12, 1882. The Burlingame Treaty was passed with the stipulation that naturalization *would not* automatically extend to the Chinese. This joint agreement, however, was perceived by white labor as a pro-Chinese piece of legislation. During the mid-1880s there was a resurgence in anti-Chinese sentiment. For manifestations in Arizona, see "Meeting of Chinese," *Daily Tombstone*, February 17, 1886, p. 3; and "The Chinese Must Go," March 4, 1886; and "The Anti-Chinamen: Language More Vigorous Than Polite Freely Used," *Arizona Daily Star*, April 4, 1886, p. 3.

42. "Editor Epitaph," *Tombstone Daily Epitaph*, July 30, 1880, p. 2; "Anti-Chinese Meeting," *Tombstone Daily Epitaph*, July 29, 1880, p. 4; and "The Boycott: John P. Clum's Opinion of the Blackmail Business," *Tombstone Daily Epitaph*, April 4, 1886, p. 2.

43. Lillian Grossetta Barry, Tucson Oral History Project, AV-0358–05 (AHS); and Albert Buehman, "Arizona Album," *Tucson Citizen*, February 27, 1953, p. 674.

44. "Bisbee, No Good for Chinaman," *Douglas Dispatch*, January 11, 1910. Also cited in Stokes, "Bisbee, No Good for Chinaman," p. 8.

45. *Arizona Daily Star*, March 15, 1893.

46. *El Fronterizo*, August 4, 1894, p. 2. For more on anti-Chinese feeling, see *El Fronterizo*, August 29, 1891, p. 3; and *El Fronterizo*, August 20, 1892, p. 3.

47. Other truck farmers resided in the Sonoita Valley and irrigated the San

Pedro River for gardening use. Around 1889, five or six Chinese gardeners lived in Johnny Ward's ranch house and sold their produce along the Sonoita Valley. See Bernard L. Fontana and J. Cameron Greenleaf, "Johnny Ward's Ranch: A Study in Historic Archaeology," *Kiva* 28, no. 1–2 (1962): 26–27. On land near Tanque Verde and in the Silver Lake district near Flowing Wells, Chinese truck farmers cultivated corn, potatoes, onions, and chili peppers. See "Tanque Verde Items," *Arizona Daily Star*, November 19, 1889, p. 4.

48. The definition of laborer was specified in the Geary Act of 1893. "All classes of skilled and unskilled manual laborers, including Chinese persons employed in mining, fishing, huckstering, peddling, laundry men, or those engaged in taking, drying, or otherwise preserving shell or other fish for home consumption, shall be claimed as laborers." Cited from *Moy Shuck v. the United States*, case D52, box 1, AZ-CEC.

49. The law distinguished a merchant from a laborer. A merchant was one "engaged in buying and selling merchandise at a fixed place of business which business is conducted in his name, and who, during the time he claims to be engaged as a merchant, does not engage in the performance of any manual labor, except such as is necessary in the conduct of his business as such merchant." Cited from *U.S. v. Sim Lee*, AZ-CEC.

50. Chin Tin Wo's personal wealth is impressive. He took out a three-year lease from the merchandising firm of Allison and Son to invest in the carp industry and "furnish Tucson with fresh carp at all times." For a reference to Chin Tin Wo's entrepreneurial ventures, see "Chin tin Wo Took Three Years Lease from Allison & Son," *Arizona Daily Star*, December 7, 1889, p. 4; and *City of Tucson General and Business Directory for 1897–98, Containing 2600 Names of Citizens, with Their Occupations and Places of Residence, the Public Officers, Secret Societies and Churches, Together with Other Useful Information Concerning the City* (Tucson, AZ: Citizen Printing and Publishing, 1897), AHS.

51. Julius Goldbaum Papers, MS 0289, folder 3, box 3, AHS. For other Chinese merchants supplied by Goldbaum, see the correspondences between the Tucson merchant and Wing Chong Company, located in Harshaw, Arizona, folder 35, box 67, AHS.

52. Pima County, Justice of the Peace, SG 1, Justice Dockets, 1873–1919, September 26, 1884, "Justice's Court, Precinct No. One, County of Pima, A.T.," roll 12, RG 110, ASLAPR.

53. "Biographical Sketch of Don Chun Wo," Don Chun Wo, Biographical File, 3, AHS; from here on referred to as DCWBF. Although Don Chun Wo filled out the information in this biographical sketch himself, the merchant did not state his birth name anywhere in the document. Don Chun Wo's father's name was Don Doan Yook, his mother was Chew Shee. Don Chun Wo had one older brother, Don Hong Chuen, and two older sisters, Don Doo Bow and Don Song Bow, who were born in China, which was also their place of death. It seems probable that Don Chun Wo was not the only sibling in his family to come to the United States. He was nonetheless the only male sibling living after 1895.

54. "Arizona Pioneer Historical Society," DCWBF, 1.

55. For more on the life of Don Chun Wo, see Wang, "The First Chinese in

Tucson," pp. 369–375. It is notable that Chin Tin Wo's family name was different from the family name of his brother, Don Doak Yook. When the nephew of Chin Tin Wo changed his name to honor his uncle, the nephew maintained what was probably Chin Tin Wo's original family name, which was "Don." However, there is no existing documentation that verifies a name change by Chin Tin Wo.

56. DCWBF, p. 2.

57. U.S. Census Bureau, *Twelfth Census of the United States, 1900*, "Population of Tucson, Pima County," T-1032, rolls 18–20.

58. *1899–1900 Tucson City Directory* (1900), *Tucson City Directory* (1901), and *1902 Tucson City Directory* (n.d.); available at the AHS.

59. "City Council," *Arizona Citizen*, March 7, 1893, p. 3. See also minutes, Tucson City Council, March 6, April 3, 1893, in Drachman Papers, MS 0226, AHS.

60. Lucy Salyer, *Laws Harsh as Tigers: Chinese Immigrants in the Shaping of Modern Immigration Law* (Chapel Hill: University of North Carolina Press, 1995), p. 43.

61. U.S. Census Bureau, "Foreign-Born Population by Country of Birth, for the United States and Divisions, 1890–1910," *Thirteenth Census of the United States, 1910*, p. 207.

62. "The Chinese Situation: Tucson Claims the First Chinaman of the United States to Register," *Arizona Daily Citizen*, May 16, 1893, p. 3; and "War in Chinatown: Celestials After the Man Who Advised Them Not to Register," *Arizona Daily Citizen*, May 18, 1893, p. 3.

63. "War in Chinatown," p. 3.

64. For a deft discussion of the Geary Act and of previous laws that affected the 1892 law, see Salyer, *Laws Harsh as Tigers*, 51–68; and Daniel Kanstroom, *Deportation Nation: Outsiders in American History* (Cambridge, MA: Harvard University Press, 2010), pp. 118–130.

65. The Scott Act of 1888 prevented all laborers who had left the country from returning and caused all valid certificates to become invalid. As a result, more than twenty thousand Chinese laborers were prevented from returning to the United States. This decision was reversed in 1894 when China and the United States signed a treaty granting entry to the United States to Chinese laborers who had certificates of return. In 1904, however, China ended the treaty because of the poor treatment of its countrymen in the United States. Upon notification of China's decision, Congress extended, reenacted, and continued all previous exclusion laws that did not require special legislation for renewal. The exclusion act of 1904, which fixed the Chinese quota of admissions at 105 a year, remained in effect until its repeal in 1943.

66. This general fact is derived from a database of more than six hundred Chinese exclusion and criminal case files from the Arizona Territory and Southern District Court of California. Compiled by the author, the database highlights twenty-three fields of information, such as place of arrest, Chinese interpreter, deportation destination, and commissioner. It allows the author to discern general patterns of immigration, deportation, and location. The database draws from the following files of RG 21: Records of the District Court of the United States for the Territory of Arizona, First Judicial District, Chinese Criminal Case Files, 1882–1912 (AZ-CCCF); Chinese Exclusion Cases, 1886–1906 (AZ-CEC); Com-

missioners' Early Case Files (AZ-CECF); Commissioners' Dockets (AZ-CD); Commissioners' Case Files, 1882–1912, (AZ-CMCF); NARA-PR. Hereafter the database is referred to as CEDAZCA (the Chinese Exclusion Case File Database for Southern Arizona and Southern California). See CEDAZCA, 1894–1905.

67. Chinese cases D1–D88, boxes 1 and 2, CEDAZCA.

68. *U.S. v. Lee King*, case 295, CEDAZCA.

69. See cases from 1894–1905, CEDAZCA.

70. Statistics compiled from Chinese cases D1–D88, boxes 1 and 2, CEDAZCA.

71. Letter from George Webb to Morris Hunter Jones, October 9, 1906, Morris Hunter Jones Collection, MS 0393, AHS.

72. *The United States v. Joseph Con*, case D13, box 1, AZ-CEC. Con was arrested on August 2, 1902. Con's name is also spelled *Coun* and *Conn*.

73. *The United States v. Joseph Con*, case D14, box 1, AZ-CEC. See "Testimony of W. F. Mannsfield," September 12, 1902.

74. Compare the cases of Ah Tin and Jim Lee as they relate to Chinese crossing into Sonora, Mexico, and then being detained in southern Arizona. Records of the District Court of the United States for the Territory of Arizona, Second Judicial District, 1886–1911, "Civil and Chinese Exclusion Cases, 1–13," folder 2, box 1, RG 21, NARA-PRl from here on referred to as AZ-SDCCEC.

75. Lease 794-795, LM-PCRO.

76. *Los Angeles Times*, January 27, 1931, and *Los Angeles Examiner*, December 26, 1928, in folder 2 of Charles Connell Papers, MS 0166, Connell Family Scrapbook, AHS; from here on referred to as CCP. Probably compiled by Connell's wife, the scrapbook contains clippings of Connell's activities as a Chinese Inspector at the border. It also contains a few clippings about other members of the Connell family (such as announcements of the marriage of Connell and his bride, and of the marriage of his daughter to Tucson immigration inspector John Murphy), but for the most part the contents address Connell's career with the Bureau of Immigration. Many of the clippings have no page numbers or authors. To make citations of these clippings as thorough as possible, the author has attempted to locate information from other sources.

77. *The United States v. Ng Jan*, case D61, box 2, AZ-CEC; and *The United States v. Chan Cheong*, case 1711, box 19, AZ-CCF. For the final order of deportation, see "Appendix B: Chinese Exclusion Violations and Deportations, Arizona Territory," p. 4, First Judicial District, 1907–1922, RG 21, NARA-PR.

78. *U.S. v. Wong Poy*, case 0111, box ??, CEDAZCA.

79. *The United States v. Lee Sing*, 1412, box 14, AZ-CCF.

80. *The United States vs. Lee Sing [alias Gee Sing]*, case 823, box 8, AZ-CCF. Sing's testimony of citizenship and merchant status aided his entry into the United States. Records of the District Court of the United States for the Territory of Arizona, First Judicial District, Criminal Case Files, 1882–1912, case 823, RG 21, NARA-PR.

81. David Gutiérrez, *Walls and Mirrors: Mexican Americans, Mexican Immigrants, and the Politics of Ethnicity* (Berkeley: University of California Press, 1995), pp. 39–68; Ettinger, *Imaginary Lines*, 123–135; and Sánchez, *Becoming Mexican American*, pp. 17–62.

82. Anna Pegler-Gordon, *In Sight of America: Photography and the Develop-

*ment of U.S. Immigration Policy* (Berkeley: University of California Press, 2009), pp. 22–37; Lee, *At America's Gates*, pp. 33–35.

83. *The United States v. Lee Sing*, case 1412, box 14, AZ-CCF.

84. *The United States v. Ah Chung*, case 1099, box 11; *The United States v. Hi Chung*, case 1100, box 11; *The United States v. Wong Nam*, case 1300, box 13; *The United States v. Ah Suey*, case 1101, box 11; and *The United States v. Mary Fong and Wong Fong*, case 1291, box 14, AZ-CCF.

85. *The United States v. Mary Fong and Wong Fong*, case 1291, box 14, AZ-CCF.

86. *The United States v. Lee Sing*, case 1422, box 14, AZ-CCF.

87. Letter from Alexander Willard to the Secretary of State, September 26, 1885, General Records of the Department of State, Dispatches from United States Consuls in Guaymas, Sonora, Mexico, 1832–1896, reel 6, RG 59; from here on referred to as USCGMEX.

88. Letter from Nogales consulate J. F. Darnell to J. B. Moore, Assistant Secretary of State, "Visaing Chinese Papers," October 31, 1898, General Records of the Department of State, Dispatches from United States Consuls in Nogales, Sonora, Mexico, 1889–1906, reel 1, RG 59; from here on referred to as USCNMEX. Lau Chi was one of the first organizers of the firm of Juan Lung Tain. In 1892, Chan and Jin joined the business by investing more than $4,000.

89. Corral, Ramón. *Memoria de la administración pública del estado de Sonora, presentada a la legislatura del mismo por el Gobernador Ramón Corral*, Vol. 1 (Guaymas, Mexico: Imprenta de E. Gaxiola y Compañía, 1891), p. 586; and Alexander Willard to the Secretary of State, September 18, 1889, reel 8, USCGMEX.

90. Dambourges, "The Anti-Chinese Campaigns in Sonora," p. 27. Dambourges cites Private Papers of Jorge Corral, Hermosillo, Sonora, Mexico, letter from Ramon Corral to Governor Rafael Izabal, Hermosillo, July 26, 1903.

91. Willard to the Secretary of State, reel 8, September 18, 1889, USCGMEX.

92. Letter from William Wallace Bowers to the Commissioner General of Immigration, May 20, 1902, San Diego Collection District, Trends in the Outgoing General Correspondence (9L-38), 1885–1909, RG 36, NARA-PR; from here on referred to as SDCD-TOGC.

93. U.S. House of Representatives, Select Committee on Immigration and Naturalization, *Investigation of Chinese Immigration with Testimony*, 51st Cong., 2d sess., 1890–1891, March 2, 1891, H. Rept. 4048, serial 2890, volume 6, p. 327; from here on referred to as *Investigation of Chinese Immigration*.

94. Until 1891 there were two reported inconsistencies in deportation location of Chinese migrants claiming Mexican residency. In one case the attorney general ordered the deportation of twenty-four men detained in Tucson for crossing illegally into the United States from Mexico. In another case, more Chinese came up from Mexico to Nogales, Arizona, and were ordered to return to Mexico, although this decision was rejected by American officials who were unwilling to send Chinese to Sonora. See *Investigation of Chinese Immigration*, pp. 327–329.

95. Ibid., p. 328.

96. *The United States v. Ah Hoon [alias Ning Hoon and Ning Ah Goon]*, case 0398, box 4, AZ-CCF.

97. *The United States v. Chu Yun [alias Chin Yan]*, case 387, box 4; *The United States v. Sam Hing*, case 413, box 4; *The United States v. Charley Quong*, case 416, box 4; *The United States v. Charley Ah Fong*, case 417, box 4, AZ-CCF.

98. *The United States v. Chu Yun [alias Chin Yan]*, case 387, box 4, AZ-CCF. For other cases where this occurred, see, for example, *The United States v. Ah Chung*, case 1099, box 11; *The United States v. Ah Chee*, case 1363, box 14, AZ-CCF; *The United States v. Ah Hing*, case 0101, box 1, AZ-CD; and *The United States v. Ah Jim*, case D64 D64, box 2; *The United States v. Ah Jueng*, case D87, box 2, AZ-CEC.

99. Letter from John R. Berry to William Windom, April 3, 1890, SDCD-TOGC.

CHAPTER 3

A portion of this chapter was originally published as Grace Peña Delgado, "At Exclusion's Southern Gate: Changing Categories of Race and Class Among Chinese *Fronterizos, 1882–1904*," in *Continental Crossroads*, ed. Samuel Truett and Elliott Young, pp. 183–207. Copyright 2004, Duke University Press. All Rights Reserved. Reprinted by permission of the publisher.

1. Letter from Anthony Godbe to John R. Berry, April 16, 1890, San Diego Collection District, Special Agents Letters Sent 1885–1909 (9L-40), RG 36, NARA-PR; from here on referred to as SDCD-SALS.

2. Letter from John R. Berry to Anthony Godbe, December 8, 1890, SDCD-SALS.

3. Anthony Godbe to State Department, April 21, 1890, General Records of the Department of State, Dispatches from United States Consuls in Ensenada, Mexico, 1832–1896, RG 59; from here on referred to as USCEMEX.

4. Letter from Delos H. Smith to William F. Wharton, Assistant Secretary of State, "Chinamen Crossing into the United States," January 28, 1890, General Records of the Department of State, USCNMEX, RG 59.

5. See the provisions of the Chinese Exclusion Act in Bill Ong Hing, *Making and Remaking Asian America Through Immigration Policy, 1850–1990* (Stanford, CA: Stanford University Press, 1993), p. 204, Appendix C. For legal and social history of Chinese exclusion laws, see Charles J. McClain, *In Search of Equality: The Chinese Struggle Against Discrimination in Nineteenth-Century America* (Berkeley: University of California Press, 1994), esp. pp. 145–221; Lee, *At America's Gates*; Salyer, *Laws Harsh as Tigers*; Gyory, *Closing the Gate*; Chan, *This Bittersweet Soil*; Chen, *Chinese San Francisco*; Saxton, *The Indispensable Enemy*; Emily Ryo, "Through the Back Door: Applying Theories of Legal Compliance to Illegal Immigration During the Chinese Exclusion Era," *Law & Social Inquiry* 31, no. 1 (2006): 109–146; and Kitty Calavita, "Paradoxes of Race, Class, Identity, and 'Passing': Enforcing the Chinese Exclusion Acts, 1882–1910," *Law & Social Inquiry* 25, no. 1 (2000): 1–40.

6. Letter from Delos H. Smith to William F. Wharton, Assistant Secretary of State, January 28, 1890, USCNMEX.

7. Letter from Delos H. Smith to William F. Wharton, Assistant Secretary of State, "Chinamen Visiting the U.S.," February 8, 1890, USCNMEX.

8. The *New Bernal* plied between Mexican ports and San Francisco, although it was unclear if the ship was engaged in the smuggling of Chinese into the United States from Mexico. The *New Bernal* did land approximately one hundred Chinese in Baja California Norte, ostensibly to work on development projects in Ensenada. See "Disputes Dispatch no. 265, from La Paz Consular," November 23, 1889; "Increase in Chinese Population as a Result of *Bernal*," February 23, 1890; and Letter from John R. Fisher to Anthony Godbe, December 8, 1890, SDCD-TOGC.

9. For more on the early development of the California routes (coastal and eastern) and the Sonoran overland route see March 15, 1886; June 9, 1887; May 11, 1888; and September 16, 1889, in SDCD-TOGC; U.S. House of Representatives, Committee on Foreign Affairs, *Resolution on negotiations with Mexico and Great Britain, to prevent entry of Chinese laborers from Canada and Mexico into United States*, 51st Cong., 1st sess., March 2, 1890, H. mis. doc. 202, serial 2775, volume 16; from here on referred to as *Concurrent Resolution Relating to Negotiations with Great Britain and Mexico*. Also, U.S. Senate, Committee on Immigration, *Report on Immigration of Chinese*, 51st Cong., 1st sess., 1891. S. ex. doc. 97, serial 2686, volume 9; from here on referred to as *Report on Immigration of Chinese*.

10. Letter from John R. Berry to J. G. Carlisle, Secretary of the Treasury, April 1, 1893. Record Group 36, San Diego Collection District, Letters Sent to the Secretary of the Treasury, 1892–1908 (9L-39), NARA-PR; from here on referred to as SDCD-LSST.

11. U.S. House of Representatives, Committee on Foreign Affairs, *Preventing Immigration of Chinese Labor from Canada and Mexico*, 51st Cong., 2d sess., 1889–1890, H. Rep. 1925, serial 2812, vol. 6, May 8, 1890. In his plea to the House, Morrow did not mention that the vast majority of illegal immigration from Canada was not from China but from Great Britain, principally the Irish and English. For more, see U.S. House of Representatives, Select Committee on Investigation of Foreign Immigration, *To Regulate Immigration*, 50th Cong., 2d sess., H. Rep. 3972, January 19, 1889; from here on referred to as *To Regulate Immigration*.

12. U.S. House of Representatives, Committee on Immigration and Naturalization, *Report of the Select Committee on Immigration and Naturalization, and testimony taken by the Committee on Immigration of the Senate and the Select Committee on Immigration and Naturalization of the House of Representatives under concurrent resolution of March 12, 1890*, 51st Cong., 2d. sess., January 14, 1891, H. Rept. 3472, serial 2886, volume 2, pp. 64, 233, 328–600, 981; from here on referred to as *Immigration Investigation: Report, Testimony, and Statistics*. On public hysteria on illegal Chinese immigration from Canada, see Julian Ralph, "The Chinese Leak," *Harper's New Monthly Magazine* 82, no. 490 (1891): 515–525; Matthew Annis, "The 'Chinese Question' and the Canada-U.S. border, 1885: 'Why Don't Governor Squire Send His Troops to Semiahmoo to Prevent the Twelve or Fifteen Thousand Pagans from Crossing Our Borders from British Columbia?'" *American Review of Canadian Studies, 1943–99*54 40, no. 3 (2010): 351–361; and Shauna Lo, "Chinese Women Entering New England: Chinese Exclusion Act Case Files, Boston, 1911–1925," *New England Quarterly* 81, no. 3 (2008): 383–409.

13. U.S. House of Representatives, Select Committee on Immigration and

Naturalization, *Immigration Investigation, Report, Testimony, and Statistics*, 51st Cong., 2d sess., January 14, 1891, H. Rept. 3472, serial 2886, volume 2, pp. 52, 233, 981; from here on referred to as *Imigration Investigation, Report, Testimony, and Statistics*.

14. Ibid., pp. 269–270, 281.

15. The New Orleans port of entry was also of concern to Congress. See U.S. Senate, Committee on Immigration, *Transit of Chinese Through United States*, 51st Cong., 1st sess., April 19, 1890, S. ex. doc. 106, serial 2686, volume 9.

16. See the Chinese Exclusion Act of 1882, 22 Stat. 58 (May 6, 1882); and the Scott Act, September 13, 1888, ch. 1015, 25 Stat. 476; and October 1, 1888, 25 Stat. 504. For more on the impact of the Scott Act, see Salyer, *Laws Harsh as Tigers*, pp. 22–24; Lee, *At America's Gates*, pp. 66–70; and McClain, *In Search of Equality*, pp. 192–196, 348.

17. "Abstract of the Fourteenth Census of the United States, 1920," p. 24. These numbers are also cited by Lee, *At America's Gates*, pp. 67–68; Philip A. Kuhn, *Chinese Among Others: Emigration in Modern Times* (Lanham, MD: Rowman and Littlefield, 2008), p. 218; and Morrison G. Wong, "Chinese Americans," in *Asian Americans: Contemporary Trends and Issues*, ed. Pyong Gap Min, pp. 110–145 (London: Sage, 2006), pp. 112–115.

18. Antonio Peñafiel, *Censo general de la República Mexicana verificado el 20 de octubre de 1895, resumen del censo de la República. Dirección General de Estadística, 1899* (Mexico City: Oficina Tipografía de la Secretaría de Fomento, 1899), p. 119. San Diego customs officials enumerated more than one hundred Chinese in Baja California Norte during the late 1880s; many of them ostensibly worked in the mining and fishing enterprises of the Chinese Six Companies. Although the demand for labor may have lured more Chinese onto the peninsula, these projects eventually collapsed. Over the next decade, the lack of employment and investment opportunities stunted the growth of the Chinese population. See letter from Thomas Arnold to the Secretary of the Treasury, February 25, 1890, SDCD-TOGC.

19. Antonio Peñafiel, *Resumen general del censo de la Republica Mexicana verificado el 28 de octubre de 1900* (Mexico City: Impr. de la Secretaría de fomento, 1905), pp. 29–30.

20. Romero, *Geographical and Statistical Notes on Mexico*, p. 34.

21. "Anti-Chinese Feeling in Mexico," *San Francisco Call*, April 7, 1886, p. 2; *Philadelphia Press*, April 13, 1886; *Philadelphia Times*, April 13, 1886; and the *Philadelphia Public Ledger*, April 30, 1886. For reports of a so-called Chinese invasion from Mexico, see U.S. Department of the Treasury, Select Committee on Immigration and Naturalization, *Immigration Investigation*.

22. The hiring of temporary inspectors was the norm at the San Diego customs office from August 1889 to July 12-11890. See letters from this period in SDCD-TOGC, especially *Congressional Record*, October 1886, vol. 19, no. 239, pp. 10297, 10303. See also letter from A. Mariscal to Romero, October 3, 1888, 15:2:69, AHSRE.

23. Kornel Chang, "Enforcing Transnational White Solidarity: Asian Migration and the Formation of the U.S.-Canadian Boundary," *American Quarterly* 60, no. 3

(2008): 671–696. For more on Canada border crossings, see U.S. Department of the Treasury, Bureau of Immigration, *Report of the Immigrant Inspector in Charge of Canadian Border Inspection, 1902* (Washington, DC: U.S. Government Printing Office, 1902); U.S. Senate, Committee on Immigration. *Letters from Secretary of State and Secretary of Treasury on act providing for inspection of immigrants by United States consuls*, 53rd Cong.,3d. sess., 1894, S. mis. doc. 253, serial 3171, volume 5; and U.S. House of Representatives, Committee to Inquire into Alleged Violation of Laws Prohibiting Importation of Contract Laborers, Paupers, Convicts, and Other Classes, *Report of the Select Committee to Inquire into the Alleged Violation of the Laws Prohibiting the Importation of Contract Laborers, Paupers, Convicts, and Other Classes, Together with the Testimony, Documents, and Consular Reports*, 50th Cong., 1st sess., H. Rept. 12291; and U.S. Senate, Select Committee on Relations with Canada, *Relations with Canada*, 51st Cong., 1st sess., April 26, 1890, HRG-1890–RCA-0001.

24. William Paul Dillingham, *The Immigration Situation in Canada* (Washington, DC: U.S. Government Printing Office, 1910), 62–64; Marian L. Smith, "Immigration and Naturalization Service (INS) at the U.S.-Canadian Border, 1893–1993: An Overview of Issues and Topics," *Michigan Historical Review* 26, no. 2 (2000): 127–147; and Lee, *At America's Gates*, pp. 176–179.

25. Letter from Major General William Tecumshe Sherman to Matías Romero, December 11, 1897; letter to A. Mariscal from U.S. Ambassador, March 24, 1899, 15:7:94, AHSRE.

26. Letter from A. Mariscal to Matías Romero, October 3l, 1888, 15:2:69, AHSRE.

27. Letter from Senate Chamber of the United States to Matías Romero, January 16, 1891, 7:11:28, AHSRE.

28. There are many sources that address this migration stream. On the earliest known report of Chinese headed toward San Diego from Mexico, see letter from San Diego Collector, March 15, 1886; letter from San Diego Collector to U.S. Attorney, November 16, 1887; and letter from J. D. Putnam to J.C. Cline, January 14, 1899, box 14, Bureau of Customs, Los Angeles Collection District, Incoming Letters: 1883–1908, RG 36, NARA-PR; from here on referred to as BC-LACD. Also, Datus E. Coon to John R. Berry, April 9, 1890, "Report on Immigration of Chinese," pp. 20–23; letter from W. W. Bowers to the Commissioner General of Immigration, April 5, 1902, SDCD-TOGC; U.S. Department of the Treasury, Select Committee on Immigration and Naturalization, *Immigration Investigation; Investigation of Chinese Immigration;* U.S. Senate, Committee on Immigration, *Regulation of Immigration of Aliens: Statements Before the Committee on Immigration, United States Senate, on the Bill H.R.12199 to Regulate the Immigration of Aliens into the United States*, 57th Cong., 1st sess., 1902, S. Rept. 2119; James Bronson Reynolds, "Enforcement of the Chinese Exclusion Law," *Annals of the American Academy of Political and Social Science* 34, no. 2 (1909): 148–149; and Marcus Braun, "How Can We Enforce Our Exclusion Laws?" *Annals of the American Academy of Political and Social Science* 34, no. 2 (1909): 140–142.

29. For a sense of the Sonora-Arizona overland route, see U.S. Senate, Committee on Immigration, *Report on Immigration of Chinese*, 51st Cong., 1st sess.,

1890, S. doc. 97, serial 2686; CCP; AZ-CCF, especially cases 672, 673, 674, 686, 683, 693, 698, and 701, boxes 4–5; and AZ-CEC, especially cases 209, 690, and 681. There was a Mexico-Texas overland route that generally ran from Veracruz to Tampico to El Paso via Ciudad Juárez. For more information, see Ettinger, *Imaginary Lines,* pp. 60–62, 102–119, and 132–133; Marilyn Dell Brady, *The Asian Texans* (San Antonio: University of Texas Institute of Texan Cultures, 2004); Nancy Farrar, *The Chinese in El Paso* (El Paso: Texas Western Press, 1972); Edward J. M. Rhoads, "The Chinese in Texas," in *Chinese on the American Frontier,* ed. Arif Dirlik (Lanham, MD: Rowman and Littlefield, 2001), pp. 165–181; Edward Eugene Briscoe, "Pershing's Chinese Refugees in Texas," *Southwestern Historical Quarterly* 62, no. 4 (1959): 467–488; Edward C. M. Chen and Fred R. von der Mehden, *Chinese in Houston* (Houston, TX: Center for the Humanities, 1982); and Amy Elizabeth Nims, "Chinese Life in San Antonio" (master's thesis, Southwest Texas State Teachers College, 1941).

30. "Information Relating to the Family of Lee Kwong and Lai Ngan from Interview with Marian Lim," February 27, 1979; and two other documents authored by Marian Lim, the fifth daughter of Lai Ngan and Lee Kwong, MS 1242, folder 38. For photographic evidence see MS 1242, folder 105, Oversize Box 9, AHS. See also Fong, "Sojourners and Settlers," pp. 26–30.

31. In 1891, the secretary of the treasury supervised immigration, and a year later established twenty-four customs inspection stations, including those in the border districts in San Diego and Nogales. The primary focus of these districts, in terms of immigration, was to enforce the Chinese exclusion laws. The collector of customs also received applications for return certificates from Chinese individuals wishing to travel abroad.

32. For a sense of the understaffing of customs stations, see House Select Committee on Investigation of Foreign Immigration, *To Regulate Immigration,* 50th Cong., 2d sess., H. Rep. 3972, January 19, 1889; and U.S. Department of the Treasury, Select Committee on Immigration and Naturalization, *Immigration Investigation.*

33. This fact comes from my counting the number of mounted inspectors, collectors of customs, and Chinese inspectors who consistently handled border enforcement from 1882 to 1912. See CEDAZCA, 1882–1912.

34. U.S. Senate, "Letter from the Acting Secretary of the Treasury Relative to the Necessity for an Appropriation to Carry into Effect the Chinese Exclusion Act," 50th Cong., 1st sess., S. ex. doc. 275, October 9, 1888.

35. Letter from John R. Berry to L. S. Irvin, April 3, 1890; and letter from John R. Berry to William Windom, April 7, 1890, SDCD-TOGC.

36. Letter from John R. Berry to the Secretary of the Treasury, April 7, 1890, SDCD-TOGC

37. Letter from John R. Berry to the Secretary of the Treasury, April 10, 1890; April 14, 1890; April 30, 1890; May 2, 1890; and July 12, 1890, SDCD-TOGC.

38. Letter from John R. Berry to M. G. Montaño, June 17, 1890, SDCD-SALR.

39. Letter from John R. Berry to General Luis E. Torres, June 19, 1890, SDCD-SALS.

40. *San Diego Union,* May 21, 1890, p. 2. For a discussion of open borders

during the Apache Wars, see Shelley Bowen Hatfield, *Chasing Shadows: Indians Along the United States-Mexico Border, 1876–1911* (Albuquerque: University of New Mexico Press, 1998), pp. 22–28, 40–54; James E. Pilcher, "Outlawry on the Mexican Border" *Scribner's Magazine* 1, no. 1 (1891): 78–87; and H. Henrietta Stockel, *Shame and Endurance: The Untold Story of the Chiricahua Apache Prisoners of War* (Tucson: University of Arizona Press, 2006).

41. *San Diego Union*, May 23, 25, and 27, 1890.

42. Letter from John R. Berry to T. J. Monahau, November 18, 1890, SDCD-SALS.

43. Letter from John R. Berry to William Windom, June 2, 1890, SDCD-TOGC.

44. Letter from A. E. Higgins to William Windom, July 12, 1890, SDCD-TOGC.

45. Letter from John C. Fisher to Anthony Godbe, June 25, 1897; July 6, 1897; and letter from Frank P. Flint to John C. Fisher, August 31, 1897, SDCD-SALS.

46. Letter from John C. Fisher to Anthony Godbe, September 11, 1897; and "Insert of Payment," John C. Fisher to R. Smith, September 10, 1897, SDCD-SALS.

47. Chinese Exclusion Act Case Files of the Los Angeles Local Office, "Administrative History, 1920–1943," RG 85, NARA-PR. See also Survey of Federal Archives, *Inventory of Federal Archives in the States, Department of Labor, California*, Series IX (Boston, MA: National Archives Project, Work Projects Administration, 1940), p. 5; Jim Brown, *Riding the Line: The United States Customs Service in San Diego, 1885–1930* (Washington DC: Department of the Treasury, United States Customs Service, 1991).

48. Letter from J. D. Putnam to J. C. Cline, February 16, 1899, box 14, BC-LACD.

49. U.S. Industrial Commission, *Reports of the Industrial Commission on Immigration: Including Testimony, with Review and Digest, and Special Reports* (Washington, DC: U.S. Government Printing Office: 1901), p. 799.

50. Letter from John C. Cline to O. L. Spaulding, Assistant Secretary of the Treasury Department, April 10, 1899, National Archives and Records Administration Pacific Region, Laguna Niguel, Ca., Records of the US Customs Service, San Diego Collection District. "Letters Received from the Treasury Department" (9L-44), 1880–1909, RG 36 (SDCD-LRTD).

51. Letter from J. D. Putnam to J. C. Cline, January 14, 1899, box 14, BC-LACD.

52. Letter from J. D. Putnam to J. C. Cline, February 13, 1899, box 14, BC-LACD.

53. *Laws, Treaties and Regulations Relating to Chinese Exclusion*, December 8, 1894, Records of the Immigration and Naturalization Service, RG 85, Series A, Subject Correspondence files, Article III, p. 6.

54. Letter from William W. Bowers to Louis Kaiser, March 7, 1899, box 3, SDCD-SALS.

55. Ibid.

56. *The United States of America v. Wong Sing Chune*, case 1207; *The United States of America v. Lu Fook Chow*, case 1208; *The United States of America v. Lue Kim Lung*, case 1209; *The United States of America v. Wong Shew*, case 1211; and *The United States of America v. Tom Kim Poy*, 1210, in Records of District

Courts of the United States, Southern District of California, RG 21, NARA-PR; from here on referred to as RDC-SDC.

57. Letter from J. D. Putnam to J. C. Cline, February 16, 1899, box 14, BC-LACD.

58. Although the Courts did rule in *Nishimura Ekiu v. United States* (1892), 142, U.S. 651, that the U.S. government had the right to take away constitutional rights from aliens not yet admitted, the courts also held that immigrants, once admitted, became lawful residents entitled to the protections of the Constitution. In the case of the five Chinese men, because they were admitted at the border, the latter ruling applies and they were thus lawful residents entitled to constitutional protections, one of the basic of which is the presumption of innocence. See Salyer, *Laws Harsh as Tigers*, pp. 51–53, for a discussion of the constitutional parameters of legal status and protection.

59. Salyer, *Laws Harsh as Tigers*, p. 59.

60. Scrapbook of Charles Connell, folder 2, untitled news clipping, CCP, although located under the article entitled "One Less Chink: Lee Quong Ordered Deported by Commissioner Pirtle," undated, Scrapbook of Charles Connell, CCP.

61. Four exceptional cases are *The United States v. Fong Soon*, case 568; *The United States v. Ah Loo*, case 944; *The United States v. Hop Sam*, case 1585; and *The United States v. Yee Kim*, case 1588, CEDAZCA.

62. The U.S. Immigration Service, U.S. Immigration and Customs Enforcement, and U.S. Customs and Border Protection, all under Homeland Security, have a long history of bureaucratic instability. In 1891, the Bureau of Immigration was established under the Treasury Department and enforcement of the Chinese exclusion laws remained under the jurisdiction of customs officials. In 1900, the general supervision of Chinese exclusion laws was transferred to the Bureau of Immigration, where they remained bureaucratically distinct from European immigration laws. In 1903, the Chinese exclusion laws were no longer set apart from European immigration laws, and enforcement and supervision of all immigration laws fell under the newly created Department of Commerce and Labor.

63. U.S. House of Representatives, Committee on Foreign Affairs, *Compilation from the Records of the Bureau of Immigration of Facts Concerning the Enforcement of the Chinese Exclusion Laws*, 59th Cong., 1st sess., H. doc. 847, May 18, 1906, serial 4990, volume 50, pp. 16–17; from here on referred to as *Facts Concerning Enforcement of Chinese Exclusion Laws*. Historian Erika Lee asserts that from 1882 to 1900, at least 17,300 Chinese immigrants entered the United States from Canada and Mexico. Because illegal immigration is difficult to quantify, this estimate is speculative. No full record exists for both northern and southern border crossings, but several sources can begin to illuminate just how many Chinese crossed into the United States from Mexico and Canada. From 1901 to 1903, the U.S. Bureau of Immigration reported that 3,445 Chinese crossed the Canadian border and entered the United States. See U.S. Department of Commerce and Labor, Bureau of Immigration and Naturalization, "Arrests of Chinese Persons Crossing the Land Boundaries of the United States," AR-CGI, p. 102.

64. *Facts Concerning Enforcement of Chinese Exclusion Laws*, pp. 13–14. One Arizona immigration official reported that some six thousand Chinese crossed the

border between 1882 and 1910, and about half were caught and deported. See George E. Paulsen, "The Yellow Peril at Nogales: The Ordeal of Collector William M. Hoey," *Arizona and the West* 13, no. 2 (1971): 113–128. In 1910, an additional 713 Chinese were arrested at the Arizona line for unlawful entry from Mexico. See AR-CGI, 1910, p. 146. The other main artery was from Mexico to El Paso. Significant numbers of Chinese were still crossing into the United States from Canada. For more information, see U.S. House of Representatives, Select Committee on Immigration, Subcommittee on Chinese Exclusion Bill, Committee on Foreign Affairs. Hearing, 59th Cong., 1st sess., February 15; March 14, 29; April 9, 11, 1906, HRG-1906–FOA-0001, esp. p. 181.

65. U.S. Senate, Committee on Immigration, *Chinese Exclusion*, hearing, 57th Cong., 1st sess., January and February 1902, 57 S. 2960, pp. 292, 441. Mexican scholar Lawrence Douglas Taylor Hansen suggests that the Chinese Six Companies may have been responsible for smuggling approximately 90 percent of all illegal Chinese immigrants who made their way into the United States. See Taylor, "El contrabando de Chinos a lo largo de la frontera." *Frontera Norte* (enero-junio 1994): 54–86."El contrabando de Chinos a lo largo de la frontera entre México y Estados Unidos, 1882–1931," *Frontera Norte* 6, no. 9 (1994): 41–57.

66. *Arizona Daily Star*, March 26, 1899, p. 2.

67. *The United States v. William M. Hoey and B. F. Jossey*, case 1568, box 16, "Final Recognizance of the Accused," October 7, 1901, AZ-CCF. See also *The United States v. William M. Hoey*, cases 1594, 1595, and 1569, box 16, AZ-CCF.

68. *Arizona Daily Star*, August 31, 1901, p. 2; and Paulsen, "The Yellow Peril, p. 115.

69. *The United States v. William Hoey and B. F. Jossey*, "Charles R. Hood, Being First Duly Sworn," September 18, 1905, case 1590, box 16, AZ-CCF.

70. "Smuggling Chinese over the Border: Nest of Corruption Unearthed by the Arrest of Collector of Customs at Nogales," *Los Angeles Herald Illustrated Magazine*, date unknown, Chinese-Arizona Ephemera File, AHS.

71. *Nogales Oasis*, January 13, 1900; May 11, July 20, and August 3, 1901.

72. See the interrogatory of alleged Chinese smuggler Frank How, October 12, 1901, case 1594, AZ-CCF; and "Chinese Enter: Bribery Found," *New York Times*, August 25, 1901, p. 6.

73. See the interrogatory of civilian John Sapunar, April 11, 1902, case 1594, AZ-CCF; and "Hoey in Trouble," *Border Vidette*, August 31, 1901, p. 1.

74. Paulsen, "The Yellow Peril, 118; esp. fns. 9, 10, 11.

75. Interrogatory of Ye Kim, by Albert R. Morawitz, U.S. Vice Consul and Commissioner, Nogales, April 11, 1902, case 1594, box 14, AZ-CCF.

76. *United States v. William M. Hoey and B. F. Jossey*, August 23, 1901, case 1568, box 16, AZ-CFF; and *Los Angeles Herald Illustrated Magazine*, p. 10. Hoey was charged with violating Section 11 of the Chinese Exclusion Act of 1884, *U.S. Statutes at Large*, XXIII, 117. Hoey was also charged with violating Sections 5440 and 5501 of the *Revised Statues of the United States*, part 1, 1060, 1072, involving conspiracy to commit an offense against the United States.

77. *Tucson Star*, April 17, 1902; and Paulsen, *The Yellow Peril*, p. 126.

78. U.S. Senate, 61st Cong., 3d sess., D. Rept. 761, *Reports of the U.S. Im-*

*migration Commission, 1907–1910: The Immigration Situation in Other Countries: Canada, Australia, New Zealand, Argentina, Brazil* (Washington, DC: U.S. Government Printing Office, 1911), p. 65. For more on in-transit situation and numbers, see U.S. Department of State, "Administrative History, 1920–1943," in *Records of the Department of State Relating to Internal Affairs of Mexico, 1910–1929* (Washington, DC: National Archives and Records Service, General Services Administration, 1955), M 274, p. 2; from here on in referred to as IAMEX. See also *ARC-GI*, 1897, p. 50; and U.S. Department of the Treasury, *Letter from the Secretary of the Treasury, transmitting to the Senate the departmental regulations relating to Chinese exclusion and the date and authority by which such regulations were adopted*, 57th Cong., 1st sess., April 10, 1902, S. doc. 300, serial 4239, volume 20, pp. 53–54.

79. "Smuggling Chinese over the Border," *Los Angeles Herald Illustrated Magazine*.

80. *San Francisco Examiner*, May 22, 1903; and July 25, 1903, CCP.

81. "Smuggling Chinese over the Border," p. 11.

82. *Border Vidette*, August 21, 1901, CCP, folder 2. See also "Delivered the Goods: Louis Greenwalt's Collosal Smuggling Scheme Nipped in the Bud," *Border Vidette*, June 18, 1904, CCP, folder 2.

83. "Wrecking of the 'Chinese Underground Route,'" *San Francisco Bulletin*, August 21, 1904, John Murphy Scrapbook, CCP, folder 4.

84. Lee Quong was also referred to as Lee Quan. For more on Lee Quan, see "Important Arrest of Chinese Smuggler: Inspector Connell Captures Lee Quan on the San Pedro River Sunday," *Bisbee Daily Review*, August 18, 1903, CCP, folder 2.*Bisbee Daily Review*, August 18, 1903, p. 7.

85. "Smuggling of Chinese: Powerful Gang at the Border Is Broken Up," *San Francisco Examiner*, June 13, 1904, CCP, folder 2.

86. "Chinese Ring Broken Up: Agent of Smugglers' Chief, Who Is a San Franciscan, Arrested and Outfit for Making Bogus Certificates Seized," CCP, folder 2.

87. "Forging Chinese Papers," *San Francisco Examiner*, June 13, 1904; and "Noted Smuggler's Capture Certain," June 25, 1904, *Los Angeles Examiner*, CCP, folder 2. Blank certificates were purchased from Greenwaldt and Springstein for fifty dollars each. See "Certificates Were Bogus," *Los Angeles Times*, June 15, 1904, CCP, folder 2.

88. "Important Arrest of Chinese Smuggler: Inspector Connell Captures Lee Quan [sic] on the San Pedro River," John Murphy Scrapbook, folder 4, AHS.

89. "Wrecking of the 'Chinese Underground Route.'"

90. "Letter 'M' Is Undoing of Syndicate," *Los Angeles Examiner*, June 13, 1904, CCP, folder 2.

91. "Smuggling of Chinese," *San Francisco Examiner*, June 13, 1904; "Chinese Inspectors Break Up Gang of Smugglers That Has Operated on Mexican Border," *San Francisco Bulletin*, June 13, 1904; and "Greenwalt Sails with Unlawful Load," *Los Angeles Examiner*, all in CCP, folder 2. The evidence included a camera and several fountain pens. Inspector Clark made Springstein demonstrate how he filled out the certificates, placed the seal on the document, and took photographs of the fraudulent certificates of residence.

92. For more on Connell's exploits, see "Chinese Inspectors Break Up Gang of Smugglers That Has Operated on Mexican Border," *San Francisco Bulletin*, June 13, 1904; "Certificates Were Bogus," *Los Angeles Times*, June 15, 1904; and "Connell Makes Sensational Raid, Captures Counterfeit 'Chok Chees' and Opens Up Many Large Frauds," *Bisbee Daily Review*, June 10, 1904, p. 1, CCP, folder 2. The *San Francisco Bulletin* reports quite a different story about the breakup of the ring. The newspaper attributes the undoing of the ring to the daring persistence of Charles Connell. One day Connell pulled a lone Chinaman who was en route to Fairbank off a boxcar at Naco, Sonora. In the man's possession was a paper that bore the name Lee Quong. Connell, pursing his suspicions, discovered that Quong had also been harboring Chinese nationals at Crance Ranch. See August 21, 1904, newspaper articles entitled "Connell Meets a Wily Chink," and "An Elusive Chink Caught" (CCP, folder 2) for the chivalrous portrayal of the inspector's exploits. The use of *chink* was quite common when referring to Chinese border crossers in Arizona newspapers. For those Chinese established as legal residents in Tucson, Arizona newspapers did not use these racial epithets.

93. "Lee Quong to Be Deported: Three Americans Testify Positively to His Identity," newspaper article, undated, in Scrapbook of Charles Connell, CCP. The letter written by Quong to Kwong is dated April 23, 1903. *The Bisbee Review* reported on June 10, 1904, that only three hundred certificates were confiscated during the raid. Yet another account reveals how the Chinese were smuggled into the United States, embarking in El Paso and traveling via Yuma to San Francisco—the final destination. Connell has reported several incidents in which Chinese who were loaded into boxcars died of thirst very quickly.

94. "Noted Smuggler's Capture Certain."

95. See "One Less Chink." For an account of the smuggling of Chinese into the United States, see letter from W. W. Husband to Henry L. Stimson, Secretary of State, June 6, 1929. The Chinese Six Companies remain complicit in the smuggling rings that were expanded to include underground routes of passage into Lower California.

96. Letter from General Powell Clayton to John Hay, February 6, 1904, General Records of the United States Department of State, Dispatches from United States Consuls in Mazatlan, Mexico, M 159, RG 59, from here on referred to as USCMMEX; and letter from Vice President Ramon Corral to Governor Rafael Izabal, June 22, 1904, tomo 1900, paquete 35, Archivo General del Estado de Sonora, Hermosillo, Sonora; from here on referred to as AGES.

97. "In a Matter of the Chinese Person Law Yoke Who," in Jared Taylor Papers, Manuscript Collection, 1078, March 17, 1911, folder 50, Box 3, AHS.

98. "In a Matter of the Chinese Person Law Yoke Who," Box 3.

99. "Tourist Attractions Today, Border Ports Have Colorful History of Mounted Patrols," newspaper article in Chinese-Tucson Ephemera File, AHS.

100. CEDAZCA, 1905–1910. This estimate was reached by counting the number of cases involving an individual of Chinese descent who was charged criminally, which included violations for Chinese exclusion laws as well as crimes not related to the Chinese exclusion laws.

101. Letter from Louis Kaiser to the Secretary of State, March 17, 1904, USCMMEX.

102. José Covarrubias, "La inmigración china considerada desde los puntos de vista intelectual y moral," in *Varios informes, sobre tierras y colonización* (Mexico City: Imprenta y Fototipia de la Secretaría de Fomento, 1912), 208–210; and José María Romero, *Comisión de Inmigración, dictamen del vocal ingeniero José María Romero encargado de estudiar la influencia social y económica de la inmigración asiática en México* (Mexico City: Imprenta de A. Carranza e Hijos, 1911).

103. Covarrubias, "La inmigración china," pp. 124–126, 205–209.

104. Ibid., pp. 2–9; 211; Mexico, Romero, *Comisión de Inmigración*, pp. 121–122.

105. Ley de Inmigración, México, December 1908, vol. 2337, folder 18, AGES; and Secretaría de Gobernación, "Ley de inmigración de los Estados Unidos Mexicanos," in *Colección de leyes, decretos, reglamentos, y acuerdos, serie I, leyes, y decretos de la federación* (Mexico City: Imprenta del Gobierno Federal, 1909).

106. Secretaría de la Economía Nacional, Mexico, *Quinto censo de población 1930, resúmen general* (Mexico City: Dirección General de Estadística, 1932–1936), pp. 235, 277, 299.

CHAPTER 4

1. "Flee Across Line: Chinamen in Sonora Feel Effect of Race Hatred in Fear of Their Lives," *Prospector*, June 23, 1911; and "Chinese on Long Ride: A Carload of Celestials Behind Barred Windows Pass Benson," *Prospector*, June 16, 1911.

2. "Chinamen Flee from Trouble," *Prospector*, April 20, 1911.

3. Wilfley and Bassett, law firm, *On the Law and the Facts in the Matter of the Claim of China Against Mexico for Losses of Life and Property Suffered by Chinese Subjects at Torreón on May 13, 14 [and] 15, 1911* (Mexico City: American Book & Printing, 1911), p. 8; Leo Michael Jacques Dambourges, "The Chinese Massacre in Torreón (Coahuila) in 1911," *Arizona and the West* 16, no. 3 (1974): 233–246.

4. Wilfley and Bassett, law firm, *Showing Extent of Destruction of Life and Property of Chinese Subjects During the Recent Revolution in Mexico and Mexico's Responsibility Therefore Together with Citation of Authorities* (Mexico City: American Book & Printing, 1911), p. 3. Property damage at Torreón equaled $849,923.69 whereas in all other Mexican states combined it totaled only $287,298.35. For a poignant discussion of the human toll, see Wilfley and Bassett, *On the Law and the Facts*, pp. 4–6.

5. For more on violent incidents targeting the Chinese, see Dambourges, "The Anti-Chinese Campaigns in Sonora," p. 270, Table A. 4; "Chinos de Sonora," *El Imparcial*, August 23, 1911; and *Prospector*, May 22, 1911, pp. 24–25.

6. "Note to Index Bureau," 312.93/172–312.93/181, Records of the Department of State Relating to the Chinese Question in Mexico, 1910–1930, RG 59; from here on referred to as CQM.

7. For a distillation of anti-Chinese sentiment, see "Document Regarding Report by Cesario G. Soriano," April 4, 1918, folder 3, 1918, José María Arana Papers, University of Arizona Library, Special Collections; from here on referred to as JMAP. See also José Ángel Espinoza, *El Ejemplo de Sonora* (Mexico City: n.p., 1932), pp. 31–41; Izquierdo, *El movimiento antichino en México*, pp. 83–110; and Romero, *Chinese in Mexico*, pp. 145–190.

8. "The Act of Installation of the Commercial and Businessman's Junta," Magdalena, Sonora, Mexico, February 5, 1916, tomo 3038, paquete 1, expediente 2, AGES.

9. *International Chinese Business Directory*, 1568–1589, Tucson Chinese Research Collection, MS 1242, AHS; from here on referred to as TCRC.

10. Letter from Juan Lung Tain to Governor Plutarco Elías Calles, November 24 1917, tomo 3138, paquete 4, AGES.

11. Letter from Ignacio Burgos to José María Arana, September 7, 1917, JMAP.

12. Letter from Aurelio Millán to José María Arana, October 25, 1917; and letter from Ignacio Barba to José María Arana, November 6, 1917, JMAP.

13. José María Arana, *Pro-Patria*, August 22, 1917, p. 1; and Dambourges, "Anti-Chinese Campaigns," pp. 44, 69–71, 107–108.

14. Letter from José Barnal to José María Arana, September 12, 1917, JMAP.

15. "Memorial Presented to the Governor of the State by the Great Commercial and Businessman's Assembly," Magdalena, Sonora, Mexico, March 16, 1916, tomo 3038, paquete 1, expediente 2, AGES; from here on referred to as "Memorial Presented to the Governor"; reprinted in *Pro-Patria*, August 15, 1917, and August 22, 1917.

16. "Memorial Presented to the Governor," AGES.

17. Speech of José María Arana at Cananea, April 29, 1916, tomo 3083, paquete 1, expediente 2, AGES.

18. William H. Beezely, "The Role of State Governors in the Mexican Revolution," in *State Governors in the Mexican Revolution, 1910–1952: Portraits in Conflict and Courage and Corruption*, ed. Jürgen Buchenau and William H. Beezley (New York: Rowman and Littlefield, 2009), pp. 4–10; and José María Arana, *Pro Patria*, July 25, 1917, p. 1.

19. Letter from José María Arana to Governor Adolfo de la Huerta, Magdalena, Sonora, Mexico, June 2, 1916, tomo 3083, paquete 1, expediente 2, AGES.

20. Letters from Reynaldo Macillas to José María Arana, May 3, 1919, and May 6, 1919, JMAP.

21. Letter from Two Hundred and Twenty-Five Small Merchants to Governor Nacozari de García, Mexico, January 1, 1917, tomo 3124, paquete 1, AGES.

22. Letter from Secretary of Foreign Relations, Mexico, to Governor de la Huerta, February 8, 1917, tomo 3313, paquete 8, expediente 1, AGES; letter from Francis J. Dyer to Secretary of State, December 27, 1919, 812.5593/13; and letter from Dyer to Secretary of State, January 29, 1920, 812.5593/23, IAMEX.

23. This was the motto of *Pro-Patria* and it appeared on the first page of every issue. See *Pro-Patria* from July to September 1917.

24. "Document Regarding Report by Cesario G. Soriano," April 4, 1918, JMAP.

25. José María Arana, *Pro-Patria*, July 25, 1917, p. 1.

26. Ibid., August 1, 1917, p. 1.

27. Anti-Chinese speech by María de Jesús Váldez, 1917, folder 1, 1904–1916, JMAP.

28. Ibid.

29. The law of dependent citizenship derives from President Antonio López de

Santa Anna's 1854 Governmental Decree on Foreigners and Nationality, which echoed the 1804 Napoleonic Code on citizenship and marriage: "For the purposes of law, . . . a Mexican woman who marries a foreigner . . . must follow the condition of her husband." See the discussion on legal definitions of marriage and the "Ley de Santa Anna, 30 de enero 1854, Decreto del gobierno sobre extranjeros y nacionalidad, Art. 1." in *Orden social e identidad de género Mexico, siglos XIX y XX*, ed. María Teresa Fernández Aceves, Carmen Ramos Escandón, and Susie Porter (Hidalgo: Centro de Investigaciones y Estudios Superiores en Antropología Social, 2006), pp. 68–71.

30. Kif Augustine-Adams, "Constructing Mexico: Marriage, Law and Women's Dependent Citizenship in the Late-Nineteenth and Early-Twentieth Centuries," *Gender and History* 18, no. 1 (2006): 20–34, esp. 22–27. On repatriation, see Jocelyn Olcott, "Worthy Wives and Mothers: State-Sponsored Women's Organizing in Postrevolutionary Mexico," *Journal of Women's History* 13, no. 4 (2002): 106–131; and Augustine-Adams, "Making Mexico: Legal Nationality, Chinese Race, and the 1930 Population Census," *Law and History Review* 27, no. 1 (2009): 113–144, esp. 140. Mexican women were certainly not the only ones to experience dependent citizenship. In 1907, the U.S. Expatriation Act passed codes on "derivative citizenship" that, until 1931, yoked citizenship to marriage. See Ann Marie Nicolosi, "'We Do Not Want Our Girls to Marry Foreigners': Gender, Race, and American Citizenship," *National Women's Studies Association Journal* 13, no. 3 (2001): 1–21; and Nancy F. Cott, "Marriage and Women's Citizenship in the United States, 1830–1934," *American Historical Review* 103, no. 5 (1998): 1440–1474.

31. Letter from Francisco Ibáñez to José María Arana, October 20, 1917, JMAP.

32. Letter from Enrique S. Gin, President, Chinese Fraternal Union, Nacozari, to Governor, September 17, 1917, expediente 12, tomo 3141; and letter from E. Andrade, Municipal President, nacozari, to Cesareo R. Soriano, Interim Governor, AGES.

33. Letter from Lawton to Secretary of State, September 21, 1917, 312.93/1965.

34. Letter from R. Ruiz, Municipal President, Huatabampo, to Governor Cesareo Soriano, September 18, 1917, expediente 1, tomo 3146; and letter from Cesareo Soriano to R. Ruiz, September 19, 1917, AGES.

35. Letter from Martin Wong, merchant, Guaymas, to Governor, September 30, 1917, expediente 4, tomo 3141, AGES.

36. For activities of General, later President, Álvaro Obregón in saving the Chinese of Huatabampo from harm, see letters from Francisco L. Yuen, President, Chinese Fraternal Union, Nogales, to Governor Cesareo Soriano; and from R. Ruiz, Municipal President, Huatabampo, to Governor Soriano, September 18, 1917, expediente 1, tomo 3146; letters from Cesareo Soriano to R. Ruiz, September 19, 1917, and November 30, 1917, paquete 4, tomo 3138; and letter from Soriano to Yuen, October 5, 1917, tomo 3146, AGES.

37. Letter from R. Ruiz, Municipal President, Huatabampo, to Governor Cesareo Soriano, September 18, 1917, expediente 1, tomo 3146; and letter from Soriano to Ruiz, September 19, 1917, AGES.

38. Letter from Juan Lung Tain, Guaymas, to Governor Cesareo Soriano, November 9, 1917, paquete 4, tomo 3138, AGES.

39. Ibid.

40. Some of the newspapers that followed Arana and his campaign were *Orientación* (Hermosillo), *La Palabra* (Nogales), and *El Malcriado* (Nacozari de García).

41. Letter from Arana to Soriano, November 24, 1917, paquete 4, tomo 3138, AGES.

42. See "Postcard from Ju Kun Lee, Image of an Asian Girl" and "Postcard from Senorita Hing Lung," folder 2, 1917, JMAP.

43. Letter from Fu Fon Culong to Arana, April 15, 1917, folder 2, 1917, JMAP.

44. Letter from Governor Cesareo Soriano to Arana, December 12, 1917, paquete 5, tomo 3138, AGES.

45. Letter from Interim Governor Soriano to Arana, December 5, 1917, box 1, folder 2, JMAP.

46. Letter from Cesario Soriano, circular to Municipal Presidents, December 4, 1917, paquete 5, tomo 3138, AGES.

47. Letter from Plutarco Elías Calles to José María Arana, July 17, 1917, box 1, folder 2, JMAP.

48. Letter from Guadalupe de Pradeau to Tacha Arana, March 6, 1918, box 1, folder 3, p. 1, JMAP.

49. Document regarding report by Cesario Soriano, April 4, 1918, box 1, folder 3, p. 10, JMAP.

50. Ibid.

51. Letter from Oficial Primero, Hermosillo, to Attorney General, January 15, 1919, tomo, 3313, AGES.

52. Archivo General del Poder Judicial (Supremo Tribunal de Justicia), Hermosillo, Sonora, Juzgado de Alamos, Ramo Penal, 1925–1926, tomo 2192; from here on referred to as AGPJ.

53. Municipal Court of Caborca, Ramo Penal, 1921, tomo 2467, AGPJ.

54. Municipal Court of Arizpe, Ramo Penal, 1923, tomo 2808, AGPJ.

55. The so-called 80 percent law (Labor and Social Provision Law, or Article 106) was passed in Sonora in March 1919. See Labor Law, April 13, 1919, tomo 3291, AGES. Limits to hiring foreigners were also part of the southern Arizona labor landscape, especially in Bisbee, where in 1914 residents passed the Alien Labor Act, which severely limited the use of foreign labor in all areas of employment. For a deft discussion of this law, see Benton-Cohen, *Borderline Americans*, pp. 200–205.

56. Labor and Social Provision Law, April 13, 1919, tomo 3291, AGES. Report from Consul Henry C. A. Damm entitled "Anti-Chinese Legislation by the State of Sonora, Mexico," February 6, 1924, National Archives Record Group 59, 812.4016/5.

57. Letter from R. R. González, Muncipal President of Cananea, to Governor Plutarco Elias Calles," July 29, 1919, tomo 3449, AGES.

58. "Plutarco Elias Calles to R. R. González," July 15, 1919, tomo 3449, AGES.

59. Letter from Bartley F. Yost to Secretary of State to William Dawson, July 28, 1919, 812.5593/54a, IAMEX.

60. Ibid.

61. Letter from William Dawson to Secretary of State, April 26, 1919, 812.504/85; and letter from Claude E. Guyant to Secretary of State, December 20, 1913, USCGMEX.

62. Letter from George T. Summerlin to Secretary of State, December 31, 1919, 812.5593/21; and letter from Bartley F. Yost to Secretary of State, December 25, 1919, 812.5593/19, USCGMEX.

63. Carlos Sánchez Mejorada, "The Writ of Amparo: Mexican Procedure to Protect Human Rights," *Annals of the American Academy of Political and Social Science* 243: Essential Human Rights (January 1946): 107–111.

64. Letter from Vice Consul Blocker to Secretary of State, December 31, 1919, 812.00/009, IAMEX.

65. Letter from Francis J. Dyer to Secretary of State, December 28, 1919, 812.5593/17, USCGMEX. Letter from Bartley F. Yost to Secretary of State, January 15, 1920, 812.5593/22, USCGMEX.

66. Letter from Frederick Simpich, U.S. Consul, Nogales, to the Secretary of State, June 23, 1919, 312.93/32; and June 24 1913, 312.93/34, IAMEX. Also letter from Simpich to Secretary of State, February 27, 1914, IAMEX.

67. Letter from William Dawson to Secretary of State, April 26, 1917, 812.504/85; and letter from Claude E. Guyant to Secretary of State, December 20, 1913, USCGMEX.

68. Letter from Hum Fook and José Chang, Nogales, September 17, 1916, tomo 3076, expediente 35; and letter from Municipal President, Magdalena, to Governor, October 31, 1916, tomo 3071, expediente 33, AGES.

69. Letter from Wilbur J. Carn for Secretary of State to American Consul General Alexander W. Weddell, March 26, 1928, 812.5593/54a, enclosure, USCGMEX.

70. Letter from James B. Stuart to Secretary of State, March 31, 1924, 812.4016/6, IAMEX.

71. Letter from Bartley F. Yost to Secretary of State, January 15, 1920, 812.5593/22, USCGMEX.

72. Juzgado de Nogales, Ramo Penal, 1919, tomo 2333, AGPJ.

73. Juzgado de Guaymas, Ramo Penal, 1921, tomo 2008, AGPJ.

74. Juzgado de Hermosillo, Ramo Penal, 1920, tomo 1141, AGPJ.

75. Espinoza, *El ejemplo de Sonora*, pp. 33, 77, 172; letter from José F. Barifel to Senor Director de *Pro-Patria*, Magdalena, September 12, 1917; Reynaldo Villalobos to José M. Arana, Culiacan, May 4, 1919, folder 4; letter from Junta Central Nacionalista to Presidente de la Republica Mexicana, Culiacan, October 25, 1920, folder 5; letter from Ramon García to José María Arana, folder 6, JMAP.

76. Letter from José F. Barifel to Senor Director de *Pro-Patria*, Magdalena, September 12, 1917; letter from Junta Central Nacionalista to Presidente de la Republica Mexicana, Culiacan, October 25, 1920, JMAP.

77. Extracto de una comunicacion de Vito Aguirre, Presidente de la Alianza Nacionalista de Chihuahua y Comites al Presidente Abelardo L. Rodriguez, dirigida desde Chihuahua, Chihuahua, June 17, 1933; extracto de un telegrama de Manuel Romero, miembro del Comite Nacionalista Pro-Raza dirigido al Presidente

de la Republica desde Santiago Ixcuintla, Nayarit, November 22, 1933; and extracto de un telegrama de José Angel Espinoza dirigido al Secretario particular del presidente de la Republica, fechado en la ciudad de Mexico, November 28, 1933. Espinoza, *El ejemplo de Sonora*, pp. 121–123; Barón Rux, "Carisimos Ninos, Amigos Nuestros," *El Nacionalista*, November 22, 1925, pp. 3, 5; "Pocas palabras y mucha accion," *El Nacionalista*, November 22, 1925, pp. 1, 4; and José Ángel Espinoza, "Actas de la 2a Gra: Convencion Antichina," *El Nacionalista*, November 22, 1925. A copy of the November 23, 1925, edition of *El Nacionalista* can also be found in the JMAP.

78. Espinoza, *El ejemplo de Sonora*, 165–166, 177.

79. Linda Hall, *Oil, Banks, and Politics: The United States and Postrevolutionary Mexico* (Austin: University of Texas Press, 1995), p. 67.

80. Mexico, Secretaria de Gobernacion, *El Servicio de Migracion en Mexico por Landa y Pina jefe del Departamento de Migracion* (Mexico City: Talleres Graficos de la Nacion, 1930), pp. 38–39.

81. José María Romero, *Comisión de inmigración: dictamen del vocal ingeniero José María Romero, encargado de estudiar la influencia social y económica de la inmigración asiatica en México* (Mexico City: Imprenta de A. Carranza e Hijos, 1911), 12–15; and "El sol chino III," Monteón González and Trueba Lara, *Chinos y antichinos*, p. 50.

82. Cott, "Mexican Diplomacy and the Chinese Issue," p. 65.

83. Romero, *Comisión de Inmigración*, pp. 14–15.

84. Clifford Alan Perkins, *Border Patrol: With the U.S. Immigration Service on the Mexican Boundary, 1910–1954* (El Paso: Texas Western Press, 1978), p. 4. In the early years of the agency, immigrant inspectors were expected to provide their own gun and uniform. A common uniform for the region included casual work clothes made of cotton or light wool to temper the extreme heat and bitter cold, a Stetson hat, and high-heeled riding boots. For the inspection of freight cars, inspectors usually changed into their oldest clothing and heavy soled army boots. Perkins remarked that "there was many a day when one more change of clothing would have finished me with the Service" (pp. 16–17). For more on the institutionalization of the Chinese division and their eventual transformation into the Immigration and Naturalization Service in 1924, see Roscoe G. Willson, "The Old 'Mounted Guards' Gave Way to the 'Border Patrol," *Arizona Days and Ways* (September 1960), pp. 32–33.

85. John Martínez, *Mexican Emigration to the U.S.: 1910–1930* (San Francisco: R and E Research Associates, 1971), p. 10. Juan Gómez-Quiñones also estimated that between 1910 and 1917, an average of 53,000 Mexicans per year fled into the United States. See *Mexican and American Labor, 1790–1990* (Albuquerque: University of New Mexico Press, 1994), p. 93. For other arrests made by Heath and other inspectors, see Jared D. Taylor, Attorney, Immigration and Naturalization Cases, 1908–1927, "Complaint Against a Chinese Person," March 11, 1911, folder 50, box 4; "In the matter of a Chinese Person," March 17, 1911; and memos from Taylor to Alfred E. Burnett, March 24, 1911; June 27, 1911; and June 30, 1911, Jared Taylor Papers, MS 1078, AHS. In the same collection but for earlier cases of deportation, see "Order of Deportation," August 5, 1906, folder 49, box 4; and *United States vs. Ah Ming*, November 4, 1904. See also *Fong Coon v. the*

*United States*, folder 125, pp. 1–9, especially "Order of Deportation," pp. 8. The Ellinwood Papers also detail the deportation of several Chinese in 1906; see "In the District Court of the United States, in and for the Southern District of California, Southern Division," November 6, 1906, 1–4, folder 120, box 17, MS 0243, AHS.

86. David E. Lorey, *United States-Mexico Border Statistics Since 1900* (Los Angeles: UCLA Latin American Center Publications, 1993), p. 7, Table 100.

87. Monteón González and Trueba Lara, *Chinos y antichinos*, p. 50.

88. Gutiérrez, *Walls and Mirrors*, pp. 44–45.

89. Perkins, *Border Patrol*, pp. 19–20.

90. Ibid., pp. 23, 26–32.

91. Pegler-Gordon, *In Sight of America*, pp. 193, 197. For more on the medicalization of the U.S. border patrol, see Alexandra Minna Stern, "Buildings, Boundaries, and Blood: Medicalization and Nation-Building on the U.S.-Mexico Border, 1910–1930," *Hispanic American Historical Review* 79, no. 1. (1999): 41–81; and Stern, *Eugenic Nation: Faults and Frontiers of Better Breeding in Modern America* (Berkeley: University of California Press, 2005), pp. 57–81.

92. Letter from William Wilson to John Burnett, Chairman, House Committee on Immigration and Naturalization, May 31, 1917, file 54261-202, entry 9, reel 6, RG 85, Records of the Immigration and Naturalization Service; from here on referred to as RINS.

93. Hunter Morris Jones Papers, folder 1, box 1, 93–94, MS 0393, AHS.

CHAPTER 5

1. Letter from Vice Consul Blocker to the Secretary of State, January 12, 1971, file no. 812.00/20260, p. 905, U.S. Department of State, *Papers Relating to the Foreign Relations of the United States with Mexico*; from here on referred to as FRUSMX.

2. Letter from Special Agent Carothers to the Secretary of State, March 9, 1916, file no. 81200/17382; and letter from Consul Letcher to the Secretary of State, March 9, 1916, file no. 81200/17383, FRUSMX.

3. Friedrich Katz, *The Life and Times of Pancho Villa* (Stanford, CA: Stanford University Press, 1998), p. 583. For more on Villa's raid of Columbus, see Alan Knight, *The Mexican Revolution*, vol. 2 (Cambridge, UK: Cambridge University Press, 1986), pp. 348–354.

4. Collector Cobb to the Secretary of State, March 9, 1916, file no. 81200/17377, FRUSMX. The number of Villa's troops varied. Pershing later reported that Villa entered Columbus with five hundred to one thousand men. See letter from General Pershing to General Funston, file no. 812.00/17450, FRUSMX.

5. Letter from Special Agent Silliman to the Secretary of State, March 10, 1916, file no. 812.00/17415, FRUSMX.

6. "Chinese on Army's Hands: Three Hundred with Pershing Fear Mexicans If Americans Withdraw," *New York Times*, July 18, 1916, p. 4.

7. Ibid.

8. Letter from John J. Pershing to F. W. Berkshire, Supervising Inspector, Department of Immigration, El Paso, January 25, 1917, 54152/79–A, box 2645, RINS; and Rhoads, "Chinese in Texas," pp. 18–20.

9. Letter from John J. Pershing to F. W. Berkshire, Supervising Inspector, Department of Immigration, El Paso, Texas, January 25, 1917, 54152/79–A, box 2645, RINS.

10. Letter from John J. Pershing to the Adjutant General of the Army, April 12, 1917, 54152/79–B, box 2645, RINS; and Briscoe, "Pershing's Chinese Refugees," p. 2.

11. "Five Hundred Chinese Refugees," *Overland Monthly and Out West Magazine* 71, no. 4, (1918).

12. Letter from Ed F. Beasley, Missouri Laundry Owners' Association, to Hon. Jacob E. Meeker, February 2, 1917, 54152/79–A, box 2645, RINS.

13. Memorandum of A. Caminetti, Commissioner-General to the Secretary, February 1, 1917, 54152/79–A, box 2645, RINS; letter from Pershing to Anthony Caminetti, November 6, 1919; and letter from Pershing to Albert Johnson, November 7, 1921, in House Committee on Immigration and Naturalization, *Registration of Refugee Chinese*, November 16, 1921, H. Rept. 471, 67th Cong., 1st sess., serial 7921.

14. Letter from E. W. Smith to E. J. Henning, October 7, 1921, House Committee on Immigration and Naturalization, *Registration of Refugee Chinese*, Hearings on S.J.Res. 33, *Permitting Chinese to Register Under Certain Provisions and Conditions*, November 8, 1921; also statements of A. Warner Parker and E. J. Henning, 67th Cong., 1st sess., serial 8. To a great extent, the origins of Public Law No. 29 lie in the final steps of World War I, which prompted the reduction of military establishments throughout the United States. Labor was needed to take down encampments, and the Chinese seemed to fill this void in San Antonio, Texas. After the war ended, the same dilemma existed: What to do with these Chinese immigrants? Returning to Mexico was not an option for them because of endemic anti-Chinese violence. When Washington began to take action to appropriate funds for deporting the refugees to China in August of 1921, both the military and civilians advocated for other remedies, and Public Law No. 29 was subsequently passed. See House Committee on Immigration and Naturalization, *Inquiry into Activities of Charles F. Hille with Relation to Certain Chinese Refugees; Hearing before Subcommittee*, January 24, 1922, with Subcommittee Report, 67th Cong., 2d sess., serial 2–B. In the end, approximately 50 percent of the Chinese refugees settled permanently in San Antonio.

15. Edward Eugene Briscoe, "Pershing's Chinese Refugees in Texas," *Southwestern Historical Quarterly* 62, no. 4 (1959): 488; and Briscoe, "Pershing's Chinese Refugees: An Odyssey of the Southwest" (master's thesis, Saint Mary's University, 1947), pp. 133–134.

16. The text reads as follows: "Whereas three hundred and seventy-nine Chinese men, some of them merchants and others of the laborer class, attached themselves to the punitive military expedition under the command of Gen. Pershing, which entered Mexico in 1916, and when said expedition returned from Mexico were temporarily admitted to the United States as refugees; and Whereas the said Chinese performed extensive services and rendered valuable assistance to the punitive expedition in Mexico at the time impossible by attaching themselves to the expedition and rendering such services; and Whereas the said Chinese after tem-

porary admission to the United States as refugees continued to render and are now rendering services to the military branch of the United States Government, such services being valuable, unusual, and in some instances of a hazardous nature; and Whereas the said Chinese can not [sic] return to their former homes in Mexico with safety and can not [sic] at this time be deported to any other places justly and humanely; Now, therefore, be it resolved, etc., That the Commissioner General of Immigration be, and he hereby is, authorized and directed to permit the said Chinese to register under the terms of and in accordance with the provisions of section 6, of the act approved May 5, 1892 (Twenty-seventh Statutes at Large, page 25), as amended by section 1 of the act approved November 3, 1893 (Twenty-eight Statutes at Large, page 7). Passed the Senate August 15, 1921." U.S. House of Representatives, Committee on Immigration and Naturalization, *Registration of Refugee Chinese*, hearing, 67th Cong., 1st sess., November 8, 1921 (Washington, DC: U.S. Government Printing Office, 1921).

17. Li Weikun (Lee Wee Kuan), "U.S. Department of Labor: Chinese Check-Out Notice," April 28, 1917, MS 1242, Folder 91, p. D, AHS.

18. Armentrout Ma, "Chinatown Organizations and the Anti-Chinese Movement, 1882–1914, in *Entry Denied: Exclusion and the Chinese Community in America, 1882–1943*, ed. Sucheng Chan (Philadelphia: Temple University Press, 1991), p. 155.

19. U.S. Bureau of the Census, *Twelfth Census of the United States, 1900*, Arizona (Washington, DC: 1980), pp. 265, 278–288. The census indicates that 4,122 Mexicans resided in Tucson in 1900. For more on the Mexican population in Tucson, see Sheridan, *Los Tucsonenses*, pp. 132–141.

20. "Alien Land Act, Sec. 2784," in *Revised Statutes of Arizona*, 1913: Penal Code (Phoenix: McNeil, 1913), pp. 646–648. For more on California, see Franklin Hichborn, *Story of the Session of the California Legislature of 1913* (San Francisco: Press of the James H. Barry Company, 1913), pp. 213–226.

21. *Arizona Daily Citizen*, July 15, 1906, p. 2.

22. B. A. Pletcher, Notarized Affidavit from the State of Arizona, County of Pima, October 22, 1919, Li Weikun (Lee Wee Kuan) Legal Papers, box 4, folder 5, AZ 376, Chinese Manuscript Collection, Special Collections, University of Arizona Libraries; from here on referred to as CMCUALSC.

23. "Merchant Domiciled and Engaged in the Mercantile Business," October 16, 1919, Li Weikun (Lee Wee Kuan) Personal Papers, 1917–1957, folder 1, box 4, CMCUALSC.

24. Untitled newspaper article adjoining notarized documents, box 4, folder 5, CMCUALSC.

25. "Wong Shee, Wife of Merchant, Application for Admission to the United States," May 6, 1924, folder 5, box 4, CMCUALSC. For more on the importance of Section Six status and Chinese marriage in the United States, see Todd Stevens, "Husbands' Rights and Racial Exclusion in Chinese Marriage Cases, 1882–1924," *Law & Social Inquiry* 27, no. 2 (2002): 271–305; David Beesley, "From Chinese to Chinese American: Chinese Women and Families in a Sierra Nevada Town," *California History* 67, no. 3 (1988): 168–179; Adam McKeown, "Transnational Chinese Families and Chinese Exclusion, 1875–1943," *Journal of American Ethnic*

*History* 18, no. 2 (1999): 73–110; and Huping Ling, "Family and Marriage of Late-Nineteenth and Early-Twentieth Century Chinese Immigrant Women," *Journal of American Ethnic History* 19, no. 2 (2000): 43–63.

26. Letter from Hongjing to Li Weikun, July 28, 1934, folder 5, box 4, CMCUALSC.

27. Letter from Qu Xijun to Li Weikun, March 23, 1935, folder 5, box 4, CMCUALSC.

28. "Store Lease," November 5, 1932, folder 5, box 4, CMCUALSC.

29. "General Exchange Insurance Corporation," February 9, 1933, folder 5, box 4, CMCUALSC.

30. Sheridan, *Los Tucsonenses*, p. 5.

31. AR-CGI, 1927, p. 7; and Gutiérrez, *Walls and Mirrors*, p. 23.

32. AR-CGI, 1926, p. 10; of those Mexicans who were barred from entry, 131 were classified as "mentally or physically defective," 86 were unable to read, and 63 were of the "criminal and immoral classes."

33. AR-CGI, 1927, p. 7; and Pegler-Gordon, *In Sight of America*, p. 212.

34. U.S. Census Bureau, *Fourteenth Census of the United States, 1920* (Washington, DC: U.S. Government Printing Office, 1921), Census Schedules, T623, roll 50 and 51, Pima County, Tucson, Arizona, Records of the Bureau of the Census, RG 29.

35. In 1901, chairman George P. Blair introduced this harsher anti-miscegenation law titled "An Act to Revise and Codify the Laws of the Territory of Arizona, with Reference to Marriage and Divorce," in Arizona, *The Revised Statutes of Arizona Territory: Containing Also the Laws Passed by the Twenty-First Legislative Assembly, the Constitution of the United States, the Organic Law of Arizona and the Amendments of Congress Relating Thereto* (Columbia, MO: E. W. Stephens, 1901), sec. 6, p. 3092, AHS; from here on referred to as *Revised Statutes of Arizona*.

36. *Revised Statutes of Arizona*, Sec. 11, 3097. By stipulating marriage laws in this way, legislators placed a person of mixed heritage in an untenable situation. If the individual descended from a Chinese father and Mexican mother, by extension of the law he or she was prevented from marrying a white person or other Mexican, or another person of mixed heritage. In effect, this person could not legally marry any Arizonan! For a similar discussion of the implications of this marriage law, see Roger D. Hardaway, "Unlawful Love: A History of Arizona's Miscegenation Law," *Journal of Arizona History* 27, no. 4 (1986): 379.

37. Compiled from U.S. Census Bureau, *Twelfth Census of the United States, 1900*, Census Schedules, T623, roll 47, Pima County, Tucson, Arizona; and from *Thirteenth Census of the United States, 1910*, Census Schedules, T625, roll 41, Pima County, Tucson, Arizona.

38. Arizona's miscegenation laws did provoke court challenges, especially from individuals with indigenous and African ancestry. See Hardaway, "Unlawful Love," pp. 379–338. The extent of legislators' actions to keep the white race pure was captured in the following quote by Justice Henry D. Ross, who advocated that a percentage of blood be stipulated to gauge the validity of marriage: "In trying to prevent the white race from interbreeding with Indians, Negroes, Mongolians, etc., it has made it unlawful for a person with 99% Indian blood and 1% Caucasian

blood to marry an Indian, or a person of 99% Caucasian blood and 1% Indian blood to marry a Caucasian. We mention this and the absurd situations it creates believing and hoping that the legislature *will correct it by naming the percentage of Indian and other tabooed blood that will invalidate marriage*" (Hardaway, "Unlawful Love," p. 384; italics added). Anti-miscegenation laws were lifted on April 28, 1942.

39. U.S. Census Bureau, *Twelfth Census of the United States, 1900*; and Lister and Lister, *The Chinese of Early Tucson*, p. 5, Table 1.2.

40. U.S. Census Bureau, *Thirteenth Census of the United States, 1910*.

41. Although Chinese men in San Francisco turned to prostitution for sexual gratification, I have found no proof that such activity took place in Tucson on a regular basis. For a discussion of the relationship between Chinese bachelor communities and prostitution in San Francisco and the West, see Judy Yung, *Unbound Feet: A Social History of Chinese Women in San Francisco* (Berkeley: University of California Press, 1999), pp. 24–52, 169–170; Lucie Cheng Hirata, "Free, Indentured, Enslaved: Chinese Prostitutes in Nineteenth-Century America," *Signs* 5, no. 1, Special Section: Women in Latin America (1979): 3–29; and George Anthony Peffer, "Forbidden Families: Emigration Experiences of Chinese Women Under the Page Law," *Journal of American Ethnic History* 6, no. 1 (1986): 28–46.

42. Lily Olivaras Valenzuela Liu, oral history interview, July 5, 1984, Southern Pacific Railroad Project, AV-0001-15, pp. 6, 8, 15, 19, 21, AHS. Sylvia and Stella were raised Roman Catholic. Lily's sister Amelia also married a Mexican man with the surname Mendez. Another incident of Chinese-Mexican marriage was that of merchant Hi Wo and his Mexican wife. Wo started a grocery business in Tucson and Benson, where he raised four daughters and a son. For photographic evidence, see Hatch, "The Chinese in the Southwest, p. 269; Hardaway, "Unlawful Love," p. 381. For other outcomes of and responses to miscegenation, see "Sing King and Ah Song Evade Arizona Law," *Prescott Courier*, September 2, 1891, p. 3; "Wife of Tucson's First Citizen Let Out with a White Man," *Prescott Courier*, March 24, 1883, p. 3; "First Chinese Wedding in Tucson," *Arizona Star*, March 29, 1905, p. 8; the *Arizona Citizen*, February 18, 1901; and Gladys Franklin Carroll, oral history interviews, Tucson Oral History Project, AV-0359-12, p. 81; and AV-0368-03, AHS.

43. Valenzuela Liu, oral history interview, pp. 15, 26.

44. Lister and Lister, *The Chinese of Early Tucson*, pp. 12–13. They also pointed out that "with penetration of a Hispanicized territory came gradual acquisition of Spanish, merchandising skills necessary to cultivate a consumer base there, and occasional intermarriage with Hispanic women" (p. 12).

45. *Tucson Citizen*, February 18, 1925; and February 22, 1935, Eleventh Annual Rodeo Edition, Chinese Section; *Arizona Star*, February 20, 1937, and March 24, 1991.

46. Don Wah was born with the name Dong Wah. According to his daughter, Esther Don Tang, her father changed his name because the new name was easier for Americans to pronounce and remember. See "In the Matter of the Identity of Dong Wah," EDTC, box 12, folder 1, MSS 94, AHF, Hayden Library, Tempe, Arizona, p. 5.

47. "In the Matter of the Identification of Fok Yut," March 14, 1908, box 1, folder 4, EDTC.

48. "Panel I, Barrio Reunion," October 27, 1986, EDTC.

49. Ibid., p. 3.

50. "Biographical Information," Don Wah, Biographical File, p. 2, AHS; and "Experiences of Chinese in Arizona," box 12, folder 1, EDTC.

51. "Certificate of Birth, Office of the County Recorder, Dong Wah," February 16, 1899, folder 4, box 1, EDTC. The case of *United States v. Wong Kim Ark,* 169 U.S., 649 (1897), affirmed that birthright citizenship extended to all Chinese born *jus solis* in the United States. Chinese born outside U.S. territory, however, remained ineligible for naturalization until the repeal of the Chinese Exclusion Law in 1943. For more on the Wong Kim Ark decision, see Thomas Brook, "China Men, United States v. Wong Kim Ark, and the Question of Citizenship," *American Quarterly* 50, no. 4 (1998): 689–717; John Hayakawa Torok, "Reconstruction and Racial Nativism: Chinese Immigrants and the Debates on the Thirteenth, Fourteenth, and Fifteenth Amendments and Civil Rights Laws," *Asian Law Journal* 3 (1996): 55–104; and Marshall B. Woodworth, "Who Are Citizens of the United States—Wong Kim Ark Case—Interpretation of Citizenship Clause of the Fourteenth Amendment," *American Law Review* 32 (1898): 554–561.

52. Esther Don Tang, undated speech, "Good Morning Friends . . . ," folder 1, box 12, EDTC, p. 2.

53. Abraham Chanin with Mildren Chanin, "Esther Tang: A Chinese Success Story," in *This Land, These Voices: A Different View of Arizona History in the Words of Those Who Lived It* (Flagstaff: Northland Press, 1977), p. 206.

54. "Panel I, Barrio Reunion," EDTC, p. 3.

55. Chanin, *This Land, These Voices,* pp. 204–206. For other accounts of Chinese children working as grocers, see Paul Lim, oral history interview, Tucson Oral History Project, AV-0452, AHS.

56. Esther Tang, Tucson Oral History Project, AV-0505-16 (from here on referred to as ETTOHP), p. 9; and undated speech, EDTC, p. 2.

57. ETTOHP, 10; and undated speech, EDTC, p. 3.

58. Undated speech, EDTC, p. 7.

59. Thomas E. Sheridan, *Arizona: A History* (Tucson: University of Arizona Press, 1995), p. 215.

60. Speech of Harry Gin, retired Pima Court Superior Judge, entitled, "Remembrances from Tucson's Chinese Community," Don Wah, Biographical File, p. 13, AHS. On the resettlement of Mexicans in the South Meyer District, see Sheridan, *Los Tucsonenses,* p. 186; and Lister and Lister, *The Chinese of Early Tucson,* p. 16.

61. "Panel I, Barrio Reunion," EDTC, p. 2.

62. "Biographical Sketch of Don Chun Wo," Don Chun Wo, Biographical File, p. 5.

63. Quote taken from Ellen Gail Harkness, "Culture and Role of Chinese Health Professionals with Multi-Ethnic Clients," (PhD diss., University of Arizona, 1973), p. 92.

64. ETTOHP, 8; and undated speech, EDTC, p. 3.

65. As early as 1900, the Chinese of Tucson were given the opportunity to learn English free of charge. A "Chinese school" was established in the Old Pueblo to teach the "Chinamen of this nationality the language of our country that they

might be lifted to a higher standard of life." However, it remains unknown how many Chinese took advantage of the missionary school. See "Brief News Items of the Town, *Arizona Daily Citizen*, December 17, 1900, p. 4.

66. "Total of 85 Chinese Pupils Enrolled in Tucson Schools," *Arizona Citizen*, Eleventh Annual Rodeo Edition, Chinese Section, February 22, 1935.

67. George Lim, "Tiny Shops of the Past Are Now Modern Stores," *Arizona Citizen*, Eleventh Annual Rodeo Edition, Chinese Section, February 22, 1935.

68. "Chinese Part in Community Is Discussed," *Arizona Citizen*, Eleventh Annual Rodeo Edition, Chinese Section, February 22, 1935.

69. *Tucson Citizen*, March 4, 1929. On January 18, 1926, the original Chinese Evangelical Church was founded, although Esther Don Tang places its founding on January 16, 1926. See "Chinese in Southwest," folder 1, box 12, EDTC.

70. Speech of Harry Gin, retired Pima Court Superior Judge, entitled, "Remembrances from Tucson's Chinese Community," Don Wah, Biographical File, 13.

71. Letter from Binglun to Zhenran, July 10, 1929, folder 11, box 1, CMCUALSC.

72. Binglun, Journal Entry, July 7, 1927, folder 11, box 1, CMCUALSC.

73. Letter from Ji Xianxing to Binglun, June 8, 1927, CMCUALSC.

74. Letter from Ji Xianxing to Binglun, June 3, 1927, CMCUALSC.

75. Letter from Ji Xianxing to Binglun, June 19, 1927, CMCUALSC.

76. For such details, see the June 3, 1927; June 19, 1927; and January 19, 1928 letters cited in the preceding notes, CMCUALSC.

77. Letter from Ji Xianxing to Binglun, June 13, 1927, CMCUALSC.

78. Letter from Ji Xianxing to Binglun, June 19, 1927; and Letter from Ji Xianxing to Binglun, May 17, 1927, CMCUALSC.

79. Letter from Ji Xianxing to Binglun, June 19, 1927, CMCUALSC.

80. Letter from Ji Xianxing to Binglun, May 9, 1927, CMCUALSC.

81. Letter from Ji Xianxing to Binglun, June 19, 1927, CMCUALSC.

82. Letter from Ji Xianxing to Binglun, August 4, 1927, CMCUALSC.

83. Letter from Ji Xianxing to Binglun, July 29, 1927, CMCUALSC.

84. Ibid.

85. Ibid.

86. Letter from Ji Xianxing to Binglun, September 17, 1927, CMCUALSC.

87. *Sixteenth Census of the United States, 1940*, vol. 2, 376, 526. In 1930, there were 162 Chinese males and 66 Chinese females living in Tucson; by 1940, 239 Chinese men and 108 Chinese women lived in the Old Pueblo.

88. Letter from Ji Xianxing to Binglun, June 13, 1927, CMCUALSC.

CHAPTER 6

1. Law 27, passed by the Sonora state legislature on December 8, 1923, was originally numbered Law 29, although in all petitions I have encountered it is referred to as Law 27. I therefore refer to what some have referred to as Law 29 as Law 27, which is consistent with what Chinese petitioners and their Sonoran challengers called the *barrioization*. See José Ángel Espinoza, *El Ejemplo de Sonora*, 34. For American reports on barrioization, see letter from Consul Henry C. A. Damm entitled "Anti-Chinese Legislation by the State of Sonora, Mexico,"

812.4016/5, February 6, 1924; and from Bartley F. Yost entitled, "Segregation of Chinese in Sonora," January 5, 1924, 812.4016/3, IAMEX.

2. "Se comunica la parte considerativa de la sentencia dictada en el Amparo de Hip Lee y co-agraviados al C. Gobernador del Estado, Hermosillo," número 12864, March 25, 1924, tomo 3645, AGES.

3. "El Amparo de Hip Lee y co-agraviados," March 25, 1924, tomo 3645, AGES.

4. The AGES is rich in primary sources documenting the personal and political rights of Chinese from their own perspective. See letters from José Sujo, Gee Lee Kee, Francisco Jo, and others to the Nogales District Judge, March 5, 1924, tomo 495; from Jim Joe to the District Judge of the State, February 24, 1924, tomo 3645; from Quong Lee, Manuel Lee, and Miguel Chon to District Judge of Sonora, March 11, 1924, tomo 3645, AGES.

5. Letter from Bartley F. Yost to Secretary of State, Report from "Guaymas Municipal Council," December 25, 1919, 812.5593/19, IAMEX.

6. Espinoza, *El ejemplo de Sonora*, p. 186.

7. Tong organizations should not be mistaken for *huigans*, or district organizations. Tongs were secret societies that had their roots in ancient China. In the United States and Mexico, tongs came to dominate many aspects of both Chinese recreational activity and illegal economic pursuits. Surname organizations provided economic support to village or family members, whereas *huigan* associations offered comparable aid but were usually larger than surname organizations and therefore could afford to assist members with legal counsel as well as economic aid. For a more thorough discussion, see Armentrout Ma, "Urban Chinese at the Sinitic Frontier: Social Organizations in United States' Chinatowns, 1849–1898," *Modern Asian Studies* 17 no. 1 (1983): 107–135; Armentrout Ma, *Revolutionaries, Monarchists, and Chinatowns: Chinese Politics in the Americas and the 1911 Revolution* (Honolulu: University of Hawaii Press, 1990); Mak Lau-fong, "Chinese Secret Societies: Criminologically Defined," *Bulletin of the Institute of Ethnology Academia Sinica* 59 (1985): 143–161; and Chueng, "Performing Exclusion and Resistance.

8. Letter from Chinese Miners to Municipal President, Mazatlán, July 25, 1922, tomo, 3524, paquete 4, AGES. Under Sun Yat-sen, China achieved a unified republican government based in Guangzhou, while in Mexico his short-lived presidency enjoyed relatively strong support among Chinese nationals and Mexican officials alike.

9. Ko-Lin Chin, "Chinese Triad Societies, Tongs, Organized Crime, and Street Gangs in Asia and the United States" (PhD diss., University of Pennsylvania, 1986), pp. 68–73. For more on tongs in Canada, see Wing Chung Ng, *The Chinese in Vancouver, 1945–1980: The Pursuit of Identity and Power* (Vancouver: University of British Columbia Press, 2000); on Mexico, see Evelyn Hu-Dehart, "Voluntary Associations in a Predominantly Male Immigrant Community: The Chinese on the Northern Mexican Frontier, 1880–1930," in *Voluntary Organizations in the Chinese Diaspora*, ed. Khun Eng Kuah-Pearce and Evelyn Hu-Dehart (Hong Kong: Hong Kong University Press, 2006), pp. 141–168. For more on 1922 tong wars from Sonora archives, see "Asunto: Extranjeros, empleados," tomo 495; "Asunto:

Permiso y naturalización de extranjeros, leyes profesiones y militar," tomo 506; and "Asunto: Ordenes, Extranjeros, y tranquilidad pública," tomo 510, AGES.

10. Letter from Yost to the Secretary of State, May 20, 1922, 312.93/211, US-CMMEX. For more on the internal structures of Chinese associations in Mexico, see Hu-Dehart, "Voluntary Associations in a Predominantly Male Immigrant Community," pp. 151–153.

11. Letter from Alfonso Almada, President, Supreme Tribunal, Hermosillo, to Governor, October 6, 1922, paquete 3, tomo 3524, AGES; letter from Francis J. Dyer to the Secretary of State, May 5, 1922, 312.93/209, USCMMEX. For more on tong wars throughout northern Mexico, see Catalina Velázquez Morales, "Diferencias Políticas entre los Inmigrantes Chinos del Noroeste de México (1920–1930): El Caso de Francisco L. Yuen," *Historia Mexicana* 15 (October-December, 2005): 461–512.

12. Mensaje del Senador A. Magallón a Alberto J. Pani, secretario de Relaciones Exteriores, el 10 de noviembre de 1921, Caja 28, CH-1, expediente 106, legajo 1, Fondo Obregón-Calles, Archivo General de la Nación (from here on referred to as AGN). See also "Mexico to Deport Chinese," *New York Times*, August 9, 1922, p. 12.

13. Telegrams from Francisco Elías to Obregón, June 23, 1922; June 24, 1922; and June 27, 1922, Fondo Obregon-Calles, AGN.

14. The Mexican Constitution of 1917, chapter 3, article 33. See *The Mexican Constitution of 1917 Compared with the Constitution of 1857*, trans. H. H. Branch (Philadelphia: American Academy of Political and Social Science, 1917), 29. The exact quote is as follows: "but the Executive shall have the exclusive right to expel from the Republic forthwith, and without judicial process, any foreigners whose presence he may deem inexpedient."

15. Letter from Juan Lin Fu to President Obregón, July 27, 1922, caja 28, expediente 104, legajo 1, Fondo Obregón-Calles, AGN.

16. Letter from President Obregón to Juan Lin Fu, July 28, 1922, caja 28, expediente 104, legajo 1, Fondo Obregón-Calles, AGN.

17. Letter from Juan Lin Fu to President Obregón, July 29, 1922, caja 28, expediente 104, legajo 1, Fondo Obregón-Calles, AGN.

18. Letter from Francisco Elías to Francisco Barreras, Presidente Municipal, Guaymas, August 17, 1922, paquete 3, tomo 3524, AGES. For Obregón's order of Article 33, see *Boletín Oficial* 39 (January-July 1922): 147–148.

19. Espinoza, *El ejemplo de Sonora*, 246.

20. Letter from Undersecretary of the State of Mexico to Elías, November 23, 1922, paquete 1, tomo 3523, AGES.

21. Letter from Yost to the Secretary of State, June 10, 1922, 312.93/213, IAMEX.

22. Espinoza, *El ejemplo de Sonora*, pp. 26, 228–229.

23. Telegram from Governor of Sonora, Francisco Elías Calles, to President, June 23, 1922; Telegram from H. Quihuia, General Secretary of the Communist Party, to the President, June 24, 1922; and Telegram from the Governor of Sonora, Francisco Elías Calles, to the President, June 27, 1922, Fondo Obregón-Calles, AGN.

24. Letter from Eduardo Arias, Municipal President of Magdalena, to Governor, June 21, 1922, tomo 3523, AGES.

25. Mexico, *Colonization and Naturalization Laws*, 15–16.

26. Alfonso J. Ben and George On al C. Juez de Distrito en el Estado, no date, tomo 3645, AGES. For more on a similar assertion of rights, see Wat Fat al Sr. Juez de la Instancia del Ramo Civil, en funciones de Juez de Distrito, May 12, 1924; and Chin Qui al C. Juez de Distrito en el Estado, February 25, 1924, tomo 3645, AGES.

27. Espinoza, *El ejemplo de Sonora*, p. 327. On naturalized Chinese Mexicans in Sonora, see "Enterado de que esa Presidencia se impuso de of. que dirigió a esta Gobno. la Sría. De Gobernación, relativo a Cartas de Naturalización Mexicana," April 10, 1924; "Ent. de que el Gob. de su cargo se dirije [sic] al Pdt.Mpal.de Cananea, para que previa just. fiere su Of. de haber obtenido carta de naturalización mexicana, les otorgue garantías," April 10, 1924; and Amparo Administrativo, "Khaki Mar and L. C. Quintero, chinos de origen y mexicanos por naturalización y R. G. Quinero, Pedro C. Fong, Juan Mar . . . ," March 24, 1924, AGES.

28. "Alfonso J. Ben y George On, mayores de edad, casados, comerciantes, chinos de origen y mexicanos por naturalización . . . al C. Juez de Distrito en el Estado," undated, AGES.

29. Edwin Ray Lankester, *Degeneration: A Chapter in Darwinism* (London: Macmillan, 1880), p. 32.

30. My definition of *indigenismo* borrows from Alan Knight, "Racism, Revolution, and *Indigenismo*: Mexico, 1910–1940," in *The Idea of Race in Latin America, 1870–1940*, ed. Richard Graham (Austin: University of Texas Press, 1990), p. 77; and Gonzalo Aguirre Beltrán, *La población negra de México* Compare Peter Wade, *Race and Ethnicity in Latin America* (London: Pluto Press, 1997), pp. 32–33.

31. José Vasconcelos, "The Latin-American Basis of Mexican Civilization," in *Aspects of Mexican Civilization*, ed. José Vasconcelos and Manuel Gamio (Chicago: University of Chicago Press, 1926), pp. 3–74.

32. José Vasconcelos, *La Raza Cósmica: Misión de la raza Iberoamericana y Notas de viajes a la América del sur* (Barcelona: Agencia de Liberia, 1925), pp. 38–40.

33. Anthropologist Manuel Gamio best captures how the intelligentsia elevated the Mexican Indians as a means of achieving racial homogeneity in the form of the *mestizo*. See Gamio, *Forjando Patria*, pp. 93–96. Compare Basave Benítez and Enríquez, *México mestizo*; and Enríquez, *Los grandes problemas nacionales*, pp. 312–313, 345–346, 357–360.

34. Knight, "Racism, Revolution, and *Indigenismo*," p. 71.

35. Law 31, "Prohibition of Marriage Between Mexican Women with Chinese Individuals," signed into law on December 20, 1923, by Governor Alejo Bay; *Boletín Oficial* (Hermosillo), p. 27, December 31, 1923. Also cited in Espinoza, *El ejemplo de Sonora*, p. 35. For references to marriage and degeneration, see letter to Obregón from the Liberal Party of Sonora, Hermosillo, Sonora, May 22, 1922; letter to Obregón from the Labor Trade Union of Sonora, Hermosillo, October 16, 1923, Fondo Obregón-Calles, AGN. For a deft discussion on Mexican and Chinese marriage see Augustine-Adams, "Making Mexico," pp. 111–144.

36. Law 31, *Boletín Oficial* 27 (December 1923), 3. See also "Cinco Chinos y Cinco Mujeres Mexicanas Fueron Penados por Infracción a la Salvadora Ley No. 31," *El Intruso*, February 29, 1924, pp. 1, 2.

37. Mexico, *Colonization and Naturalization Laws*, pp. 13–14.

38. "María Escalante muchacha de corta edad fue vendida al chino Luis Chan: La venta lo consumaron los padres de la muchacha en Estación Esperanza, R.Y.," *El Nacionalista*, July 4, 1924. *El Nacionalista* reported that the story originated on June 30, 1924.

39. Alejo Bay, Governor of Sonora, "El H. Congreso del Estado ha mandado al Ejecutivo del mismo para sus sanción y observancia, La Ley No. 27 que a la letra," December 13, 1924, tomo 3645, AGES. See also *Boletín de la Cámara de Diputados del Estado de Sonora*, XXVII Legislatura, December 6, 1923, p. 5. From here on referred to as BCDS. See also *Boletín Oficial*, Hermosillo, December 7, 1923, p. 26.

40. "Aviso" from Francisco Barreras, Muncipal President of Guaymas, February 15, 1924, tomo 3645, AGES. For the physical parameters of the *barrio chino* in Sahuaripa, see "From Carlos Trujillo, Municipal President of Sahuaripa, to Governor of the State," March 10, 1924, AGES.

41. "Asunto: Se comunica lo conducente de la resolución dictada en el Amparo de Juan Hong y Adela Barrio de Hong," July 19, 1924, tomo 3523, AGES.

42. Letter from Pacifica Morales and Adela Barrios to the Judge of the First Instance, Nogales, June 1, 1922, tomo 3523, AGES.

43. Florencio Frisby, "List of Cumpas Chinese," June 27, 1922, tomo 3523, AGES.

44. Al Gobernador del Estado de Francisco L. Chin, September 30, 1924, tomo 3645, AGES. See also Velázquez Morales, "Diferencias políticas," pp. 461–512.

45. Letter from Secretary of Interior, Mexico, to Governor, Sonora, October 12, 1924, expediente 2035, tomo 3645, AGES. On the confiscation of arms, see Circular #204 to all municipal presidents, October 3, 1924; and letter to Citizens of Naco to Governor, September 20, 1924, and October 20, 1924, expediente 2033, tomo 3645, AGES.

46. For the first quote, see letter from Clara V. de Gámez to the Governor of Sonora, "Comité Femenil Pro-Raza de Pueblo Nuevo," Nacozari de García, September 23, 1924, tomo 3645, AGES; for the second quote, see Chinese Legation, from Deputy Alejandro C. Villaseñor, "Las Razones que se Aducen Para Dictar una Ley Contra Esos Peligrosos Inmigrantes Demuestran que Esta no se Halla en Pugna con la Constitución," not dated, p. 4, tomo 3645, AGES; see also original in *Excélsior* (Mexico City), January 4, 1924.

47. José Ángel Espinoza, *El problema Chino en México* (Mexico City: n.p., 1931); and *El ejemplo de Sonora*.

48. "Programa que se desarrollara en la CONVENCIÓN ANTI-CHINA que tendrá verificativo en esta Ciudad, principiando el día 1o. de Febrero de 1925," tomo 3645, AGES.

49. Al Gobernador C. Alejo Bay de G. Hsiang Hu, El Cónsul de China en Sonora y Sinaloa, January 30, 1924, no. 745/0.124, tomo 3645, AGES.

50. It was common for labor unions to fall in step with El Sindicato Laboralista de Sonora (the Trade Union of Sonora) and the Partido Liberal Sonorense (Sonoran Liberal Party) complain about unfair marketplace competition and Chinese-Mexican intermarriage. Message from C. González Tijerina and Bernabé A. Soto

to the President of the Republic, January 20, 1925, Fondo Obregón-Calles, 104, ch. 1, AGN.

51. President Salvador Múñoz Tostado "Comité de Salud Publica," January 29, 1924, JMAP.

52. L. Villareal, letter from Silvano B. Figueroa to Sr. José María Arana, Tuxpan, Nayarit, January 1, 1921; letter from José María Arana to H. Junta Nacionalista de Culiacán, Magdalena, November 24, 1920; letter from El Club del Pueblo to H. Congreso del Estado, Magdalena, September 12, 1918; *El Nacionalista*, November 22, 1925, p. 3, JMAP.

53. Letter from Licenciado C. González Tijerina and Bernabé A. Soto to the President of the Republic, "Program That the Convention of Anti-Chinese Committees Will Develop," January 20, 1925, Fondo Obregón-Calles, p. 104, ch. 1, AGN.

54. Letter from Licenciado C. González Tijerina and Mr. B. A. Soto to Presidente Plutarco Elías Calles, February 4, 1925, in Monteón González, *Chinos y Antichinos*, p. 90.

55. "Circular 50 remitida por el Congreso de Zacatecas a los Diputados de Sonora," May 5, 1925, caja 127, tomo 257, El Archivo del Congreso del Estado de Sonora, Hermosillo; from here on referred to as ACES.

56. "Acuerdo. Se dice a la Presidenta del Sub-Comité Femenino Antichino No. 2 en Nogales," May 19, 1925, caja 127, tomo 258, ACES.

57. Letter to Obregón from the Trade Union Party of Sonora, Hermosillo, October 16, 1923; and to Obregón from the Sonora Liberal Party, Hermosillo, Sonora, May 22, 1922, Fondo Obregón-Calles, AGN.

58. Compiled from censuses of Cananea, Pilares de Nacozari, and Nogales, in "Censo de Sonora, municipios," tomo 3569, AGES.

59. Letter from Francis J. Dyer to Secretary of State, December 30, 1919, 812.5593/17, reel 204, IAMEX.

60. Dambourges, "The Anti-Chinese Campaigns," p. 210. Dambourges arrives at this statistic by compiling the number of Chinese and Mexican merchants and grocers in Sonora during 1924. See p. 211, Table 6.

61. Letter from James B. Stewart to Secretary of State, March 31, 1924, 812.4016/6, IAMEX. For a similar response to Chinese merchant competition in Chihuahua, see letter from Charles A. Bay to Secretary of State, February 8, 1926, 812.4016/17, IAMEX.

62. Letter from M. Durón, Municipal President, to Secretary of Government, February 17, 1925, expediente 1230, tomo 3750, AGES.

63. For more on Hermosillo, see letter from Minister Consul Timothy T. M. Wang to Governor Alejo Bay, June 8, 1925, and June 9, 1925, expediente 1244, tomo 3750, AGES.

64. Declaration of Juan Calderón, July 23, 1925; and letter from Calderón to Interim Governor Manuel Montoya, July 29, 1925, expediente 1244, tomo 3750, AGES.

65. Letter from Calderón to the People of Nacozari, August 25, 1925, tomo 3750, AGES.

66. Letter from A. P. Martínez, Municipal President, Nacozari, to Governor,

August 27, 1925; letter from Montoya to Martínez, August 28, 1925; and letter from Pedro Felix to Governor, August 28, 1925, tomo 3570, AGES.

67. Letter from Secretary of the Interior, Mexico, to Governor, September 8, 1925; letter from Carlos González Tijerina, President, Board of Governors, National Anti-Chinese Movement, Nogales, to Governor September 1, 1925; and letter from State Congress to Governor, October 27, 1925, tomo 3750, AGES.

68. "Circular 2 remitida por el Presidente del Comité Directivo del Anti-Chinismo Nacional," October 15, 1925, caja 127, tomo 257, ACES.

69. Susan Bordo, "The Body and the Reproduction of Femininity: A Feminist Appropriation of Foucault," in *Gender/Body/Knowledge: Feminist Reconstructions of Being and Knowing,* ed. Alison M. Jaggar and Susan R. Bordo (New Brunswick, NJ: Rutgers University Press), pp. 13–33.

70. Espinoza, *El ejemplo de Sonora,* p. 327.

71. Jürgen Buchenau, "Plutarco Elías Calles of Sonora: A Mexican Jacobin," in *State Governors in the Mexican Revolution, 1910–1952: Portraits in Conflict and Courage and Corruption,* ed. Jürgen Buchenau and William H. Beezley, pp. 59–75 (New York: Rowman and Littlefield, 2009), p. 59.

72. Letter from President Plutarco Elías Calles, Mexico, to Governor, Sonora, September 23, 1925, tomo 3750; and letter from Francisco Amparon, Substitute Municipal President, Navojoa, to Secretary of Government, January 26, 1926, AGES, tomo 20, expediente 169, AGES.

73. Address by Felipe González Cortés, Sanitation Inspector, Hermosillo, December 20, 1925, in letter from Wang to Governor, December 25, 1925, AGES, tomo 3750.

74. The full paragraph in Spanish reads as follows: "En diferentes Estados se han organizado agrupaciones anti-chinas que, lejos de concretarse a defender sus miras dentro del orden y la ley, han cometido un sinnúmero de atropellos en las personas e intereses de los nacionales chinos que viven en nuestro país y que tienen derecho, conforme a los principios establecidos pro nuestra Constitución, a gozar de las mismas garantías individuales que los mexicanos." Oficio del Presidente de la República a los Gobernadores de los Estados, September 23, 1925, Fondo Obregón-Calles, 104, ch. 1, p. 2, AGN.

75. Oficio del Presidente de la República a los Gobernadores de los Estados, September 23, 1925, expediente 1244, tomo 3750, AGES.

76. Correspondence of American Consul at Ciudad Juárez, John W. Dye, to the Secretary of State, November 4, 1926, 812.55/107, IAMEX. For the status of tourists and immigrants not exceeding six months' residency, see Article 28 of "The Mexican Immigration Law of 1926," 812.55/110. Mexicans reentering from the United States were subject to sanitation inspections and were required to fill out the immigrant questionnaire, but nothing else.

77. Harry L. Walsh, "A Reply to Colonel Tejada," dispatch no. 3828, IAMEX. See also *Excélsior* (Mexico City), January 24, 1927, for original correspondence in Spanish.

78. "The Mexican Immigration Law of 1926," Article 29, Section VIII, 812.55/110; for the prohibitive powers of the Department of the Government, see Article 64, IAMEX.

79. After July 1927, Syrian, Lebanese, Armenian, Palestinian, Arabian, and Turkish immigrants entering Mexico were required to possess at least ten thousand pesos; almost all did not. The ascendants and descendants of those already in Mexico legally and who had an honest means of earning their living and were in a good financial position could join their relatives. See Alexander W. Weddell, American General Consul to Secretary of State, "Economic Matters: Immigration; Executive Order Restricting the Immigration of Laborers of Syrian, Libanese [sic], Armenian, Palestinian, Arabian, and Turkish Origin into Mexico," July 28, 1927, 812.55, IAMEX. See also the full text of the law, published in *Diario Oficial de la Federación* (Hermosillo), July 15, 1927. For more on Lebanese immigration in Mexico, see Alfaro-Velcamp, *So Far from Allah*, pp. 31–69.

80. Weddell, American General Consul to Secretary of State, "Economic Matters," July 28, 1927, 812.55, IAMEX.

81. "The Mexican Immigration Law of Mexico of 1926," 812.55/110, IAMEX.

82. Al Jefe de la Oficina de Secretaría de Gobernación del Abogado Consultar, July 1, 1927, Dirección General de Gobernación, Extranjeros, 9:33:2.360 (3) 3, AGN.

83. For an analysis of Calles's presidency and the drive for American and international recognition, see Jean Meyer, "La reconstrucción de los años veinte: Obregón y Calles," in *Historia de México*, ed. Timothy E. Anna, Jan Bazant, and Friedrich Katz, pp. 215–249 (Barcelona: Crítica, 2001). Throughout 1924, the front page of *El Nacionalista* advocated for the abrogation of the Treaty of Amity, Commerce, and Navigation, as did *El Intruso* (Cananea) and *El Diario de Coahuila* (Saltillo, Coahuila).

84. "Se comunica la parte considerativa de la sentencia dictada en el Amparo de Hip Lee y co-agraviados," p. 2.

85. Mexico, *Convenciones y Tratados Imperio chino: Tratado de Amistad, comercio y navegación entre los Estados Unidos Mexicanos y el Imperio chino* (Mexico City: Imprenta del Gobierno en el ex Arzobispado, Secretaría de Relaciones Exteriores de los Estados Unidos Mexicanos, 1900), p. 23. See also Vera Valdéz Lakowsky, *Estudio histórico del tratado sino mexicano de 1899* (Mexico City: Colegio de Historia, 1979), p. 205.

86. John E. Jones, "Immigration of Chinese into Mexico," April 18, 1928, 812.5593/61, NARA-DC.

87. Beezley, "The Role of State Governors in the Mexican Revolution, pp. 9–14.

88. William Dawson to Secretary of State, "Regulations Supplementing Order Prohibiting Temporary Immigration to Mexico of Manual Laborers," 812.5511/60, IAMEX.

89. Alexandra Minna Stern, "From Mestizophilia to Biotypology: Racialization and Science in Mexico, 1920–1960," in *Race and Nation in Modern Latin America*, ed. Nancy P. Applebaum, Anne S. Macpherson, and Karin Alejandra Rosemblatt, pp. 187–210 (Chapel Hill: University of North Carolina Press, 2003), p. 189.

90. Nancy Leys Stepan, *The Hour of Eugenics: Race, Gender, and Nation in Latin America* (Ithaca, NY: Cornell University Press, 1996), pp. 55–58, 81, 129–133, 150–153; Stern, "From Mestizophilia to Biotypology," pp. 187–210, esp.

190–196; Renique, "Race, Region, and Nation," pp. 220, 229; and Romero, *Chinese in Mexico*, pp. 89–92.

91. Caleb Williams Saleeby, *The Progress of Eugenics* (New York: Funk and Wagnalls, 1914), p. 112. Saleeby also cites lead and malaria as racial poisons. For more on the concept of racial poisons, see Saleeby, "Racial Poison," *Eugenics Review* 2 (April 1910–January 1911): 30–52; and Stepan, *The Hour of Eugenics*, p. 85.

92. Dr. Antonio Quiroga, "Aviso a los comerciantes de abarrotes en general, dictado por el director general de Salubridad Publica en el Estado," November 12, 1930, in Espinoza, *El ejemplo de Sonora*, 65–68. See the following for an earlier newspaper portrayal of Chinese as carriers of disease: "El Resultado de los Examenes Medicos Practicados en los Chinos mas Sanos," *El Nacionalista*, March 21, 1924, p. 1.

93. Dr. Antonio Quiroga, "Aviso a los comerciantes firmado por el director de Salubridad Pública del Estado de Sonora," October 29,1930, Espinoza, *El ejemplo de Sonora*, pp. 63–64.

94. Mexico, *El Servicio de Migración en Mexico por Andrés Landa y Piña jefe del Departamento de Migración* (Mexico City: Talleres Gráficos de la Nación, 1930), p. 5.

95. Izquierdo, *El movimiento antichino en México*, p. 135; and 2.362.2 (29) 223, expediente 44, caja 22, Archivo General de la Nación, Dirección General del Gobierno; from here on referred to as AGN-DGG.

96. "Circular número 278, Matrimonios chino-mexicano," and "Circular número 277, Sección de Registro Civil," in Espinoza, *El ejemplo de Sonora*, pp. 55, 57. Also, fines were increased from five hundred to one thousand pesos for those who performed such nuptials. See also "Asks Mexico Ban Chinese: Former Senator Sees Menace to Nationality in Intermarriages," *New York Times*, November 19, 1930, p. 10.

97. Espinoza, *El ejemplo de Sonora*, Circular número 278, Sección del Registro Civil, Hermosillo, October 7, 1930, p. 55.

98. Circular número 308, Sección de los todos Presidentes Municipales, Hermosillo, November, 13, 1930, in *Bound Circulars*, 1930, AGES.

99. "Ley número 89," *Boletín Oficial*, tomo 27, número 39, May 16, 1931; also in Espinoza, *El ejemplo de Sonora*, pp. 74–75.

100. Circular número 141, in Espinoza, *El ejemplo de Sonora*, p. 89; and "De Los Chinos: Circular Número 141," *El Universal*, July 15, 1925.

101. "Chinese Fail in Mexico: Radical Campaign Results in Closing of Many Shops," *New York Times*, August 10, 1931, p. 10.

102. "Scores Chinese Expulsion: Mexican Official Says Sonora's Business Now Is Stagnant," *New York Times*, December 26, 1931, p. 6. Chinese Vice Consul to the United States, C. K. Wong, estimated losses near ten million pesos. See also "Mexico City Halts Chinese Oustings: The Federal Government Takes Hand in Expulsions as Break with China Seems Near," *New York Times*, September 4, 1931, p. 7, for a temporary stay of expulsion and for a report on the losses of Juan Lung Tain. For more on an estimated twenty million pesos in losses, see "Orientals' Loss Is Large," *New York Times*, September 4, 1931, p. 7; and "Federal Troops on Bor-

der Sent into Interior to Protect Celestials After Reports of Confiscation of Land and Property," *Arizona Daily Star*, September 4, 1931, p. 1.

103. *Douglas Dispatch*, August 27, 1931, p. 2; and August 29, 1931, p. 6; *Arizona Daily Star*, August 29, 1931.

104. "Mexico City Halts Chinese Oustings," *New York Times*, September 4, 1931, p. 7.

105. "Employment, Sonora and the Chinese," *Arizona Daily Star*, September 5, 1931, pp. 8–9.

106. Camacho, "Traversing Boundaries," pp. 118–119.

107. Correspondence of Mauricio Fresco, Vice Consul, Shanghai, to Mexico Foreign Affairs Minister, 2.360 (29) 8109, Caja 10, Expediente 5, AGN-DGG.

108. *San Francisco Chronicle*, September 2, 1931; *Arizona Daily Star*, September 3, 1931; "Los Chinos de Sonora Sin Ayuda," *El Provenir*, September 3, 1931, p. 6; and "Chinca Will Ask U.S. to Help in Mexico," *New York Times*, September 3, 1931, p. 12.

109. "U.S. to Aid Chinese in Sonora Case," *Tucson Citizen*, September 3, 1931. Under normal circumstances, immigration inspectors required a $500 dollar bond for temporary entry of any Chinese into the United States. Under this agreement, the Chinese originating from Sonora required no such bond.

110. "Mexican Wives Leaving Sonora: Have Right to Remain, but Follow Husbands to Old Country," *Arizona Daily Star*, September 5, 1931, p. 1.

111. "Five Mexican States Cleared of Chinese," *New York Times*, October 18, 1931, p. 2.

112. "Mexican Labor Law Threatens Complications on the Border," *New York Times*, March 20, 1932, p. E8; "3,000 Chinese Flee Mexico, Cross into the U.S.," *Chicago Daily Tribune*, March 18, 1932, p. 1.

113. For 1930 statistics for Coahuila, see Secretaria de Economía Nacional, Dirección General de Estadística, Mexico, *Quinto censo general de población*, Estado de Coahuila, vol. 2, tomo 5 (Mexico City: Estados Unidos Mexicanos, 1933). For 1940 statistics, see Secretaría de la Economía Nacional, Dirección General de Estadística, Mexico, *Sexto censo de población*, vol. 5 (Mexico City: Estados Unidos Mexicanos, 1940).

For 1930 statistics for Sinaloa, see Secretaria de Economía Nacional, Dirección General de Estadística, Mexico, *Quinto censo general de población*, Estado de Sinaloa, vol. 25, tomo 7 (Mexico City: Estados Unidos Mexicanos, 1933). For 1940 statistics for Sonora, see Secretaría de la Economía Nacional, Dirección General de Estadística, Mexico, *Sexto censo de población*, vol. 24 (Mexico City: Estados Unidos Mexicanos, 1940).

114. For 1932 statistics for Baja California, see Secretaria de Economía Nacional, Dirección General de Estadística, Mexico, *Quinto censo general de población*, vol. 1, tomo 3 (Mexico City: Estados Unidos Mexicanos, 1934). For 1940 statistics, see Secretaría de la Economía Nacional, Dirección General de Estadística, Mexico, *Sexto censo de población*, vol. 1, Baja California, territorios norte y sur (Mexico City: Estados Unidos Mexicanos, 1940).

115. For 1930 statistics, see Secretaría de Economía Nacional, Dirección General de Estadística, Mexico, *Quinto censo de población, 15 de mayo de 1930*, vol.

26 (Mexico City: Estados Unidos Mexicanos, 1934). For 1940 statistics, see Secretaria de la Economía Nacional, Dirección General de Estadística, Mexico, *Sexto censo de población*, Estado de Sonora, vol. 24 (Mexico City: Estados Unidos Mexicanos, 1940).

116. Espinoza, *El ejemplo de Sonora*.

117. "Scores China Expulsion: Mexican Officals Say Sonora's Business Now Stagnant," *New York Times*, December 26, 1931, p. 6.

EPILOGUE

1. Gordon V. Kurtz, "Chinese Labor, Economic Development and Social Reaction," *Ethnohistory* 18, no 4 (1971): 331.

2. George Lim, "Chinese Part in Community Is Discussed," *Arizona Citizen*, Eleventh Annual Rodeo Section, Chinese Section, February 22, 1935, p. 2.

3. For instances of abuse, see Asunto: "Problema Chino," 1927, caja 362, tomo 1166, AGES; Camacho, "Crossing Boundaries, Claiming a Homeland," pp. 163–164, 558–560; and Pardinas, *Relaciones diplomáticas entre China y México*, pp. 475–477.

4. Rénique, "Anti-Chinese Racism," 124; Héctor Aguilar Camín, "The Relevant Tradition: Sonoran Leaders in the Revolution," in *Caudillo and Peasant in the Mexican Revolution*, ed. D. A. Brading, 90–114 (New York: Cambridge University Press, 1980), p. 98.

5. Lyndon B. Johnson, "Remarks at the Signing of the Immigration Bill, Liberty Island, New York, October 3, 1965," *Public Papers of the Presidents of the United States: Lyndon B. Johnson, 1965*, vol. II, entry 546 (Washington, DC: U.S. Government Printing Office, 1966), p. 1038.

6. Eithne Luibhéid, "The 1965 Immigration and Nationality Act: An 'End' Exclusion," *Positions* 5, no. 2 (1997): 501–522; and Ngai, *Impossible Subjects*, pp. 258–264.

# Glossary of Chinese Names and Terms

| | |
|---|---|
| bao | 寶 |
| Binglun | 炳倫 |
| ganqing | 敢情 |
| guanxi | 關係 |
| hai jin | 金海 |
| hanjian | 漢奸 |
| hong | 香港 |
| huigan | 會館 |
| Ji Xianxing | 姬禎祥 |
| Liangban | 良扳 |
| Liangxiu | 良秀 |
| Lisheng | 立勝 |
| Lunwei | 倫渭 |
| Shengzhao | 滲著 |
| Zhenran | 甄然 |

# Bibliography

ARCHIVES: UNITED STATES

Arizona Historical Foundation, Hayden Library, Tempe, Arizona
Arizona Historical Society, Tucson, Arizona
Arizona State Library, Archives and Public Records, Phoenix, Arizona
Bancroft Library, Berkeley, California
National Archives of the United States, College Park, Maryland
National Archives of the United States, Pacific Region, Laguna Niguel, California
National Archives of the United States, Washington, DC
University of Arizona Libraries, Special Collections, Tucson, Arizona

ARCHIVES: MEXICO

Archivo del Congreso del Estado de Sonora, El, Hermosillo, Sonora
Archivo General del Estado de Sonora, Hermosillo, Sonora
Archivo General de la Nación, Mexico City, Mexico
Archivo General del Poder Judicial (Supremo Tribunal de Justicia), Hermosillo, Sonora
Biblioteca de El Colegio de Mexico, Mexico City, Mexico
Biblioteca Dirección General de Estadística, Mexico City, Mexico
Secretaría de Relaciones Exteriores, Dirección General del Acervo Histórico Diplomático, Mexico City, Mexico

MANUSCRIPT COLLECTIONS

Allison Family Papers, MS 0013 (AHS)
Bisbee Research Collection, MS 0189 (AHS)
Charles Drake Collection, MS 0228(AHS)
Charles T. Connell, Biographical File (AHS)
Charles T. Connell Papers, MS 0166 (AHS)
Chinese Manuscript Collection, AZ 375 (UALSC)
Clera Ferrin Bloom, Biographical File (AHS)
Don Chun Wo, Biographical File (AHS)
Don Wah, Biographical File (AHS)
Ellinwood Papers, MS 0243 (AHS)
Estevan Ochoa, Biographical File (AHS)
Esther Don Tang Collection, MSS 94 (AHF)
Esther Tang, Tucson Oral History Project, AV-0505-16 (AHS)
Fallis Photograph Collection, PC 042 (AHS)
Final Mittimus Records, MS 0073 (AHS)
Gladys Franklin Carroll, Tucson Oral History Project, AV-0359-12 (AHS)

Hunter Morris Jones Papers, MS 0393 (AHS)
James Chester Worthington Letters, MS 0890 (AHS)
James Chester Worthington Papers, MS 0890 (AHS)
Jared Taylor Papers, MS 1078 (AHS)
José María Arana Papers, MS 9 (UALSC)
Julius Goldbaum Papers, MS 0289 (AHS)
Leopoldo Carrillo, Biographical File (AHS)
Lillian Grossetta Barry, Tucson Oral History Project, AV-0358-05 (AHS)
Lily Olivaras Valenzuela Liu, Southern Pacific Railroad Project, AV-0001-15 (AHS)
Paul Lim, Tucson Oral History Project, AV-0452 (AHS)
Pima County Departments, MS 0183 (AHS)
Tucson Chinese Research Collection, MS 1242 (AHS)
U.S. Marshal Records, MS 0820 (AHS)

NEWSPAPERS AND MAGAZINES

*Arizona Citizen* (Tucson)
*Arizona Daily Citizen* (Tucson)
*Arizona Daily Star* (Tucson)
*Arizona Enterprise* (Florence)
*Arizona Republic* (Phoenix)
*Arizona Sentinel* (Arizona City–Yuma)
*Arizona Star* (Tucson)
*Arizona Weekly Citizen* (Tucson)
*Arizona Weekly Star* (Tucson)
*Bisbee Daily Review* (Bisbee)
*Boletín Oficial* (Hermosillo, Mexico City, Ures)
*Border Vidette, The* (Nogales)
*Bulletin: Sunday Magazine, The* (Los Angeles)
*Californian* (San Francisco)
*Cananea Heraldo* (Cananea)
*Chicago Daily Tribune*
*China Weekly Review* (Shanghai)
*Cochise Quarterly* (Douglas)
*Congressional Globe* (Washington, DC)
*Congressional Record* (Washington, DC)
*Daily Arizona Miner* (Prescott)
*Douglas Daily Dispatch* (Douglas)
*Douglas Daily International* (Douglas)
*El Correo del Comercio* (Mexico City)
*El Diario de Coahuila* (Saltillo)
*El Fronterizo* (Tucson)
*El Heraldo* (Cananea)
*El Heraldo de Cananea* (Cananea)
*El Imparcial* (Guaymas, Hermosillo, Mexico City)
*El Intruso* (Cananea)
*El Machete* (Mexico City)

*El Malcriado* (Nacozari de García)
*El Monitor Republicano* (Mexico City)
*El Municipio* (Guaymas)
*El Nacionalista* (Cananea)
*El Provenir* (Monterrey)
*El Tráfico* (Guaymas)
*El Universal* (Mexico City)
*Excélsior* (Mexico City)
*Galveston Daily News* (Galveston)
*Harper's Magazine* (New York)
*La Constitución* (Hermosillo)
*La Era Nueva* (Hermosillo)
*La Estrella de Occidente* (Ures)
*La Libertad* (Mexico City)
*La Palabra* (Nogales)
*La Sonora* (Hermosillo)
*Los Angeles Examiner* (Los Angeles)
*Los Angeles Herald Illustrated Magazine* (Los Angeles)
*Los Angeles Times* (Los Angeles)
*National Post* (Ontario, Canada)
*New York Herald, The* (New York)
*New York Times* (New York)
*New Yorker, The* (New York)
*Nogales Oasis* (Nogales, Arizona)
*Nogales Record* (Nogales, Arizona)
*Orientación* (Hermosillo)
*Overland Monthly and Out West Magazine* (San Francisco)
*Philadelphia Press* (Philadelphia)
*Philadelphia Public Ledger* (Philadelphia)
*Philadelphia Times* (Philadelphia)
*Phoenix Herald* (Phoenix)
*Prescott Courier* (Prescott)
*Pro Patria* (Magdalena)
*Prospector, The* (Tombstone)
*Revista Universal* (Mexico City)
*Salt River Herald* (Phoenix)
*San Diego Union* (San Diego)
*San Francisco Bulletin* (San Francisco)
*San Francisco Call* (San Francisco)
*San Francisco Chronicle* (San Francisco)
*San Francisco Examiner* (San Francisco)
*San Francisco Post* (San Francisco)
*South China Morning News* (Shanghai)
*St. Louis Globe–Democrat* (St. Louis)
*Tombstone Daily Nugget* (Tombstone)
*Tombstone Epitaph* (Tombstone)

*Tombstone Daily Epitaph* (Tombstone)
*Tombstone Weekly Epitaph* (Tombstone)
*Tucson Citizen* (Tucson)
Tucson Daily Citizen (Tucson)
*Tucson Star* (Tucson)
*Weekly Arizona Miner* (Prescott)
*Weekly Nugget* (Tombstone)
*World Journal, The*

PRIMARY SOURCES

Alexander, R., Major General. *British Opium Smuggling: The Illegality of the East India Company's Monopoly of the Drug; and Its Injurious Effects upon India, China, and the Commerce of Great Britain.* London: Judd and Glass Printers, 1856.

Arizona. *The Revised Statutes of Arizona Territory: Containing Also the Laws Passed by the Twenty-First Legislative Assembly, the Constitution of the United States, the Organic Law of Arizona and the Amendments of Congress Relating Thereto.* Columbia, MO: E. W. Stephens, 1901.

Borchard, Montefiore Edwin. *The Diplomatic Protection of Citizens Abroad: Or the Law of International Claims.* New York: Banks Law, 1915.

Branch, Hilarion Noel. *The Mexican Constitution of 1917 Compared with the Constitution of 1857.* Philadelphia: American Academy of Political and Social Science, 1917.

Browne, J. Ross. "Explorations in Lower California." *Harpers Magazine* 37 (1868): 740–752.

———. *Adventures in Apache Country: A Tour Through Arizona and Sonora, with Notes on the Silver Regions of Nevada.* New York: Harper, 1869.

California, State Board of Control. *California and the Oriental: Japanese, Chinese and Hindus. Report of State Board of Control of California to Gov. Wm. D. Stephens. June 19, 1920.* Sacramento: California State Printing Office, 1970.

*City of Tucson General and Business Directory for 1897-1898 Containing 2600 Names of Citizens, with Their Occupations and Places of Residence, the Public Officers, Secret Societies and Churches, Together with Other Useful Information Concerning the City.* Tucson, AZ: Citizen Printing and Publishing, 1897.

Committee of the Senate of the State of California. *Chinese Immigration: The Social, Moral, and Political Effect of Chinese Immigration.* Sacramento: State Printing Office, 1876.

Corral, Ramón. *Memoria de la administración pública del estado de Sonora, presentada a la legislatura del mismo por el Gobernador Ramón Corral,* Vol. 1. Guaymas, Mexico: Imprenta de E. Gaxiola y Compañía, 1891.

———. *Obras históricas.* Hermosillo: Publicaciones del Gobierno del Estado, 1981.

Covarrubias, José. "La inmigración china considerada desde los puntos de vista intelectual y moral," in *Varios informes, sobre tierras y colonización.* Mexico City: Imprenta y Fototipia de la Secretaría de Fomento, 1912.

Davis, John Francis. *The Chinese: A General Description of the Empire of China and Its Inhabitants.* New York: Harper, 1836.

de Arona, Juan. *La Inmigración en el Perú : Monografía Histórico-Crítica.* Lima, Peru: Imprenta del Universo, de Carlos Prince, 1891.

Dillingham, William Paul. *The Immigration Situation in Canada.* Washington, DC: U.S. Government Printing Office, 1910.

Dirección General de Estadística, Mexico. *Anuario estadístico de la República Mexicana.* 5 vols. Mexico: n.p., 1886.

Division of Women's and Professional Projects, Works Progress Administration. *The 1864 Census of the Territory of Arizona.* Phoenix: Historical Records Survey, 1938.

Eitel, Ernest John. *Europe in China: The History of Hongkong from the Beginning to the Year 1882.* London: Luzac, 1895.

Fortune, Robert. *Two Visits to the Tea Countries of China and the British Tea Plantations in the Himalaya with a Narrative of Adventures, and a Full Description of the Culture of the Tea Plant, the Agriculture, Horticulture, and Botany of China.* London: W. Clowes, 1852.

Hichborn, Franklin. *Story of the Session of the California Legislature of 1913.* San Francisco: Press of the James H. Barry Company, 1913.

Johnson, Lyndon B. "Remarks at the Signing of the Immigration Bill, Liberty Island, New York, October 3, 1965." In *Public Papers of the Presidents of the United States: Lyndon B. Johnson, 1965,* vol. II, entry 546. Washington, DC: U.S. Government Printing Office, 1966.

Katz, Friedrich. *The Life and Times of Pancho Villa.* Stanford, CA: Stanford University Press, 1998.

Kino, Eusebio. *Kino's Historical Memoir of Pimería Alta,* trans. Herbert Eugene Bolton. Cleveland, OH: Arthur H. Clark, 1919.

———. *Kino's Plan for the Development of Pimería Alta, Arizona and Upper California: A Report to the Mexican Viceroy,* trans. Ernest J. Burrus. Tucson: Arizona Pioneers' Historical Society, 1961.

La Motte, Ellen N. *The Opium Monopoly.* New York: Macmillan, 1920.

Lankester, Edwin Ray. *Degeneration: A Chapter in Darwinism.* London: Macmillan, 1880.

*Laws of the Territory of Arizona: Thirteenth Legislative Assembly; Also Memorials and Resolutions.* San Francisco: H. S. Crocker, 1885.

Legislative Assembly of the Territory of Arizona. *The Territory of Arizona: A Brief History and Summary.* Tucson: Citizen Office, 1874.

Lloyd, B. E. *Lights and Shades in San Francisco.* San Francisco: A. L. Bancroft, 1876.

Matheson, Donald. *What Is the Opium Trade?* Edinburgh, Scotland: Thomas Constable, 1857.

Maude, Frederic Phillip, and Charles Edward Pollock. *A Compendium of the Law of Merchant Shipping: With Appendix Containing All the Statutes, Orders in Council and Forms of Practical Utility,* Vol. 1. London: Henry Sweet, 1881.

McDonald, William, ed. *Select Statutes and Other Documents Illustrative of the History of the United States, 1861–1898.* New York: Macmillan, 1898.

*Mexican Yearbook: A Financial and Commercial Handbook Compiled from Official and Other Returns.* London: McCorquodale, 1908.

Mexico. "Corresponde al año trascurrido de diciembre de 1876 a noviembre de 1877." In *Memoria presentada al Congreso de la Unión por el Secretario de Fomento, Colonización, Industria, y Comercio,* pp. 14–21. Mexico City: 1877.

———. *Convenciones y Tratados Convenciones y Tratados Imperio chino: Tratado de Amistad, comercio y navegación entre los Estados Unidos Mexicanos y el Imperio chino.* Mexico City: Imprenta del Gobierno en el ex Arzobispado, Secretaría de Relaciones Exteriores de los Estados Unidos Mexicanos, 1900.

———. *Colonization and Naturalization Laws of the Republic of Mexico with Amendments.* Mexico City: n.p., 1905.

———. *Manual del Extranjero.* Mexico City: Antigua Librería Robredo, 1949.

———. *Maximilian's Asiatic Colonization Scheme,* trans. Richard H. Dillon. Chicago: 1952. Available at Bancroft Library, Berkeley, CA.

Mexico Foreign Relations Office. *Correspondencia Diplomática Cambiada entre el Gobierno de los Estados Unidos Mexicanos y Los Varias Potencias Extranjeras,* vol. 4. Mexico City: Tipografía La Luz, 1887.

Ministerio de Fomento, Mexico. *Boletín de la dirección general de estadística de la República Mexicano, 1888–1891.* 8 vols. Mexico City: n.p., 1888–1891.

Peñafiel, Antonio. *Censo general de la República Mexicana verificado el 20 de octubre de 1895, resumen del censo de la República. Dirección General de Estadística, 1899.* Mexico City: Oficina Tipografía de la Secretaría de Fomento, 1899.

———. *Resumen general del censo de la Republica Mexicana verificado el 28 de octubre de 1900.* Mexico City: Impr. de la Secretaría de fomento, 1905.

Ralph, Julian. "The Chinese Leak." *Harper's New Monthly Magazine* 82, no. 490 (1891): 515–525.

Rockhill, William Woodville, ed. *Treaties and Conventions with or concerning China and Korea, 1894–1904, Together with Various State Papers and Documents Affecting Foreign Interests.* Washington, DC: U.S. Government Printing Office, 1904.

Romero, José María. *Comisión de inmigración, dictamen del vocal ingeniero José María Romero, encargado de estudiar la influencia social y económica de la inmigración asiática en México.* Mexico City: Imprenta de A. Carranza e Hijos, 1911.

Romero, Matías, ed. *Correspondencia de la legación mexicana durante la intervención extranjera, 1860–1868,* 10 vols. Mexico City: Imprenta de Gobierno, 1870–1892.

———. *Geographical and Statistical Notes on Mexico, 1837–1898.* New York: Putnam, 1898.

———. *Mexico and the United States: A Study of Subjects Affecting Their Political, Commercial, and Social Relations, Made with a View to Their Promotion.* New York: Knickerbocker Press, 1898.

Secretaría de Agricultura y Fomento, Mexico. *Tercer censo de población de los Estados Unidos Mexicanas, verificado el 27 de octubre 1910.* Mexico City: Dirección General de Estadística, 1911.

Secretaría de la Economía Nacional, Dirección General de Estadística, Mexico. *Anuario estadístico de la República Mexicana 1901*. Mexico City: Dirección General de Estadística, 1902.

———. *Anuario estadístico de la República Mexicana 1905*. Mexico City: Dirección General de Estadística, 1906.

———. *Anuario estadístico de la República Mexicana 1907*. Mexico City: Dirección General de Estadística, 1908.

———. *Anuario estadístico de la República Mexicana 1913*. Mexico City: Dirección General de Estadística, 1914.

———. *Censo de poblacíon 1910, resúmen general*. Mexico City: Dirección General de Estadística, 1918–1920.

———. *Anuario estadístico de la República Mexicana 1930*. Mexico City: Dirección General de Estadística, 1931.

———. *Quinto censo de poblacíon 1930, resúmen general*. Mexico City: Dirección General de Estadística, 1932–1936.

———. *Quinto censo general de población*. Estado de Coahuila, vol. 2, tomo 5. Mexico: Estados Unidos Mexicanos, 1933.

———. *Quinto censo general de población*, vol. 1. Mexico: Estados Unidos Mexicanos, 1934.

———. *Sexto censo de población*, Vol. 1. Baja California, territorios norte y sur. Mexico: Estados Unidos Mexicanos, 1940.

———. *Sexto censo de población, 1940: Resúmen general*. Mexico City: Talleres Gráficos de la Nación, 1943.

———. *Estados Unidos Mexicanos: Sexto censo de poblacíon 1940, resúmen general*. Mexico City: Dirección General de Estadística, 1943.

———. *Estadísticas sociales del Porfiriato: 1877–1910*. Mexico City: Dirección General de Estadística, 1956.

Secretaría de Gobernación, Mexico. "Ley de inmigración de los Estados Unidos Mexicanos." In *Colección de leyes, decretos, reglamentos, y acuerdos, serie I, leyes, y decretos de la federación*. Mexico City: Imprenta del Gobierno Federal, 1909.

———. *El Servicio de Migración en Mexico por Andrés Landa y Piña jefe del Departamento de Migración*. Mexico City: Talleres Gráficos de la Nación, 1930.

*Sonora, 1856–1877. Biografía de José María Leyva Cajeme*. Hermosillo: Publicaciones del Gobierno del Estado, 1981.

Staunton, George Thomas (trans.). *Ta Tsing Leu Lee: Being the Fundamental Laws, and a Selection from the Supplementary Statutes, of the Penal Code of China*. London: Cadell and Davis, 1810.

Stone, Charles Pomeroy. *Notes on Sonora*. Washington, DC: Henry Polkinhorn, 1861.

Thelwall, Algernon Sydney. *The Iniquities of the Opium Trade with China; Being a Development of the Main Causes Which Exclude the Merchants of Great Britain from the Advantages of an Unrestricted Commercial Intercourse with That Vast Empire*. London: William H. Allen, 1839.

U.S. Census Bureau. "Chinese Population by Decades and Geographical Divisions." *Population Census of the United States, 1870*. Washington, DC: U.S. Government Printing Office, 1872.

————. "Sex, General Nativity, and Color: Chinese Population by Counties." *Population Census of the United States, 1870*. Washington, DC: U.S. Government Printing Office, 1872.

————. Eleventh Census of the United States (Washington, DC: Government Printing Office, 1895.

————. *Thirteenth Census of the United States, 1910*. Washington, DC: U.S. Government Printing Office, 1914.

————. *Fourteenth Census of the United States, 1920*. Washington, DC: U.S. Government Printing Office, 1921.

————. *Sixteenth Census of the United States, 1940*. Washington, DC: U.S. Government Printing Office, 1943.

————. *Tenth Census of the United States, 1880*. Washington, DC: U.S. Government Printing Office, 1957.

————. *Twelfth Census of the United States, 1900*. Washington, DC: U.S. Government Printing Office, 1957.

U.S. Department of Commerce and Labor, Bureau of Immigration and Naturalization. *First Annual Report of the Commissioner-General of Immigration for the Fiscal Year Ending June 30, 1903*. Washington, DC: U.S. Government Printing Office, 1903.

————. *Annual Report of the Commissioner-General of Immigration, 1903–1911*. Washington, DC: U.S. Government Printing Office, 1903–1911.

————. *Immigration: Laws and Regulations, 1906*. Washington, DC: Government Printing Office, 1906.

————. *Treaty, Laws, and Regulations Governing the Admission of Chinese*. Washington, DC: Government Printing Office, 1909.

U.S. Department of Justice, Immigration and Naturalization Service. *Development of Immigration and Naturalization Laws and Service History*. Washington, DC: Department of Justice, 1966.

U.S. Department of State. Dispatches from United States Consuls in Guaymas, Sonora, Mexico, 1832–1896. M 284. Washington, DC: National Archives and Records Service, General Services Administration, 1955.

————. Dispatches from United States Consuls in Hermosillo, Sonora, Mexico, 1905–1906. M 293. Washington, DC: National Archives and Records Service, General Services Administration, 1955.

————. General Records of the United States Department of State, Dispatches from United States Consuls in Mazatlan, Mexico, 1826–1906. M 281. Washington, DC: National Archives and Records Service, General Services Administration, 1955.

————. *Records of the Department of State Relating to Internal Affairs of Mexico 1910–1929*. M 274. Washington, DC: National Archives and Records Service, General Services Administration, 1955.

————. Despatches from United States Consuls in Nogales, Sonora, Mexico, 1889–1906. M 283. Washington, DC: National Archives and Records Service, General Services Administration, 1959.

————. Dispatches from the United States Consul in Ensenada, Mexico, 188

8–1906. M 291. Washington, DC: National Archives and Records Service, General Services Administration, 1964.

———. General Records of the Department of State, Dispatches from United States Consuls in Acapulco, Mexico, 1823–1906. M 143. Washington, DC: National Archives and Records Service, General Services Administration, 1965.

U.S. Department of the Treasury. *Annual Report of the Commissioner-General of Immigration, 1894–1902.* Washington, DC: U.S. Government Printing Office, 1894–1902.

U.S. Department of the Treasury. *Letter from the Secretary of the Treasury, transmitting to the Senate the departmental regulations relating to Chinese exclusion and the date and authority by which such regulations were adopted.* 57th Cong., 1st sess., April 10, 1902, S. doc. 300, serial 4239, vol. 20.

U.S. Department of the Treasury, Bureau of Immigration. *Report of the Immigrant Inspector in Charge of Canadian Border Inspection, 1902.* Washington, DC: U.S. Government Printing Office, 1902.

U.S. Department of the Treasury, Committee on Appropriations, Organization of the Immigration on Service. Letter from the Secretary of the Treasury, transmitting a plan for the organization of the Immigration Service of the United States, *Plan for Organization of Immigration Service.* 53rd Cong., 3rd. sess., 1895. H. Rep. 206.

U.S. Department of the Treasury, Committee on Foreign Affairs. *To Regulate Coming of Chinese into the United States.* 56th Congress, 2nd sess., 1901, 4213, H. Rep. 2503, January 25, 1901.

U.S. Department of the Treasury, Committee on Immigration and Naturalization. *Hearings on Immigration Investigation.* 51st Cong., 2nd sess., HRG.1890-IMH-0001.

U.S. Department of the Treasury, Select Committee on Immigration and Naturalization. *Immigration Investigation.* 51st Cong., 2nd sess., 1891. H. Rep. 3472., January 15, 1891.

U.S. Department of the Treasury, Select Committee on Investigation of Foreign Immigration. *Hearings on the Importation of Contract Laborers, Paupers, Convicts, and Other Classes.* 50th Cong., 2nd sess., 1889.

U.S. House of Representatives, Committee on Foreign Affairs. *Regulating Immigration.* 49th Cong., 1st sess., H. ex. doc. 141, May 25, 1886.

———. *Preventing Immigration of Chinese Labor from Canada and Mexico.* 51st Cong., 2nd sess., 1889–1890, H. Rep. 1925, serial 2812, vol. 6, May 8, 1890.

———. *Resolution on negotiations with Mexico and Great Britain, to prevent entry of Chinese laborers from Canada and Mexico into United States.* 51st Cong. 1st sess., 1890, H. mis. doc. 202, serial 2775, vol. 16, March 2, 1890.

———. *Compilation from the Records of the Bureau of Immigration of Facts Concerning the Enforcement of the Chinese Exclusion Laws,* 59th Cong., 1st sess., H. doc. 847, May 18, 1906.

U.S. House of Representatives, Committee on Immigration and Naturalization, Investigation of Chinese immigration, with testimony. 51st Cong., 2nd. sess., H. Rep. 3472, serial 2890, vol. 6, March 2, 1891.

———. Hearing. 67th Cong., 1st sess., November 8, 1921. HRG-1921-IMN-0012.

————. *Inquiry into Activities of Charles F. Hille with Relation to Certain Chinese Refugees*, hearing, 67th Cong., 2nd Sess., January 24, 1922. HRG-192 2-IMN-0001.

U.S. House of Representatives, Committee to Inquire into Alleged Violation of Laws Prohibiting Importation of Contract Laborers, Paupers, Convicts, and Other Classes, *Report of the Select Committee to Inquire into the Alleged Violation of the Laws Prohibiting the Importation of Contract Laborers, Paupers, Convicts, and Other Classes, Together with the Testimony, Documents, and Consular Report.* 50th Cong., 1st sess., H. Rept. 12291.

U.S. House of Representatives, Select Committee on Immigration. *Immigration Investigation, Report, Testimony, and Statistics.* 51st Cong., 2nd. sess., H. Rept. 3472, serial 2886, vol. 2, January 14, 1891.

U.S. House of Representatives, Select Committee on Immigration, Subcommittee on Chinese Exclusion Bill, Committee on Foreign Affairs. Hearing, 59th Cong., 1st sess., February 15; March 14, 29; April 9, 11, 1906, HRG-1906-FOA-0001.

U.S. House of Representatives, Select Committee on Investigation of Foreign Immigration. *Hearings on the Importation of Contract Laborers, Paupers, Convicts, and Other Classes.* 50th Cong., 2nd sess., HRG-1888-IAV-0001 1, January, August, and December 1888.

————. *To Regulate Immigration.* 50th Cong., 2d sess., H. Rep. 3972, January 19, 1889.

U.S. House of Representatives, Subcommittee on Chinese Exclusion Bill, Committee on Foreign Affairs. Hearing. 59th Cong., 1st sess., Feb. 15, Mar. 14, 29, April 9, 11, 1906, HRG-1906-FOA-0001.

U.S. Secretary of State. *Annual Report of the Commercial Relations Between the United States and Foreign Nations.* Washington, DC: U.S. Government Printing Office, 1869–1912.

U.S. Senate. "Letter from the Acting Secretary of the Treasury Relative to the Necessity for an Appropriation to Carry into Effect the Chinese Exclusion Act," 50th Cong., 1st sess., S. ex. doc. 275, October 9, 1888.

U.S. Senate, Committee on Immigration. *Report on Immigration of Chinese,* 51st Cong., 1st sess., S. ex. doc. 97, serial 2686, vol. 9, 1890.

————. *Transit of Chinese Through United States.* 51st Cong. 1st sess., S. ex. doc. 106, serial 2686, vol. 9, April 19, 1890.

————. *Report of the Select Committee on Immigration and Naturalization, and testimony taken by the Committee on Immigration of the Senate and the Select Committee on Immigration and Naturalization of the House of Representatives under concurrent resolution of March 12, 1890.* 51st Cong., 2nd. sess., H. Rep. 3472, serial 2886, vol. 2, January 14, 1891.

————. *Letters from Secretary of State and Secretary of Treasury on act providing for inspection of immigrants by United States consuls,* 53rd Cong., 3d. sess., S. mis. doc. 253, serial 3171, vol. 5., 1894.

————. *Chinese Exclusion.* Hearing, 57th Cong., 1st sess., 57 S. 2960, January and February 1902.

————. *Regulation of Immigration of Aliens: Statements Before the Committee on Immigration, United States Senate, on the Bill H.R.12199 to Regulate the Im-*

*migration of Aliens into the United States*, 57th Cong., 1st sess., S. Rept. 2119, 1902.

U.S. Senate, Select Committee on Relations with Canada. *Relations with Canada*, 51st Cong., 1st sess., April 26, 1890, HRG-1890–RCA-0001.

———. *Compilation of the Laws, Treaty, and Regulations and Rulings of the Treasury Department Relating to the Exclusion of Chinese*. 57th Cong., 1st sess., 1903. S. doc. 291.

Velasco, Alfonso Luis. *Geografía y estadística del Estado de Sonora*. Mexico: Tipografía T. González, 1895.

Velasco, José Francisco. *Noticias estadísticas del Estado de Sonora*. Hermosillo: Gobierno del Estado de Sonora, 1850.

———. *Sonora: Its Extent, Population, Natural Productions, Indian Tribes, Mines, Mineral Lands, etc.* San Francisco: H. H. Bancroft and Company, 1861.

Wilfley and Bassett, Law Firm. *On the Law and the Facts in the Matter of the Claim of China Against Mexico for Losses of Life and Property Suffered by Chinese Subjects at Torreón on May 13, 14 and 15, 1911*. Mexico City: American Book & Printing, 1911.

———. *Showing Extent of Destruction of Life and Property of Chinese Subjects During the Recent Revolution in Mexico and Mexico's Responsibility Therefore Together with Citation of Authorities*. Mexico City: American Book & Printing, 1911.

Willoughby, Westel W. *Foreign Rights and Interests in China*. Baltimore, MD: Johns Hopkins University Press, 1920.

SECONDARY SOURCES

Aceves, María Teresa Fernández, Carmen Ramos Escandón, and Susie Porter, eds. *Orden social e identidad de género Mexico, siglos XIX y XX*. Hidalgo: Centro de Investigaciones y Estudios Superiores en Antropología Social, 2006.

Adelman, Jeremy, and Stephen Aron. "From Borderlands to Borders: Empires, Nation-States, and the Peoples in Between in North American History." *American Historical Review* 104, no. 3 (1999): 814–817.

Aguilar Camín, Héctor. *La frontera nómada: Sonora y la Revolución Mexicana*. Mexico City: Siglo XXI, 1977.

———. "The Relevant Tradition: Sonoran Leaders in the Revolution." In *Caudillo and Peasant in the Mexican Revolution*, ed. D. A. Brading, 90–114. New York: Cambridge University Press, 1980.

Aguilar Camín, Héctor, and Lorenzo Meyer. *A la sombra de la Revolución Mexicana: Un ensayo de historia contemporánea de México, 1910–1989*. Mexico City: Cal y arena, 1989.

Alfaro-Velcamp, Theresa. *So Far from Allah: Middle Eastern Immigrants in Modern Mexico*. Austin: University of Texas Press, 2007.

Almada Bay, Ignacio, and José Marcos Medina Bustos. *Historia Panorámica del del Estado de Sonora, 1825–2000*. Mexico City: Cal y Arena, 2001.

Anaya, Delia Salazar. *La población extranjera en México (1895–1990): Un recuento con base en los censos generales de población*. Mexico City: Instituto Nacional de Antropología e Historia, 1996.

Anderson, Benedict. *Imagined Communities: Reflections on the Origin and Spread of Nationalism*. London: Verso, 1983.

Annis, Matthew. "The 'Chinese Question' and the Canada-U.S. Border, 1885: 'Why Don't Governor Squire Send His Troops to Semiahmoo to Prevent the Twelve or Fifteen Thousand Pagans from Crossing Our Borders from British Columbia?'" *American Review of Canadian Studies, 1943–1954*, 40, no. 3 (2010): 351–361.

Arizona State Historic Preservation Office. *The Chinese in Arizona, 1870–1950*, prepared by Melissa Keane, A. G. Rogge, and Bradford Luckingham. Phoenix: Arizona State Parks Board, 1992.

Armentrout Ma, L. Eve. "Urban Chinese at the Sinitic Frontier: Social Organizations in United States' Chinatowns, 1849–1898." *Modern Asian Studies* 17, no. 1 (1983): 107–135.

———. *Revolutionaries, Monarchists, and Chinatowns: Chinese Politics in the Americas and the 1911 Revolution*. Honolulu: University of Hawaii Press, 1990.

———. "Chinatown Organizations and the Anti-Chinese Movement, 1882–1914." In *Entry Denied: Exclusion and the Chinese Community in America, 1882–1943*, ed. Sucheng Chan, 147–169. Philadelphia: Temple University Press, 1991.

Aron, Stephen. "Lessons in Conquest: Towards a Greater Western History." *Pacific Historical Review* 63 (May 1994): 125–147.

Augustine-Adams, Kif. "Constructing Mexico: Marriage, Law and Women's Dependent Citizenship in the Late-Nineteenth and Early-Twentieth Centuries." *Gender and History* 18, no. 1 (2006): 20–34.

———. "Making Mexico: Legal Nationality, Chinese Race, and the 1930 Population Census." *Law and History Review* 27, no. 1 (2009): 113–144.

Auyón, Eduardo Gerardo. *El dragón en el desierto, los primeros chinos en Mexicali, 1903–1991*. Mexicali, Baja California:, Instituto de Cultura de Baja California, 1991.

Bancroft, Hubert Howe. *The New Pacific*. New York: Bancroft, 1915.

Bantjes, Adrian A. *As If Jesus Walked on Earth: Cardenismo, Sonora, and the Mexican Revolution*. Wilmington, DE: Scholarly Resources, 1998.

Barkow, Patricia Irma Figueroa. "El movimiento antichino en México de 1916–1935: Un caso de 'racismo económico,'" master's thesis, Universidad Nacional Autónoma de México, 1976.

Barrett, James, David Roediger, and Klaus Unger. "In-Between Peoples: Race, Nationality, and the 'New Immigrant' Working Class in the United States." *Werkstatt Geschichte* 14, no. 39 (2005): 7–34.

Basave Benítez, A. F., and Andrés Molina Enríquez. *México mestizo: análisis del nacionalismo mexicano en torno a la mestizofilia de Andrés Molina Enríquez. Sección de obras de historia*. Mexico City: Fondo de Cultura Económica, 1992.

Bayly, C. A., Sven Beckert, Matthew Connelly, Isabel Hofmeyr, Wendy Kozol, and Patricia Seed. "AHR Conversation: On Transnational History," *American Historical Review* 111, no. 5 (2006): 1141–1165.

Beckert, Sven. "Featured Review: Thomas Bender, *A Nation Among Nations*:

*America's Place in World History." American Historical Review* 112, no. 4 (2007): 1123–1125.

Beesley, David. "From Chinese to Chinese American: Chinese Women and Families in a Sierra Nevada Town." *California History* 67, no. 3 (1988): 168–179.

Beezley, William H. "The Role of State Governors in the Mexican Revolution." In *State Governors in the Mexican Revolution, 1910–1952: Portraits in Conflict and Courage and Corruption*, ed. Jürgen Buchenau and William H. Beezley, 4–10. New York: Rowman and Littlefield, 2009.

Beltrán, Gonzalo Aguirre. *La población negra de México: Estudio etnohistórico.* Mexico City: Fondo de Cultura Económica, 1989.

———. "The Slave Trade in Mexico." *Hispanic American Review* 24, no. 3 (1994): 412–431.

Bender, Thomas. *Rethinking American History in a Global Age.* Berkeley: University of California Press, 2002.

———. *A Nation Among Nations: America's Place in World History.* New York: Hill and Wang, 2006.

Benton-Cohen, Katherine. *Borderline Americans: Racial Division and Labor War in the Arizona Borderlands.* Cambridge, MA: Harvard University Press, 2009.

Berninger, George Dieter. *La inmigración en México, 1821–1857. La inmigración en México, 1821–1857* (Mexico D. F.: 1974) Mexico City: 1970.

Bjork, Katharine. "The Link That Kept the Philippines Spanish: Mexican Merchant Interests and the Manila Trade, 1571–1815." *Journal of World History* 9, no. 1 (1998): 25–51.

Blanton, Carlos K. "George I. Sánchez, Ideology, and Whiteness in the Making of the Mexican American Civil Rights Movement, 1930–1960." *Journal of Southern History* 72, no. 3 (2006): 569–604.

Bliss, Katherine Elaine. *Compromised Positions: Prostitution, Public Health, and Gender Politics in Revolutionary Mexico City.* University Park: Pennsylvania State University Press, 2001.

Bordo, Susan. "The Body and the Reproduction of Femininity: A Feminist Appropriation of Foucault." In *Gender/Body/Knowledge: Feminist Reconstructions of Being and Knowing*, ed. Alison M. Jaggar and Susan R. Bordo, 13–33. New Brunswick, NJ: Rutgers University Press.

Boyd-Bowman, Peter. "Two Country Stores in XVIIth Century Mexico." *Americas* 28, no. 3 (1972): 237–251.

Bradley, Anita. *Trans-Pacific Relations of Latin America: An Introductory Essay and Selected Bibliography.* New York: Institute of Pacific Relations, 1942.

Brady, Marilyn Dell. *The Asian Texans.* San Antonio: University of Texas Institute of Texan Cultures, 2004.

Braun, Marcus. "How Can We Enforce Our Exclusion Laws?" *Annals of the American Academy of Political and Social Science* 34, no. 2 (1909), 140–142.

Briscoe, Edward Eugene. "Pershing's Chinese Refugees: An Odyssey of the Southwest," master's thesis, Saint Mary's University, 1947.

———. "Pershing's Chinese Refugees in Texas." *Southwestern Historical Quarterly* 62, no. 4 (1959): 467–488.

Brook, Thomas. "China Men, United States v. Wong Kim Ark, and the Question of Citizenship." *American Quarterly* 50, no. 4 (1998): 689–717.

Brooks, James F. *Captives and Cousins: Slavery, Kinship, and Community in the Southwest Borderlands.* Chapel Hill: University of North Carolina Press, 2002.

Brown, Jim. *Riding the Line: The United States Customs Service in San Diego, 1885–1930.* Washington, DC: Department of the Treasury, United States Customs Service, 1991.

Buchenau, Jürgen. "Plutarco Elías Calles of Sonora: A Mexican Jacobin." In *State Governors in the Mexican Revolution, 1910–1952: Portraits in Conflict and Courage and Corruption,* ed. Jürgen Buchenau and William H. Beezley, 59–75. New York: Rowman and Littlefield, 2009.

Calavita, Kitty. "Paradoxes of Race, Class, Identity, and 'Passing': Enforcing the Chinese Exclusion Acts, 1882–1910." *Law & Social Inquiry* 25, no. 1 (2000): 1–40.

Camacho, Julia María Schiavone. "Traversing Boundaries: Chinese, Mexicans, and Chinese Mexicans in the Formation of Gender, Race, and Nation in the Twentieth-Century U.S.-Mexican Borderlands." PhD diss., University of Texas at El Paso, 2006.

————. "Crossing Boundaries, Claiming a Homeland: The Mexican Chinese Transpacific Journey to Becoming Mexican, 1930s–1960s." *Pacific Historical Review* 78, no. 4 (2009): 545–577.

Campbell, Persia Crawford. *Chinese Coolie Emigration to Countries with the British Empire.* Charleston, SC: BiblioLife, 2009.

Cardiel Marín, Rosario. "La migración china en el norte de Baja California, 1877–1949." In *Destino México: un estudio de las migraciones asiáticas a México, siglos XIX y XX,* ed. María Elena Ota Mishima, 189–255. Mexico City: El Colegio de México, 1997.

Cardoso, Lawrence A. *Mexican Emigration to the United States, 1897–1931: Socio-Economic Patterns.* Tucson: University of Arizona Press, 1980.

Carlos, Manuel L. "Kinship and Modernization in Mexico: A Comparative Analysis." *Anthropological Quarterly* 46, no. 2 (1973): 75–91.

Chan, Sucheng. *This Bittersweet Soil: The Chinese in California Agriculture, 1860–1910.* Berkeley: University of California Press, 1986.

————. ed. *Entry Denied: Exclusion and the Chinese Community in America, 1882–1943.* Philadelphia: Temple University Press, 1991.

Chang, Ching-chieh. "The Chinese in Latin America: A Preliminary Geographical Survey with Special Reference to Cuba and Jamaica." PhD diss., University of Maryland, 1956.

Chang, Kornel. "Enforcing Transnational White Solidarity: Asian Migration and the Formation of the U.S.-Canadian Boundary." *American Quarterly* 60, no. 3 (2008): 671–696.

Chang-Rodriguez, Eugenio. "Chinese Labor Migration into Latin America in the Nineteenth Century." *Revista de Historia de America* 46 (December 1958): 375–397.

Chanin, Abraham S., with Mildren Chanin. *This Land, These Voices: A Different View of Arizona History in the Words of Those Who Lived It.* Flagstaff: Northland Press, 1977.

Chen, Edward C. M., and Fred R. von der Mehden. *Chinese in Houston*. Houston, TX: Center for the Humanities, 1982.

Chen, Yong. *Chinese San Francisco, 1850–1943—A Transpacific Community.* Stanford, CA: Stanford University Press, 2002.

Cheong, Weng Eang. *The Hong Merchants of Canton: Chinese Merchants in Sino-Western Trade, 1684–1798*. New York: Routledge, 1997.

Chien, Chiao. "The Continuation of Tradition: Navajo and Chinese Models." PhD diss., Cornell University 1969.

Chin, Ko-lin. *Smuggled Chinese: Clandestine Immigration to the United States.* Philadelphia: Temple University Press, 1999.

———. "Chinese Triad Societies, Tongs, Organized Crime, and Street Gangs in Asia and the United States." PhD diss., University of Pennsylvania, 1986.

Chinn, Thomas W., H. Mark Lai, and Philip P. Choy, eds. *A History of the Chinese in California: A Syllabus.* San Francisco: Chinese Historical Society of America, n. d.

Chou, Diego L. "The Chinese in Mexico (1876–1931)." *Cuadernos americanos* 15, no. 89 (2001): 73–85.

Chueng, Floyd. "Performing Exclusion and Resistance: Anti-Chinese League and Chee Kung Tong Parades in Territorial Arizona." *Drama Review* 46, no. 1 (2002): 39–59.

Cohen, Lucy M. *The Chinese in the Post-Civil War South: A People Without History.* Baton Rouge: Louisiana State University Press, 1984.

Conner, Ruth. "Charlie Sam and the Sojourners." *Journal of Arizona History* 14, no. 4 (1973): 303–316.

Coolidge, Mary Roberts. *Chinese Immigration*. New York: Arno Press and *New York Times*, 1909.

Cooper, Frederick, Thomas C. Holt, and Rebecca Scott, eds., *Beyond Slavery: Explorations of Race, Labor, and Citizenship in Postemancipation Societies*. Chapel Hill: University of North Carolina Press, 2000.

Cortina-Borja, Mario and Leopoldo Valiñas C., "Some Remarks on Uto-Aztecan Classification." *International Journal of American Linguistics* 55, no. 2 (1989): 214–239.

Corwin, Arthur F. "Historia de la emigración mexicana, 1900–1970: literatura e investigación." *Historia mexicana* 22 (October-December 1972): 188–220.

Cott, Kennett. "Mexican Diplomacy and the Chinese Issue, 1876–1910." *Hispanic American Historical Review* 67, no. 1 (1987): 63–85.

Cott, Nancy F. "Marriage and Women's Citizenship in the United States, 1830–1934." *American Historical Review* 103, no. 5 (1998): 1440–1474.

Cox, Annie M. "History of Bisbee, 1877–1937," master's thesis, University of Arizona, 1938.

Craib, Raymond B. "Chinese Immigrants in Porfirian Mexico: A Preliminary Study of Settlement, Economic Activity, and Anti-Chinese Sentiment." *Latin American Institute Research Paper Series*, no. 28. Albuquerque: University of New Mexico, 1996: 1–33.

Crissman, Lawrence W. "The Segmentary Structure of Urban Overseas Chinese Communities," *Man* 1 (1967): 185–204.

Cronon, William, George Miles, and Jay Gitlin. "Becoming West: Toward a New Meaning for Western History." In *Under an Open Sky: Rethinking America's Western Past*, ed. William Cronon, George Miles and Jay Gitlin, 10–11. New York: Norton, 1992.

Cumberland, Charles. "The Sonoran Chinese and the Mexican Revolution." *Hispanic American Historical Review* 40, no. 2 (1960): 191–205.

Curtis, James R. "Mexicali's Chinatown." *Geographical Review* 85, no. 3 (1995): 335–348.

da Cunha Reis, D. Manuel B. *Estatutos de la Compañía de Colonización Asiática*. Mexico City: Imprenta de J. M. Lara, 1866.

Dambourges, Leo Michael Jacques. "The Anti-Chinese Campaigns in Sonora, Mexico, 1900–1931." PhD diss., University of Arizona, 1974.

———. "The Chinese Massacre in Torreón (Coahuila) in 1911." *Arizona and the West* 16, no. 3 (1974): 233–246.

———. "Have Quick More Money Than Mandarins: The Chinese in Sonora," *Journal of Arizona History* 17, no. 3 (1976): 201–218.

———. "Chinese Merchants in Sonora, 1900–1931." In *Asiatic Migrations in Latin America*, ed. Luz M. Martínez Montiel (Mexico City 1981): 13–20.

Davis, James J. "Bootleg Immigrants." *American Review of Reviews* 67, no. 6 (1923): 615–617.

de la Riva, Juan Pérez. *Los culíes chinos en Cuba*. La Habana: Editorial de Ciencias Sociales, 2000.

DeLay, Brian. *War of a Thousand Deserts: Indian Raids and the U.S.-Mexican War*. New Haven, CT: Yale University Press, 2008.

Delgado, Grace Peña. "In the Age of Exclusion: Race, Region, and Chinese Identity in the Making of the Arizona-Sonora Borderlands, 1863–1943." PhD diss., University of California, Los Angeles, 2000.

———. "At Exclusion's Southern Gate: Changing Categories of Race and Class Among Chinese *Fronterizos*, 1882–1904." In *Continental Crossroads: Remapping U.S.-Mexico Borderlands History*, ed. Samuel Truett and Elliott Young, 183–207. Durham, NC: Duke University Press, 2004.

———. "Of Kith and Kin: Land, Leases, and Guanxi in Tucson's Chinese and Mexican Communities, 1880s–1920s." *Journal of Arizona History* 46, no. 1 (2005): 33–54.

Dennis, Phillip A. "The Anti-Chinese Campaigns in Sonora, Mexico." *Ethnohistory* 26, no. 1 (1979): 65–80.

Deutsch, Karl. *Nationalism and Social Communication: An Inquiry into the Foundations of Nationality*. 2nd ed. Boston: MIT Press, 1966.

Duara, Prasenjit. *Rescuing History from the Nation: Questioning Narratives of Modern China*. Chicago: University of Chicago Press, 1997.

———. "The Regime of Authenticity: Timelessness, Gender, and National History in Modern China." *History and Theory* 37 (1998): 287–308.

———. "Civilizations and Nations in a Globalizing World." In *Reflections on Multiple Modernities*, ed. Dominic Sachsenmeier, Jens Reidel, and Shmuel Eisenstadt, 79–99. Berlin: Brill Academic, 2002.

———. "Transnationalism and the Challenge to National Histories." In *Rethink-*

*ing American History in a Global Age*, ed. Thomas Bender, 25–46. Berkeley: University of California, 2002.

———. *Sovereignty and Authenticity: Manchukuo and the East Asian Modern.* New York: Rowman & Littlefield, 2004.

Dubs, Homer H., and Robert S. Smith. "The Chinese in Mexico City in 1635." *Far Eastern Quarterly* 1, no. 4 (1942): 387–389.

Duncan, Robert H. "The Chinese and the Economic Development of Northern Baja California." *Hispanic American Historical Review* 74, no. 4 (1994): 615–647.

Enríquez, Andrés Molina. *Los grandes problemas nacionales.* Mexico City: Imprenta de A. Carranza e hijos, 1909.

Espinoza, José Ángel. *El problema Chino en México.* Mexico City: n.p., 1931.

———. *El Ejemplo de Sonora.* Mexico: n.p., 1932.

Ettinger, Patrick. *Imaginary Lines: Border Enforcement and the Origins of Undocumented Immigration, 1882–1930.* Austin: University of Texas Press, 2009.

Fairbank, John King. *Trade and Diplomacy on the China Coast: The Opening of the Treaty Ports, 1842–1854.* Cambridge, MA: Harvard University Press, 1964)

Farrar, Nancy. *The Chinese in El Paso.* El Paso: Texas Western Press, 1972.

Fay, Peter Ward. *The Opium War, 1840–1842: Barbarians in the Celestial Empire in the Early Part of the Nineteenth Century and the War by Which They Forced Her Gates.* Chapel Hill: University of North Carolina Press, 1997.

Félix, Maricela González. "Los inmigrantes chinos y la hacienda pública del Distrito Norte de la Baja California, 1910–1920." In *China en las Californias.* Colección Divulgación. Mexico City: Consejo Nacional para la Cultura y las Artes, 2002.

———. *El proceso de aculturación de la población de origen chino en la ciudad de Mexicali.* Mexicali: Universidad Autónoma de Baja California, Instituto de Investigaciones Sociales, 1990.

Foley, Neil. "Becoming Hispanic: Mexican Americans and the Faustian Pact with Whiteness." In *Reflexiones 1997: New Directions in Mexican American Studies*, ed. Neil Foley, 53–70. Austin: University of Texas Press, 1998.

———. *White Scourge: Mexicans, Blacks, and Poor Whites in Texas Cotton Culture.* Berkeley: University of California Press, 1999.

Fong, Lawrence Michael. "Sojourners and Settlers: The Chinese Experience in Arizona." *Journal of Arizona History* 21, no. 3 (1980): 1–30.

Fontana, Bernard L., and J. Cameron Greenleaf. "Johnny Ward's Ranch: A Study in Historic Archaeology." *Kiva* 28, no. 1–2 (1962): 26–27.

Fredrickson, George M. "From Exceptionalism to Variability: Recent Developments in Cross-National Comparative History." *Journal of American History* 82, no 2 (1995): 587–604.

Fry, Luther C. "Illegal Entry of Orientals into the United States Between 1910 and 1920." *Journal of the American Statistical Association* 23, no. 162 (1928): 173–177.

Gamio, Manuel. *Forjando Patria (pro nacionalismo).* Mexico City: Porrúa Hermanos, 1916.

Gellner, Ernest. *Nations and Nationalism.* Ithaca, NY: Cornell University Press, 1983.

Gerardo, Eduardo Auyón. *El dragón en el desierto: los pioneros chinos en Mexicali.* Mexicali: Instituto de Cultura de Baja California, 1991.

Gitlin, Jay. "On the Boundaries of Empire: Connecting the West to Its Imperial Past." In *Under an Open Sky: Rethinking America's Western Past,* ed. William Cronon, George Miles, and Jay Gitlin, 71–89. New York: Norton, 1992.

Gold, Thomas, Doug Guthrie, and David Wank. *Social Connections in China: Institutions, Culture, and the Changing Nature of Guanxi.* Cambridge, UK: Cambridge University Press, 2002.

Gómez-Quiñones, Juan. *Mexican and American Labor, 1790–1990.* Albuquerque: University of New Mexico Press, 1994.

González Navarro, Moisés. *El Porfiriato: La vida social,* Vol. 4. Mexico City: Hermes, 1957.

———. *La colonización en Mexico, 1877–1910.* Mexico City: Talleres de Impresión de Estampillas y Valores, 1960.

———. "Xenofobia y xenofilia en la Revolución Mexicana." *Historia Mexicana* 18, no. 72 (1969): 569–614.

———. *Los extranjeros en México y los mexicanos en el extranjero, 1821–1970.* Mexico City: Colegio de México, Centro de Estudios Históricos, 1993.

González Navarro, Moisés, and Delia Salazar Anaya. *Xenofobia y xenofilia en la historia de México, siglos XIX y XX: homenaje a Moisés González Navarro.* Mexico City: SEGOB, Instituto Nacional de Migración, Centro de Estudios Migratorios, 2006.

Goodman, John Kestner. "Race and Race Mixture as the Basis of Social Status in Tucson, Arizona," master's thesis, Yale University, 1942.

Gootenberg, Paul. *Imagining Development: Economic Ideas in Peru's "Fictitious Prosperity" of Guano, 1840–1880.* Berkeley: University of California Press, 1993.

Gordon, Linda. *The Great Arizona Orphan Abduction.* Cambridge, MA: Harvard University Press, 1999.

Guterl, Matthew. "After Slavery: Asian Labor, the American South, and the Age of Emancipation." *Journal of World History* 14, no. 2 (2003): 209–242.

Gutiérrez, David. *Walls and Mirrors: Mexican Americans, Mexican Immigrants, and the Politics of Ethnicity.* Berkeley: University of California Press, 1995.

Gyory, Andrew. *Closing the Gate: Race, Politics and the Chinese Exclusion Act.* Chapel Hill: University of North Carolina Press, 1998.

Hall, Linda. *Oil, Banks, and Politics: The United States and Postrevolutionary Mexico.* Austin: University of Texas Press, 1995.

Hall, Linda B., and Don M. Coerver. *Revolution on the Border: The United States and Mexico, 1910–1920.* Albuquerque: University of New Mexico Press, 1988.

Hämäläinen, Pekka. *The Comanche Empire.* New Haven, CT: Yale University Press, 2008.

Hardaway, Roger D. "Unlawful Love: A History of Arizona's Miscegenation Law." *Journal of Arizona History* 27, no. 4 (1986): 377–390.

Harkness, Ellen Gail. "Culture and Role of Chinese Health Professionals with Multi-Ethnic Clients." PhD diss., University of Arizona, 1973.

Hatch, Heather S. "The Chinese in the Southwest: A Photographic Record." *Journal of Arizona History* 21, no. 3 (1980): 256–274.

Hao, Yen-p'ing. *The Commercial Revolution in Nineteenth-Century China: The Rise of Sino-Western Mercantile Capitalism.* Berkeley: University of California Press, 1986.

Haney-López, Ian F. *White by Law: The Legal Construction of Race.* New York: New York University Press, 1997.

Hansen, Lawrence Douglas Taylor. "El contrabando de Chinos a lo largo de la frontera entre México y Estados Unidos, 1882–1931." *Frontera Norte* 6, no. 9 (1994): 41–57.

———. "The Chinese Six Companies of San Francisco and the Smuggling of Chinese Immigrants Across the U.S.-Mexico Border 1882–1930." *Journal of the Southwest* 48, no. 1 (2006): 37–61.

Hatfield, Shelley Bowen. *Chasing Shadows: Indians Along the United States-Mexico Border, 1876–1911.* Albuquerque: University of New Mexico Press, 1998.

Heatwole, Thelma. "An Old Chinese Custom." *Arizona Days and Ways* (1960): 32–33.

Helly, Denise. *The Cuba Commission Report: A Hidden History of the Chinese in Cuba.* Baltimore, MD: Johns Hopkins University Press, 1993.

Hernández, Kelly Lytle. *Migra! A History of the U.S. Border Patrol.* Berkeley: University of California Press, 2010.

Heyman, Josiah M. *Life and Labor on the Border: Working People of Northeastern Sonora, Mexico, 1886–1986.* Tucson: University of Arizona Press, 1991.

Hing, Bill Ong. *Making and Remaking Asian America Through Immigration Policy, 1850–1990.* Stanford, CA: Stanford University Press, 1993.

Hirata, Lucie Cheng. "Free, Indentured, Enslaved: Chinese Prostitutes in Nineteenth-Century America." *Signs* 5, no. 1, Special Section: Women in Latin America (1979): 3–29.

Hsu, Madeline Y. *Dreaming of Gold, Dreaming of Home: Transnationalism and Migration Between the United States and South China, 1882–1943.* Stanford, CA: Stanford University Press, 2000.

Hu-Dehart, Evelyn. "Immigrants to a Developing Society: The Chinese in Northern Mexico, 1875–1932." *Journal of Arizona History* 21, no. 1 (1980): 49–86.

———. "Racism and Anti-Chinese Persecution in Sonora, Mexico, 1876–1932." *Amerasia Journal* 9, no. 4 (1982): 1–28.

———. "The Chinese of Baja California Norte, 1910–1934." *Proceedings of the Pacific Coast Council on Latin American Studies* 12 (1985–1986): 9–30.

———. "Coolies, Shopkeepers, Pioneers: The Chinese of Mexico and Peru (1849–1930)." *Amerasia* 15, no. 2 (1989): 91–116.

———. "Chinese Coolie Labor in Cuba and Peru in the Nineteenth Century: Free Labor or Neoslavery?" *Journal of Overseas Chinese Studies* 2, no. 2 (1992): 149–181.

———. "Chinese Coolie Labour in Cuba in the Nineteenth Century: Free Labour or Neo-Slavery?" *Slavery and Abolition: A Journal of Slave and Post-Slave Studies* 14, no. 1 (1993): 67–83.

———. "Los chinos del norte de México, 1875–1930: la formación de una pequeña burguesía regional." In *China en las Californias.* Colección Divulgación. Mexico City: Consejo Nacional para la Cultura y las Artes, 2002.

————. "*Huagong* and *Huashang*: The Chinese as Laborers and Merchants in Latin America and the Caribbean." *Amerasia Journal* 28, no. 2 (2002): 64–90.

————. "Voluntary Associations in a Predominantly Male Immigrant Community: The Chinese on the Northern Mexican Frontier, 1880–1930." In *Voluntary Associations in the Chinese Diaspora*, ed. Khun Eng Kuah-Pearce and Evelyn Hu-Dehart, 141–168. Hong Kong: Hong Kong University Press, 2006.

Hunter, Tera W. *To 'Joy My Freedom: Southern Black Women's Lives and Labors After the Civil War*. Cambridge, MA: Harvard University Press, 1997.

Hurtado, Albert L. "Parkmanizing the Spanish Borderlands: Bolton, Turner, and the Historians' World." *Western Historical Quarterly* 26, no. 2 (1995): 149–167.

Hwang, Ching Yen. *Coolies and Mandarins: China's Protection of Overseas Chinese in the Late Ch'ing Period, 1851–1911*. Singapore: University of Singapore Press, 1985.

Instituto Matías Romero (Mexico) and Rosario Green. *Instituto Matías Romero: XXV aniversario*. Mexico City: Secretaría de Relaciones Exteriores, 1999.

Irick, Robert L. *Ch'ing Policy Toward the Coolie Trade, 1847–1878*. Taipei, Taiwan: Chinese Material Center 1982.

Iriye, Akira. "The Internationalization of History." *American Historical Review* 94, no. 1 (1989): 1–10.

Izquierdo, José Jorge Gómez. *El movimiento antichino en México (1871–1934): Problemas de racismo del nacionalismo durante la Revolución Mexicana*. Mexico City: Instituto Nacional Antropología e Historia, 1991.

Jacoby, Karl. *Shadows at Dawn: A Borderlands Massacre and the Violence of History*. New York: Penguin Press, 2008.

Johnson, Benjamin Heber. *Revolution in Texas: How a Forgotten Rebellion and Its Bloody Suppression Turned Mexicans into Americans*. New Haven, CT: Yale University Press, 2003.

Jung, Moon-Ho. *Coolies and Cane: Race, Labor, and Sugar in the Age of Emancipation*. Baltimore, MD: Johns Hopkins University Press, 2006.

Kanstroom, Daniel. *Deportation Nation: Outsiders in American History*. Cambridge, MA: Harvard University Press, 2010.

Keefe, Patrick Radden. *The Snakehead: An Epic Tale of the Chinatown Underworld and the American Dream*. New York: Doubleday, 2009.

Kim, Jaeyoon. "The Heaven and Earth Society and the Red Turban Rebellion in Late Qing China." *Journal of Humanities and Social Sciences* 3, no. 1 (2009): 1–35.

Kirk, Andrew Taylor. "Radical Labor, Racism, and the Preservation of Hegemony in Ogden, Territorial Utah, 1885–1886." *American Journalism* 24, no. 4 (2007): 149–173.

Klein, Herbert S. *African Slavery in Latin America and the Caribbean*. Oxford, UK: Oxford University Press, 1986.

Knight, Alan. *The Mexican Revolution*, vol. 2. Cambridge, UK: Cambridge University Press, 1986.

————. "Racism, Revolution, and *Indigenismo*: Mexico, 1910–1940." In *The Idea of Race in Latin America, 1870–1940*, ed. Richard Graham, 71–114. Austin: University of Texas Press, 1990.

Kuhn, Philip A. *Chinese Among Others: Emigration in Modern Times.* Lanham, MD: Rowman and Littlefield, 2008.

Kurtz, Gordon V. "Chinese Labor, Economic Development and Social Reaction." *Ethnohistory* 18, no 4 (1971): 331–333.

———. *The Mexican Revolution: Counter-revolution and Reconstruction.* 2 vols. New York: Cambridge University Press, 1986.

Lai, Walton Look. *Indentured Labor, Caribbean Sugar: Chinese and Indian Migrants to the British West Indies, 1838–1918.* Baltimore: Johns Hopkins University Press, 1993.

Lakowsky, Vera Valdéz. *Estudio histórico del tratado sino mexicano de 1899.* Mexico City: Colegio de Historia, 1979.

———. "Estudio historicó del tratado sino-mexicano de 1899." PhD diss., Universidad Nacional Autónoma de México, Mexico City, 1979.

Lamar, Howard. *The Far Southwest, 1846–1912: A Territorial History.* Albuquerque: University of New Mexico Press, 1991.

LaTorre, Germán. *Relaciones geográficas de Indias (contenidas en el Archivo General de Indias de Sevilla: La Hispanoamérica del siglo XVI): Virreinato de Nueva España,* vol. 4, no. 4. Mexico City: Censos de población, 1920.

Lau-fong, Mak. "Chinese Secret Societies: Criminologically Defined." *Bulletin of the Institute of Ethnology Academia Sinica* 59 (1985): 143–161.

Lee, Erika. "Enforcing the Borders: Chinese Exclusion Along the U.S. Borders with Canada and Mexico, 1882–1924." *Journal of American History* 89, no. 1 (2002): 54–86.

———. *At America's Gates: Chinese Immigration During the Exclusion Era, 1882–1943.* Chapel Hill: University of North Carolina Press, 2003.

———. "Orientalisms in the Americas: A Hemispheric Approach to Asian American History." *Journal of Asian American Studies* 8, no. 3 (2005): 235–256.

Leonard, Karen Isaksen. *Making Ethnic Choices: California's Punjabi Mexican Americans.* Philadelphia: Temple University Press, 1992.

Lesser, Jeffrey. *Negotiating National Identity: Immigrants, Minorities, and the Struggle for Ethnicity in Brazil.* Durham, NC: Duke University Press, 1999.

———. *Searching for Home Abroad: Japanese-Brazilians and Transnationalism.* Durham, NC: Duke University Press, 2003.

Lim, Julian. "Chinese and *Paisanos*: Chinese Mexican Relations in the Borderlands." *Pacific Historical Review* 78, no. 1 (2010): 50–85.

Limerick, Patricia Nelson. *The Legacy of Conquest: The Unbroken Past of the American West.* New York: Norton, 1987.

———. "Going West and Ending Up Global." *Western Historical Quarterly* 32, no. 1 (2001): 5–23.

Ling, Huping. "Family and Marriage of Late-Nineteenth and Early-Twentieth Century Chinese Immigrant Women." *Journal of American Ethnic History* 19, no. 2 (2000): 43–63.

Lister, Florence C., and Robert H. Lister. *The Chinese of Early Tucson: Historic Archaeology from the Tucson Urban Renewal Project.* Tucson: University of Arizona Press, 1989.

Lo, Shauna. "Chinese Women Entering New England: Chinese Exclusion Act Case Files, Boston, 1911–1925." *New England Quarterly* 81, no. 3 (2008): 383–409.

Loewen, David. *Mississippi Chinese: Between Black and White.* Cambridge, MA: Harvard University Press, 1971.

Lorey, David E. *United States-Mexico Border Statistics Since 1900.* Los Angeles: UCLA Latin American Center Publications, 1993.

Luibhéid, Eithne. "The 1965 Immigration and Nationality Act: An 'End' Exclusion." *Positions* 5, no. 2 (1997): 501–522.

————. *Entry Denied: Controlling Sexuality at the Border.* Minneapolis: University of Minnesota Press, 2002.

MacMurray, John V. A. *Treaties and Agreements with and Concerning China, 1894–1919.* New York: Oxford University Press, 1921.

Mann, Dean E. *The Politics of Water in Arizona.* Tucson: University of Arizona Press, 1963.

Martínez, John. *Mexican Emigration to the U.S.: 1910–1930.* San Francisco: R and E Research Associates, 1971.

Martínez, Ma. Isabel Chong. *La migración china hacia Cuba 1850–1930.* Mexico City: Facultad de Ciencias Políticas y Sociales-UNAM, 1986.

Massey, Douglas. "Theories of International Migration: A Review and Appraisal." *Population and Development Review* 19, no. 3 (1993): 431–466.

Masterson, Daniel M. with Sayaka Funada-Classen. *The Japanese in Latin America.* Champaign: University of Illinois Press, 2004.

McClain, Charles J. *In Search of Equality: The Chinese Struggle Against Discrimination in Nineteenth-Century America.* Berkeley: University of California Press, 1994.

————, ed. *Chinese Immigrants and American Law.* New York: Garland Publishing Inc., 1994.

McGerr, Michael. "The Price of the 'New Transnational History.'" *American Historical Review* 96, no. 4 (1991): 1057–1067.

McKeown, Adam. "Conceptualizing Chinese Diasporas, 1842–1949." *Journal of Asian Studies* 58, no. 2 (1999): 306–337.

————. "Transnational Chinese Families and Chinese Exclusion, 1875–1943." *Journal of American Ethnic History* 18, no. 2 (1999): 73–110.

————. *Chinese Migrant Networks and Cultural Change: Peru, Chicago, Hawaii, 1900–1936.* Chicago: University of Chicago Press, 2001.

————. *Melancholy Order: Asian Migration and the Globalization of Borders.* New York: Columbia University Press, 2008.

————. "Chinese Emigration in Global Context, 1850–1940." *Journal of Global History* 5 (2010): 95–124.

Meagher, Arnold. *The Coolie Trade: The Traffic in Chinese Labors to Latin America 1847–1874.* Bloomington, IN: Xlibris, 2008.

Meeks, Eric. *Border Citizens: The Making of Indians, Mexicans, and Anglos in Arizona.* Austin: University of Texas Press, 2007.

Mejorada, Carlos Sánchez. "The Writ of Amparo: Mexican Procedure to Protect Human Rights." *Annals of the American Academy of Political and Social Science* 243: Essential Human Rights (January 1946): 107–111.

Meyer, Jean. "La reconstrucción de los años veinte: Obregón y Calles." In *Historia de México*, ed. Timothy E. Anna, Jan Bazant, and Friedrich Katz, 215–249. Barcelona: Crítica, 2001.

Miller, Wick R. "The Classification of the Uto-Aztecan Languages Based on Lexical Evidence." *International Journal of American Linguistics* 50 (January 1984): 1–24.

Monteón González, Humberto, and José Luis Trueba Lara, eds. *Chinos y antichinos en México: Documentos para su estudio.* Guadalajara: Gobierno de Jalisco, Secretaría General, Unidad Editorial, 1988.

Mora, Juan Flores. *The Making of the Mexican Border: The State, Capitalism, and Society in Nuevo Leon, 1848–1910.* Austin: University of Texas Press, 2001.

Morales, Catalina Velázquez. "Diferencias Políticas entre los Inmigrantes Chinos del Noroeste de México (1920–1930): El Caso de Francisco L. Yuen," *Historia Mexicana* 55, no. 2 (October-December 2005): 461–512.

Ng, Wing Chung. *The Chinese in Vancouver, 1945–1980: The Pursuit of Identity and Power.* Vancouver: University of British Columbia Press, 2000.

Ngai, Mae. "The Strange Career of the Illegal Alien: Immigration Restriction and Deportation Policy in the United States, 1921–1965, *Law and History Review* 21, no. 1 (2003): 169–107.

———. *Impossible Subjects: Illegal Aliens and the Making of Modern America.* Princeton, NJ: Princeton University Press, 2004.

Nicolosi, Ann Marie. "'We Do Not Want Our Girls to Marry Foreigners': Gender, Race, and American Citizenship." *National Women's Studies Association Journal* 13, no. 3 (2001): 1–21.

Nims, Amy Elizabeth. "Chinese Life in San Antonio," master's thesis, Southwest Texas State Teachers College, 1941.

Nutini, Hugo G., and Douglas R. White. "Community Variations and Network Structure in the Social Functions of Compadrazgo in Rural Tlaxcala, Mexico." *Ethnology* 16, no. 4 (1977): 353–384.

Officer, James. *Hispanic Arizona, 1536–1856.* Tucson: University of Arizona Press, 1987.

Olcott, Jocelyn. "Worthy Wives and Mothers: State-Sponsored Women's Organizing in Postrevolutionary Mexico." *Journal of Women's History* 13, no. 4 (2002): 106–131.

Oreenstein, Dara. "Void for Vagueness: Mexicans and the Collapse of Miscegenation Law in California." *Pacific Historical Review* 74, no. 3 (2005): 367–407.

Ota Mishima, María Elena, Moisés González Navarro, Sergio Camposortega Cruz, and Javier Rodríguez Chávez, eds. *Destino México: Un estudio de las migraciones asiáticas a México, siglos IX y XX.* Mexico City: El Colegio de México, Centro de Estudios de Asia y África, 1997.

Otero, Lydia R. *La Calle: Spatial Conflicts and Urban Renewal in a Southwest City.* Tucson: University of Arizona Press, 2010.

Pardinas, Felipe. *Relaciones diplomáticas entre China y México, 1898–1948*, vol. 1. Mexico City: Secretaría de Relaciones Exteriores, 1982.

Pascoe, Peggy. *What Comes Naturally: Miscegenation Law and the Making of Race in America.* Oxford, UK: Oxford University Press, 2009.

Paulsen, George E. "The Yellow Peril at Nogales: The Ordeal of Collector William M. Hoey." *Arizona and the West* 13, no. 2 (1971): 113–128.

Peck, Martin Edward. "Chinese Coolie Emigration to Latin America," master's thesis, Ohio State University, 1934.

Peffer, George Anthony. "Forbidden Families: Emigration Experiences of Chinese Women Under the Page Law." *Journal of American Ethnic History* 6, no. 1 (1986): 28–46.

Pegler-Gordon, Anna. *In Sight of America: Photography and the Development of U.S. Immigration Policy*. Berkeley: University of California Press, 2009.

Perkins, Clifford Alan. "Reminiscences of a Chinese-Immigration Inspector." *Journal of Arizona History* 17, no. 2 (summer 1976): 180–200.

———. *Border Patrol: With the U.S. Immigration Service on the Mexican Boundary 1910–1954*. El Paso: Texas Western Press, 1978.

Pilcher, James E. "Outlawry on the Mexican Border." *Scribner's Magazine* 1, no. 1 (1891): 78–87.

Pisani, Donald J. "Enterprise and Equity: A Critique of Western Water Law in the Nineteenth Century," *Western Historical Quarterly* 18, no. 1 (1987): 16–21.

Portes, Alejandro, and Julia Sensenbrenner. "Embeddedness and Immigration: Notes on the Social Determination of Economic Action." *American Journal of Sociology* 98, no. 6 (1993): 1320–1350.

Pugsley, Andrea. "'As I Kill This Chicken So May I Be Punished If I Tell an Untruth': Chinese Opposition to Legal Discrimination in the Arizona Territory." *Journal of Arizona History* 44, no. 2 (2003): 170–190.

Puig, Juan. *Entre el río Perla y el Nazas: la China decimonónica y sus braceros emigrantes, la colonia China de Torreón y la matanza de 1911*. Mexico City: Consejo Nacional para la Cultura y las Artes, 1993.

Radding, Cynthia. *Wandering Peoples: Colonialism, Ethnic Spaces, and Ecological Frontiers in Northwestern Mexico, 1700–1850*. Durham, NC: Duke University Press, 1997.

———. *Landscapes of Power and Identity: Comparative Histories in the Sonoran Desert and the Forests of Amazonia from Colony to Republic*. Durham, NC: Duke University Press, 2005.

Radding, Murrieta Cynthia. *Ciclos demográficos, trabajo y comunidad en los pueblos serranos de la Provincia de Sonora, siglo XVIII (Congreso sobre a História da População da América Latina*. Ouro Preto, Brazil: Fundação SEADE, 1990.

———. *Entre el desierto y la sierra: las naciones o'odham y tegüima de Sonora, 1530–1840*. Mexico City: Centro de Investigaciones y Estudios Superiores en Antropología, 1995.

Reilly, Thomas H. *The Taiping Heavenly Kingdom: Rebellion and the Blasphemy of Empire*. Seattle: University of Washington Press, 2004.

Rénique, Gerardo. "Anti-Chinese Racism, Nationalism, and State Formation in Post-Revolutionary Mexico, 1920s–1930s." *Political Power and Social Theory* 14 (2001): 91–140.

———. "Race, Region, and Nation: Sonora's Anti-Chinese Racism and Mexico's Postrevolutionary Nationalism, 1920s–1930s." In *Race and Nation in Modern Latin America*, ed. Nancy P. Appelbaum, Anne S. Macpherson, and Karin

Alejandra Rosemblatt, 211–237. Chapel Hill: University of North Carolina Press, 2003.

Reséndez, Andrés. *Changing National Identities at the Frontier: Texas and New Mexico, 1800–1850*. Cambridge, UK: Cambridge University Press, 2005.

Reynolds, James Bronson. "Enforcement of the Chinese Exclusion Laws." *Annals of the American Academy of Political and Social Science* 34, no. 2 (1909): 143–154.

Rhoads, Edward J. M. "The Chinese in Texas." In *Chinese on the American Frontier*, ed. Arif Dirlik, 165–181. Lanham, MD: Rowman and Littlefield Publishers, 2001.

Rodgers, Daniel T. "Exceptionalism." In *Imagined Histories: American Historians Interpret the Past*, ed. Anthony Molho and Gordon S. Wood, 21–40. Princeton, NJ: Princeton University Press, 1998.

Romero, Matías. *Diario Personal, 1855–1865*, ed. Emma Cosío Villegas. Mexico City: El Colegio de México, 1960.

Romero, Robert Chao. Transnational Chinese Immigrant Smuggling to the United States via Mexico and Cuba, 1882–1916," *Amerasia Journal* 30, no. 3 (2004/2005): 1–16.

———. *The Chinese in Mexico, 1882–1940*. Tucson: University of Arizona Press, 2010.

Ryo, Emily. "Through the Back Door: Applying Theories of Legal Compliance to Illegal Immigration During the Chinese Exclusion Era." *Law & Social Inquiry* 31, no. 1 (2006): 109–146.

Sacks, B. *Be It Enacted: The Creation of the Territory of Arizona*. Phoenix: Arizona Historical Foundation, 1964.

Saleeby, Caleb Williams. "Racial Poison." *Eugenics Review* 2 (April 1910–January 1911): 30–52.

———. *The Progress of Eugenics*. New York: Funk and Wagnalls, 1914.

Salyer, Lucy. *Laws Harsh as Tigers: Chinese Immigrants in the Shaping of Modern Immigration Law*. Chapel Hill: University of North Carolina Press, 1995.

Sánchez, George. *Becoming Mexican American: Ethnicity, Culture, and Identity in Chicano Los Angeles, 1900–1945*. New York: Oxford University Press, 1993.

Sangren, P. Steven. "Traditional Chinese Corporations: Beyond Kinship." *Journal of Asian Studies* 43 (1984): 391–415.

Santamaría, Alberto, O. P., "The Chinese Parian (El Parian de Los Sangeleyes)." In *The Chinese in the Philippines: 1570–1770*, ed. Alfonso Felíx Jr., 76–81. Manila: Solidaridad, 1966.

Sato, Kanji. "Formation of La Raza and the Anti-Chinese Movement in Mexico." *Transforming Anthropology* 14, no. 2 (2006): 181–186.

Saxton, Alexander. *The Indispensable Enemy: Labor and the Anti-Chinese Movement in California*. Berkeley: University of California Press, 1971.

Schmidt-Nowara, Christopher, and John M. Nieto-Philips, eds. *Interpreting Spanish Colonialism: Empires, Nations, and Legends*. Albuquerque: University of New Mexico Press, 2005.

Schneider, David M. "Kinship and Biology." In *Aspects of Analysis of Family Structure*, ed. Ansley J. Coale, 83–101. Princeton, NJ: Princeton University Press, 1965.

Schurz, William Lytle. *The Manila Galleon.* New York: E. P. Dutton, 1939.

Scott, David. *China and the International System, 1840–1949: Power, Presence, and Perceptions in a Century of Humiliation.* Albany: State University of New York Press, 2008.

Scott, Rebecca. *Slave Emancipation in Cuba: The Transition to Free Labor, 1860–1899.* Princeton, NJ: Princeton University Press, 1985.

Sheridan, Thomas E. *Los Tucsonenses: The Mexican Community in Tucson, 1854–1941.* Tucson: University of Arizona Press, 1986.

———. *Arizona: A History.* Tucson: University of Arizona Press, 1995.

Sierra, Justo. *The Political Evolution of the Mexican People,* trans. Charles Ramsdell. Austin: University of Texas Press, 1969.

Siu, Lok. *Memories of a Future Home: Diasporic Citizenship of Chinese in Panama.* Stanford, CA: Stanford University Press, 2005.

Skinner, G. William. *Chinese Society in Thailand: An Analytical History.* Ithaca, NY: Cornell University Press, 1957.

Smith, Marian L. "Immigration and Naturalization Service (INS) at the U.S.-Canadian Border, 1893–1993: An Overview of Issues and Topics." *Michigan Historical Review* 26, no. 2 (2000): 127–147.

Spence, Jonathan D. *God's Chinese Son: The Taiping Heavenly Kingdom of Hong Xiuquan.* New York: Norton, 1996.

Stepan, Nancy Leys. *The Hour of Eugenics: Race, Gender, and Nation in Latin America.* Ithaca, NY: Cornell University Press, 1996.

Stern, Alexandra Minna. "Buildings, Boundaries, and Blood: Medicalization and Nation-Building on the U.S.-Mexico Border 1910–1930." *Hispanic American Historical Review* 79, no. 1 (1999): 41–81.

———. "From Mestizophilia to Biotypology: Racialization and Science in Mexico, 1920–1960." In *Race, and Nation in Modern Latin America,* ed. Nancy P. Appelbaum, Anne S. Macpherson, and Karin Alejandra Rosemblatt, 187–210. Chapel Hill: University of North Carolina Press, 2003.

———. *Eugenic Nation: Faults and Frontiers of Better Breeding in Modern America.* Berkeley: University of California Press, 2005.

Stevens, Todd. "Husbands' Rights and Racial Exclusion in Chinese Marriage Cases, 1882–1924." *Law & Social Inquiry* 27, no. 2 (2002): 271–305.

Stewart, Watt. *La servidumbre china en el Perú: una historia de los culíes chinos en el Perú, 1849–1874.* Lima, Peru: Mosca Azul Editores, 1976.

Stockel, H. Henrietta. *Shame and Endurance: The Untold Story of the Chiricahua Apache Prisoners of War.* Tucson: University of Arizona Press, 2006.

Stokes, Richard. "Bisbee No Good for Chinamen," *Cochise Quarterly* 3, no. 4 (1973): 6–9.

Survey of Federal Archives. *Inventory of Federal Archives in the States, Department of Labor, California,* Series IX. Boston, MA: National Archives Project, Work Projects Administration, 1940.

Takaki, Ronald. *Strangers from a Different Shore: A History of Asian Americans.* New York: Little, Brown, 1989.

Territory of Arizona, Second Legislative Assembly. *Acts, Resolutions, and Memo-*

*rials Adopted by the Second Legislative Assembly of the Territory of Arizona.* Prescott: Office of the Arizona Miner, 1866.

———. *Acts, Resolutions, and Memorials Adopted by the Sixth Legislative Assembly of the Territory of Arizona.* Tucson: Office of the Arizona Citizen, 1871.

Thelen, David. "Audiences, Borderlands, and Comparisons: Toward the Internationalization of American History." *Journal of American History* 79, no. 2 (1992): 432–462.

———. "Rethinking History and the Nation-State: Mexico and the United States as a Case Study: A Special Issue" (September 1999): 439–452.

———. "The National and Beyond: Transnational Perspectives on United States History: A Special Issue." *Journal of American History* 86, no. 3 (1999): 965–975.

Thiel, J. Homer. *Archaeological Investigations of a Chinese Gardener's Household, Tucson, Arizona.* Tucson: Center for Desert Archaeology, 1997.

Tinker Salas, Miguel. *In the Shadow of the Eagles: Sonora and the Transformation of the Border During the Porfiriato.* Los Angeles: University of California Press, 1997.

Toro, Alfonso. "Influencia de la raza negra en las formación del pueblo mexicanos." *Ethnos. Revista para la vulgarización de Estudios Antropológicos sobre México y Centro América* 1, no. 8–12 (1920–1921): 215–218.

Torok, John Hayakawa. "Reconstruction and Racial Nativism: Chinese Immigrants and the Debates on the Thirteenth, Fourteenth, and Fifteenth Amendments and Civil Rights Laws." *Asian Law Journal* 3 (1996): 55–104.

Trouillot, Michel-Rolph. *Silencing the Past: Power and the Production of History.* Boston: Beacon Press, 1995.

Trueba Lara, José Luis. "La xenofobia en la legislación sonorense: el caso de los chinos." In *Memoria del XIII Simposio de Historia y Antropología de Sonora.* Hermosillo: Universidad de Sonora, 1989.

———. *Los chinos en Sonora: Una historia olvidada.* Hermosillo: Instituto de Investigaciones Históricas, Universidad de Sonora, 1990.

Truett, Samuel. "Epics of Greater America: Herbert Eugene Bolton and the Quest for a Transnational American History." In *Interpreting Spanish Colonialism: Empires, Nations, and Legends,* ed. Christopher Schmidt-Nowara and John M. Nieto Phillips, 213–247. Albuquerque: University of New Mexico Press, 2005.

———. *Fugitive Landscapes: The Forgotten History of the U.S.-Mexico Borderlands.* New Haven, CT: Yale University Press, 2006.

Tyrell, Ian. "American Exceptionalism in an Age of International History." *American Historical Review* 96, no. 4 (1991): 1031–1055.

———. "Ian Tyrell Responds." *American Historical Review* 96, no. 4 (1991): 1068–1072.

U.S. Industrial Commission. *Reports of the Industrial Commission on Immigration: Including Testimony, with Review and Digest, and Special Reports.* Washington, DC: U.S. Government Printing Office: 1901.

U.S. Senate. *Reports of the U.S. Immigration Commission, 1907–1910: The Immigration Situation in Other Countries: Canada, Australia, New Zealand, Argentina, Brazil.* Washington, DC: U.S. Government Printing Office, 1911.

Valdés, Dennis N. "The Decline of Slavery in Mexico." *The Americas* 44, no. 2 (1987): 167–194.

Van Den Berghe, Pierre L. "The African Disapora in Mexico, Brazil, and the United States." *Social Forces* 54, no. 3 (1976): 530–545.

Van Dyke, Paul Arthur. *The Canton Trade: Life and Enterprise on the China Coast, 1700–1845.* Hong Kong: Hong Kong University Press, 2005.

Van Hear, Nicholas. *New Diasporas: The Mass Exodus, Dispersal and Regrouping of Migrant Communities.* Seattle: University of Washington Press, 1998.

Vasconcelos, José. *La Raza Cósmica: Misión de la raza Iberoamericana y Notas de viajes a la América del sur.* Barcelona: Agencia de Liberia, 1925.

———. "The Latin-American Basis of Mexican Civilization." In *Aspects of Mexican Civilization,* ed. José Vasconcelos and Manuel Gamio, 3–74. Chicago: University of Chicago Press, 1926.

Veysey, Laurence. "The Autonomy of American History Reconsidered," *American Quarterly* 31, no. 4 (1979): 455–477.

Vinson, Ben, III, and Matthew Restall, eds. *Black Mexico: Race and Society from Colonial to Modern Times.* Albuquerque: University of New Mexico Press, 2009.

Voss, Stuart F. *On the Periphery of Nineteenth-Century Mexico: Sonora and Sinaloa, 1810–1877.* Tucson: University of Arizona Press, 1982.

Wade, Peter. *Race and Ethnicity in Latin America.* London: Pluto Press, 1997.

Walker, Francis A, Superintendent of Census. *A Compendium of the Ninth Census.* Washington, DC: U.S. Government Printing Office, 1872.

Wang, Guanhua. *In Search of Justice: The 190 5–1906 Chinese Anti-American Boycott.* Cambridge, MA: Harvard University Asia Center and Harvard University Press, 2001.

Wang, Joan S. "Race, Gender, and Laundry Work: The Roles of Chinese Laundrymen and American Women in the United States, 1850–1950." *Journal of American Ethnic History* 24, no.1 (2004): 58–99.

Wang, Wengsheng. "The First Chinese in Tucson: New Evidence on a Puzzling Question." *Journal of Arizona History* 43, no. 3 (2002): 369–380.

Weber, David J. "Turner, the Boltonians, and the Borderlands." *American Historical Review* 91 (February 1986): 66–81.

Weil, Samuel C. *Water Rights in the Western States.* San Francisco: Bancroft-Whitney, 1908.

Williams, Frederick Wells. *Anson Burlingame and the First Chinese Mission to Foreign Powers.* New York: Scribner's, 1912).

Willson, Roscoe G. "Secret Service Men Foil Border Smuggling Racket." *Arizona Days and Ways* (January 1957): 24–25; and (January 1957): 16–17.

———. "The Old 'Mounted Guards' Give Way to the 'Border Patrol.'" *Arizona Days and Ways* (September 1960): 32–33.

———. "They All Look Alike." *Arizona* (December 1967): 56–57.

———. "The Smuggled Chinese." *Arizona* (June 1975): 46–47.

Wilson, Andrew R. *Ambition and Identity: Chinese Merchant Elites in Colonial Manila, 1880–1916.* Honolulu: University of Hawai'i Press, 2004.

———, ed. *The Chinese in the Caribbean.* Princeton, NJ: Markus Weiner, 2004.

Woodworth, Marshall B. "Who Are Citizens of the United States—Wong Kim Ark Case—Interpretation of Citizenship Clause of the Fourteenth Amendment." *American Law Review* 32 (1898): 554–561.

Wong, Marie Rose. *Sweet Cakes, Long Journey: The Chinatowns of Portland, Oregon.* Seattle: University of Washington Press, 2004.

Wong, Morrison G. "Chinese Americans." In *Asian Americans: Contemporary Trends and Issues,* ed. Pyong Gap Min, 110–145. London: Sage, 2006.

Worster, Donald. "New West, True West: Interpreting the Region's History." *Western Historical Quarterly* 18 (April 1987): 141–156.

———. "Herbert Eugene Bolton: The Making of a Western Historian," In *Writing Western History: Essays on Major Western Historians,* ed. Richard W. Etulain, 193–213. Albuquerque: University of New Mexico Press, 1991.

Wu, Ching-ch'ao. "Chinese Immigration in the Pacific Area." *The Chinese Social and Political Science Review* 12 (1928): 550–573.

Wu, Paak-shing. "China's Diplomatic Relations with Mexico." *The China Quarterly* 4 (1939): 1–21.

Yun, Lisa. *The Coolie Speaks: Chinese Indentured Laborers and African Slaves of Cuba.* Philadelphia: Temple University Press, 2007.

Yun, Lisa, and Ricardo René Laremont. "Chinese Coolies and African Slaves in Cuba, 1847–1874." *Journal of Asian American Studies* 4, no. 2 (2001): 99–122.

Yung, Judy. *Unbound Feet: A Social History of Chinese Women in San Francisco.* Berkeley: University of California Press, 1995.

Zeraoui, Zidane. "Los arabes en Mexico: el perfil de la migración." In *Destino México: un estudio de las migraciones asiaticas a México siglos XIX y XX,* ed. Maria Elena Ota Mishima, 257–304. Mexico: El Colegio de Mexico, 1997.

Zhang, Sheldon. *Chinese Human Smuggling: Families, Social Networks, and Cultural Imperatives.* Stanford, CA: Stanford University Press, 2009.

Zhu, Leiping. *A Chinaman's Chance: The Chinese on the Rocky Mountain Mining Frontier.* Boulder: University of Colorado, 1997.

Zhu, Leiping, and Rose Estep Fosha. *Ethnic Oasis: The Chinese in the Black Hills.* Pierre: South Dakota State Historical Society Press, 2004.

# Index

Page numbers in *italics* represent illustrations. *Italicized* page numbers followed by *m* or *t* indicate illustrative maps or tables, respectively.

All Chinese proper names in English are alphabetized according to the traditional Chinese ordering of the family name (or surname) and given name/s (or first name/s). For example, Chin Tin Wo is alphabetized as Chin (family name), Tin Wo (given names). When Chinese Hispanicized their names (e.g., Benjamín Ungson or Juan Lung Tain), the same alphabetizing format is used with the recognition that the Hispanicized first name of a Chinese person is a westernized first name (e.g., Benjamín Ungson or Juan Lung Tain). Therefore, in the index these names appear as Ungson (family name), Benjamin (Hispanicized given name); and Tain (family name), Juan (Hispanicized given name) Lung (Chinese given name). When Mexican women married Chinese men and took their husband's family name like in the case of Adela Barrios de Hong, her name is alphabetized to maintain her marital status to Hong (de Hong, Adela Barrios).